SOCIAL ISSUES IN DEVELOPMENTAL PSYCHOLOGY

Social Issues in Developmental Psychology

HELEN L. BEE

Harper & Row, Publishers
New York, Evanston, San Francisco, London

Sponsoring Editor: George A. Middendorf
Project Editor: Cynthia Hausdorff
Designer: T. R. Funderburk
Production Supervisor: Will Jomarron

Library of Congress Cataloging in Publication Data
Bee, Helen L   1939–   comp.
    Social issues in developmental psychology.

    1. Parent and child (Psychology)   2. Sex differ-
ences (Psychology)   3. Poverty—Psychological aspects.
4. Education, Preschool.   I. Title.   [DNLM: 1. Child
development.   2. Social problem.   WS105   B414s 1974]
BF723.P25B4   155.4   73-21846
ISBN 0-06-040581-3

contents

preface

This book, like many textbooks, grew out of my own needs as a teacher. At many colleges and universities, the developmental psychology course is excessively large—up to 450 students per quarter in my own experience—and there is little or no opportunity for class discussion. In part to solve this problem, classes are often divided once a week into smaller groups, with the sessions taught by graduate student assistants. But what should be done in these small classes? What should be discussed? After trying out various strategies, I concluded several years ago that the most interesting and useful approach for the students was to use the discussion time to explore the application of course material to real "social" problems. So my assistants and I began to devise different formats, including debates and discussions of various types. The problem, always, was lack of available material. No one book contained the information we wanted the students to discuss, so we assigned individual students to dig into particular areas. That worked fine for the student doing the digging, but made any kind of intelligent discussion difficult because the majority of the students were relying only on their own opinions and not on any reading. This book is an attempt to fill the gap and make it possible for groups of students to have at least some common reading background on some of the major social issues of our day.

I have quite intentionally organized each section so as to foster debate, and at the end of each overview I have offered hopefully provocative questions around which such debate might be structured. In each instance I have tried to cast the issues as clearly as I could, and as fairly as I could, although I am sure that my own opinions show through. In selecting articles to exemplify research and thinking on the various issues, I have again tried to be as fair as I could and to choose material that reflected several points of view.

My fundamental purpose in this book is to show the beginning psychology student that it is possible to address important social issues from a scientific point of view. In many cases, of course, we know less than we would like to know, but in every case there is a scientific literature and some important research findings. I hope that students will be stimulated by reading the research and, further, that they will come away from the book with a greater understanding of the ways in which social scientists go about exploring difficult social questions.

My thinks to all the authors who allowed their work to be reprinted in this book. I hope that their work can have greater exposure because of it. Thanks too, to all those former students whose enthusiasm for or total boredom with previous sets of "debate topics" helped to determine the final selection of topics for the book.

HELEN L. BEE

part I
sex differences
in development

sex differences

HELEN L. BEE

Whatever your position on the real causes of sex differences, there are two facts we must live with—at least for now. First, there are clear stereotypes in our culture about men and women—about their characteristics and what is expected of them. (See Broverman, Vogel, Broverman, Clarkson, and Rosenkrantz, 1972, for a review.) Men are seen as, and are expected to be, competent, aggressive, logical, emotionally unexpressive, nonsensitive to the feelings of others, interested in math and science, and not very talkative. Women are seen as, and are expected to be, essentially the opposite: emotionally expressive, sensitive to others' feelings, nonaggressive, less logical, less competent, more talkative, and uninterested in math and science. Second, these stereotypes are not all that far off; in fact, men and women *do* differ on many (but by no means all) of the dimensions mentioned, and in the expected directions in most cases.[1]

Where do the stereotypes—and the differences—come from? Do they merely mirror fundamental, perhaps biologically inevitable, differences between men and women? Or do we find differences between

---

[1]Why then do we call the opinions about sex differences stereotypes? Why not consider them reflections of reality? Because, like all stereotypes, expectations about sex differences are applied uniformly to all men and women, despite the fact that the observed differences do not apply equally to all men and women.

the sexes in part because there *are* stereotypes and people are trained to fill societal expectations?

There has been more heat than light generated in current popular discussions of these questions, undoubtedly because people (especially women) feel very strongly about the matter. To many, any assertion that there are fundamental, biological differences (other than sexual differences) between the sexes is a statement justifying what is seen by many as the oppression of women. There is also more heat than light because there is far less good data available than one would like, and what there is is almost always open to several interpretations. In the discussion that follows, I have attempted to avoid the usual polemical traps (although I may not have succeeded) and to remain open to the several possible interpretations of the findings. To facilitate that, I've divided the discussion into several parts. First we'll look at the evidence on existing sex differences. Then we'll examine the arguments proposed by the advocates of essentially biological explanations and the arguments proposed by those advocating an environmental explanation, and finally a synthesis of sorts will be offered.

CURRENTLY OBSERVED
SEX DIFFERENCES

In order to simplify the mountain of material documenting sex differences, I've reduced the available information to two summary tables. Table 1 gives the observed differences in the area of personality and social behavior, and Table 2 gives observed differences in cognitive functioning. You will note that I have divided the age ranges into four periods, in part because it is convenient to do so and in part because the data suggest that such a division is worthwhile. In general, as you will see by examining the tables, there are very few clear differences prior to adolescence and even fewer prior to age six or so. Before school age the clearest difference is that boys are more aggressive; there is some indication that at the very young ages girls may be ahead in verbal development (although that isn't as obvious as we once thought it was) and that girls may be more nurturant and affiliative. For children 6–12 the difference in aggressiveness is still strong; the nurturance and affiliative differences are clearer; and some of the cognitive differences are beginning to emerge: Boys, in some studies of this age group, are better at mathematical tasks, set-breaking tasks, reasoning problems, and spatial skills, but for no one of these skills are the sex differences found consistently in every study.

By adolescence the differences are very much larger and clearer. At this age boys are more aggressive, less nurturant, less affiliative, less suggestible, less anxious, better at mathematical reasoning tasks, better

Table 1 Summary Table of Sex Differences in Social and Personality Dimensions[a]

Observed difference	Age of subjects			
	0–6	6–12	12–adult	Adult
Aggression	boys; strong effect	boys; strong effect	boys	men
Aggression anxiety	no data	no data	girls (one study)	women
Dependency on others	mixed; probably none	no good data	no good data; girls by self-report	
Activity level	probably none	no good data	no good data	no good data
Nurturance (not very good measure)	maybe girls	girls	girls	women
Conformity and suggestibility	probably none	probably none	girls (not good data)	women
Anxiety, particularly test anxiety	no good data	girls usually	girls usually	women usually
Fear of success	no data	no data	no data	women

[a]The primary source for this information and that contained in Table 2 is Maccoby (1966), with some updating from the unpublished paper by Maccoby and Jacklin (1972).

at all tasks involving spatial relationships and at set-breaking problems, more "field independent," more "analytic" in cognitive style, and somewhat less verbal, and they achieve less highly in school. Girls are the converse: less aggressive; more nurturant; more affiliative; more suggestible; more anxious (particularly about test and task situations); not as good at mathematical reasoning, spatial relations, and set-breaking problems; more "field dependent"; and less "analytic" in cognitive style. They are more verbal and higher in school achievement. Girls' verbal abilities are in some dispute. They seem to be better at the fluency and grammar and spelling aspects of language, but it's not clear whether they are also good at verbal reasoning. In several earlier studies (McNemar, 1942; Klausmeier and Wiersma, 1964, 1965), adolescent boys were found to be better at verbal analogies and at such tasks as the water-jar problems from the Stanford-Binet. (I'm sure you know these problems: A child is sent to the river with a 13-oz. jar, and a 3-oz. jar, and is supposed to come back with 10 oz. of water—to use a simple example.) But Raaheim (1963) finds that Scandinavian post-adolescent girls and adult women are as good or better at verbal problem solving, and Droege (1967) found that American high-school girls, whose progress he followed throughout high school, were slightly and increasingly better on the verbal aptitude measure of the General Aptitude Test Battery, which includes some complex kinds of verbal tasks, including reasoning problems. It's clear from all this that adult men and late adolescent boys are better at *mathematical* reasoning tasks; it's simply not clear whether women have a parallel superiority at verbal reasoning problems, but at least women are not clearly and uniformly inferior at such tasks either, as has often been suggested. The best bet at the moment is that, except for purely mathematical tasks, women and men are probably about equivalent on reasoning problems.

The terms "field independence" and "field dependence," and "analytic cognitive style," which appear in the summary tables, may be unfamiliar to you. Field dependence and field independence refer to the ability or inability to respond to specific aspects of a stimulus situation without being confused or influenced by the background information. The classic task (developed by Witkin, Dyk, Faterson, Goodenough, and Karp, 1962) is the rod-and-frame test, in which the subject must adjust a tilted rod so that it is upright—a simple task except for the fact that the rod is enclosed in a picture-frame-like apparatus that is itself tilted off the upright. Those subjects who can deal with the position of the rod without being influenced by the frame are called field independent, and those who are more influenced by the frame are called field dependent. Girls and women, in general, are more field dependent than boys and men. Analytic cognitive style, a designation used by Kagan and his associates (Kagan, Rosman, Day,

Table 2 Summary Table of Sex Differences in Cognitive Functioning

Observed difference	Age of subjects			
	0–6	6–12	12–adult	Adult
Verbal abilities:				
Articulation	weak effect; girls	weak effect; girls; more boys with speech defects	no data	no data
Verbal fluency	maybe girls	probably none	girls	women
Vocabulary	probably none	probably none	none	women
Grammatical development in speech	probably none	no data	no data	no data
Grammatical skill, analyzing sentences	not relevant	probably none	girls	women
Spelling	not relevant	maybe girls	girls	women
Verbal reasoning	no good data	mixed; maybe boys	mixed; can't tell	maybe women
Reading	not relevant	girls	probably none	probably none
Mathematical ability:				
Counting	maybe girls	probably none	no data	no data
Computation	not relevant	probably girls	none	probably no difference
Mathematical reasoning	none	maybe boys	boys	men
Conservation	none	none	no data	no data
Spatial ability	none	maybe boys	boys	men
Breaking set	no data	probably boys	probably boys	men
Field independence	none	maybe boys	boys	men
"Analytic" style	probably none	boys	boys	no data
Total IQ	none	none	none	none
School grades	not relevant	girls	girls	not relevant

Albert, and Phillips, 1964) refers to the tendency to respond to parts of objects rather than to the whole object. If a subject is given a group of pictures and asked to select those that go together, the analytic individual will base his or her selection on some selected common element in the pictures, such as all the animals with long ears or all pictures with spirals in them. Starting somewhere during elementary school, boys show a slightly greater analytic tendency than do girls.

One final note about all these differences. I've tried to indicate where the differences are observed consistently, and where they are not, but the tables do not tell you how large the observed differences may be. In fact, most of the differences are quite small, with largely overlapping distributions. The differences in aggression are consistently quite large, and the spatial ability differences are reasonably large (perhaps a half a standard deviation on any particular test), but the other differences are small, even when they are consistent. The fact that the differences are, in general, slight does not make it any less important to be able to explain them, but the absolute size of the difference should be kept in mind, if only to keep the heat of the discussion down to a minimum.

With this background in mind, let's turn to the two very general varieties of explanations offered for the phenomena I've just described, namely biological explanations and environmental explanations.

BIOLOGICAL
EVIDENCE

There are several types of arguments offered that can be grouped roughly under the heading of "biological evidence." First, there is the evidence suggesting that observed differences are genetic in origin; second, there is evidence suggesting that hormone differences lie behind observed behavioral differences; and finally, there is a series of indirect arguments, including those based on comparisons of man to subhuman primates. Let's take each of the major biological arguments in turn.

GENETIC FACTORS

In order to attribute any sex difference in behavior to genetic difference, one must show that behavior is governed by a gene (or genes) that is carried on the X or Y chromosome, that is, a gene that is sex-linked. There has been comparatively little research of this kind, the exception being work on possible sex-linked heritability of spatial abilities (Stafford, 1961; Corah, 1965; Hartlage, 1970). The basic finding is that parent-child resemblance in spatial ability is cross sex: Boys' scores on spatial abilities are predicted best by their mothers' scores, and girls' scores are predicted best by their fathers'. This runs counter to what would be intuitively sensible for an environmental explanation and suggests the possibility of a sex-linked heritability for spatial ability. Stafford has suggested that the findings make sense if at least one important genetic component for spatial skill is carried on the X chromosome and is recessive. Girls, with two X chromosomes, would have to receive the recessive gene from both parents, which is a comparatively unlikely possibility, in order to have high spatial ability. Boys, with only one X chromosome, on the other hand, would have to receive a recessive gene from their mothers only. So boys would not only more closely resemble their mothers in spatial ability, but would be more likely to inherit the high spatial ability gene and hence have higher spacial ability as a group.

This analysis at least suggests that a genetic component in spatial ability is possible. Similar analyses of verbal or mathematical ability or field dependence and field independence are not available, so we don't know how reasonable similar genetic arguments might be in the case of other abilities.[2]

HORMONAL FACTORS

A much more common kind of biological argument is that differences in hormones produce the observed behavioral sex differences. Such arguments center around the two times in the organism's lifetime when hormones seem to play a particularly crucial role. First, early in the prenatal period, there is a point at which the normally developing male embryo receives a sharp jolt of androgen (the "male" hormone). This increase in androgen is what apparently produces the development of male physical characteristics. If androgen is not added at this time, the fetus develops as a female, even though it may be genetically XY. Similarly, a genetically female embryo (XX) can develop into a physical male if androgen is introduced into the system at the critical point. Obviously, this very early hormonal event is crucial for the development of physical sex differences, but what about behavioral or cognitive differences?

The most interesting data come from research on genetic females whose mothers were given injections of androgen or of progestins (prescribed for human mothers in some instances to prevent threatened miscarriages). The selection by Charles H. Phoenix, Robert W. Goy, and John A. Resko is an example of this kind of work with rhesus monkeys and other animals. The finding, quite simply, is that geneti-

[2]Please be clear about the fact that this discussion deals only with sex-linked genetic differences. It's entirely possible for verbal or math ability, for example, to have a strong genetic component without that genetic component being sex-linked. That is, genetic factors may contribute to overall individual differences in a trait, but not to differences between the sexes.

cally female monkeys who have experienced increased levels of andro-gen in utero show masculinized behavior as young animals: heightened aggressive play, increased mounting, and so on. In humans the number of cases is very small, since the instances are all essentially accidents. We do have, however, one study (Ehrhardt and Money, 1967) of ten girls whose mothers were given doses of progestin during the crucial part of the prenatal period. Ehrhardt and Money describe these girls as showing some behavioral masculinization. They are interested in competitive sports; they think of themselves as tomboys and are so considered by others. Unfortunately, most of the information comes from interviews and not from actual observation of behavior, so we don't know how different the behavior of these girls really is. Further, the fact that they are tomboys, and consider themselves as such may not be a result of hormone variations, but rather of social expectations. The parents know that their child is somewhat sexually ambiguous and may be more tolerant of stereotypically boyish behavior. Ehrhardt and Money did attempt to assess cognitive functioning in their sub-jects, but used only a single IQ test (on which the girls' scores were unusually high). Lacking measures of the separate kinds of intellectual tasks, we can't say whether these girls showed the "male pattern" of cognitive skills or not. (A study now underway at the University of Washington, with another group of similar subjects, may help to answer this question.)

The upshot of all this is that the subhuman data are quite clear: Hormonal injections of various kinds during the prenatal period affect later observable behavior, particularly in the area of aggressive play. Whether it is reasonable to generalize these findings to humans is more difficult to say, although we know that there is the same crucial point in early prenatal development in humans, when physical sex characteristics are determined by hormonal infusions. At this point the hypothesis that some behavioral differences between human males and females may be affected by those same prenatal hormonal infu-sions seems at least to be reasonable.

Obviously, a second time when hormone changes are evident is during adolescence, when the physical changes of puberty are evoked by sharp increases in the level of androgen for boys and estrogen for girls. We know that observable sex differences, particularly in cognitive functioning, become much sharper at about the same time. Are these two events related? Possibly. Broverman and his associates (Broverman, Klaiber, Kobayashi, and Vogel, 1968; Klaiber, Broverman, and Koba-yashi, 1967; Stenn, Klaiber, Vogel, and Broverman, 1972; Klaiber, Broverman, Vogel, Abraham, and Cone, 1971; Broverman, Broverman, Vogel, Palmer, and Klaiber, 1964) have conducted a series of studies, thus far almost entirely with male subjects, that seems to show that some kinds of cognitive skills are related to hormone levels. For example, they found that among college age males those with higher levels of androgen were relatively better at simple repetitive tasks and not as good at restructuring tasks (including tasks that assessed field independence) (Klaiber, Broverman, and Kobayashi, 1967). Further, they report that injections of testosterone in two young human males, who were slow in pubertal development, resulted in an improvement in performance on repetitive tasks. The correlations obtained between hormonal level and cognitive performance are not high in any of the Broverman studies, but their existence suggests at least the possibility of a causal relationship between the two. The puzzle, as you may have detected, is that the relationship seems to go in the wrong direction. That is, men with more androgen are better at tasks that are "female" tasks, and it is the less heavily androgenized men who are better at the set-breaking and field independence tasks, which are usually considered "male" tasks. Since a parallel set of studies on women does not exist, it is difficult to unravel this puzzle. Broverman et al (1968), in a highly complicated paper, have attempted to unravel it with only moderate success, but the line of research is worth pursuing.

OTHER BIOLOGICAL ARGUMENTS

One of the most frequent of the biological arguments, emphasized strongly in Corinne Hutt's paper, is that many of the behavioral differences we see among humans are paralleled by behavioral differences in subhuman primates. The pattern of male aggressiveness and female nurturance and affiliation is seen in most subhuman primate species studied. Furthermore, it is also found consistently across human cultures. Such inter- and intraspecies consistency is usually taken as strong evidence for a biological explanation (though not everyone agrees, as shown by Weisstein's eloquent counterargument, 1971).

We are also beginning to discover that male and female human neonates differ from one another in a variety of ways, a point that Corinne Hutt also discusses. Whether these initial differences are genetic or hormonal is not particularly crucial; the fact remains that such differences do exist, so that the caretakers have different kinds of organisms to respond to. Even if the caretakers were to attempt to treat the two sexes equivalently, different patterns of interaction might well emerge, simply because the children come equipped with different sets of responses or different response rates. To take only one example, Moss (1967) finds that at three weeks of age female infants sleep more, fuss less, and show less irritability than the male infants. Mothers hold and respond to the male more during this period, perhaps because he is awake and demands attention more. However, when the girl *is* fussy or irritable, she is more likely to get attention than the male is. Moss suggests that something like the following may build up: Girls are less fussy overall, and when they do fuss and the mother goes to them and comforts them, they are soothed more easily, so that the mother is reinforced for comforting them. Boys, on the other hand, are fussier overall and may be harder to soothe, so that over time the mother learns not to comfort them as quickly or as frequently when they are irritable. In fact, by the time the infants are three months old, the most irritable boys are the ones the mothers pay the least attention to. To be sure, the possible sequence I've just described involves a heavy dose of environment. But the fundamental point is that the differences in the way the two sexes are treated may not result from the mother's acting out of cultural stereotypes, but from differences that the two groups of infants brought with them in the first place.

Finally, there is a kind of biological-by-default argument that is offered about the observed differences in analytic cognitive style and field independence and dependence. The interesting thing about the differences in these measures is that there are no clear sex stereotypes about either. There is no evidence that I know of suggesting that men or boys are expected to be more field independent or more analytic, so it is difficult to imagine any kind of direct teaching of such skills or attitudes. Even the child's learning analytic or field independent behavior through modeling seems unlikely, since neither behavior is particularly observable and, in fact, cross sex correlations are commonly found—that is, girls' scores on field independence measures are best predicted by their fathers' scores, boys' by their mothers (Corah, 1965). Since no simpleminded environmental explanation stands out, some argue that these differences must be biological. It is of interest, in this context, that the tasks that Broverman and his associates have found to be associated with hormonal level are these very same cognitive style tasks, which lends some minimal credence to this line of argument.

But, obviously, this is a naïve way of looking at environmental influence. There are many more, indirect ways in which sex differences in cognitive styles could be acquired. Kagan and Kogan (1970) discuss most of these ways in an extensive presentation of the material on this subject. I mention this very weak biological argument only because the explanation of sex differences in field dependence and independence and analytic style is a particularly puzzling and difficult problem in any theory.

In sum, there are quite persuasive arguments for biological components in at least some of the observed sex differences, most notably in the aggression versus nurturance and affiliation dimension and in spatial abilities. There are some suggestions of possible biological effects in the cognitive area. But no biological explanations have been offered concerning the greater "fear of success," greater anxiety, or lower achievement motivation shown by women.

ENVIRONMENTAL
EVIDENCE

The fundamental task of a theorist in trying to devise a largely environmental explanation for sex differences is to specify the manner in which the observed differences in behavior may be taught to the child directly or may be learned by the growing child through imitation of adults who typify the differences, or may be acquired by the child by other, less direct, environmental influences. Several elegant attempts have been made, most notably by Mischel (1966, 1970) and Kohlberg (1966). A discussion of the learning and developmental mechanisms that have been invoked to account for the acquisition of sex differences is beyond the scope of this review. What I want to do instead is simply to highlight the sort of evidence that can be mustered in support of *any* environmental explanation. So, as in the case of the biological explanations, let us take a look at a series of pieces of evidence, or lines of argument, that have been advanced in support of an environmental view.

BEHAVIOR OF HERMAPHRODITES

As I reported in discussing the biological evidence, there are a number of studies of females (mostly subhuman primates) who have apparently been "masculinized" as a result of prenatal administration of male hormone. (See the selection by Phoenix, Goy, and Resko.) But what about after birth? Does the environment have an effect as well? Apparently it does. Money (1971) describes a series of cases of individuals with an ambiguous external genital appearance at birth. (That is, you can't tell from the appearance whether the infant is genetically male or female.) Some such children are reared as boys, some as girls, even though their physical appearance is similar. After examining matched pairs of such children (with the same diagnosis and the same external genital appearance in each pair, but one in the pair raised as a boy and the other as a girl), Money reports that the child raised as a boy considers himself a boy and behaves like a boy, and the one raised as a girl considers herself, and behaves like, a girl. Whether the two groups are similar in cognitive skill patterns, we don't know. But the evidence indicates that for noncognitive behavioral traits, the sex of *rearing* is the crucial factor within this group of anomalous children.

Money has taken this finding one step further and suggested that for all individuals,

> despite whatever sexual dimorphism may already have differentiated in the central nervous system, the human organism at birth is still largely bipotential for dimorphism of gender-identity differentiation. More

simply said, the individual's gender-identity and role . . . will differentiate in response to and in interaction with stimuli encountered after
birth [Money, 1971, p. 209].

As I read this, Money is saying that a child will consider himself or
herself to be whatever sex he or she is brought up to be and will
attempt to fill the role assigned to that sex. This may well be true, but
that doesn't tell us very much about the actual behavior of children
whose assigned sex and biological sex are at variance. A biological
female, raised as a boy, might well consider herself or himself a
boy, but would he or she show behavior patterns typical of a boy?
What about cognitive skill patterns? We simply don't know, although
such data would obviously be of importance for any environmental
theory.

SEX DIFFERENCES AT BIRTH

We know that males and females differ in some respects from birth.
If one takes a biological tack, these differences are emphasized. Obviously, when an environmental view is taken, the similarities between
the two sexes are emphasized, and in fact, there are more similarities
than differences, at least as far as our current data go. (I put in that
qualification because the better our techniques for assessing infant
behavior get, the more sex differences at that age seem to emerge.)
Both sexes have quite well developed sensory systems; both have the
same complement of reflexes and the same general repertoire of behaviors. If Piaget is correct that all later cognitive development builds
on these early sensorimotor skills, then the two sexes should turn out
to be very much alike. In any case, although there are differences
between boys and girls at birth, those differences are probably not
large enough to account, by themselves, for the larger differences we
see later; some differences in the treatment of the two sexes must
occur as well.

DIFFERENCES IN TREATMENT OF THE TWO SEXES

Obviously, one of the crucial underpinnings of an environmental argument must be evidence that boys and girls are treated differently from
birth or from some specified point in development. You will see just
this sort of reasoning in Lois Wladis Hoffman's paper. She begins with
observations about the sex differences in achievement and then
attempts to backtrack to differential early experiences of particular
kinds. She cites a number of studies that do indeed show that boys
and girls are treated differently from a very early age. The paper by
Cheryl Minton, Jerome Kagan, and Janet A. Levine provides further
support for this view. They find that "mothers were more intrusive with

sons than with daughters," where "intrusive" refers to the mother's tendency to interfere with the child's activity or prohibit something the child is doing. Boys were also punished more often.

But as usual the picture is really not all that one-sided. Maccoby (1972) has reviewed all the evidence on differential early socialization and comes to the conclusion that on the whole boys and girls are treated markedly the same during the preschool years. Many studies do show differences, but the direction of the differences is not all that consistent and seems to be affected by such variables as the ordinal position of the child, the educational level of the mother, or even whether the father or the mother is studied. For example, Moss (1967) reports that mothers more often imitate their infant daughters—when the baby makes a sound, the mother repeats the sound—but they provide more physical stimulation and arousal for their sons. Lewis (1972) reports very similar findings. On the other hand, Rebelsky and Hanks (1971) found that fathers vocalized to their sons more than to their daughters, and Maccoby (1972) cites a finding from a study by Evelyn Thoman that indicates mothers vocalized more to firstborn than to later born sons and more to later born than to firstborn daughters. Work in my own laboratory, with both infants and older preschoolers, suggests that the mother's social class and the child's ordinal position are the most crucial variables, not the child's sex. Kilbride, Johnson, and Streissguth (1971) found that mothers vocalized more to firstborn children than to later borns regardless of sex, and that college-educated mothers vocalized to their child more than less educated mothers did, again regardless of the child's sex.

Maccoby (1972) does find consistent reports in the literature of differences in treatment in two areas: (1) Boys are handled somewhat more roughly than girls, and parents indicate more concern about the daughter's physical well-being, and (2) boys are physically punished more than girls and are directed more in general. (See the study by Minton, Kagan, and Levine for an example of evidence on both points.) But there are apparently no consistent differences in warmth or affection; nor are the findings consistent in suggesting differential parental treatment of aggression or dependence and independence.

The findings on differential treatment of aggression, or rather the lack of it, are worth examining, since we know that there is a clear sex difference in aggressive behavior from very early. The Newsons, in their major study in England (1963), found no difference in the parental treatment of aggression in boys and girls; nor did Sears, Rau, and Alpert (1965) in their American study. The complexity of the situation is suggested by Rothbart and Maccoby's finding (1966) that mothers were more willing to accept aggressive behavior directed toward themselves from a male child than from a female child, and for fathers the reverse was true. All of this does not add up to the sort of systematically differential treatment we would need to account for differences in aggressive behavior from an environmental point of view.

Maccoby concludes that during the preschool years there are really very few differences in treatment of boys and girls; the exceptions seem to be greater punitiveness toward boys and greater physical protectiveness toward girls. If further data substantiate this generalization, where does that leave an environmental viewpoint? There are several options. First, take another look at Tables 1 and 2. You will notice that during the preschool period very few sex differences are observable in children. So we have few behavioral differences and few treatment differences, which is surely a reasonable combination. The behavioral differences and the differences in cognitive measures do not really emerge strongly until about age ten or into adolescence (with aggressive differences being the marked exception to that generalization). Most of the information we have about differential rearing of boys and girls—and it is slim at best—comes from studies of preschool age children. We have little comparable information about school age or adolescent children. Perhaps differences in rearing patterns that correspond to the developing behavioral and cognitive differences are to be found in later periods. Some support for this notion comes from the Newsons' study in England. They found no differences in the permissiveness mothers showed toward independence and free physical movement when the children were young, but they did find differences starting when the children were about seven. At this point the mothers began to "chaperone" the daughters more. Hoffman also discusses studies of achievement training with older children that suggest differential treatment of the two sexes in elementary school years. Perhaps, then, we should look for environmental differences at the point in time when the behavioral difference emerges, rather than looking to the early childhood period.

Alternatively, one may choose to emphasize the sex differences in treatment that do exist during the preschool period and argue that even though these differences are small and in some cases subtle, they do convey information to the child about what is expected of each sex. As our measures of early parent-child interaction get more sophisticated, perhaps we will begin to pick up some indication of subtle cues that we are simply missing with our grosser measures.

VARIATIONS IN ENVIRONMENTAL CONDITIONS

More persuasive evidence in favor of an environmental view comes from analyses of alterations in observed sex differences under varying environmental conditions. First off, cognitive sex differences are not the same in children living in poverty as they are in middle-class children. Hoffman discusses this and makes a very solid point: Among (lower-class) blacks it is the girls who are better at most things, including math and verbal skills, whereas among whites it tends to be the boys who are better at math and maybe verbal reasoning. Thus the behavior of black males and white females tends to be more alike. But there is a possible biological explanation of this, as well as the environmental one that Hoffman offers. We know that males, in general, are more susceptible to various kinds of environmental traumas, including prenatal traumas. We also know that among poverty-level groups, particularly among blacks (see Herbert G. Birch's paper in Part III), there is a higher rate of various kinds of prenatal traumas and birth complications, and the boys are more likely to be adversely affected by these events. So it may well be that the generally lower cognitive performance of poverty-level males is due to the inclusion in this group of an unusually large number of boys who suffered some kind of prenatal or perinatal trauma. In order to test this, one would have to study a group of black children from which all children with "at risk" prenatal or birth histories had been eliminated, so that only those subjects who seem to be physiologically intact would be tested. If, under these conditions, girls did better on tests that usually show boys higher, the potential biological explanation would not hold, and an environmental explanation (such as Hoffman's) would begin to look very good indeed. Unfortunately, I know of no study of this kind.

A second environmental variation that appears to alter the relative cognitive performance of males and females is rearing without a father. Take a look at Lyn Carlsmith's paper in Part V. She finds that boys reared without a father, particularly if the father was absent early in the child's life, are more likely to show the "typically feminine" pattern of being better at verbal than at mathematical tasks. Furthermore, Barclay and Cusumano (1967) report that boys reared in homes without a father are more field dependent. So here we have a purely environmental variation that seems to produce alterations not in the *level* of cognitive functioning, but in the *pattern* of cognitive functioning, a series of findings that provide strong support for an environmental view.

SYNTHESIS

The customary comment to make at this point—which I have made in some of the other introductory chapters—is that the whole issue is not an either/or question. The standard follow-up is to invoke the notion of interaction: The observed differences are obviously a result of a combination of biological and environmental forces.

Well, I'm not going to say that. At least not in the customary form. I'm going to suggest, instead, that for some of the observed differences, the cause is largely biological; for others it is largely environmental; and for some it is a combination or interaction of the two. One of the fallacies in the usual discussion, from my point of view, is that an effort is made to explain all the observed differences with the same theory. That's parsimonious, perhaps, even elegant, but it's probably not right in this case.

To me the evidence suggests that some of the observed differences are heavily influenced by biological factors. Most notable among these is aggression, but possibly spatial ability belongs here too. More tentatively, I would place nurturance and affiliation in this category as well, although here the evidence is simply not as good or as clear. We do know that nonhuman primate females show more nurturance and affiliative behavior than do males, but males will adopt such a role when no females are available to take care of the young. This observation suggests that the male animal has all of the responses, but that nurturance and affiliative responses are not very high in the hierarchy of his preferred behaviors.

On the other side, it seems to me that one whole cluster of behaviors seen in women—anxiety, fear of success, low achievement motivation, conformity, and suggestibility—is best understood as an environmentally produced set of traits. Hoffman's paper is really a discussion of this cluster of behaviors and how they may interfere with the attainment of excellence and productivity in women.

What remains is primarily the group of cognitive differences (minus the spatial differences, which I've tentatively listed as primarily biological). For the verbal, math, and cognitive style skills, there *may* be both biological and environmental sources, although here the data are really not good at all. Broverman's scant data suggest that there *may* be hormonal correlates of cognitive abilities, but virtually all other evidence points to environmental origins for the observed cognitive differences. What is lacking is not only further research on the relationship of cognitive functioning and hormone balance, but also research on the interpersonal and environmental origins of different patterns of cognitive skill. Aside from the evidence from studies of father-absent families and one rare study by Bing (1963) of children with differential patterns of skill (high verbal–low math and high math–low verbal), there is little evidence bearing on the question. We are beginning to accumulate evidence about the relationship between parent-child interaction and *general* levels of cognitive performance (see Freeberg and Payne, 1967, or Streissguth and Bee, 1972, for reviews), but this won't help us much in analyzing sex differences, since the sexes do not differ in overall cognitive performance.

Finally, I do not want to leave you with the impression, in this discussion, that interaction effects are unimportant. The differences that the children bring into the world with them clearly influence the way they are treated. The Moss work (1967) is only one example. Minton, Kagan, and Levine's paper gives further examples of the same thing. Boys do not comply as quickly with their mothers' requests, so some escalation of intervention occurs, and this escalation more frequently ends up with some kind of punishment for the boy. These differences in treatment, resulting from differences in the child's pattern of responses, obviously make a difference in the long run. Hopefully, we will have more research like Minton's in the future, enabling us to build up a better and better picture of the nature of the interaction, and the contributions to that interaction of the child's initial proclivities and of the mother's differential responses.

SOME PARTING SHOTS

After all is said and done, I find there are two other comments I must make—perhaps less "scientific" and "well-balanced," but needed.

First, even though it is not presently possible to document many clear differences in treatment of young boys and girls in such areas as independence training or dependency or aggression, it is nonetheless true that from the very beginning parents know whether their infant is a boy or a girl and act accordingly in some ways. Girls wear pink and have bows in their hair; boys wear blue and have their hair cut short (or at least they used to). In buying clothing for our four-year-old daughter, I have found that girls' clothing is constructed for looks, not for durability, whereas boys' clothing is made to last through lots of rough outdoor play. Take a look at a Sears' catalog sometime (or Wards' or any of them). For little girls, they have pages of pants suits, coordinated knits, dresses, and such and only one page of clothing they call "rugged"; in the boys' section for the same ages, there are half a dozen pages of rugged clothing with all sorts of extra layers of material, reinforced knees, extra stitching at stress points, and so on—none of which is present in the "rugged" clothing for girls. The obvious implication is that boys are expected to play outdoors and more roughly than girls. (My solution is to buy boys' clothing for my daughter.) Whether the differences in clothing are in response to real differences in play patterns, which already exist at age three or four, or whether such play differences are in part determined by differences in clothing and the stereotypes such differences represent we can't say. But I find it interesting that clothing for infants and for toddlers does not show nearly as much sex differentiation. Except for color, babies wear much the same clothing, and the clothing described in the catalog is designed for either sex. It's when the age of about three or four is reached that clear differentiation in clothing appears.

The point I am trying to make is that sex typing is going on in various ways from very early; the puzzle is that this early sex typing in clothing and other externals does not at this point appear to be matched by clear sex typing in training practices, at least not at the very early ages.

Second, I must go back to the point I made at the very beginning: The sex differences we have been discussing are quite small, and the distributions invariably overlap. The presence of persistent differences, even if they are small, does require *explanation,* but it need not lead us to conclude that women (or men) are necessarily as a group suited or unsuited to particular jobs. Perhaps a few thousand years ago, or even a hundred years ago, differences in aggressiveness or physical strength mattered a great deal; our role assignments to men and women may well date from that period. But strength is a requirement in very few jobs now, and even where it does matter, there are enough technical advances to provide the less strong woman with mechanical assistance when needed. And in what kind of jobs does aggression matter? Spatial ability probably matters for some kinds of jobs, such as drafting or perhaps architecture, but keep in mind again that the male and female distribution of skills on this variable overlap, so there are many women with the requisite basic spatial ability for such jobs.

What I am arguing for is the separation of the scientific questions about the observed sex differences and their origins from the practical and social questions of the roles available to men and women in our society. The two sets of questions cannot be totally separated, but they can be separated to the extent that an open-minded examination of the possibilities of biological differences is not taken as support for the "suppression" or subjugation of women. And to the extent that good evidence for the existing differences is not used in support of advocacy of discriminatory job practices.

QUESTIONS FOR DEBATE OR DISCUSSION

1. If a woman you know was denied a top level executive job on the grounds that, because of her sex, she was not capable of holding such a job, what would your comment be? What evidence pro or con could you muster?

2. Based on the (admittedly scanty) evidence, what sort of rearing conditions would you recommend as being best designed to produce males and females who are most alike?

ADDITIONAL REFERENCES USEFUL IN PREPARATION
FOR DEBATE OR DISCUSSION

Broverman, D. M., Klaiber, E. L., Kobayashi, Y., and Vogel, W. Roles of activation and inhibition in sex differences in cognitive abilities. *Psychological Review*, 1968, **75**, 23–50.

This is a very difficult article, but probably worth exploring if you are interested in this side of the question. They are making an attempt at a synthesizing theory that would account for cognitive sex differences biologically.

Garai, J. E., and Scheinfeld, A. Sex differences in mental and behavioral traits. *Genetic Psychology Monographs*, 1968, **77**, 169–299.

This is the paper that is always referred to in discussions of neonatal sex differences.

Kagan, J., and Kogan, N. Individual variation in cognitive processes. In P. H. Mussen (Ed.), *Carmichael's manual of child psychology*. (3rd ed.) Vol. 1. New York: Wiley, 1970, pp. 1273–1365.

A review of all the evidence on all varieties of individual differences in cognitive functioning, including sex differences as only part of the discussion. A tough paper, but worth your while.

Maccoby, E. E. (Ed.) *The development of sex differences*. Stanford, Calif.: Stanford University Press, 1966.

A collection of six articles, all prepared especially for this book and all worthwhile. There is also an absolutely marvelous annotated bibliography covering all research on sex differences up to about 1965, with summary tables (from which most of the information in the summary tables in this chapter was extracted.)

Mednick, M. S., and Tangri, S. S. (Eds.) New perspective on women. *The Journal of Social Issues*, 1972, **28**(2).

This issue includes 14 papers discussing various aspects of the problems of sex differences. Of particular interest (in addition to the Hoffman paper, which came from this volume) are papers by Broverman et al. and by Horner. A number of papers describe sex roles in other countries.

Money, J. (Ed.) Sex research, new developments. New York: Holt, Rinehart and Winston, 1965.

A series of papers, mostly discussing research with primates.

Money, J. Sexually dimorphic behavior, normal and abnormal. In N. Kretchmer and D. N. Walcher (Eds.), *Environmental influences on genetic expression: Biological and behavioral aspects of sexual differentiation*. (Fogarty International Center Proceedings No. 2) Washington, D.C.: United States Government Printing Office, 1971.

An excellent presentation of the various literature on hermaphrodites, both human and subhuman.

Weisstein, N. Psychology constructs the female. In M. H. Garskof (Ed.), *Roles women play*. Belmont, Calif.: Brooks-Cole, 1971.

A *well-argued paper, in which the author takes the position among others that biological arguments based on comparisons of man with subhuman primates are fundamentally invalid.*

REFERENCES

Barclay, A., and Cusumano, D. R. Father absence, cross-sex identity, and field-dependent behavior in male adolescents. *Child Development*, 1967, **38**, 243–250.

Bing, E. Effect of childrearing practices on development of differential cognitive abilities. *Child Development*, 1963, **34**, 631–648.

Broverman, D. M., Broverman, I. K., Vogel, W., Palmer, R. D., and Klaiber, E. L. The automatization cognitive style and physical development. *Child Development*, 1964, **35**, 1343–1359.

Broverman, D. M., Klaiber, E. L., Kobayashi, Y., and Vogel, W. Roles of activation and inhibition in sex differences in cognitive abilities. *Psychological Review*, 1968, **75**, 23–50.

Broverman, I. K., Vogel, S. R., Broverman, D. M., Clarkson, F. E., and Rosenkrantz, P. S. Sex role stereotypes: A current appraisal. *Journal of Social Issues*, 1972, **28**(2), 59–78.

Carlsmith, L. Effects of early father absence on scholastic aptitude. *Harvard Educational Review*, 1964, **34**, 3–21.

Corah, N. L. Differentiation in children and their parents. *Journal of Personality*, 1965, **33**, 301–308.

Droege, R. C. Sex differences in aptitude maturation during high school. *Journal of Counseling Psychology*, 1967, **14**(5), 407–411.

Ehrhardt, A. A., and Money, J. Progestin induced hermaphroditism: I.Q. and psychosexual identity in a study of ten girls. *The Journal of Sex Research*, 1967, **3**, 83–100.

Freeberg, N. E., and Payne, D. T. Parental influence on cognitive development in early childhood: A review. *Child Development*, 1967, **38**, 65–87.

Hartlage, L. C. Sex-linked inheritance of spatial ability. *Perceptual and Motor Skills*, 1970, **31**, 610.

Kagan, J., and Kogan, N. Individual variation in cognitive processes. In P. H. Mussen (Ed.), *Carmichael's manual of child psychology*. (3rd ed.) Vol. 1. New York: Wiley, 1970, pp. 1273–1365.

Kagan, J., Rosman, B. L., Day, D., Albert, J., and Phillips, W. Information processing in the child: significance of analytic and reflective attitudes. *Psychological Monographs*, 1964, **78**(1, Whole No. 578).

Kilbride, H., Johnson, D., and Streissguth, A. P. Early home experiences of newborns as a function of social class, infant sex and birth order. Unpublished manuscript, University of Washington, 1971.

Klaiber, E. L., Broverman, D. M., and Kobayashi, Y. The automatization cognitive style, androgens, and monoamine oxidase. *Psychopharmacologia,* 1967, **11,** 320–336.

Klaiber, E. L., Broverman, D. M., Vogel, W., Abraham, G. E., and Cone, F. L. Effects of infused testosterone on mental performances and serum LH. *The Journal of Clinical Endocrinology and Metabolism,* 1971, **32,** 341–349.

Klausmeier, H. J., and Wiersma, W. Relationship of sex, grade level and locale to performance of high I.Q. students on divergent thinking tests. *Journal of Educational Psychology,* 1964, **55,** 114–119.

Klausmeier, H. J., and Wiersma, W. The effects of I.Q. level and sex on divergent thinking of seventh grade pupils of low, average, and high I.Q. *Journal of Educational Research,* 1965, **58,** 300–302.

Kohlberg, L. A cognitive-developmental analysis of children's sex-role concepts and attitudes. In E. E. Maccoby (Ed.), *The development of sex differences.* Stanford, Calif.: Stanford University Press, 1966, pp. 82–173.

Lewis, M. State as an infant-environment interaction: an analysis of mother-infant interactions as a function of sex. *Merrill-Palmer Quarterly,* 1972, **18,** 95–121.

Maccoby, E. E. (Ed.) *The development of sex differences.* Stanford, Calif.: Stanford University Press, 1966.

Maccoby, E. E. Differential socialization of boys and girls. Unpublished paper presented at the annual American Psychological Association meeting, Hawaii, September 1972.

Maccoby, E. E., and Jacklin, C. N. Sex differences in intellectual functioning. Unpublished paper presented at Educational Testing Service invitational conference on testing problems, October 28, 1972.

McNemar, Q. *The revision of the Stanford-Binet scale: An analysis of the standardization data.* Boston: Houghton Mifflin, 1942.

Mischel, W. A social-learning view of sex differences in behavior. In E. E. Maccoby (Ed.), *The development of sex differences.* Stanford, Calif.: Stanford University Press, 1966, pp. 56–81.

Mischel, W. Sex-typing and socialization. In P. H. Mussen (Ed.), *Carmichael's manual of child psychology.* (3rd ed.) Vol. 2. New York: Wiley, 1970, pp. 3–72.

Money, J. Sexually dimorphic behavior, normal and abnormal. In N. Kretchmer and D. N. Walcher (Eds.), *Environmental influences on genetic expression: biological and behavioral aspects of sexual differentiation.* (Fogarty International Center Proceedings No. 2) Washington, D.C.: United States Government Printing Office, 1971, pp. 201–212.

Moss, H. A. Sex, age, and state as determinants of mother-infant inter-action. *Merrill-Palmer Quarterly*, 1967, **13**, 19–36.

Newson, J., and Newson, E. *4 year old in an urban community.* London: G. Allen & Unwin, 1963.

Raaheim, K. Sex differences on problem-solving tasks. *Scandinavian Journal of Psychology*, 1963, **4**, 161–164.

Rebelsky, F., and Hanks, C. Fathers' verbal interactions with infants in the first three months of life. *Child Development*, 1971, **42**, 63–68.

Rosenkrantz, P. S., Vogel, S. R., Bee, H., Broverman, I. K., and Brover-man, D. M. Sex role stereotypes and self-concepts in college students. *Journal of Consulting and Clinical Psychology*, 1968, **32**, 287–295.

Rothbart, M. K., and Maccoby, E. E. Parents' differential reactions to sons and daughters. *Journal of Personality and Social Psychology*, 1966, **4**, 237–243.

Sears, R. R., Rau, L., and Alpert, R. *Identification and child rearing.* Stanford, Calif.: Stanford University Press, 1965.

Stafford, R. E. Sex differences in spatial visualization as evidence of sex-linked inheritance. *Perceptual and Motor Skills*, 1961, **13**, 428.

Stenn, P. G., Klaiber, E. L., Vogel, W., and Broverman, D. M. Testos-terone effects upon photic stimulation of the electroencephalogram (EEG) and mental performance of humans. *Perceptual and Motor Skills*, 1972, **34**, 371–378.

Streissguth, A. P., and Bee, H. L. Mother-child interactions and cogni-tive development in children. In W. W. Hartup (Ed.), *The young child.* Vol. 2. Washington, D.C.: National Association for the Educa-tion of Young Children, 1972, pp. 158–183.

Weisstein, N. Psychology constructs the female. In M. H. Garskof (Ed.), *Roles women play.* Belmont, Calif.: Brooks-Cole, 1971.

Witkin, H. A., Dyk, R. B., Faterson, H. F., Goodenough, D. R., and Karp, S. A. *Psychological differentiation.* New York: Wiley, 1962.

Yarrow, L. J., Rubenstein, J. L., Pederson, F. A., and Jankowski, J. J. Dimensions of early stimulation and their differential effects on in-fant development. *Merrill-Palmer Quarterly*, 1972, **18**, 205–218.

sex differences in human development[*]

CORINNE HUTT   *Department of Psychology, University of Reading, Reading, Berks*

During the past two decades there has been a regrettable silence on the subject of sex differences in human development in the psychological literature. What reports there were, clearly influenced by the 'psychosexual-neutrality-at-birth' theory (Diamond, 1965), dealt mainly with questions of sex-role identification, sex-role adoption, learning of appropriate sex-role behaviours, and so on.

Two timely rebukes were administered recently by Garai and Scheinfeld (1968) and Carlson and Carlson (1960). Each pair of authors was lamenting the lack of attention paid to sex differences in their own field—the former in developmental psychology and the latter in social psychology. They noted that in each area a large number of studies failed to look for sex differences; others used single-sex samples, and some were even unaware of the sex of their subjects. Since these two areas account for a substantial proportion of psychological research undertaken, the neglect of sex differences seems to have been particularly regrettable.

A turning-point in this trend was the publication in 1966 of

Hutt, Corinne. Sex differences in human development. *Human Development*, 1972, **15**, 153–170.
*Based, in part, on a paper read to the Annual Conference of the British Psychological Society, Exeter, 1971, in a symposium on 'The biological bases of psychological sex differences' convened by the author.

the book *The development of sex differences* edited by Eleanor Maccoby. Although still reflecting a predominantly 'psychosexual-neutrality-at-birth' orientation, it nevertheless brought to light a large amount of incriminating evidence. Then followed the third edition of *The psychology of human differences* (Tyler, 1965) which contained a cogent review of cognitive sex differences, and more recently, the impressive monograph by Garai and Scheinfeld (1968). Since then, and given an ironic fillip by the Women's Liberation Movement no doubt, many reports acknowledging the presence of sex differences have once again appeared in the literature. It is notable that, since its inception two years ago, the journal *Developmental Psychology* has contained one or more reports on sex differences in nearly every issue.

In many ways, however, psychological sex differences are the tip of the iceberg. By the time differences in behavior and performance manifest themselves, so much differentiation has already taken place. As contributors to the symposium on *The biological bases of psychological sex differences* made only too clear, many of these differences are determined from the moment an ovum is fertilised by a sperm carrying an X or a Y chromosome. Possession of a Y chromosome, for example, confers a particular flavour on the development of the male zygote and embryo—an effect more pervasive than would result from simply the determination of masculinity (Ounsted and Taylor, 1972). Subsequently, the gonadal hormones exert their organisational influence on reproductive structures and, more significantly, on the central nervous system (Harris, 1964, 1970; Levine, 1966; Whalen, 1968; Hutt, 1972a; Michael, 1971).

In this paper, therefore, I would like to discuss some empirical results of behavioural and intellectual sex differences in early human development in the context of what is known about the biological determination of such differences.

EMBRYOLOGICAL DEVELOPMENT

As Garai and Scheinfeld (1968) point out, from the moment of conception males and females exhibit radically different patterns of development. The neuroendocrinological processes and their influence on early development are essentially the same in all placental mammals and these have been adequately described elsewhere (Harris, 1964, 1970; Gorski and Wagner, 1965; Whalen, 1968; Hutt, 1972a).

The most notable feature of mammalian development is that there is no *neuter* sex. In the presence of a Y chromosome, the male gonad differentiates and then produces the androgenic evocator substance which exerts its action upon hypothalamic centres to produce the acyclic pattern of gonadotrophic hormone release characteristic of the male. In the absence of a Y chromosome, or more specifically, early androgenic influence, the natural propensity of mammalian creatures is to differentiate as *females*. This is so even in the case of a genetic male in whom, due to early castration or some disorder, the testicular hormone is absent or ineffective. Such an instance occurs in humans in the syndrome of testicular feminisation, where, due to a recessive disorder, the testes of the genetic male often develop in an inguinal hernia and the gonadal hormone, if produced at all, is without effect (Federman, 1967). This individual differentiates as a female. Conversely, in the presence of androgens during the critical period, even the genetic female will differentiate as a male, as happens in the case of the adrenogenital syndrome (Wilkins, 1962; Bongiovanni and Root, 1963; Federman, 1967). Curiously, in the absence of *any* gonadal hormone, the development might be described as excessively 'feminine': this happens in the case of Turner's syndrome, where one sex chromosome is lacking, the karyotype being XO, and there is gonadal dysgenesis. The comparison of behavioural and psychological features in androgenised females and in cases of Turner's syndrome made by Money and Ehrhardt (1968) is most instructive.

The particular interest of the processes and determinants of sexual differentiation to psychologists lies in the fact that it is not merely the reproductive structures which are organised in a typically male or female pattern, but higher neural centres as well. Characteristic differences appear, therefore, in patterns of sexual behaviour as well as in non-sexual behaviour. The behavioural differences are particularly striking in the higher mammals, namely, the primates (see Hamburg and Lunde, 1966; Goy, 1966, 1968, for informative reviews).

PHYSICAL GROWTH, MATURATION AND SUSCEPTIBILITY

From very early in uterine life males show their characteristic vulnerability: on average 120 males are conceived for every 100 females and by term this ratio has decreased to 110: 100 (Glenister, 1956). The majority of spontaneous abortions (miscarriages), therefore, are of male foetuses (Stevenson and McClarin, 1957). In terms of live births the ratio is only 106: 100, which indicates a greater male susceptibility to perinatal complications such as anoxia (Stevenson, 1966; Stevenson and Bobrow, 1967). Throughout life males remain more vulnerable to a variety of disorders, e.g., cerebral palsy, viral infections, ulcers, coronary thrombosis and some forms of mental illness (Taylor and Ounsted, 1972; Garai, 1970). In fact the male's longevity is so curtailed that by the 6th and 7th decades of life the sex ratio is reversed in favour of the females. The sex-linked recessive disorders like haemophilia and colour-blindness predominantly affect the males; the recessive genes being carried on the X chromosome, males manifest the disorder even in the heterozygotic condition, whereas females are protected, other than in the homozygous condition, by the normal allele on the other X chromosome. The adage of the male being the stronger sex requires a very literal interpretation indeed.

At birth, males are heavier and longer than females (Ounsted, 1972). From infancy on boys have a consistently higher basal metabolism and greater vital capacity, develop proportionately larger hearts and lungs, and have a higher concentration of haemoglobin, notably after puberty (Hutt, 1972). Moreover, the male hormone facilitates protein synthesis whereas the female hormones have no such direct action. All these features characterise the male for a more active and strenuous life.

In sharp contrast to his physical advantages, however, is the male's developmental retardation: growth velocity lags nearly 2 years behind the female's (Tanner, 1970), bone ossification is completed much later (see Hutt, 1972b) and puberty is attained about 2½ years after the girl (Nicholson and Hanley, 1953). The onset of walking and talking, as well as aspects of dentition occur earlier in girls than in boys. In terms of maturity the newborn girl is equivalent to a 4- to 6-week-old boy (Garai and Scheinfeld, 1968).

BEHAVIOUR DIFFERENCES IN INFANCY

MOTOR ACTIVITY AND SENSORY CAPACITIES

In general, male newborn infants exhibit more spontaneous motor activity and this consists predominantly of gross movements, whereas the activity of the female infants consists typically of finer movements, largely of the facial area, e.g., mouthing, smiling or sucking (Korner, 1969). Female neonates have lower tactual and pain thresholds (Lipsitt and Levy, 1959) and this sex difference very probably obtains throughout the lifespan since Galton observed it in adults and specifically commented upon it as early as 1894. Female infants also react more irritably to tactual stimulation (Bell and Costello, 1964).

There is now substantial evidence that the visual acuity of males is superior to that of females, at least from adolescence on (Burg and Hulbert, 1961), whereas females have better auditory discrimination and localisation (Corso, 1959; Schaie et al., 1964). The results obtained by Lewis suggest that such sensory proficiency and preferences may be evident even in early infancy: he found that male infants showed greater interest in visual patterns generally, while female infants attended more to auditory sequences (Kagan and Lewis, 1965); of visual patterns female infants found *facial* configurations most interesting and at 3, 6 and 9 months of age they were able to differentiate between such patterns more effectively than the males (Lewis, 1969).

On the basis of results obtained from 3-month-old infants, Moss and Robson (1970) concluded that, whereas social experience and learning appeared to have a strong influence upon the visual behaviour of females, that of the males was more a function of endogenous attributes like state. These several results illustrate not merely the sex-dependent sensory capacities but also the differences in those influences to which they are amenable. Such differences, however, are not peculiar to the human species—very similar behaviour is shown by monkeys (Mitchell and Brandt, 1970).

The early dependence on particular sensory modalities has the consequence that auditory and visual stimuli have different reinforcing properties, depending on the sex of the subject. For instance, Watson (1969) found that visual fixation on a target could be operantly conditioned in 14-week-old infants, the effective reinforcers being visual for males and auditory for females. Moreover, the boys failed to learn under conditions of auditory reinforcement. This reliance of males and females on visual and auditory channels, respectively, is observable throughout childhood and adolescence (Stevenson et al., 1963) and persists in adulthood (Miller, 1963; Pishkin and Shurley, 1965).

MOTHER-INFANT INTERACTION

The earliest social behaviour displayed by the human infant is in the context of the mother-infant interaction. Many studies reporting differences in the way mothers handle their male and female infants, or for that matter, any sex differences in human behaviour, tend to account for such differences in terms of the mothers' expectations of a son or a daughter, of her greater affinity for the same-sex infant, or else in terms of the reinforcement of sex-appropriate behaviours. A study by Moss (1967) is notable, therefore, for the demonstration that considerable differences in the behaviour of male and female infants exist at the age of 3 weeks. The differential reactions of the mother are very probably contingent upon these behaviours and not contrariwise, as commonly supposed. Two of Moss' findings seem particularly significant, especially since they were also apparent at the age of 3 months:

mothers stimulated their infant sons more, and imitated the vocalisations of their daughters more. The first of these raises the interesting possibility that we may have here the human analogue of the 'early-handled' animals described by Levine (1960), Denenberg (1964) and others. If such findings are replicated, we may seriously have to inquire whether the early experience of male infants in any way contributes to their subsequent lower emotionality (Gray, 1971a; Gray and Buffery, 1971; Buffery and Gray, 1972). Secondly, the fact that mothers imitated, and thereby very probably reinforced, their daughters' vocalisations is surprising, since the actual amounts of vocalisation by boys and by girls were almost identical. Since a similar finding was also reported by Goldberg and Lewis (1969), it immediately raises the question as to what parameters of infants' vocal behaviour the mothers were responding. May this fact also explain, in part, the earlier acquisition of speech in girls?

Goldberg and Lewis (1969) were able to demonstrate striking sex differences in infants of 13 months, both in their behavior towards their mothers as well as in the character of their play. Girls were more reluctant than boys to leave their mothers, tended to stay near them when playing and sought physical reassurance more frequently.

FEAR

Analysing data from the Berkeley Growth Study, Bronson (1969) found sex differences in the onset of the fear-of-stranger reaction: fear at 10–15 months was positively correlated with fear and shyness at a later age in *boys* but not in girls. This was chiefly due to a sub-group of boys who showed a precocious onset of fear (4–6 months) and remained so throughout childhood. Thus, an early onset of fear-of-novelty in male infants was predictive of fearfulness during the entire pre-school period.

BEHAVIOURAL DIFFERENCES IN CHILHOOD

SOCIAL INTERACTIONS

In an investigation of the types of activity boys and girls generally engaged in (Brindley et al., 1972), it was found that girls engaged in social interactions much more frequently than boys—a dramatic illustration of the early differentiation of masculine and feminine interests, boys being interested in objects or 'things' and girls in people (Little, 1968). Honzik (1951) and Hattwick (1937) observed very similar differences in older children, as did Farrell (1957).

More specifically, *aggression* is an aspect of social behaviour that has interested many students of child behaviour and a number of studies have shown boys to be more aggressive than girls (Green, 1933; Dawe, 1934; Jersild and Markey, 1935; Hattwick, 1937; Walters et al., 1957; Jegard and Walters, 1960; Bandura et al., 1963; Digman, 1963; Pederson and Belling, 1970). Many of these results, however, were interpreted in terms of sex-role expectations and conventions, with no reference made to the fact that the males of most mammalian species are more aggressive than the females, nor was surprise expressed at the apparent universality of male aggression —despite differences in culture-patterns, conventions and social norms. In our own study of nursery school children (Brindley et al., 1972), we found that two thirds of all aggressive acts were initiated by boys. Moreover, not only did boys *display* more aggression, but they also *elicited* aggression. Many of such disputes arose over the possession of toys, equipment or territory. Girls, whose aggression generally found verbal expression, were equally aggressive to other girls, boys, teachers or objects. Boys retaliated more and hence prolonged such encounters whereas the girls usually submitted or else employed more devious strategies to secure their objectives (McCandless et al., 1961). These sex-dependent features of aggression are observable in older children as well as in adults. In experiments which allowed subjects to mete out punishment to a mock opponent, adult males gave bigger shocks when they thought their opponent was a male than when they thought it was a female (Buss, 1963; Taylor and Epstein, 1967). In a similar experiment 10- and 11-year-olds, using noise as punishment, behaved exactly as the adults had done (Shortell and Biller, 1970).

Male monkeys engage in threat displays while the females show fear grimaces, and in a male monkey group the dominance hierarchy is established by the aggressive behaviour and threat displays of the ascendant male while in female groups the hierarchy is established and maintained by the submissive behaviours of the non-dominant females (Angermeier et al., 1968). Thus, when the human results are considered in the general context of primate social behaviour, any purely cultural or environmental sex-role theory of sexual differentiation becomes difficult to countenance. Elsewhere (Hutt, 1972a, b), I have also presented the experimental evidence for regarding aggressive behaviour as primarily a function of the early sexual differentiation of the brain, and secondarily as an effect of circulating hormone levels.

Another aspect of early social behaviour that we studied was cooperative or mutual behaviour (Brindley et al., 1972), where children joined each other, either spontaneously or at the request of one of them, to engage in some mutual activity. Girls initiated such acts much more than boys, and directed their attention in this respect predominantly towards *younger* children (chiefly girls), thus manifesting their proclivities for fulfilling a nurturant and protective role (Mischel, 1970). This is evident in many ways: readiness to help younger ones carry things, to button pinafores or tie aprons, and to comfort a hurt or distressed child. The boys appear to show a remarkable indifference to a peer's discomfort or distress. McGrew (1972) has also described the characteristic tendency of the girls to shepherd and care for a new entrant to the nursery group, whereas boys manifest their customary indifference to such a newcomer. The boys in our study tended to direct their cooperative acts primarily towards other *older* boys, usually attempting to join a game or excursion already in progress. Similar sex-typical behaviours have been described in many infra-human primate groups too (DeVore and Jay, 1963; Harlow, 1962; Goodall, 1968).

In general, there is a marked tendency in humans—children and adults alike (Hutt, 1972; Tiger, 1969)—to interact with others of their own sex. The men's club, the officers' mess, the women's institute, all clearly have their ontogenetic origins in the kindergartens and their phylogenetic origins in diverse primate groups.

. . .

CONCLUDING DISCUSSION

The foregoing discussion of the process of sexual differentiation and the phenomena of sex differences has been an attempt to reiterate the many biological and psychological differences that characteristically differentiate males and females in our species. These particular properties have clearly been selected in accordance with, on the one hand, certain morphological features, and on the other, with the particular roles human males and females fulfill. That these morphological and functional requirements are not unique to a particular society, nor even to the human species is evident in the fact that very similar differences are demonstrable in infra-human primate species. This fact alone makes an exclusively environmental theory of sex differences difficult to countenance. Moreover, as Buffery and Gary (1972) point out, such similarities behove us to seek a more appropriately biological explanation for the phenomena. Gray himself has discussed the endocrinological, neural and adaptive bases for sex differences in mammals generally (Gray, 1971a, b; Gray and Buffery, 1971; Buffery and Gray, 1972). The evidence reviewed by both Gray and myself (Hutt, 1972) shows that not only is behaviour affected by circulating hormones, but that these hormones have an important formative and organisational influence on brain function and structure.

It is a common, but nonetheless fallacious, assumption that the recognition of individual differences, be they sex- or personality-dependent, is to commit oneself to a psychological or behavioural determinism. On the contrary, the recognition of such differences and their possible determinants enables individuals to modify and/or exploit environmental circumstances to profitable advantage.

The conformity and consistency of the female's behaviour in fulfilling a predominantly nurturant role makes her a stable and reliable support for the dependent infant. Even her distractability (Garai and Scheinfeld, 1968) appears to be adaptive. In her intellectual faculties too the human female seems to have exploited those facets that ensure the optimal execution of her primary role—the maternal role. For more effective communication increasing reliance is placed on linguistic skills, and it is noteworthy that in verbal functions as in non-verbal ones, it is in *execution* that the female excels. The male on the other hand, and necessarily, excels in spatial and numerical abilities, is divergent in thought and action, and is generally superior in *conceptualisation*. The fact that such functional dimorphism exists may be unacceptable to many, but it is a dimorphism that has been uniquely successful.

REFERENCES

Angermeier, W. F.; Phelps, J. B.; Murray, S. and Howanstine, J.: Dominance in monkeys: sex differences. Psychon. Sci. **12:** 344 (1968).

Bandura, A.; Ross, D. and Ross, S. A.: Transmission of aggression through imitation of aggressive models. J. abnorm. soc. Psychol. **63:** 575–582 (1961).

Bayley, N.: Developmental problems of the mentally retarded child; in Philips: Prevention and treatment of mental retardation (Basic Books, New York 1966).

Bayley, N. and Schaefer, E. S.: Correlations of maternal and child behaviours with the development of mental abilities: data from the Berkeley Growth Study. Monogr. Soc. Res. Child Develop. **29:** 1–80 (1964).

Bell, R. Q. and Costello, N. S.: Three tests for sex differences in tactile sensitivity in the newborn. Biol. Neonat. **7:** 335–347 (1964).

Bennett, G. K.; Seashore, H. G. and Wesman, A. G.: Differential aptitude tests. Manual, 3rd ed. (Psychological Corporation, New York 1959).

Bhavnani, R. and Hutt, C.: Divergent thinking in boys and girls. J. child Psychol. Psychiat. (1972, in press).

Bongiovanni, A. M. and Root, A. W.: The adrenogenital syndrome. New Engl. J. Med. **268:** 1283 (1963).

Brindley, C.; Clarke, P.; Hutt, C.; Robinson, I. and Wethli, E.: Sex differences in the activities and social interactions of nursery school children; in Michael and Crook: Comparative ecology and behaviour of primates (Academic Press, London 1972, in press).

Bronson, G. W.: Fear of visual novelty: developmental patterns in males and females. Develop. Psychol. 1: 33–40 (1969).

Buffery, A. W. H.: Sex differences in cognitive skills. Paper Ann. Conf. Brit. Psychol. Soc., Exeter; in Symp. on Biological bases of psychological sex differences (1971).

Buffery, A. W. H. and Gray, J. A.: Sex differences in the development of perceptual and linguistic skills; in Ounsted and Taylor: Gender differences—their ontogeny and significance (Churchill, London 1972).

Burg, A. and Hulbert, S.: Dynamic visual acuity as related to age, sex and static acuity. J. appl. Psychol. 45: 111–116 (1961).

Buss, A. H.: Physical aggression in relation to different frustrations. J. abnorm. soc. Psychol. 67: 1–7 (1963).

Carlson, E. R. and Carlson, R.: Male and female subjects in personality research. J. abnorm. soc. Psychol. 61: 482–483 (1960).

Clark, A. H.; Wyon, S. M. and Richards, M. P.: Free-play in nursery school children. J. child Psychol. Psychiat. 10: 205–216 (1969).

Corso, J. F.: Age and sex differences in pure-tone thresholds. J. acoust. Soc. Amer. 31: 489–507 (1959).

Dawe, H. C.: An analysis of 200 quarrels of preschool children. Child Develop. 5: 139–156 (1934).

Denenberg, V. H.: Animal studies on developmental determinants of behavioural adaptability; in Harvey: Experience, structure and adaptability, pp. 123–147 (Springer, New York 1966).

De Vore, I. and Jay, P.: Mother-infant relations in baboons and langurs; in Rheingold: Maternal behaviour in mammals (Wiley & Sons, 1963).

Diamond, M.: A critical evaluation of the ontogeny of human sexual behaviour. Quart. Rev. Biol. 40: 147–175 (1965).

Digman, J. M.: Principal dimensions of child personality as inferred from teachers' judgments. Child Develop. 34: 43–60 (1963).

Farrell, M.: Sex differences in block play in early childhood education. J. educ. Res. 51: 279–284 (1957).

Federman, M. D.: Abnormal sexual development (Saunders, Philadelphia 1967).

Galton, F.: The relative sensitivity of men and women at the nape of the neck by Webster's test. Nature, Lond. 50: 40–42 (1894).

Garai, J. E.: Sex differences in mental health. Genet. Psychol. Monogr. 81: 123–142 (1970).

Garai, J. E. and Scheinfeld, A.: Sex differences in mental and behavioural traits. Genet. Psychol. Monogr. 77: 169–299 (1968).

Glenister, T. W.: Determination of sex in early human embryos. Nature, Lond. **177:** 1135 (1956).

Goldberg, S. and Lewis, M.: Play behaviour in the year-old infant: early sex differences. Child Develop. **40:** 21–31 (1969).

Goodall, J. L. van: The behaviour of free-living chimpanzees in the Gombi Stream Reserve. Anim. Behav. Monogr. **1:** 161–311 (1968).

Gorski, R. A. and Wagner, J. W.: Gonadal activity and sexual differentiation of the hypothalamus. Endocrinology **76:** 226–239 (1965).

Goy, R. W.: Role of androgens in the establishment and regulation of behavioural sex differences in mammals. J. anim. Sci. **25:** suppl., pp. 21–35 (1966).

Goy, R. W.: Organising effects of androgen on the behaviour of rhesus monkeys; in Michael: Endocrinology and human behaviour (Oxford University Press, London 1968).

Gray, J. A.: Sex differences in emotional behaviour in mammals including man: endocrine bases. Acta psychol., Amst. **35:** 29–46 (1971a).

Gray, J. A.: The psychology of fear and stress (Weidenfeld and Nicolson, London 1971b).

Gray, J. A. and Buffery, A. W. H.: Sex differences in emotional and cognitive behaviour in mammals including man: adaptive and neural bases. Acta psychol., Amst. **35:** 89–111 (1971).

Green, E. H.: Friendships and quarrels among preschool children. Child Develop. **4:** 236–252 (1933).

Hamburg, D. A. and Lunde, D. T.: Sex hormones in the development of sex differences in human behaviour; in Maccoby: The development of sex differences (Tavistock, London 1966).

Harlow, H. F.: Development of affection in primates; in Bliss: Roots of behaviour (Harper, New York 1962).

Harris, G. W.: Sex hormones, brain development and brain function. Endocrinology **75:** 627–648 (1964).

Harris, G. W.: Hormonal differentiation of the developing central nervous system with respect to patterns of endocrine function. Philos. Trans. B **259:** 165–177 (1970).

Hattwick, L. A.: Sex differences in behavior of nursery school children. Child Develop. **8:** 343–355 (1937).

Heilman, J. D.: Sex differences in intellectual abilities. J. educ. Psychol. **24:** 47–62 (1933).

Hobson, J. R.: Sex differences in primary mental abilities. J. educ. Res. **41:** 126–132 (1947).

Honzik, M. P.: Sex differences in the occurrence of materials in the play constructions of pre-adolescents. Child Develop. **22:** 15–35 (1951).

Hudson, L.: Contrary imaginations (Methuen, London 1966).

Hudson, L.: Frames of mind (Methuen, London 1968).

Hutt, C.: Specific and diversive exploration; in Reese and Lipsitt: Advances in child development and behaviour, vol. 5 (Academic Press, London 1970a).

Hutt, C.: Curiosity in young children. Sci. J. **6**: 68–72 (1970b).

Hutt, C.: Neuroendocrinological, behavioural and intellectual aspects of sexual differentiation in human development; in Ounsted and Taylor: Gender differences—their ontogeny and significance (Churchill, London 1972a).

Hutt, C.: Males and females (Penguin Books, 1972b, in press).

Jegard, S. and Walters, R. H.: A study of some determinants of aggression in young children. Child Develop. **31**: 739–747 (1960).

Jersild, A. T. and Markey, F. V.: Conflicts between preschool children. Child Develop. Monogr. 21 (1935).

Kagan, J. and Lewis, M.: Studies of attention in the human infant. Behav. Develop. **11**: 95–127 (1965).

Klein, V.: The demand for professional Woman I power. Brit. J. Sociol. **17**: 183 (1966).

Korner, A. F.: Neonatal startles, smiles, erections, and reflex sucks as related to state, sex and individuality. Child Develop. **40**: 1039–1053 (1969).

Levine, S.: Stimulation in infancy. Sci. Amer. **202**: 80–86 (1960).

Levine, S.: Sex differences in the brain. Sci. Amer. **214**: 84–90 (1966).

Lewis, M.: Infants' responses to facial stimuli during the first year of life. Dev. Psychol. **1**: 75–86 (1969).

Lipsitt, L. P. and Levy, N.: Electrotactual threshold in the neonate. Child Develop. **30**: 547–554 (1959).

Little, B.: Psychospecialisation: functions of differential interest in persons and things. Bull. Brit. psychol. Soc. **21**: 113A (1968).

Maccoby, E. E. (ed.): The development of sex differences (Tavistock, London 1966).

McCandless, B. R.; Bilous, B. and Bennett, H. L.: Peer popularity and dependence on adults in preschool age socialisation. Child Develop. **32**: 511–518 (1961).

McGrew, W. C.: Aspects of social development in nursery school children with emphasis on introduction to the group; in Blurton-Jones: Ethological studies of child behaviour (Cambridge University Press, London 1972).

Michael, R. P.: The endocrinological bases of sex differences. Paper Ann. Conf. Brit. Psychol. Soc., Exeter, in Symp. on Biological bases of psychological sex differences (1971).

Miller, A.: Sex differences related to the effect of auditory stimulation on the stability of visually fixed forms. Percept. Mot. Skills **16**: 589–594 (1963).

Mischel, W.: Sex-typing and socialisation; in Mussen: Carmichael's manual of child psychology, vol. 2 (Wiley, London 1970).

Mitchell, G. and Brandt, E. M.: Behavioural differences related to experience of mother and sex of infant in the rhesus monkey. Develop. Psychol. **3:** 149 (1970).

Money, J. and Ehrhardt, A. A.: Prenatal hormonal exposure: possible effects on behaviour in man; in Michael: Endocrinology and human behaviour (Oxford University Press, London 1968).

Moore, T.: Language and intelligence: a longitudinal study of the first 8 years. I. Patterns of development in boys and girls. Human Develop. **10:** 88–106 (1967).

Moss, H.: Sex, age and state as determinants of mother infant interaction. Merrill-Palmer Quart. **13:** 19–36 (1967).

Moss, H. A. and Robson, K. S.: The relation between the amount of time infants spend at various states and the development of visual behaviour. Child Develop. **41:** 509–517 (1970).

Nicolson, A. B. and Hanley, C.: Indices of physiological maturity: derivation and interrelationships. Child Develop. **24:** 3–38 (1953).

Ounsted, C. and Taylor, D. C.: The Y chromosome message: a point of view; in Ounsted and Taylor: Gender differences—their ontogeny and significance (Churchill, London 1972).

Ounsted, M.: Sex differences in intrauterine growth; in Ounsted and Taylor: Gender differences—their ontogeny and significance (Churchill, London 1972).

Pedersen, F. A. and Bell, R. Q.: Sex differences in preschool children without histories of complications of pregnancy and delinquency. Develop. Psychol. **3:** 10–15 (1970).

Pishkin, V. and Shurley, J. T.: Auditory dimensions and irrelevant information in concept identification of males and females. Percept. Mot. Skills **20:** 673–683 (1965).

Schaie, K. W.; Baltes, P. and Strother, C. R.: A study of auditory sensitivity in advanced age. J. Geront. **19:** 453–457 (1964).

Shortell, J. R. and Biller, H. B.: Aggression in children as a function of sex of subject and sex of opponent. Develop. Psychol. **3:** 143–144 (1970).

Shouksmith, G.: Intelligence, creativity and cognitive style (Batsford, London 1970).

Stevenson, A. C.: Sex chromatin and the sex ratio in man; in Moore: The sex chromatin (Saunders, Philadelphia 1966).

Stevenson, A. C. and Bobrow, M.: Determinants of sex proportions in man, with consideration of the evidence concerning a contribution from x-linked mutations to intrauterine death. J. med. Genet. **4:** 190–221 (1967).

Stevenson, A. C. and McClarin, R. H.: Determination of the sex of human abortions by nuclear sexing the cells of the chorionic. Nature, Lond. **180:** 198 (1957).

Stevenson, H. W.; Keen, R. and Knights, R. W.: Parents and strangers as reinforcing agents for children's performance. J. abnorm. soc. Psychol. **67**: 183–186 (1963).

Tanner, J. M.: Physical growth; in Mussen: Carmichael's manual of child psychology, 3rd ed. (Wiley, New York 1970).

Taylor, D. C.: Differential rates of cerebral maturation between sexes and between hemispheres. Lancet **iii**: 140–142 (1969).

Taylor, D. C. and Ounsted, C.: The nature of gender differences explored through ontogenetic analyses of sex ratios in disease; in Ounsted and Taylor: Gender differences—their ontogeny and significance (Churchill, London 1972).

Taylor, S. P. and Epstein, S.: Aggression as a function of the interaction of the sex of the aggressor and sex of the victim. J. Personality **35**: 474–486 (1967).

Tiger, L.: Men in groups (Nelson, London 1969).

Tyler, L.: The psychology of human differences, 3rd ed. (Appleton-Century-Crofts, New York 1965).

Wallach, M. A. and Kogan, N.: Modes of thinking in young children (Holt, Rinehart & Winston, New York 1965).

Walters, J.; Pearce, D. and Dahms, L.: Affectional and aggressive behaviour of preschool children. Child Develop. **28**: 15–26 (1957).

Watson, T. S.: Operant conditioning of visual fixation in infants under visual and auditory reinforcement. Develop. Psychol. **1**: 508–516 (1969).

Wechsler, D.: The measurement of adult intelligence (Williams & Wilkins, Baltimore 1941).

Wechsler, D.: The measurement and appraisal of adult intelligence, 4th ed. (Williams & Wilkins, Baltimore 1958).

Werner, E. E.: Sex differences in correlations between children's IQ and measures of parental ability, and environmental ratings. Develop. Psychol. **1**: 280–285 (1969).

Whalen, R. E.: Differentiation of the neural mechanisms which control gonadotropin secretion and sexual behaviour; in Diamond: Reproduction and sexual behaviour (Indiana University Press, Bloomington 1968).

Wilkins, L.: Adrenal disorders. II. Congenital virilizing adrenal hyperplasia. Arch. Dis. Childh. **37**: 231 (1962).

psychosexual differentiation as a function of androgenic stimulation*

CHARLES H. PHOENIX
ROBERT W. GOY
JOHN A. RESKO

Among mammals the sex of an individual is generally said to be dependent upon contribution of either an X or Y chromosome by the male. However, the mechanism whereby these chromosomes determine the sex of the individual has until recently received little attention. In practice, the sex of an individual is commonly decided upon by the appearance of the external genitalia without reference to the chromosomal status.

To each sex is ascribed a characteristic pattern of reproductive behavior which varies from one species to another. In addition, other behavioral characteristics are commonly attributed to members of a given sex. For example, the bitch is commonly thought to be more gentle than the dog, and the bull to be dangerously aggressive when compared to the cow. These behavioral characteristics, or in many cases what amounts only to expectations, are assumed to follow from the appearance of the external genitalia. In man, an

Reprinted from M. Diamond (Ed.) *Reproduction and sexual behavior.* Copyright © 1969, Indiana University Press. By permission.
*Publication No. 320 of the Oregon Regional Primate Research Center supported in part by Grant MH-08634 of the National Institutes of Health, and in part by Grant FR-00163.

elaborate set of behaviors and attitudes are labeled as masculine and another constellation of behaviors are considered feminine. The behavior expected of an individual within a given society is determined by assignment to the class male or female.

Very little is known about what determines masculinity or femininity. Because research on problems of sexuality in the human is virtually impossible, researchers have looked to mammals lower on the phylogenetic scale for answers to some of the basic questions. For example, what are the biological mechanisms by which sexual and sex related behaviors are determined?

From research on adult laboratory animals and from clinical observations it has long been believed that hormones do not establish patterns of behavior but only serve to bring to expression previously established behavior patterns. The consensus of opinion is that gonadal hormones themselves are not masculine or feminine; they only permit the masculine or feminine pattern of behavior that exists within the individual to be brought to expression. The question arises as to whether or not the hormones, especially the gonadal hormones, play any role at all in establishing the basic sexuality of the individual.

We approached this question by first studying sexual behavior, that is, behavior instrumental to reproduction of the species, and initially directed our attention to the guinea pig. Much was known about the reproductive behavior of this species (Young, 1961), and it seemed to be a model eminently suited to the investigation.

Our first series of studies on the guinea pig led us to conclude that the gonadal hormones did indeed play a role in establishing basic patterns of reproductive behavior. We learned that when pregnant female guinea pigs are injected with testosterone propionate, the genetic female offspring from such pregnancies are masculinized (Phoenix et al., 1959). The masculinization included not only morphological characteristics which had previously been demonstrated (Dantchakoff, 1938) but, more significantly, physiological and psychosexual masculinization as well. Such experimentally produced pseudohermaphrodites possess ovaries, although there is evidence of ovarian disfunction (Tedford and Young, 1960). The external vaginal orifice is completely obliterated, and a well-developed penis is formed. The genital tract shows variable abnormalities. The O_2 consumption rate resembles that of the male rather than that of the female (Goy et al., 1962). The spayed, adult pseudohermaphrodite when injected with estrogen and progesterone fails to display estrous behavior characteristic of the normal spayed female similarly injected with estrogen and progesterone. Not only is responsiveness to the female hormones suppressed but there is heightened sensitivity to testosterone propionate as evidenced by the increase in mounting frequency. Furthermore, the effect of the prenatal treatment is permanent. Thus, although it is possible to increase the frequency of mounting behavior in a normal female by treating the animals with testosterone propionate in adulthood, the effect is transient and mounting frequency returns to pretreatment levels when treatment is discontinued (Phoenix et al., 1959). Informal observation of the behavior of the female pseudohermaphrodite reveals a level of aggression not unlike that observed in male guinea pigs.

In producing masculinization of the genetic female both the stage of fetal development and the hormonal dosage are critical. Treatments confined to very early or late stages in fetal development are ineffective with the dosages that have been used (Goy et al., 1964). Maximum masculinization in the guinea pig was obtained when treatment with 5 mg of testosterone propionate was started at day 30 of gestation and continued daily for 6 days, followed by 1 mg per day to day 55. Other times and dosages produced variable degrees of modification. In general, the animals displaying the highest degree of psychosexual modification were also the most modified morphologically. These findings from our early research on the guinea pig led us to conclude that the gonadal hormones, especially testosterone, had a dual function. During the period of differentiation the gonadal hormones, we hypothesized, had an organizing action on the central neural tissues that controlled the display of sexual behavior. This function we contrasted to the action of the same hormones in the adult, where the hormones functioned to bring to expression patterns of behavior that had been previously established during development (Young, 1961). We viewed the action of the gonadal hormones on the central neural tissues in the developing fetus as analogous to their action on genital tract tissue, including those tissues constituting the external genitalia.

In further study of the role that testosterone plays in organizing the neural tissues that underlie reproductive behavior, genetic male rats were castrated on the day of birth and at various times to maturity (Grady et al., 1965). When rats were castrated on the day of birth and injected as adults with estrogen and progesterone, they responded much as did genetic females. Males that were castrated after the first 10 days of life failed to give typical female responses when injected in adulthood with the ovarian hormones. The results supported our hypothesis that it is the presence of the testicular hormone during the period of differentiation that masculinizes the individual whether that individual is genetically male or female.

From our work with the rat it become obvious that it was not prenatal treatment per se that was critical but treatment during the period of psychosexual differentiation. Generally one might expect that in long gestation animals such as the guinea pig, monkey, and man, the critical stage of development would occur during the prenatal period, whereas, in short gestation animals such as the mouse, rat, and hamster, the critical period for psychosexual differentiation might occur during the late fetal and early postnatal period. If one compares the ages at which psychosexual differentiation is found to occur in the rat, guinea pig, and monkey on the basis of post-fertilization age, the differences among these species become relatively small. More work is needed, especially in the monkey, to establish the critical time limits of psychosexual differentiation, and virtually nothing is known about man.

. . .

Largely as a result of aggressive behavior observed among pseudohermaphroditic guinea pigs we suggested in our first definitive paper on the organizing action of testosterone (Phoenix et al., 1959) that the ". . . masculinity or femininity of an animal's behavior beyond that which is purely sexual has developed in response to certain hormonal substances within the embryo and fetus." Considerable evidence gathered on the rodent has confirmed our suggestion. Cyclic running activity (Harris, 1964; Kennedy, 1964) and open-field behavior (Gray et al., 1965; Swanson, 1966, 1967) have been shown to be dependent upon the presence or absence of androgen during the period of psychosexual differentiation.

. . .

The success achieved with work on the rodent led us to pursue the work on a species which in a number of respects was more similar to man (Young et al., 1964). We chose to work with the rhesus monkey in which sexually dimorphic social behavior in the infant had been demonstrated (Rosenblum, 1961; Harlow, 1965). If, as we had postulated, behaviors other than those instrumental to reproduction were determined by the action of testosterone during differentiation, the rhesus, because of its rich behavioral repertoire, would prove an ideal model for study.

We set about producing female pseudohermaphroditic rhesus monkeys by injecting pregnant females with testosterone propionate.* The procedure followed essentially that reported by Wells and van Wagenen (1954) in which they produced animals described as showing marked morphological masculinization. Pregnant rhesus were given daily intramuscular injections of 20 mg of testosterone propionate beginning on day 40 and extending through day 69 of pregnancy. The average gestation period in the monkey is approximately 168 days. Using this treatment we obtained two female pseu-

---

*Testosterone propionate (Perandren) was supplied by courtesy of Ciba, Inc., Summit, N.J.

dohermaphrodites. Both animals possessed well-developed scrota and well-formed but small penes. The external urethral orifice was located at the tip of the penis as in the normal male. Testes could not be palpated as they can be in the genetic male, buccal smears were 34 to 37 percent sex-chromatin positive, and it was assumed that the animals possessed ovaries and Müllerian derivatives such as described by Wells and van Wagenen for the pseudohermaphroditic monkey and as we had observed in the pseudohermaphroditic guinea pig. We have had the opportunity to study the internal genital morphology of several treated fetuses that were aborted and in a few female pseudohermaphrodites that died shortly after birth. We confirmed the presence of an ovary in these pseudohermaphroditic animals but have not studied the internal morphology on any of the living pseudohermaphrodites whose behavior is reported here.

All the evidence from work on the guinea pig and rat in which we varied dosage and time of treatment suggested that for each species there is an optimal regimen for maximum behavioral and morphological modification. The opportunity to explore various treatments on the monkey has been sorely limited because of the few animals available coupled with the relatively high abortion rates we have encountered. It should be recalled that approximately half of the offspring from treated mothers are genetic males thus further reducing the pseudohermaphroditic females available for study. Evidence thus far assembled suggests that the original treatment was less than optimal both for morphological and behavioral modification. We also know from our limited experience that the animal with greatest penis development is not necessarily the animal showing the greatest behavioral modification. We assume that as the number of animals we study increases there then will be a correlation between the extent of morphological and behavioral modification. This was the situation that prevailed in our research on the guinea pig and there is no evidence for believing that the relationship will not hold for the rhesus.

The various treatment parameters employed for each surviving treated animal are indicated in Table 1. It is obvious from the table that few dosages and time periods are represented among the pseudohermaphrodites. It may be noted in the table that the mother of pseudohermaphrodite 1239 was treated with testosterone 6 days per week. This procedure followed exactly one of the treatments described by Wells and van Wagenen (1954). The abortion rate in animals so treated was as high as in animals treated 7 days per week and thus the 7-day-per-week treatment schedule was followed in all other animals. Animal 1656, who received hormone through day 111 of fetal life, possesses the most extensively modified external genitalia. However, its initial dosage level was low and the total

Table 1 Amount and Temporal Distribution of Prenatal Injections of Testosterone Propionate in Rhesus Monkeys

No. of off-spring	Genetic sex	Gesta-tional age Rx started	Gesta-tional age Rx ended	Amount and no. of injections of TP into mother			Total mg
				Mg × days	Mg × days	Mg × days	
828	♀	40	69	20 × 30			600
829	♀	40	69	20 × 30			600
1239	♀	38	66	25 × 25[a]			625
1656	♀	40	111	10 × 50 →	5 × 22		610
836	♀	40	89	25 × 10 →	15 × 20 →	10 × 20	750
1616	♀	39	88	25 × 10 →	15 × 20 →	10 × 20	750
1619	♀	39	88	25 × 10 →	15 × 20 →	10 × 20	750
1640	♀	39	88	25 × 10 →	15 × 20 →	10 × 20	750
1558	♂	42	92	25 × 10 →	15 × 20 →	10 × 20	750
1561	♂	39	45	25 × 7			175
1618	♂	43	92	25 × 10 →	15 × 20 →	10 × 20	750
1644	♂	44	113	10 × 50 →	5 × 20		600
1645	♂	39	129	25 × 10 →	10 × 19[b]→	5 × 22[b]	550
1648	♂	39	119	25 × 3 →	5 × 78		465
1653	♂	43	134	25 × 10 →	10 × 17 →	5 × 24	540
1966	♂	40	109	15 × 10 →	10 × 40 →	5 × 20	650

[a]Injected 6 days per week.
[b]Injected on alternate days.

amount received was also relatively low. We are now preparing a series of treatment schedules which will extend later into pregnancy. The rationale for adopting the more protracted treatment procedure is based upon evidence obtained in our laboratory. Using the gas chromatographic technique, testosterone has been shown to be present in the plasma of the male rhesus fetus late in gestation and even on the day of birth. In small samples of plasma that have been analyzed at intervals during the first 30 days of life no detectable amounts of testosterone were found, whereas comparable-sized samples of plasma from adult male rhesus did reveal the presence of testosterone. By continuing testosterone treatment during late pregnancy we hope to produce conditions which resemble more closely the hormonal environment of the genetic male, thus maximizing degree of modification of the genetic female. In a proportionate sense, the situation for the rhesus may not be greatly different from that which exists for the guinea pig. In that species, the best psychological modifications of the genetic female were obtained with treatments extending to day 55 or 65 of the 68-day gestational period. The organizing action of testosterone is therefore very likely completed at or shortly after birth in the rhesus.

The first two pseudohermaphrodites studied by us and the two untreated females with whom they were studied were taken from their mothers at birth and fed at appropriate intervals by nursery technicians. The animals were housed in individual cages that contained a terry-cloth surrogate mother such as described by Harlow (1961). The four animals constituting the study group were placed together for approximately 30 minutes each day to avoid isolation effects. The animals were taken from their mothers at birth, because we were particularly concerned that whatever sexually dimorphic behavior patterns might be observed would not be the result of differential treatment of the sexes by the mother. The behavior displayed by these two pseudohermaphrodites has been reported previously (Young et al., 1964).

All other animals, experimental and control, have been permitted to remain with the mother for the first 3 months of life. At that time the infant is taken from the mother, placed in a separate cage, and weaned to solid food. Peer groups are formed consisting of four to six animals each. The animals continue to be housed individually, but each weekday the members of a group are brought together in a 6 ft. by 10 ft. experimental room for observation. Each subject in a group of peers is observed for 5 consecutive minutes. The behavior of each subject is recorded on an inventory check list for the 5 minutes during which it is observed. To eliminate a possible time effect, the order of observation within a group is rotated daily. Each group is observed at approximately the same time each day. During the first year of life the subjects are studied for 100 days in the same social setting and for 50 days during the second and each subsequent year. During the interval between yearly tests just described, the animals are tested for social and sexual behavior

Table 2 Frequency of Social Behavior During the First Year of Life by Male and Female Rhesus Monkeys

		Frequency per block of 10 trials			
		Threat	Play initiation	Rough and tumble play	Chasing play
Males (N = 20)	Mean	24.2	37.5	30.5	8.2
	Median	18.3	29.5	27.6	7.7
	Semi- inter- quartile range	7.9 → 35.8	22.2 → 46.3	16.7 → 40.5	4.4 → 11.8
Females (N = 17)	Mean	6.1	9.2	8.9	1.3
	Median	4.2	8.8	6.6	0.8
	Semi- inter- quartile range	1.9 → 10.0	3.4 → 15.1	2.5 → 13.2	0.1 → 2.4

in pairs. All pair combinations possible within a given peer group are studied.

Our findings have confirmed those reported by Rosenblum (1961) and Harlow (1965) with respect to sexual dimorphism in play behavior of young rhesus. We have compared the frequency of occurrence of threat, play initiation, rough and tumble play, and chasing play for 20 normal males and 17 females during the first year of life (Table 2). The mean performance level for males in each successive block of 10 daily trials over the 100 days of observation is clearly above that of the female. Males also show a greater frequency of mounting behavior than do females (Table 3). This higher level of performance is maintained by males during the second year of life as well as for all the behavior items mentioned above.

Our purpose in studying the rhesus monkey was not simply to confirm the observation that differences in sexual behavior and other behaviors not directly associated with reproduction existed between male and female but to determine whether or not these differences could be accounted for by the organizing action of testosterone. Our observations of female pseudohermaphrodites over the past few years substantiates our initial hypothesis. Not

Table 3   Total Number of Mounts Displayed in 100 Daily
Observations During the First Year of Life

Normal males		Normal females	
Animal no.	Total frequency of mounting	Animal no.	Total frequency of mounting
839	19	830	0
1242	117	831	0
1243	169	1252	1
1617	44	1551	1
1620	11	1642	0
1625	4	1649	0
1636	0	1654	0
1657	5	1769	0
1658	12	1838	0
1662	1	2362	1
1954	18	2369	0
1958	28	2539	0
1960	40	2551	0
2354	4	2569	0
2356	12	2575	0
2358	2	2577	0
2359	15	2580	0
2552	8	Median	0
2555	3		
2557	25		
Median	12.0		

Table 4   Total Number of Mounts Displayed in Pseudohermaphroditic Females in 100 Daily Observations During the First Year of Life

Animal no.	Total frequency of mounting
828	20
829	7
836[a]	4
1239	9
1616	9
1619	22
1640	33
1656	0
Median	9.0

[a]Data obtained between $10\frac{1}{2}$ and 16 months of age rather than $3\frac{1}{2}$ to 9 months as in all other cases.

only is sexual behavior, such as mounting, increased in the female pseudohermaphrodite compared with that of untreated female rhesus, but their play behavior also resembles that of the genetic male rather than that of the genetic female (Table 4 and Fig. 1).

The augmentation of mounting behavior of the pseudohermaphrodite compared with the normal female seems to be a specific effect of androgenic stimulation during the prenatal period of development. When large amounts of testosterone propionate are injected into each member of three pairs of adult female rhesus monkeys mounting activity is not increased (Phoenix et al., 1967). Recently we have extended these tests of adult females by adding a fourth pair to the experiment. Our procedure, briefly, was to test compatible pairs of females by bringing them together in a neutral observation cage for 10 minutes each weekday. Following 1 or 2 weeks of such tests, the subordinate member of each pair was injected for two weeks with 5 mg of testosterone propionate daily followed by two additional weeks with 10 mg daily of the same hormone. One week later, exactly the same sequence of injections was administered to the more dominant member of the pair, and the daily observations were continued. Our analysis of the results obtained from these observations show that dominant females mounted their partners about 0.8 times per test without androgen treatment. When they were injected with testosterone, the average frequency for these same females increased to 1.2 mounts per test, but the increase was not statistically significant. The subordinate females mounted less than once in every 10 tests prior to treatment with testosterone, and no increase was observed during treatment. The results suggest that testosterone does not augment mounting behavior in the adult female primate regardless of her dominance

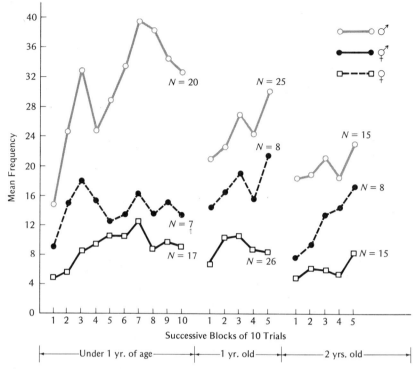

Figure 1 Frequency of rough and tumble play by infant and juvenile monkeys studied from 3 months of age to approximately 2½ years of age.

status in the testing situation, and the lack of effect in the adult clearly contrasts with the marked effect of prenatally administered androgen on the mounting behavior of the developing infant female pseudohermaphrodite.

We find no differences in the kind of frequency of social or sexual behavior displayed by normal males and males whose mothers were injected with testosterone propionate during pregnancy. We have not discounted the possibility, however, that differences may eventually appear.

From our work with the female pseudohermaphrodite monkey we feel reasonably certain that not only are patterns of sexual behavior determined by the presence of testosterone during development, but that other behaviors not directly associated with reproduction are also influenced by the action of androgens during the period of psychosexual differentiation.

We do not know the limits of this organizing action. It may, in fact, extend to behaviors we had not initially anticipated as being influenced by hormone action. We have suspected the frequency of display of aggression and fighting in general to be related to the presence of testosterone during psychosexual development and this indirectly to dominance. We have barely started to tease out the complex social interactions that account for dominance in a group. In other areas, too, we have just begun. For example, we are investigating the role of prenatal testosterone on what may be loosely termed parental behavior. In fact, our approach to the broad problem of the organizing action of prenatal testosterone has led us to look more closely and carefully at sex differences and similarities as they exist in the untreated population.

The simple cataloguing of sex differences is not being pursued as an end in itself. The aim rather is to investigate the array of behaviors which come under hormonal influence during the period of psychosexual differentiation. What has been found thus far in our investigations broadens our initial hypothesis such that we now suggest that testosterone not only organizes the tissues that mediate patterns of sexual behavior but many other sex-related behaviors. In this regard it is important to emphasize that the organizing actions of testosterone are not manifested on certain types or classes of behaviors independently of the species. For example, aggressiveness cannot be said to be enhanced by early treatment with androgen. In species like the monkey and the guinea pig a relationship between early androgen and aggressiveness may in fact exist, but in species like the hamster, in which the female is normally more aggressive than the male, early androgen may reduce the level and frequency of aggressive displays. Correspondingly, urinary postures which are sex-related in dogs (Martins and Valle, 1948; Berg, 1944) and other Canidae may be influenced in a male direction by early androgen, but urinary postures in general cannot be said to be susceptible to the same kind of influence. In short, androgens can be shown to act organizationally only upon those behaviors which exist as dimorphisms in the species. Those behavioral characteristics which the sexes display with equal frequency (such as huddling, grooming, withdrawing, and fear-grimacing—to mention only a few in the rhesus monkey) are not influenced in any detectable manner by the early administration of androgens.

The term "organizing action of testosterone" is used in the sense of setting a bias on a system such that differential sensitivity and responsiveness are built into the mechanism. Being ignorant of the specific body parts that constitute the control mechanisms we have referred simply to the tissues that mediate, in this instance, sexual behavior. From what is known about the role of the hypothalamus in the control of sexual behavior it is an easy step to assume that testosterone acts to organize tissues of the hypothalamus. Learning that an ovary implanted in a male rat castrated on the day of birth would ovulate and produce corpora lutea, Harris

(1964) has suggested (in view of the evidence of hypothalamic control of the pituitary) that castration on the day of birth in the rat prevents masculinization of the hypothalamus, and the work of Barraclough and Gorski (1962) supports such a view. Our findings of modified play behavior in the female pseudohermaphroditic rhesus monkey suggests that other areas of the central nervous system in addition to the hypothalamus are also modified by the prenatal treatment with testosterone. It is premature to conjecture just how widespread modification of central neural tissues might be, but the neural modifications obviously have relatively extensive effects on behavior.

The phenomena with which we are dealing are broad and their implications probably not yet fully appreciated. As more investigators from more disciplines become involved with the problem, its total scope and limits will become delineated.

In describing the research that has been done we have for the most part referred to the organizing action of *testosterone*. This was done primarily to simplify presentation. We have not established that it is testosterone per se and none of its metabolites that produces the many effects we have observed. We do not know, nor do we claim, that in the intact genetic male it is testosterone alone to the exclusion of other fetal morphogenic substances that masculinizes the nervous system controlling patterns of behavior. Those investigators familiar with hormone action are especially aware of the complex interrelationships that exist and of the need for caution in assuming that the injected material itself is producing the effect observed. This limitation does not detract from the generality of the findings, but rather suggests the need for additional research to spell out the complete and specific hormonal condition that accounts for the observed behavioral modifications.

REFERENCES

Barraclough, C. A., and R. A. Gorski. 1962. Studies on mating behaviour in the androgen-sterilized female rat in relation to the hypothalamic regulation of sexual behaviour. *J. Endocrinol.*, **25:** 175–182.

Beach, F. A., and A. M. Holz. 1946. Mating behavior in male rats castrated at various ages and injected with androgen. *J. Exptl. Zool.*, **101:** 91–142.

Berg, I. A. 1944. Development of behavior: The micturition pattern in the dog. *J. Exptl. Psychol.*, **34:** 343–368.

Dantchakoff, V. 1938. Rôle des hormones dans la manifestation des instincts sexueles. *Compt. Rend.*, **206:** 945–947.

Feder, H. H. 1967. Specificity of testosterone and estradiol in the differentiating neonatal rat. *Anat. Rec.,* **157:** 79–86.

Feder, H. H., and R. E. Whalen. 1965. Feminine behavior in neonatally castrated and estrogen-treated male rates. *Science,* **147:** 306–307.

Gerall, A. A., and I. L. Ward. 1966. Effects of prenatal exogenous androgen on the sexual behavior of the female albino rat. *J. Comp. Physiol. Psychol.,* **62:** 370–375.

Goy, R. W., W. E. Bridson, and W. C. Young. 1964. Period of maximal susceptibility of the prenatal female guinea pig to masculinizing actions of testosterone propionate. *J. Comp. Physiol. Psychol.,* **57:** 166–174.

Goy, R. W., J. C. Mitchell, and W. C. Young. 1962. Effect of testosterone propionate on O_2 consumption of female and female pseudohermaphroditic guinea pigs. *Am. Zoologist,* **2:** 525 (Abstr.).

Gradey, K. L., C. H. Phoenix, and W. C. Young. 1965. Role of the developing rat testis in differentiation of the neural tissues mediating mating behavior. *J. Comp. Physiol. Psychol.,* **59:** 176–182.

Gray, J. A., S. Levine, and P. L. Broadhurst. 1965. Gonadal hormone injections in infancy and adult emotional behavior. *Animal Behavior,* **13:** 33–43.

Harlow, H. F. 1961. The development of affectional patterns in infant monkeys. In *Determinants of Infant Behaviour* (B. M. Foss, ed.). Wiley, New York, pp. 75–97.

Harlow, H. F. 1965. Sexual behavior in the rhesus monkey. In *Sex and Behavior* (F. A. Beach, ed.). Wiley, New York, pp. 234–265.

Harris, G. W. 1964. Sex hormones, brain development and brain function. *Endocrinology,* **75:** 627–647.

Kennedy, G. C. 1964. Mating behaviour and spontaneous activity in androgen-sterilized female rats. *J. Physiol. (London).* **172:** 393–399.

Martins, T., and J. R. Valle. 1948. Hormonal regulation of the micturition behavior of the dog. *J. Comp. Physiol. Psychol.,* **41:** 301–311.

Neumann, F., and W. Elger. 1965. Physiological and psychical intersexuality of male rats by early treatment with an anti-androgenic agent (1,2α-methylene-6-chloro-Δ-hydroxyprogesterone-acetate). *Acta Endocrinal. Suppl.,* **100:** 174 (Abstr.).

Neumann, F., and W. Elger. 1966. Permanent changes in gonadal function and sexual behavior as a result of early feminization of male rats by treatment with an anti-androgenic steroid. *Endocrinology,* **50:** 209–225.

Phoenix, C. H., and K. L. Grady. 1964. Inhibitory effects of estradiol benzoate administered prenatally on the sexual behavior of female rats. *Anat. Rec.,* **148:** 395 (Abstr.).

Phoenix, C. H., R. W. Goy, A. A. Gerall, and W. C. Young. 1959. Organizing action of prenatally administered testosterone propionate on the tissue mediating mating behavior in the female guinea pig. *Endocrinology,* **65:** 369–382.

Phoenix, C. H., R. W. Goy, and W. C. Young. 1967. Sexual behavior: General aspects. In *Neuroendocrinology,* Vol. II (L. Martini and W. F. Ganong, eds.). Academic Press, New York, pp. 163–196.

Resko, J. A., H. H. Feder, and R. W. Goy. 1968 Androgen concentrations in plasma and testis of developing rats. *J. Endocrinol.,* **40:** 485–491.

Rosenblum, L. 1961. The development of social behavior in the rhesus monkey. Unpublished doctoral dissertation, Univ. of Wisconsin Libraries, Madison.

Swanson, H. H. 1966. Modification of sex differences in open field and emergence behaviour of hamsters by neonatal injections of testosterone propionate. *J. Endocrinol.* **34:** vi–vii.

Swanson, H. H. 1967. Alteration of sex-typical behavior of hamsters in open field and emergence by neo-natal administration of androgen or oestrogen. *Animal Behavior,* **15:** 209–216.

Tedford, M. D., and W. C. Young. 1960. Ovarian structure in guinea-pigs made hermaphroditic by the administration of androgen prenatally. *Anat. Rec.,* **136:** 325 (Abstr.).

Wells, L. J., and G. van Wagenen. 1954. Androgen-induced female pseudohermaphroditism in the monkey (*Macaca mulatta*): Anatomy of the reproductive organs. *Carnegie Inst. Wash. Publ. 235; Contribut. Embryol.,* **35:** 95–106.

Whalen, R. E. 1964. Hormone-induced changes in the organization of sexual behavior in the male rat. *J. Comp. Physiol. Psychol.,* **57:** 175–182.

Whalen, R. E., and R. D. Nadler. 1963. Suppression of the development of female mating behavior by estrogen administered in infancy. *Science,* **141:** 272–275.

Young, W. C. 1961. The hormones and mating behavior. In *Sex and Internal Secretions* (W. C. Young, ed.). Williams & Wilkins, Baltimore, 3rd ed., pp. 1173–1239.

Young, W. C., R. W. Goy, and C. H. Phoenix. 1964. Hormones and sexual behavior. *Science,* **143:** 212–218.

early childhood experiences and women's achievement motives

LOIS WLADIS HOFFMAN   *University of Michigan*

The failure of women to fulfill their intellectual potential has been adequately documented. The explanations for this are so plentiful that one is almost tempted to ask why women achieve at all. Their social status is more contingent on whom they marry than what they achieve; their sense of femininity and others' perception of them as feminine is jeopardized by too much academic and professional success; their husband's masculinity, and hence their love relationship as well as their reciprocal sense of femininity, is threatened if they surpass him; discrimination against women in graduate school admittance and the professions puts a limit on what rewards their performance will receive; their roles as wives and mothers take time from their professional efforts and offer alternative sources of self-esteem. Perhaps most important, they have an alternative to professional success and can opt out when the going gets rough. A full scale achievement effort involves painful periods of effort and many a man would drop out if that alternative were as readily available as it is to women. (Indeed, the Vietnam war and the new distrust of the old goals have provided young men with just such an opportunity and many have grabbed it.) But women's underachieve-

Reprinted from *The Journal of Social Issues*, 1972, **28**(2). By permission.

ment must have roots deeper even than these, for the precursors of the underachieving woman can be seen in the female child.

Even at preschool age girls have different orientations toward intellectual tasks than do boys. Little girls want to please; they work for love and approval; if bright, they underestimate their competence. Little boys show more task involvement, more confidence, and are more likely to show IQ increments. Girls have more anxiety than boys and the anxiety they have is more dysfunctional to their performance. There are also differences in the specific skills of each sex: Males excel in spatial perceptions, arithmetical reasoning, general information, and show less set-dependency; girls excel in quick-perception of details, verbal fluency, rote memory, and clerical skills.

Boys and girls enter the world with different constitutional make-ups, and recent studies show that parents treat boys and girls differently even from birth. Social roles are first—and most impressively—communicated through parent-child relations and events in early childhood may have an impact that cannot later be duplicated in effectiveness.

As a result, interest in women's intellectual achievement has led a number of people to look to the child development data for insights. A few of the limitations of these data will be discussed first, for a number of extravagant generalizations are being drawn from them.

LIMITATIONS OF CHILD DEVELOPMENT DATA

RELATIVITY

Child development data are often relative to a given group. Thus a statement about girls who are "high on aggression" usually means high relative to the other girls studied. If they are compared to boys who are "high on aggression" even in the same study, the actual aggressive behavior may be very different. Boys are considerably more aggressive than girls; a girl who is high on aggression may resemble a boy whose aggressive behavior is coded as average. She may also differ from the boys with respect to the form of aggression and the personality syndrome of which it is a part. It should not be surprising then to discover that the antecedent conditions of high aggression are different in boys and girls. They might very well be different even if the dependent variables were identical, but the fact is that they are not. We are comparing oranges with apples and discovering to our surprise that they grow on different trees.

This problem not only applies to the dependent variables, but also to the independent variables studied, usually parent behavior or the parent-child relationship. To use an actual finding, Kagan and Moss (1962) found that maternal protectiveness during the first three years was negatively related to adult achievement behavior for girls. This was not true for boys and in fact the relationship was positive although not statistically significant. This is an important finding to which we will return, but here it should be pointed out that we cannot tell from these correlations whether or not the actual maternal behavior is different for high achieving boys and girls. Girls are subject to more overprotection than boys and the same amount of protective behavior may be relatively low for a girl but average or high for a boy.

Baumrind (1970) has pointed out that obtaining data on the differential treatment (or behavior) of boys and girls is difficult because, even in behavioral observations, when the observer knows the sex of the child, "an automatic adjustment is made which tends to standardize judgments about the two sexes."

GENERALIZABILITY

The problem of generalizing results obtained with one population to another occurs throughout the social sciences. It is particularly acute when the variables involve relative terms. "High parental coerciveness" in a middle class sample may not be considered high in a lower class sample. Furthermore, most empirical generalizations hold only within certain contexts. Variations in social class, parent education, rural-urban residence, family structure, and ethnicity—as well as changes over time—may make the generalizations inapplicable.

As an interesting case in point, it is impossible to generalize white sex differences to blacks for the patterns of sex differences are very different in the two groups. Studies of blacks will be important in interpreting the etiology of sex differences in intellectual performance for in many ways the black male resembles the white female. For both, school performance has been largely irrelevant to adult goals and there are interesting similarities in the patterns of achievement scores that may reflect this (Tulkin, 1968; Jensen, 1970). In a study of conformity and perceptual judgments by Iscoe, Williams, and Harvey (1964), black males and white females were more influenced by others than were black females and white males. Similarities between black males and white females argue against constitutional explanations, for these two groups share neither hormones nor race—but they do share environmental handicaps.

MATURATION

Another difficulty in interpreting sex differences among children pertains to differences in the maturity of boys and girls. The newborn girl is one month to six weeks developmentally ahead of the boy. At school entrance she is about one year ahead, depending on the index of growth used. Growth does not proceed equally on all fronts and the intellectual growth rate is not related to the physical (Bayley, 1956). These different degrees of maturity complicate the comparison between the sexes.

CONCEPTUALIZATION

Ambiguous concepts are a problem in many fields. The so-called inconsistencies in the child development data often upon close examination turn out to be inconsistencies in the researcher's summaries and concluding statements rather than in the actual findings. If examined in terms of the operational definitions, contradictory studies sometimes turn out to be dealing with different phcnomena that have been given the same label. Among the particularly troublesome concepts that are important in the sex-difference literature are identification and dependency (Bronfenbrenner, 1960; Maccoby and Masters, 1970).

FEMALE ACHIEVEMENT ORIENTATIONS

There are very few studies that have empirically connected socialization experiences to sex differences in achievement orientations. As a matter of fact, there are few studies of sex differences in child-rearing practices in general, and existing data—most of which were originally collected for other purposes—are subject to the limitations mentioned above. Promising new approaches sensitive to identifying sex differences may be found in the studies of parent-child interaction with neonates (Moss, 1967; Moss and Robson, 1968; Moss, Robson, and Pedersen, 1969; Lewis, 1969; Goldberg and Lewis, 1969; Kagan, 1969; Kagan, Levinc, and Fishman, 1967). These are mainly longitudinal studies which will make their most valuable contributions in the future, but some have already examined relationships between maternal behavior and cognitive orientations.

Probably the richest current area in the study of sex differences has to do with cognitive styles. Witkin, Dyk, Faterson, Goodenough, and Karp (1962) as well as other investigators have been interested in differcnces in perceptions of and approaches to problems. For example, some people are more affected by background stimuli than others. In a task in which the subject is asked to line up a rod until it is perpendicular, the fact than the frame around the rod is tilted will affect the judgment of some respondents more than others. Those most affected by the tilting frame are said to be field dependent. This body of research has revealed a number of personality traits that are associated with performance on the task, and a number of cognitive skills such as mathematical ability that seem to be closely tied to field independence. These personality traits describe differences between the sexes; the corresponding cognitive abilities similarly differentiate.

For example, Maccoby (1963, 1966)[1] has pointed out that girls are more conforming, suggestible, and dependent upon the opinions of others. These traits in turn have been related to field dependency, inability to break the set of a task, and IQ's that tend to decrease rather than increase over the years. She suggests that these same traits in females might also account for their superior performance on spelling and vocabulary tests, and their inferior performance on tests involving analytic thinking, spatial ability, and arithmetic reasoning. Additional discussion on this issue can be found in Kagan (1964), Sherman (1967), Silverman (1970), and Kagan and Kogan (1970).

The actual linkage between these personality traits and the cognitive styles has not been established, nor has the etiology of sex differences in personality. Some of the infancy studies mentioned above are making inroads. Thus the finding that mothers spend more time in face-to-face verbalizations with infant girls (Kagan, 1969; Moss, 1967; Goldberg and Lewis, 1969) may be tied to the observation that female infants are more verbally responsive and to the later superiority of females in verbal ability. Verbal responsiveness may also result from the fact that girls' hearing is superior to that of boys (Garai and Scheinfeld, 1968). Also relevant is a study with 10-year-olds in which observations of mother–daughter interaction in task solving showed that girls good in math or spatial relations were left to solve tasks by themselves while the mothers of girls higher on verbal skills (the more typical female pattern) were more intrusive with help, suggestions, and criticism (Bing, 1963).

The present paper will focus on an area that is even less explored: the question of motivation for top intellectual performance. There are data that the very brightest women more often than comparable men stop short of operating at their top intellectual level. Terman and Oden (1947) have shown that gifted girls did not as adults fulfill their potential as often as gifted boys. Rossi (1965a, 1965b) has summarized data indicating that even those few women who do go into science and the professions rarely achieve eminence.[2]

---

[1]These reviews by Maccoby and reviews by Kagan (1964), Becker (1964), Glidewell, Kantor, Smith, and Stringer (1966), Oetzel (1966), Garai and Scheinfeld (1968), Silverman (1970), Kagan and Kogan (1970), and Bardwick (1971) will be referred to throughout the paper where a point is supported by several studies that are adequately reported in the review.

[2]Simon, Clark, and Galway (1970), on the other hand, have reported that the woman PhD who is employed full time publishes as much as her male colleagues.

These data reflect in part the factors mentioned earlier—alternative choices in life that have been available to women but not to men, barriers to career opportunities that exist because of women's family roles, and discrimination in the professions which limits the rewards obtainable. The concern here is not with these factors, however, but with a deeper, more psychologically based motivation that occurs in women. The most relevant data come from the work of Horner (1968, 1972) who has demonstrated with a projective story completion measure a "fear of success" among able college women. Furthermore, women who indicate fear of success show poorer performance in a competitive task than when the same task is performed alone. In interpreting her results, Horner suggests that this fear exists in women because their anticipation of success is accompanied by the anticipation of negative consequences in the form of social rejection or loss of femininity.

The idea that the affiliative motive can be dysfunctional to performance is supported by another of Horner's findings. Men who were motivated both to achieve and to affiliate showed a performance decrement when asked to compete with another man. Horner suggests this decrement may have resulted from a conflict of motives since "out-performing a competitor may be antagonistic to making him a friend."

AFFILIATIVE NEEDS AND ACHIEVEMENT

There is a great deal of evidence that females have greater affiliative needs than males (Oetzel, 1966; Walberg, 1969) and therefore the conflict between affiliation and achievement probably will occur more often for women. It seems that, apart from direct concerns with whether or not their behavior is sufficiently "feminine," academic and professional women frequently allow their concern with affective relationships to interfere with the full use of their cognitive capacities. In group discussion and in intellectual argument, women often seem to sacrifice brilliance for rapport.

However, while the findings of the Horner studies (1972) and our observations of professional women focus attention on the dysfunctions of affiliative motivations for performance, there are data indicating that the desire for love and approval can also have a positive effect. In fact, the Crandalls (V. J. Crandall, 1963; V. C. Crandall, 1964) as well as others (Garai and Scheinfeld, 1968) have suggested that achievement behavior in girls is motivated not by mastery strivings as with boys, but by affiliative motives.

In two very different studies, nursery school and elementary school girls' achievement efforts were motivated by a desire for social approval to a greater extent than were boys'. In the nursery school study the attempt was also made to motivate the children by appeals to mastery strivings; this technique succeeded with boys but failed with girls (Lahtinen, 1964). In the study with elementary school children, achievement motives in boys were related positively to achievement test scores. Among the girls, affiliative motives, not achievement motives, were so related (Sears, 1962, 1963). Other studies with nursery school and elementary school children found affiliative behavior and achievement efforts positively related in girls, but boys showed no such relationship (Tyler, Rafferty, and Tyler, 1962; Crandall, Dewey, Katkovsky, and Preston, 1964). Similarly with adult women, the achievement arousal techniques that are effective with males have failed with females (Veroff, Wilcox, and Atkinson, 1953; Horner, 1968), but appeals to social acceptability have been successful (Field, 1951).

There are also several studies that indicate that throughout grade school boys are more motivated than girls to master challenging tasks when social approval is not involved. When given the opportunity to perform an easy or more difficult task, to work on a puzzle they had already solved or one they had failed, to pursue further or escape a difficult problem, boys are more likely to choose the more difficult and challenging, girls to choose the task that promises easy success or to leave the scene (Crandall and Rabson, 1960; Moriarty, 1961; McManis, 1965; Veroff, 1969).

From these studies it appears that female achievement behavior even at preschool or early grade school ages is motivated by a desire for love rather than mastery. When achievement goals conflict with affiliative goals, as was the case in Horner's projective responses and in the competitive situation in which her fear-of-success girls showed less competent performance, achievement behavior will be diminished and/or anxiety result. This does not mean that academic performance is lower for females in general since it is often compatible with affiliative motives. In elementary schools, excellence is rewarded with love and approval by parents, teachers, and peers. Even in the lower socioeconomic class, sociometric studies show that academic excellence in girls is rewarded with popularity (Glidewell et al., 1966; Pope ,1953). In college, however, and in professional pursuits, love is less frequently the reward for top performance. Driving a point home, winning an argument, beating others in competition, and attending to the task at hand without being side-tracked by concern with rapport require the subordination of affiliative needs.

In short, the qualities needed for sustained top performance—especially as an adult—are not typically part of a girl's make-up. She wants approval and so she performs well in school. She works for good grades. And indeed throughout grammar school, high school, and college, she obtains higher grades than boys (Oetzel, 1966; Garai and Scheinfeld, 1968). If overachievement is thought of as grades exceeding IQ's, then girls as a group are more over-achieving than boys. But girls are less likely to become involved in their task; they are less motivated by strivings for mastery. In Mc-Clelland's sense of *achievement* (McClelland, Atkinson, Clark, and Lowell, 1953)—competition with a standard of excellence—they fall short.[3]

This affiliative need may be particularly germane to achieve-ment patterns because it may be rooted in early experiences when the child is learning patterns of effectance. When little boys are ex-panding their mastery strivings, learning instrumental indepen-dence, developing skills in coping with their environment and con-fidence in this ability, little girls are learning that effectiveness—and even safety—lie in their affectional relationships. The idea ex-pressed by Kagan (1964) that boys try to "figure the task" and girls try to "figure the teacher" seems rooted in early childrearing prac-tices and reinforced by later experiences.

STATEMENT OF THEORY

It is the thesis here that the female child is given inadequate par-ental encouragement in early independence strivings. Furthermore, the separation of the self from the mother is more delayed or incom-plete for the girl because she is the same sex with the same sex role expectations, and because girls have fewer conflicts with their parents. As a result, she does not develop confidence in her ability to cope independently with the environment. She retains her in-fantile fears of abandonment; safety and effectiveness lie in her affective ties. These points will now be elaborated and supportive data brought in where available.

THE DEVELOPMENT OF INDEPENDENCE,
COMPETENCE, AND SELF-CONFIDENCE

All infants are dependent; as the child matures his independence strivings increase. Observers have often been impressed with what White (1960) calls the *effectance motive*—the child's need to have an effect upon his environment. Thus the child grasps and releases, reaches and pulls, and in the course of doing this he learns about

[3]Women have obtained scores on McClelland's test of achievement motivation under neutral conditions that are as high or higher than those obtained by men under arousal conditions; however, researchers have questioned the validity of the measure for women (see McClelland et al., 1953; and Horner, 1968).

his environment and his ability to manipulate it. He develops cognitive abilities, and he develops a sense of effectiveness—a sense of competence through increasingly successful interaction with his environment.

As the infant matures, the feats he undertakes get scarier. Increasingly they involve separating the self from the mother and leaving the security of that unity. Early independence explorations seem to take place most successfully with the parent present; the child moves toward independence so long as the "safety man" is in sight. As he gains confidence, the parent's presence becomes less and less necessary.

Very likely this period—somewhere between a year and three or four years of age—is critical in the development of independence and competence (Erikson, 1959; Veroff, 1969; White, 1960; Stendler, 1963). By critical, we mean a period when independence and competence orientations are more efficiently learned than at other times. There is a rapid building up of notions about the self and about the world.

Although theories differ as to the exact timing and differential importance of the events occurring in this period, all would probably agree on the minimal requirements for the development of independence and competence. Thus if the infant is deprived of affection, rejected, or prematurely pushed toward independence, he will not have a secure base from which to build true independence. The dependency that results from a short shrift in early affective ties is probably of a distinct kind (Stendler, 1963). We do not think it is more characteristic of girls, nor that it is sufficiently common to the nonpathogenic middle class family to be useful in understanding prevalent female achievement orientations.

Even with an adequate affective base, independent behavior does not happen automatically. It requires not only opportunities for independent behavior but also actual parental encouragement. Evidence for this can be found in Baumrind's research (Baumrind and Black, 1967; Baumrind, 1971) which indicates that competence comes not from permissiveness but from guidance and encouragement. The first steps a child takes are exciting but also frightening, and cues from the mother can greatly influence the subsequent behavior. The mother's delight is part of her independence training; her apprehension constitutes training in dependence.

Further, if the child's early independence behaviors are to be followed by more, these ventures must be reasonably in accord with his abilities. Repeated successes such as these will have the important effect of developing in the child a sense of competence. There may be a delicate timing mechanism—premature independence can backfire; but the parent who withholds independence opportunities too long and indeed does not encourage independent behavior will also fail to produce an independent child. (It is possible that the appropriate timing is different for boys than girls due to differences in abilities and maturation rates.)

The awareness that the mother is a separate person whose wishes are not the same as his serves to increase the child's striving for autonomy and independence. Both Erikson and White see the period between one and three as the battle for autonomy. At this age the child's motoric explorations often require parental interference. The span of consecutive action is such that interference can be frustrating for the child and completions gratifying. Toilet training usually occurs around this time. The child thus enters into conflict with his mother; out of this conflict, if it does not involve his humiliation and defeat, the child will emerge with "a lasting sense of autonomy and pride (Erikson, 1959)" and "a measure of confidence in his own strength (White, 1960)."

THE EMPIRICAL FINDINGS

INDEPENDENCE TRAINING: SEX DIFFERENCES

Early exploratory behaviors in which the child interacts effectively with his environment are seen here as crucial in building up a sense of competence. In this respect males have a number of advantages.

Infant studies. Studies of neonates suggest a higher activity level on the part of the male, while females demonstrate greater tactile sensitivity and a lower pain threshold (Garai and Scheinfeld, 1968). From these predispositions alone we could expect more exploratory behavior on the part of male infants, but to compound the matter observations of mothers with neonates show that even controlling for the differences in activity levels, mothers handle and stimulate males more than females (Moss, 1967, undated). And a study by Rubenstein (1967) suggests that such maternal attentiveness facilitates exploratory behavior.

Kagan and Lewis and their associates have also reported differences in maternal behavior toward male and female infants (Kagan, Levine, and Fishman, 1967; Goldberg and Lewis, 1969). Whether the maternal behavior is primarily a response to infant predispositions or a cause of the differences is not definitely established, but there is some evidence that both influences occur. That maternal behavior is not entirely a response to the infant is indicated by relationships found between the mother's infant care and her orientations prior to the child's birth. For example. Moss (1967) reports that mothers were interviewed two years before they gave birth and rated on their attitudes toward babies. A positive attitude toward babies was found to relate significantly to the amount of responsiveness later shown to her 3-week-old infant. This same investigator also found mutual visual regard—one of the earliest forms of mother-infant communication—to be related to maternal attitudes expressed before the birth (Moss and Robson, 1968). On the other hand, that maternal behavior is not the sole determinant of the infant's behavior is indicated by the fact that the sex differences in tactile stimulation and pain thresholds mentioned above have been established for infants less than four days old and still in the hospital nursery (Garai and Scheinfeld, 1968; Silverman, 1970). An interaction hypothesis seems most tenable in the light of the present data.

One of Moss's mother-infant interaction findings is particularly pertinent to the theory presented in this paper (1967, undated). He reports data on the mother's responsiveness to the infant's cries and notes that this sequence—baby cries and mother responds with the needed care—is important in shaping the infant's response to the mother as a supplier of comfort. The more closely the mother's caretaking behavior is related to the infant's cries, the more effectively will the child "regard the mother as having reinforcing properties and respond to her accordingly (Moss, undated, p .10)." The correlation obtained between maternal contact and infant irritability was statistically significant for females but not for males. The mothers did not attend to the female infants more than the male (less, in fact) but their attention was more closely linked to the infant's state of need as expressed by crying. This finding if borne out by further research could be very important for several reasons. First, it could signify the beginning of a pattern of interaction between mothers and daughters in which the daughters quickly learn that the mother is a source of comfort; and the mother's behavior is reinforced by the cessation of crying. The sheer presence of the mother would soon signal the satisfaction of the infant's needs. Second, there is agreement among most investigators that there are critical periods in infancy when learning takes place so efficiently that long range behaviors are effected by simple but pertinently timed events; this might be such a critical period. Third, even if this is not a critical period, the finding may reflect an orientation of mothers toward daughters that is often repeated beyond the infancy period.

In any case, one thing appears certain from this body of research on early mother-infant interaction: There are sex differences in both maternal and infant behavior during the first year of life. That sex role learning is begun so early should not be surprising.

Sex is a primary status—the first one announced at birth. The mother is very much aware of it. Her early behaviors toward the infant are not deliberate efforts to teach the child his proper sex role, but she has internalized society's view and acts accordingly. She acts toward her son as though he were sturdy and active and she is more likely to show pleasure when his behavior fits this image. Her daughter is her doll—sweet and delicate and pink. The mother's behavior reflects this perception, and if the child exhibits behavior consistent with the female stereotype, such as dependency, she is not as likely to discourage it as she would with a son.

Independence training in childhood. Moving from early infancy, we find studies that link independence training and the parent's achievement orientations to the child's competence (Baumrind and Black, 1967) and achievement orientations (Winterbottom, 1958; Rosen and D'Andrade, 1959), but few examining sex differences in the independence and achievement training children receive. It is our view that because of parental attitudes toward male and female children which reflect their culturally assigned roles, males receive more effective independence training and encouragement.

An adaptation of the Winterbottom measure for use with parents of younger children was developed by Torgoff (1958). Using this measure, Collard (1964) asked mothers of 4-year-olds to indicate the ages they thought parents should expect or permit certain child behaviors. For example, the parents were asked at what age they believed parents should: (a) begin to allow their child to use sharp scissors with *no* adult supervision, (b) begin to allow their child to play away from home for long periods of time during the day without first telling his parents where he will be. The answers to these questions yielded two measures—*independence granting* and *achievement induction.* Mothers of girls responded with later ages than mothers of boys. This difference was significant for the independence-granting items and it was particularly strong in the middle class. The achievement induction scores were not significantly different for the two sexes, but close inspection of the data revealed that, for the middle class, mothers of girls indicated an earlier age for only two of the 18 items making up the scale. One of the two exceptions was "sharing toys" which may have more to do with inter-personal relationships than with achievement.

Parental anxiety and protectiveness. Still another difference in the independence training received by boys and girls may stem from parental ambivalence: Parents may show more unambivalent pleasure in sons' achievements than in daughters'. The young child's first motoric adventures can produce anxiety in the mother as well as the child, just as they produce pleasure for both. It seems likely that for the parent of a boy there is a particular pride in the achievement and less of a feeling of the child's fragility; as a result there is a clearer communication of pleasure in the achievement per se. A beaming mother when the child takes his first steps may have a very different effect than the mother who looks anxious while holding out loving arms. In the former case, the task itself becomes the source of pleasure (in reinforcement terms the reward is closer to the act). In the latter case, the mother is saying in effect, "You may break your neck en route, but I will give you love when you get here." The mother's indications of anxiety as the child moves toward independence make the child doubt his own competence, for mothers are still omniscient to the young child.

There is some indirect evidence for this view. Despite the greater maturity and sturdiness of the female infant (Garai and Scheinfeld, 1968), parents think of them as more fragile. Furthermore, behavioral observations of infants have shown that male infants are handled more vigorously (Moss, 1967). The setting of later ages for granting autonomy to girls, as indicated in the Collard (1964) study mentioned earlier, suggests that parents are more protective, if not more anxious, toward girls. For example, parents report allowing boys to cross busy streets by themselves earlier, though they are not motorically more advanced than girls and their greater motoric impulsivity would seem to make this more dangerous. And we do know that infants pick up the subtle attitudes of their caretakers. This was demonstrated in the well known study by Escalona (1945) in which the infant's preference for orange or tomato juice depended heavily on the preference of the nurse who regularly fed him. The infant had no way of knowing his nurse's preference except through sensing her attitude as she fed him.

Another kind of parent behavior that is detrimental to the development of independence might be called *over-help*. Mastery requires the ability to tolerate frustration. If the parent responds too quickly with aid, the child will not develop such tolerance. This shortcoming—the tendency to withdraw from a difficult task rather than to tackle the problem and tolerate the temporary frustration— seems to characterize females more than males. This has been demonstrated in the test situations mentioned earlier, and Crandall and Rabson (1960) have also found that, in free play, grade school girls are more likely than boys to withdraw from threatening situations and more frequently to seek help from adults and peers. The dysfunctions of this response for the development of skills and a sense of competence are clear. There are no data to indicate that over-help behavior is more characteristic of parents of girls, but such a difference seems likely in view of the greater emphasis placed on the independence training of boys.

Clearly more research is needed to identify differences in the independence and achievement training—and in any overprotection and over-help—that parents provide boys and girls. Even if the differences we have described are definitely established, it will still need to be shown that this pattern of parental protectiveness and insufficient independence training is a major contributor to an inadequate sense of personal competence in girls. It should be pointed out, however, that this inference is consistent with the findings that girls are more anxious than boys, more likely to underestimate their abilities, and more apt to lack confidence in their own judgment when it is contrary to that of others (Sarason, 1963; Sarason and Harmatz, 1965; Sears, 1964; Crandall, Katkovsky, and Preston, 1962; Hamm and Hoving, 1969). There is also evidence that the above pattern is reinforced by the later socialization experiences of girls. Several investigators report that while dependency in boys is discouraged by parents, teachers, peers, and the mass media, it is more acceptable in girls (Kagan and Moss, 1962; Kagan, 1964; Sears, Rau, and Alpert, 1965). Data from the Fels study (Kagan and Moss, 1962) are particularly interesting in this respect, reporting that childhood dependency predicted to adult dependency for females but not males, the converse being true for aggression. Their interpretation is that pressure is exerted on the child to inhibit behaviors that are not congruent with sex role standards (Kagan, 1964).

ESTABLISHING A SEPARATE SELF: SEX DIFFERENCES

Same sex parent as primary caretaker.   Separation of the self is facilitated when the child is the opposite sex of the primary caretaker. Parsons (1949, 1965) and Lynn (1962, 1969), as well as others, have pointed out that both males and females form their first attachment to the mother. The girl's modeling of the mother and maintaining an identity with her is consistent with her own sex role, but the boy must be trained to identify with his father or to learn some abstract concept of the male role. As a result, the boy's separation from the mother is encouraged; it begins earlier and is more complete. The girl, on the other hand, is encouraged to maintain her identification with the mother; therefore she is not as likely to establish an early and independent sense of self. If the early experiences of coping with the environment independently are crucial in the development of competence and self-confidence, as suggested previously, the delayed and possibly incomplete emergence of the self should mitigate against this development.

There are no studies that directly test this hypothesis. As indirect evidence, however, there are several studies showing that the more identified with her mother and the more feminine the girl is, the less likely she is to be a high achiever and to excel in mathematics, analytic skills, creativity, and game strategies. For example, Plank and Plank (1954) found that outstanding women mathematicians were more attached to and identified with their fathers than their mothers. Bieri (1960) found that females high on analytical ability also tended to identify with their fathers. Higher masculinity scores for girls are related positively to various achievement measures (Oetzel, 1961; Milton, 1957; Kagan and Kogan ,1970), as are specific masculine traits such as aggressiveness (Sutton-Smith, Crandall, and Roberts, 1964; Kagan and Moss, 1962). The relation between cross-sex identification and cognitive style for both boys and girls is discussed also by Maccoby (1966).

For several reasons the above studies provide only limited support for our view. First, there is some evidence, though less consistent, that "overly masculine" males, like "overly feminine" females, are lower on various achievement-related measures (Maccoby, 1966; Kagan and Kogan, 1970). Second, the definitions and measures of femininity may have a built-in anti-achievement bias. Third, the question of the mother's actual characteristics has been ignored; thus the significant factor may not be closeness to the mother and insufficient sense of self, as here proposed. The significant factor may be identifying with a mother who is herself passive and dependent. If the mother were a mathematician, would the daughter's close identification be dysfunctional to top achievement?

Clearly the available data are inadequate and further research is needed to assess the importance of having the same sex as the primary caretaker for personality and cognitive development.

Parent-child conflict. Establishing the self as separate from the mother is also easier for boys because they have more conflict with the mother than do girls. Studies of neonates suggest, as mentioned above, that males are more motorically active; this has also been observed with older children (Garai and Scheinfeld, 1968; Moss, 1967; Goldberg and Lewis, 1969). Furthermore, sex differences in aggressive behavior are solidly established (Oetzel, 1966; Kagan, 1964), and there is some evidence that this is constitutionally based (Bardwick, 1971). Because of these differences, the boy's behavior is more likely to bring him into conflict with parental authority. Boys are disciplined more often than girls, and this discipline is more likely to be of a power assertive kind (Becker, 1964; Sears, Maccoby, and Levin, 1957; Heinstein, 1965). These encounters facilitate a separation of the self from the parent. (While extremely severe discipline might have a very different effect, this is not common in the middle class.)

One implication of this is that girls need a little maternal rejection if they are to become independently competent and self-confident. And indeed a generalization that occurs in most recent reviews is that high achieving females had hostile mothers while high achieving males had warm ones (Bardwick, 1971; Garai and Scheinfeld, 1968; Maccoby, 1966; Silverman, 1970). This generalization is based primarily on the findings of the Fels longitudinal study (Kagan and Moss, 1962). In this study "maternal hostility" toward the child during his first three years was related positively to the adult achievement behavior of girls and negatively to the adult achievement behavior of boys. Maternal protection, on the other hand, as mentioned earlier, related negatively to girl's achievement and positively to boy's.

In discussions of these findings "maternal hostility" is often equated with rejection. There is reason to believe, however, that it may simply be the absence of "smother love." First, the sample of cooperating families in the Fels study is not likely to include extremely rejecting parents. These were primarily middle class parents who cooperated with a child development study for 25 years. They were enrolled in the study when the mother was pregnant, and over the years they tolerated frequent home visits, each lasting from 3 to 4 hours, as well as behavioral observations of their children in nursery school and camp. Second, we have already pointed out that what is "high hostility" toward girls, might not be so labeled if the same behavior were expressed toward boys. It is interesting to note in this connection that "high hostility" toward girls during these early years is related positively to "acceleration" (i.e., the tendency to push the child's cognitive and motoric development) and negatively to maternal protectiveness. Neither of these relationships is significant for the boys (Kagan and Moss, 1962, p. 207). Further, the mothers who were "hostile" to their daughters were better educated than the "nonhostile." In addition to being achievers, the daughters were "less likely to withdraw from stressful situations" as adults. The authors themselves suggest that the latter "may reflect the mother's early pressure for independence and autonomy [p. 213.]."

Our interpretation of these findings then is that many girls experience too much maternal rapport and protection during their early years. Because of this they find themselves as adults unwilling (or unable) to face stress and with inadequate motivation for autonomous achievement. It is significant that the relationships described are strongest when the early years are compared to the adult behavior. Possibly the eagerness to please adults sometimes passes as achievement or maturity during the childhood years.

While excessive rapport between mother and son occurs, it is less common and usually of a different nature. The achievement of

boys may be in greater danger from too much conflict with parents
—there being little likelihood of too little.

The danger for girls of too much maternal nurturance has been
pointed out by Bronfenbrenner (1961a, 1961b) and is consistent with
data reported by Crandall, Dewey, Katkovsky, and Preston (1964).
The finding that girls who are more impulsive than average have
more analytic thinking styles while the reverse pattern holds for
boys also fits this interpretation (Sigel, 1965; Kagan, Rosman, Day,
Phillips, and Phillips, 1964). That is, impulsive girls may be brought
into more conflict with their mothers, as in the typical pattern for
boys. Maccoby (1966) has suggested that the actual relationship
between impulsivity and analytic thinking is curvilinear: The extreme impulsivity that characterizes the very impulsive boys is
dysfunctional, but the high impulsivity of the girls falls within the
optimal range. In our view, the optimal range is enough to insure
some conflict in the mother-child relationship but not so much as
to interfere with the child's effective performance.

INADEQUATE SELF-CONFIDENCE AND DEPENDENCE ON OTHERS

Since the little girl has (a) less encouragement for independence, (b)
more parental protectiveness, (c) less cognitive and social pressure
for establishing an identity separate from the mother, and (d) less
mother–child conflict which highlights this separation, she engages
in less independent exploration of her environment. As a result she
does not develop skills in coping with her environment nor confidence in her ability to do so. She continues to be dependent upon
adults for solving her problems and because of this she needs her
affective ties with adults. Her mother is not an unvarying supply of
love but is sometimes angry, disapproving, or unavailable. If the
child's own resources are insufficient, being on her own is frustrating and frightening. Fears of abandonment are very common in
infants and young children even when the danger is remote. Involvement in mastery explorations and the increasing competence
and confidence that results can help alleviate these fears, but for
girls they may continue even into adulthood. The anticipation of
being alone and unloved then may have a particularly desperate
quality in women. The hypothesis we propose is that the all-per-
vasive affiliative need in women results from this syndrome.

Thus boys learn effectance through mastery, but girls are effective through eliciting the help and protection of others. The situations that evoke anxiety in each sex should be different and their
motives should be different.

The theoretical view presented in this paper is speculative but
it appears to be consistent with the data. In the preceding sections
we have reviewed the research on sex differences in early socializa-

tion experiences. The theory would also lead us to expect that owing to these differences females would show less self-confidence and more instrumental dependency than males.

The data on dependency are somewhat unclear largely because the concept has been defined differently in different studies. These findings have been summarized by Kagan (1964), Oetzel (1966), Garai and Scheinfeld (1968), and the concept of dependency has been discussed by Maccoby and Masters (1970). The balance of the evidence is that females are more dependent, at least as we are using the concept here, and this difference appears early and continues into maturity. Goldberg and Lewis (1969) report sex differences in dependency among one-year-olds, but Crandall and his associates (Crandall, Preston, and Rabson, 1960; Crandall and Rabson, 1960) found such differences only among elementary school children and not among preschoolers. It should be noted, however, that even differences that do not show up until later can have their roots in early experiences. For example, independence training at a later age may require a sense of competence based on early successes if it is to be effective.

The findings on self-confidence show that girls, and particularly the bright ones, underestimate their own ability. When asked to anticipate their performance on new tasks or on repetition tasks, they give lower estimates than boys and lower estimates than their performance indicates (Brandt, 1958; Sears, 1964; Crandall, Katkovsky, and Preston, 1962; Crandall, 1968). The studies that show the girls' greater suggestibility and tendency to switch perceptual judgments when faced with discrepant opinions are also consistent with their having less self-confidence (Iscoe, Williams, and Harvey, 1963; Allen and Crutchfield, 1963; Nakamura, 1958; Hamm and Hoving, 1969; Stein and Smithells, 1969).[4] Boys set higher standards for themselves (Walter and Marzolf, 1951). As mentioned earlier, difficult tasks are seen as challenging to males, whereas females seek to avoid them (Veroff, 1969; Crandall and Rabson, 1960; Moriarty, 1961; McManis, 1965). Thus the research suggests that girls lack confidence in their own abilities and seek effectance through others (Crandall and Rabson, 1960). Affective relationships under these conditions would indeed be paramount.

The findings indicating that this is the case—that affective relationships are paramount in females—were summarized earlier in this paper. The data suggest that they have affiliative needs and that achievement behavior is motivated by a desire to please. If their

---

[4]Girls do not conform more to peer standards which conflict with adult norms (Douvan and Adelson, 1966), even though they conform more when group pressure is in opposition to their own perceptual judgments.

achievement behavior comes into conflict with affiliation, achievement is likely to be sacrificed or anxiety may result.

IMPLICATIONS

If further research provides support for the present developmental speculations, many questions will still need answering before child-rearing patterns used with girls can be totally condemned. Even from the standpoint of achievement behavior, I would caution that this paper has only dealt with the upper end of the achievement curve. Indices of female performance, like the female IQ scores, cluster closer to the mean and do not show the extremes in either direction that the male indices show. The same qualities that may interfere with top performance at the highest achievement levels seem to have the effect of making the girls conscientious students in the lower grades. Is it possible for the educational system to use the positive motivations of girls to help them more fully develop their intellectual capacities rather than to train them in obedient learning? The educational system that rewards conformity and discourages divergent thinking might be examined for its role in the pattern we have described.

Although childrearing patterns that fail to produce a competent and self-confident child are obviously undesirable, it may be that boys are often prematurely pushed into independence. Because this paper has focused on achievement orientations, it may seem that I have set up the male pattern as ideal. This is not at all intended. The ability to suppress other aspects of the situation in striving for mastery is not necessarily a prerequisite for mental health or a healthy society. The more diffuse achievement needs of women may make for greater flexibility in responding to the various possibilities that life offers at different stages in the life cycle. A richer life may be available to women because they do not single-mindedly pursue academic or professional goals. And from a social standpoint, a preoccupation with achievement goals can blot out consideration of the effect of one's work on the welfare of others and its meaning in the larger social scheme.

A loss in intellectual excellence due to excessive affiliative needs, then, might seem a small price to pay if the alternative is a single-minded striving for mastery. But the present hypothesis suggests that women's affiliative needs are, at least in part, based on an insufficient sense of competence and as such they may have a compelling neurotic quality. While I have not made the very high achievement needs more characteristic of males the focus of this paper, they too may have an unhealthy base. By unraveling the childhood events that lead to these divergent orientations we may gain insights that will help both sexes develop their capacities for love and achievement.

REFERENCES

Allen, V. L., and Crutchfield, R. S. Generalization of experimentally reinforced conformity. *Journal of Abnormal and Social Psychology*, 1963, **67**, 326–333.

Bardwick, J. M. *The psychology of women: A study of biosocial conflict.* New York: Harper and Row, 1971.

Baumrind, D. Socialization and instrumental competence in young children. *Young Children*, 1970, December, 9–12.

Baumrind, D. Current patterns of parental authority. *Developmental Psychology Monograph*, 1971, **4**,(1, Pt. 2).

Baumrind, D., and Black, A. E. Socialization practices associated with dimensions of competence in preschool boys and girls. *Child Development*, 1967, **38**, 291–327.

Bayley, N. Growth curves of height and weight by age for boys and girls, scaled according to physical maturity. *Journal of Pediatrics*, 1956, **48**, 187–194.

Bayley, N. Developmental problems of the mentally retarded child. In I. Phillips (Ed.), *Prevention and treatment of mental retardation.* New York: Basic Books, 1966.

Becker, W. Consequences of different kinds of parental discipline. In M. L. Hoffman and L. W. Hoffman (Eds.), *Review of child development research.* Vol. 1. New York: Russell Sage, 1964.

Bieri. J. Parental identification, acceptance of authority and within-sex differences in cognitive behavior. *Journal of Abnormal and Social Psychology*, 1960, **60**, 76–79.

Bing, E. Effect of childrearing practices on development of differential cognitive abilities. *Child Development*, 1963, **34**, 631–648.

Brandt, R. M. The accuracy of self-estimate: A measure of self concept. *Genetic Psychology Monographs*, 1958, **58**, 55–99.

Bronfenbrenner, U. Freudian theories of identification and their derivatives. *Child Development*, 1960, **31**, 15–40.

Bronfenbrenner, U. Some familial antecedents of responsibility and leadership in adolescents. In L. Petrullo and B. M. Bass (Eds.), *Leadership and interpersonal behavior.* New York: Holt, Rinehart, & Winston, 1961. (a)

Bronfenbrenner, U. Toward a theoretical model for the analysis of parent–child relationships in a social context. In J. Glidewell (Ed.), *Parent attitudes and child behavior.* Springfield, Illinois: Thomas, 1961. (b)

Coleman, J. S. *The adolescent society.* Glencoe, Illinois: Free Press, 1961.

Collard, E. D. Achievement motive in the four-year-old child and its relationship to achievement expectancies of the mother. Unpublished doctoral dissertation, University of Michigan, 1964.

Crandall, V. C. Achievement behavior in young children. *Young Children,* 1964, **20,** 77–90.

Crandall, V. C. Sex differences in expectancy of intellectual and academic reinforcement. In C. P. Smith (Ed.), *Achievement-related motives in children.* New York: Russell Sage, 1968.

Crandall, V. J. Achievement. In H. W. Stevenson (Ed.), *Child Psychology: The 62nd Yearbook of the National Society for the Study of Education.* Part I. Chicago: University of Chicago Press, 1963.

Crandall, V. J., Dewey, R., Katkovsky, W., and Preston, A. Parents' attitudes and behaviors and grade school children's academic achievements. *Journal of Genetic Psychology,* 1964, **104,** 53–66.

Crandall, V. J., Katkovsky, W., and Preston, A. Motivational and ability determinants of young children's intellectual achievement behaviors. *Child Development,* 1962, **33,** 643–661.

Crandall, V. J., Preston, A., and Rabson, A. Maternal reactions and the development of independence and achievement behavior in young children. *Child Development,* 1960, **31,** 243–251.

Crandall, V. J., and Rabson, A. Children's repetition choices in an intellectual achievement situation following success and failure. *Journal of Genetic Psychology,* 1960, **97,** 161–168.

Douvan, E. M., and Adelson, J. *The adolescent experience.* New York: Wiley, 1966.

Erikson, E. H. Identity and the life cycle. *Psychological Issues,* 1959, **1,** 1–171.

Escalona, S. K. Feeding disturbances in very young children. *American Journal of Orthopsychiatry,* 1945, **15,** 76–80.

Field, W. F. The effects of thematic apperception upon certain experimentally aroused needs. Unpublished doctoral dissertation, University of Maryland, 1951.

Garai, J. E., and Scheinfeld, A. Sex differences in mental and behavioral traits. *Genetic Psychology Monographs,* 1968, **77,** 169–299.

Glidewell, J. C., Kantor, M. B., Smith, L. M., and Stringer, L. A. Socialization and social structure in the classroom. In L. W. Hoffman and M. L. Hoffman (Eds.), *Review of child development research.* Vol. 2. New York: Russell Sage, 1966.

Goldberg, S., and Lewis, M. Play behavior in the year old infant: Early sex differences. *Child Development,* 1969, **40,** 21–31.

Hamm, N. K., and Hoving, K. L. Conformity of children in an

ambiguous perceptual situation. *Child Development*, 1969, **40,** 773–784.

Heinstein, M. *Child rearing in California.* Bureau of Maternal and Child Health, State of California, Department of Public Health, 1965.

Horner, M. S. Sex differences in achievement motivation and performance in competitive and non-competitive situations. Unpublished doctoral dissertation, University of Michigan, 1968.

Horner, M. S. Toward an understanding of achievement related conflicts in women. *Journal of Social Issues*, 1972, **28**(2).

Iscoe, I., Williams, M., and Harvey, J. Modifications of children's judgements by a simulated group technique: A normative developmental study. *Child Development*, 1963, **34,** 963–978.

Iscoe, I., Williams, M., and Harvey, J. Age, intelligence and sex as variables in the conformity behavior of Negro and White children. *Child Development*, 1964, **35,** 451–460.

Jensen, A. R. The race × sex × ability interaction. Unpublished manuscript. University of California, Berkeley, 1970.

Kagan, J. Acquisition and significance of sex-typing and sex-role identity. In M. L. Hoffman and L. W. Hoffman (Eds.), *Review of child development research.* Vol. 1. New York: Russell Sage, 1964.

Kagan, J. On the meaning of behavior: Illustrations from the infant. *Child Development*, 1969, **40,** 1121–1134.

Kagan, J., and Kogan, N. Individuality and cognitive performance. In P. H. Mussen (Ed.), *Carmichael's manual of child psychology.* Vol. 1. New York: Wiley, 1970.

Kagan, J., Levine, J., and Fishman, C. Sex of child and social class as determinants of maternal behavior. Paper presented at the meeting of the Society for Research in Child Development, March 1967.

Kagan, J., and Moss, H. A. *Birth to maturity.* New York: Wiley, 1962.

Kagan, J., Rosman, B. L., Day, D., Phillips, A. J., and Phillips, W. Information processing in the child: Significance of analytic and reflective attitudes. *Psychological Monographs*, 1964, **78,** 1.

Lahtinen, P. The effect of failure and rejection on dependency. Unpublished doctoral dissertation, University of Michigan, 1964.

Lewis, M. Infants' responses to facial stimuli during the first year of life. *Developmental Psychology*, 1969, **1,** 75–86.

Lynn, D. B. Sex role and parental identification. *Child Development*, 1962, **33,** 555–564.

Lynn, D. B. *Parental identification and sex role.* Berkeley: McCutchan, 1969.

Maccoby, E. E. Woman's intellect. In S. M. Farber and R. H. L. Wilson (Eds.), *The potential of woman.* New York: McGraw-Hill, 1963.

Maccoby, E. E. Sex differences in intellectual functioning. In E. E.

Maccoby (Ed.), *The development of sex differences.* Stanford, California: Stanford University Press, 1966.

Maccoby, E. E., and Masters, J. C. Attachment and dependency. In P. H. Mussen (Ed.), *Carmichael's manual of child psychology.* Vol. 2. New York: Wiley, 1970.

McClelland, D. C., Atkinson, J. W., Clark, R. A., and Lowell, E. L. *The achievement motive.* New York: Appleton-Century-Crofts, 1953.

McManis, D. L. Pursuit-rotor performance of normal and retarded children in four verbal-incentive conditions. *Child Development,* 1965, **36,** 667–683.

Milton, G. A. The effects of sex-role identification upon problem solving skill. *Journal of Abnormal and Social Psychology,* 1957, **55,** 208–212.

Moriarty, A. Coping patterns of preschool children in response to intelligence test demands. *Genetic Psychology Monographs,* 1961, **64,** 3–127.

Moss, H. A. Laboratory and field studies of mother–infant interaction. Unpublished manuscript, NIMH, undated.

Moss, H. A. Sex, age, and state as determinants of mother–infant interaction. *Merrill-Palmer Quarterly,* 1967, **13,** 19–36.

Moss, H. A., and Robson, K. S. Maternal influences in early social visual behavior. *Child Development,* 1968, **39,** 401–408.

Moss, H. A., Robson, K. S., and Pedersen, F. Determinants of maternal stimulation of infants and consequences of treatment for later reactions to strangers. *Developmental Psychology,* 1969, **1,** 239–247.

Nakamura, C. Y. Conformity and problem solving. *Journal of Abnormal and Social Psychology,* 1958, **56,** 315–320.

Oetzel, R. M. The relationship between sex role acceptance and cognitive abilities. Unpublished masters thesis, Stanford University, 1961.

Oetzel, R. M. Annotated bibliography and classified summary of research in sex differences. In E. E. Maccoby (Ed.), *The development of sex differences.* Stanford, California: Stanford University Press, 1966.

Parson, T. *Essays in sociological theory pure and applied.* Glencoe, Illinois: Free Press, 1949.

Parson, T. Family structure and the socialization of the child. In T. Parsons and R. F. Bales (Eds.), *Family socialization and interaction process.* Glencoe, Illinois: Free Press, 1965.

Plank, E. H., and Plank, R. Emotional components in arithmetic learning as seen through autobiographies. In R. S. Eissler et al., (Eds.), *The psychoanalytic study of the child.* Vol. 9. New York: International Universities Press, 1954.

Pope, B. Socio-economic contrasts in children's peer culture prestige values. *Genetic Psychology Monographs*, 1953, **48**, 157–220.

Rosen, B. C., and D'Andrade, R. The psychosocial origins of achievement motivations. *Sociometry*, 1959, **22**, 185–218.

Rossi, A. S. Barriers to the career choice of engineering, medicine, or science among American women. In J. A. Mattfeld and G. G. Van Aken (Eds.), *Women and the scientific professions: Papers presented at the M.I.T. symposium on American Women in Science and Engineering, 1964.* Cambridge, Massachusetts: M.I.T. Press, 1965. (a)

Rossi, A. S. Women in science: Why so few? *Science*, 1965, **148**, 1196–1202. (b)

Rubenstein, J. Maternal attentiveness and subsequent exploratory behavior in the infant. *Child Development*, 1967, **38**, 1089–1100.

Sarason, I. G. Test anxiety and intellectual performance. *Journal of Abnormal and Social Psychology*, 1963, **66**, 73–75.

Sarason, I. G., and Harmatz, M. G. Test anxiety and experimental conditions. *Journal of Personality and Social Psychology*, 1965, **1**, 499–505.

Sears, P. S. Correlates of need achievement and need affiliation and classroom management, self concept, and creativity. Unpublished manuscript, Stanford University, 1962.

Sears, P. S. The effect of classroom conditions on the strength of achievement motive and work output of elementary school children. Final report, cooperative research project No. OE-873, U.S. Dept. of Health, Education, and Welfare, Office of Education, Washington, D.C., 1963.

Sears, P. S. Self-concept in the service of educational goals. *California Journal of Instructional Improvement*, 1964, **7**, 3–17.

Sears, R. R., Maccoby, E. E., and Levin, H. *Patterns of child rearing.* Evanston, Illinois: Row, Peterson, 1957.

Sears, R. R., Rau, L., and Alpert, R. *Identification and child rearing.* Stanford, California: Stanford University Press, 1965.

Sherman, J. A. Problems of sex differences in space perception and aspects of intellectual functioning. *Psychological Review*, 1967, **74**, 290–299.

Sigel, I. E., Rationale for separate analyses of male and female samples on cognitive tasks. *Psychological Record*, 1965, **15**, 369–376.

Silverman, J. Attentional styles and the study of sex differences. In D. L. Mostofsky (Ed.), *Attention: Contemporary theory and analysis.* New York: Appleton-Century-Crofts, 1970.

Simon, R. J., Clark, S. M., and Galway, K. The woman Ph.D.: A recent profile. Paper prepared for a workshop of the New York Academy of Sciences, New York, February 1970.

Stein, A. H., and Smithells, J. Age and sex differences in children's sex role standards about achievement. *Developmental Psychology,* 1969, **1,** 252–259.

Stendler, C. B. Critical periods in socialization. In R. G. Kuhlen and G. G. Thompson (Eds.), *Psychological studies of human development.* New York: Appleton-Century-Crofts, 1963.

Sutton-Smith, B., Crandall, V. J., and Roberts, J. M. Achievement and strategic competence. Paper presented at the meeting of the Eastern Psychological Association, April 1964.

Terman, L. M., and Oden, M. H. *The gifted child grows up.* Stanford, California: Stanford University Press, 1947.

Torgoff, I. Parental developmental timetable. Paper presented at the meeting of the American Psychological Association, Washington, D.C., August 1958.

Tulkin, S. R. Race, class, family, and school achievement. *Journal of Personality and Social Psychology,* 1968, **9,** 31–37.

Tyler, F. B., Rafferty, J. E., and Tyler, B. B. Relationships among motivations of parents and their children. *Journal of Genetic Psychology,* 1962. **101,** 69–81.

Veroff, J. Social comparison and the development of achievement motivation. In C. P. Smith (Ed.), *Achievement-related motives in children.* New York: Russell Sage, 1969.

Veroff, J., Wilcox, S., and Atkinson, J. W. The achievement motive in high school and college age women. *Journal of Abnormal and Social Psychology,* 1953, **48,** 108–119.

Walberg, H. J. Physics, femininity, and creativity. *Developmental Psychology,* 1969, **1,** 47–54.

Walter, L. M., and Marzolf, S. S. The relation of sex, age, and school achievement to levels of aspiration. *Journal of Educational Psychology,* 1951, **42,** 258–292.

White, R. W. Competence and the psychosexual stages of development. In M. Jones (Ed.), *Nebraska Symposium on Motivation.* Lincoln, Nebraska: University of Nebraska Press, 1960.

Winterbottom, M. R. The relation of need for achievement to learning experiences in independence and mastery. In J. W. Atkinson (Ed.), *Motives in fantasy, action, and society.* Princeton: Van Nostrand, 1958.

Witkin, H. A., Dyk, R. B., Faterson, H. F., Goodenough, D. R., and Karp, S. A. *Psychological differentiation.* New York: Wiley, 1962.

maternal control and obedience in the two-year-old[*][1]

CHERYL MINTON
JEROME KAGAN
JANET A. LEVINE
Harvard University

Analytic description of the mother-child interaction can inform several issues in developmental psychology. The most essential function of such knowledge is to provide data that permit the winnowing of incorrect hypotheses concerning early socialization. A second function is more provincial. It is both useful and interesting to examine child-rearing practices in our society periodically in order to determine if anything has changed. Baldwin's classic monographs on the Fels longitudinal population (Baldwin, Kalhorn,

Reprinted from *Child Development*, 1971, 42. Copyright © 1972 by the Society for Research in Child Development, Inc. By permission.
*This research was supported, in part, by research grants MH8792 from the National Institute of Mental Health and HD4299 from the National Institute of Child Health and Human Development, contract PH43-65-1009, and a grant from the Carnegie Corporation of New York. The authors are indebted to Elizabeth Anderson and Laura Levine for help in coding the home visit protocols. Reprint requests should be sent to Jerome Kagan, William James Hall, Harvard University, Cambridge, Massachusetts 02138.
[1]In abridging this article I have deleted sections describing reliability of measurement and some details of the statistical analysis. I have also cut a long and excellent section on social-class differences in mothers' behavior, not because it was not interesting, but because it did not fit with the needs of a discussion of sex differences. [Ed]

and Breese 1945, 1949) postulated a basic dimension of maternal behavior best described as egalitarian-authoritarian, with well-educated mothers favoring the former attitude and less well-educated mothers the latter. No one has seriously challenged that view in the 25 years that have elapsed. A third reason for studying parent-child interaction is based on adult despair over the behavior of contemporary youth. This behavior has generated the emotionally based hypothesis that the protest and rebelliousness are the product of overly permissive parental practices. It is implied by some that, if we had been able to view these adolescents with their parents 15 years earlier, we would have seen parental acceptance of flagrant disobdience among these 2-year-old children.

The present report contains data relevant to all three issues. It is a summary of observations made in the homes of 90 firstborn children when they were 27 months old. The observations were originally made because the subjects were participants in a longitudinal study, one purpose of which was to determine if the mother's behavior toward the 2-year-old was influenced, in any way, by the characteristics of her child during infancy. As we shall see, there was very little relation between the infant's behavior and his mother's practices with him 2 years later. However, a major dimension of difference among the mothers was reminiscent of Baldwin's earlier distinction between controlling and democratic homes. Different terms can be applied to this dimension. We might call one mode distrustful of the child and the other trustful, or adopt the more popular terminology of authoritarian versus egalitarian. In any case, mothers differ dramatically on this dimension, and maternal educational level is a strong correlate of preferred practice. The purpose of this paper is to convey how this aspect of socialization proceeds in an urban sample of lower-middle- and middle-class white mothers.

METHOD

SUBJECTS

Each of 49 boys and 41 girls, 27 months old, was visited at home on two separate occasions by a female observer who recorded aspects of the mother-child interaction for a total of about 5 hours for each family. The educational background of the parents ranged from less than 12 years of formal education to postgraduate training. Table 1 contains a summary of the educational attainment of the parents, which was subsequently used to assign each family to one of four social class groups.

Prior to the 27-month home visits, these children had been seen

Table 1 Number of Children in Each of the Four Educational Groups

Educational group	Boys	Girls
Lower: one or both parents did not complete high school	10	12
Lower-middle: both parents high school graduates; one may have post-high school training but neither parent a college graduate	21	11
Middle: both parents attended college; or one is a college graduate and the other a high school graduate; or both college graduates	9	8
Upper-middle: one parent has postcollege training; other parent ranges from some college to postcollege	9	10

in a laboratory setting when they were 4, 8, 13, and 27 months of age. In addition, some had been visited in their homes when they were 4 months old. The woman who made the home observations at 4 and 27 months had no access, at any time, to the data gathered in the laboratory, and her observations could not have been influenced by the child's laboratory performances.

PROCEDURES

The home observations were focused on socialization routines, and the observer recorded only a small portion of all that occurred in the home. The cues that prompted the observer to begin recording were either: child making a request of the mother or violating a maternal standard; or mother reprimanding, warning, or commanding the child to perform or not to perform some action. If any of these events occurred, the observer wrote down everything that happened, including verbalizations, until that interaction terminated. She indicated termination of the sequence by a special mark in the protocol and also noted, with a different mark, the end of each 15 minutes of continuous observation.

The observer also administered a vocabulary test to the child and conducted a short interview with the mother while she was in the home.

SCORING OF PROTOCOLS

All of the original protocols, which were written in longhand in the home, were typed verbatim and scored by two independent coders, neither of whom had ever visited the home or communicated with the original observer. After all the records had been scored, the two coders discussed their disagreements and arrived at a consensus.

The scoring that resulted from this discussion was used in the statistical analyses.

Variables. Initially, each sequence was scored as belonging to one of four independent categories: (1) Child violation—mother prohibits or reprimands the child for an ongoing or completed violation of one of her standards. (2) Child request—child makes a request of the mother. (3) Maternal anticipation—mother anticipates the child's violation of one of her standards. (4) Maternal command—mother orders the child to perform some action.

Second, the number of action units in each sequence was scored, where a unit was defined as an uninterrupted sequence displayed by one member of the mother-child dyad. The number of action units was a rough index of the duration of the interaction sequence. The coding of all other variables depended on which of the four sequences was involved.

Sequence type 1: child violation of maternal standards. The child's violations were of two general types. The first included aggressive or destructive behavior that had been designated, a priori, as a violation of normative standards, and included physical or verbal aggression to anyone, angry motor outbursts or tantrums, and deliberate property destruction. This category of behavior was of infrequent occurrence. The second and more frequent class of violation included all actions by the child that provoked a maternal reprimand or prohibition. If mother A chastised the child for touching a vase, it was scored as a violation, but was not so scored if mother B ignored this same action. Hence, this category reflects not only the child's tendency to violate the mother's standards but also the mother's idiosyncratic disposition to chastise her child for minor infringements of a loose code that might be called "home appropriate behavior in America 1970." The types of idiosyncratic violations occurring most frequently included: personal cleanliness, inappropriate social behavior, failure to perform a task with competence, threatening the integrity of household objects or toys, taking food without permission, interference with the mother's ongoing activity, engaging in play that was annoying to the mother, engaging in potentially dangerous activity, and making a general mess in the house.

After the specific violation was coded, the temporal relation between the mother's first response and the child's violation was noted according to the following scheme: (1) Mother reprimands child immediately after he has initiated or completed the activity. (2) Mother reprimands at some time during the violation. (3) Mother reprimands some time after the violation is over. (4) Mother does not see the violation when it begins but reprimands when she sees it.

The coder also noted the content of the first three elements in the mother's reaction. In almost all cases this covered the entire initial reaction, since the mother rarely issued more than three discrete action elements in her initial prohibition. The mother's actions were coded as follows: (1) Simple prohibition requiring only inhibition (stop that, no). (2) Directive prohibition requiring an action other than inhibition. (3) Mild, indirect prohibition (calling the child's name or discouraging him). (4) Removing an object from the child. (5) Removing the child from a situation. (6) Physical punishment. (7) Explanation of an accompanying prohibition. (8) Distraction or suggestion of an alternative activity. (9) Questioning the child about his activity.

If the mother's initial prohibition was not obeyed, all subsequent responses during that sequence were scored as "later responses." These later actions were scored only if they differed in content from the initial maternal action. The final outcome of any violation sequence was scored as follows: (1) Child inhibits the action and obeys the mother. (2) Mother forces obedience by removing the object, moving the child out of the situation, or physically punishing the child, thus stopping the activity. (3) Child disobeys but mother forces obedience (as in [2] above) after six or more action units have occurred. (4) Mother compromises or helps the child to obey. (5) Child obeys partially or after a delay and mother accepts this delay without further reprimand. (6) Mother accepts disobedience. (7) Mother reprimands after the action has terminated and hence the child has no opportunity to obey.

Sequence type 2: child request. Initially, the method or form of the child's request was coded into four categories: verbal request; verbal request issued in a whining tone; fretting, whining, or crying implying a request; and nonverbal request made by gesture or physical contact with mother.

The aim of the child's request was coded; the most frequent aims were: desire for attention, unreasonable request for help with a task the child could obviously perform alone, a reasonable request for instrumental help, a request for the mother to play with the child, request for permission to do something, request for food, request for a special object, request for help in toileting, and request for information.

The mother's response to the child's request was also scored for a large number of initial categories. However, we shall only be concerned with the final outcome of the request sequence, which was scored as follows: (1) Mother grants the child's request. (2) Mother grants the request partially (provides a substitute goal for the one requested, suggests a reasonable delay which the child accepts, assists the child without totally granting the request). (3) Mother refuses request. (4) Mother ignores request.

Sequence type 3: maternal anticipation sequence. The code for child violations was used to score those child behaviors the mother anticipated. The coder also noted whether or not the mother's anticipation was confirmed within that sequence. If the anticipation was confirmed (the child did what his mother warned him not to do), a violation sequence was scored from that point on in the same way other violation sequences were scored.

Sequence type 4: maternal command sequences. Command sequences were scored when the mother seemed to be initiating an order instead of reacting to her child's behavior. As with child request sequences, both method and aim were scored. The major types of command methods were as follows: (1) Barter: mother offers a reward for obedience as she issues a command ("If you'll bring me your cup, I'll give you some juice."). (2) Request: mother phrases her command as a request or a question ("Would you get me the broom?"). (3) Imperative: mother phrases her command in the imperative mode ("Get me the broom."). (4) Nonverbal or physical: mother moves child through desired action.

The major aims of the maternal command included commands to the child to inhibit an activity, to cooperate with the mother, to eat, to cooperate in getting dressed, to clean himself or pick up his toys, or setting limits on an otherwise acceptable activity.

If the child did not obey a maternal command immediately, the mother's subsequent responses were scored using the response categories described for violation sequences. The outcome of a command sequence was scored in the same way that violation sequences were coded.

. . .

RESULTS

FREQUENCY OF MAJOR CATEGORIES

Table 2 contains the rate values for the four basic interaction sequences as well as the proportion of the total interaction time occupied by each of the four major sequences.

Child violation and child requests occurred far more frequently than maternal anticipations or commands. Moreover, boys interacted with their mothers more than girls, and this difference was

Table 2 Rate of Occurrence of Major Variables and Proportion of Total Interaction Time for the Sequences

Variable	Boys (N = 49)			Girls (N = 41)			Sex difference	
	Range	Median	Mean	Range	Median	Mean	t	p
Rate of occurrence:								
Mother-child interaction	7.6–47	19.8	20.1	8.5–32	16.9	17.2	2.10	< .05
Child violations	1.3–31	8.8	9.7	2.2–19	7.7	7.8	2.02	< .05
Child requests	0.7–19	5.2	5.9	1.4–11	5.1	5.4	0.94	N.S.
Maternal anticipations	0.0–10	1.2	1.1	0.0–3.2	0.8	0.9	1.34	N.S.
Maternal commands	0.6–10	3.0	3.4	0.2–6.6	2.9	3.1	0.82	N.S.
Proportion of total interaction time:								
Child violations	0.13–0.76	0.47	0.47	0.16–0.70	0.44	0.44	0.84	N.S.
Child requests	0.07–0.67	0.28	0.30	0.13–0.62	0.32	0.32	−0.59	N.S.
Maternal anticipations	0.0–0.13	0.06	0.06	0.0–0.19	0.05	0.05	0.43	N.S.
Maternal commands	0.03–0.38	0.16	0.17	0.02–0.37	0.17	0.19	−0.67	N.S.

due primarily to the fact that boys had more violation sequences. In general, an event that involved a maternal prohibition, command, or child request occurred once every 3 minutes. Analysis of the temporal order of the sequences within a mother-child dyad revealed that a violation tended to follow a violation, a request was likely to follow a request (see Table 3).

In general, most of the data consisted of sequences in which a mother told a child to stop doing something or a child asked his mother for a favor. The direction of the power relationship is unambiguous.

Although sex differences in specific violations were not dramatic, boys generally had higher rates than girls for integrity of household goods ($p < .05$) and were more often reprimanded for aggression toward the mother. Girls were more often reprimanded for failing to perform a task with competence.

Anticipation sequences. The rate at which mothers anticipated child violations was generally low, and no particular action was anticipated by all mothers. The mothers of four boys and five girls never anticipated the child's violation. The two actions most often anticipated were danger to the child or to the integrity of household goods. It is of interest to note that the mothers worried more often about personal danger to their daughters, but danger to household goods with their sons.

Maternal reaction to the child's violation. Mothers typically responded to the child's violation immediately (range of 71%–100% for boys and 68%–100% for girls). The distribution of maternal responses (in proportion time) to the child's violation is contained in Table 4. Since a mother might display several acts to a particular violation, a high value for one category does not necessarily imply a low value for another. A single maternal response to a violation occurred a little more than half the time; two responses about one-third of the time; and three or more responses a little over 10% of the time. A simple prohibition was the most common maternal reaction to a violation. Mothers of girls, in contrast to mothers of boys, were a little more likely to employ directive prohibitions and a little less likely to move them from the locus of the violation.

Outcome of violation sequences. Children voluntarily obeyed maternal prohibitions about 43% of the time and were forced to obey about 18% of the time. Mothers compromised about 13% and accepted disobedience about 15% of the time. The myth of the "terrible twos" is not supported, for these children seem to have an accommodating posture to parental prohibition.

Table 3 Temporal Ordering of Sequence Types

Prior interaction	Subsequent interaction							
	Child violation		Child request		Maternal anticipation		Maternal command	
	Observed	Expected	Observed	Expected	Observed	Expected	Observed	Expected
Violation	1,799	1,527	869	1,047	182	182	514	609
Request	870	1,044	927	716	107	124	397	416
Anticipation	177	180	97	124	39	21	84	72
Command	521	616	416	422	73	73	347	245

NOTE. $\chi^2 = 266.9$, $df = 9$, $p < .001$.

Table 4 Maternal Responses to Child Violations (Frequency of Occurrence of Maternal Response/Total Child Violations)

Maternal response	Boys (N = 49)		Girls (N = 41)		Significance of sex differences	
	Median	Mean	Median	Mean	t	p
Simple prohibition	.35	.36	.32	.32	1.73	.09
Directive prohibition	.28	.27	.33	.32	-2.00	< .05
Mild negative	.16	.18	.20	.19	-0.41	N.S.
Explain	.16	.14	.14	.16	-0.58	N.S.
Question	.10	.11	.11	.11	0.03	N.S.
Move object	.09	.10	.11	.12	-1.13	N.S.
Move child	.09	.09	.05	.06	2.00	< .05
Distract	.05	.06	.03	.06	-0.04	N.S.
Physical punishment	.02	.03	.00	.02	1.72	.09

Intrasequence analysis for violations. In order to examine intrasequence relations, it was necessary to collapse categories and all the violations were placed into one of six categories. The maternal responses were placed into one of seven categories. The intrasequence analysis revealed that the mother was likely to remove the object or the child if the violation dealt with household property, use physical punishment if the child was aggressive, and respond mildly if the violation concerned socially inappropriate behavior. If the child did not obey the mother's initial prohibition, she was likely to issue a more active reprimand, but the method used later in the sequence was dependent upon her initial reaction. If she issued a mild negative statement initially, she was likely to follow it with a specific prohibition. If she used a specific prohibition initially, she was likely to remove the object or child subsequently. If a prohibition was ineffective initially, the mother might physically punish the next time. If the child disobeyed on a given sequence, the mother was more likely to use physical punishment on the next violation; but if the previous sequence ended in a compromise, she was likely to be mild in her reprimand the next time. The mother's behavior seemed to follow a graded severity of prohibitions and punishments, and there seemed to be justice in her behavior. Her behavior to any specific violation sequence was influenced by the resolution of the previous conflict with her child (see Table 5).

Maternal command sequences. The mother issued commands in the imperative mode about two-thirds of the time, in the form of a request about one-fourth of the time, and rarely bartered or moved the child. Commands were divided into two categories: those related to daily routine (dressing, eating, toileting), and all others (helping mother, picking up toys, playing a game).

In general, commands were obeyed about 60% of the time, compromised about 15%, and disobeyed about 20% of the time. Girls

Table 5 Effect of Outcome of Maternal Reprimand on Subsequent Maternal Reprimand (Observed [O] Followed by Expected [E] Frequencies)

| | Method of reprimand on subsequent violation | | | | | |
| | Mild verbal | | Strong verbal | | Physical | |
Prior outcome	O	E	O	E	O	E
Obedience	336	321	464	433	188	233
Forced obedience	97	123	152	166	130	90
Compromise	139	113	140	152	68	82
Disobedience	100	114	150	154	102	83

NOTE. $\chi^2 = 52.4$, $df = 6$, $p < .001$.

were more likely than boys to obey immediately; boys were likely to resist initially and obey later or be forced to obey. But again, the general picture is a relatively well-socialized child.

The intrasequence analyses for command revealed that the mother used mild command methods when she wanted help or was suggesting an activity to the child. She used strong command methods to obtain cooperation in daily routines or when she was setting limits.

Child request sequences.   Almost all the child's requests were verbal, and because they were not always understood immediately, the mother often asked for repetition or clarification. Requests for food were the most common; requests for help were slightly more frequent for girls than boys ($p < .10$). Requests for information and permission were more frequent for boys ($p < .10$). Mothers rarely ignored child requests and about 30% of the time granted them immediately. If the child persisted, the mother granted about half of the time. Hence, the obedient child that emerged from earlier data is complemented by a relatively obliging and nurturant mother.

The intrasequence analysis revealed that the form of the child's request varied with his intention. Although most requests were verbal, requests for attention were often sought through whining and fretting. These fretful requests were likely to be ignored or hedged, but rarely refused outright. Mothers were more likely to grant reasonable requests for help or mutual play and refuse requests for food and special objects, the latter being the most frequent types of requests. She often told the child to help himself if the request was unreasonable, and she sometimes ignored diffuse requests for attention.

A mother's response to the child's request was also affected by the outcome of the immediately preceding conflict with her child. If the child had obeyed in the preceding conflict, the mother was more likely to grant the request than if he had disobeyed. Mothers were also consistent in their reaction from one request to the succeeding request, for they were likely to grant following a prior granting and refuse a request that followed an earlier refusal.

In sum, the general impression that emerges from the data is relatively clear and not surprising. This sample of lower-middle- and middle-class first-born children tends to be obedient and nonaggressive and the mother generally nurturant and consistent. There tends to be an interaction every few minutes, either because the child has done something the mother thinks requires reprimand or because the child wants something from the mother. The event that elicits the mother's reprimand is usually a minor misdemeanor, like playing with or dirtying household objects, and the mother's modal reaction is to tell the child to "stop it," occasionally explaining why the prohibition is necessary. The child typically obeys. If he does not, she does not ignore the action but initiates stronger treatment procedures, which are usually successful. The child's requests, which are usually verbal, are for food or for a special play object, and the mother is likely to grant the request about half the time.

This is the daily drama that emerged from the observations. The reasonableness of the conclusions implies that the data are a valid reflection of daily life in these homes. Let us ask, therefore, if educational level of the mother and the child's behavior in the laboratory are correlated with these observations in the home.

SOCIAL CLASS DIFFERENCES

The single most striking difference among the mothers of different educational levels was the higher rate of maternal reprimand among the less educated mothers. Mothers who had not graduated from high school prohibited twice as frequently (about once every 5 minutes) than those who had attended college. The trend was monotonic and held for both sexes. (Analysis of variance with educational level as the independent variable yielded an F of 7.19, $p < .001$.)

. . .

DISCUSSION AND SUMMARY

Lower-middle- and middle-class mothers in an urban setting are rather intrusive with their 2-year-olds, interrupting them every 6–8 minutes to remind them of a behavior they should stop or a command they should heed. The children are disposed to obey. Since most of the misbehaviors are trivial, the mother's standards and personality seem to be a better predictor than the child's temperament of whether she will punish. The mother's education is a good predictor of her tendency to be intrusive and authoritarian. Since this pattern of results matches the earlier Baldwin data as well as those of others, faith in this empirical generalization is increased. Although the major result indicated a negative relation between educational level and intrusive prohibitions, mothers also differed in their behavior toward sons and daughters. They reprimanded sons more frequently and moved them from situations more often than they did their daughters.

One reasonable interpretation of these results relies on the parents' goals and implicit theories of child rearing. Educational differences among mothers are likely to reflect both sets of ideas. Well-educated mothers are likely to believe that a sense of autonomy and responsibility are desirable traits for their child to possess. They believe in the value of freedom, and their theory of child rearing contains the simple premise that you train for autonomy by giving the child freedom. The lower-middle-class mother may be afraid that freedom breeds rebelliousness and laziness in school (Kagan 1971; Kamii 1965; Tulkin 1970). Better-educated mothers are also more receptive to the contemporary emphasis on permissive child rearing because of the belief, attributable to psychoanalytic theory, that restrictiveness breeds fear, hostility, and, at some future date, symptoms. The lower-middle-class mother seems to hold more strongly to the doctrine that the child must be told what to do. It is perhaps paradoxical that the lower-middle-class children are given more restrictive commands but are not more obedient.

It is suggested that a mother's behavior derives, in part, from uncertainties she holds about her child's future. The middle-class mother is uncertain about the child's eventual leadership ability, eminence, and creativity. She is worried about how high and how much he will attain. It is an unrealistically optimistic attitude when contrasted with the more defensive posture of the lower-middle-class parent, who is concerned whether the child will do well in school, get into trouble, or establish friendships with bad children. This ideology leads her to make the child fearful of authority but not necessarily more obedient. One datum should not be forgotten. The middle-class children asked their mothers to play with them more often than lower-middle-class children. While we can call the former group dependent and emphasize the regressive nature of that disposition, we suggest that such a request implies that the child views the parent as a companion rather than as an object to fear. No contemporary theory of child development concerned with the future personality of the adult would prefer the latter attitude over the former.

Let us finally relate these data to the three general questions posed in the introduction. With respect to hypotheses about social-ization, the data neither support nor refute traditional social learning theory, for the relationship between the child's obedience and various maternal practices was clearly equivocal. Although social learning theory would have predicted that the lower-middle-class children who received more frequent punishment for violations should have been less mischievous, they also would have insisted that this relation is dependent on consistent awarding of reinforcements for obedient behavior. These data were not complete enough to assess the degree of consistency. Moreover, social learning theory argues that the child models his behavior on that of the parents and that the middle-class child's behavior may reflect patterns of reaction to requests and commands he has witnessed in the home.

With respect to the question of change over time, it appears that there has been little change in the relation between social class and authoritarian practices with the child over the past quarter-century. There is still a positive relation between educational level of the mother and an egalitarian attitude with the preschool child. As far as the last question is concerned, if these data reflect what happened in the homes of the middle-class children who comprise today's "rebellious" youth, it appears that these children were not flagrantly disobedient at 2 years of age; rather, they seemed to have had an accommodating and obedient posture with mothers who were neither inconsistent nor overly permissive.

REFERENCES

Baldwin, A. L., Kalhorn, J., and Breese, F. H. Patterns of parent behavior. *Psychological Monographs,* 1945, **58,** No. 3.

Baldwin, A. L., Kalhorn, J., and Breese, F. H. The appraisal of parent behavior. *Psychological Monographs,* 1949, **63,** No. 299.

Becker, W. C., and Krug, R. S. The parent attitude research instrument: a research review. *Child Development,* 1965, **36,** 329–365.

Hess, R. D., and Shipman, V. C. Cognitive elements in maternal behavior. In J. P. Hill (Ed.), *Minnesota symposia on child psychology.* Vol. 1. Minneapolis: University of Minnesota Press, 1967.

Kagan, J. *Change and continuity in infancy.* New York: Wiley, 1971.

Kamii, C. K. *Socio-economic class differences in the preschool socialization practices of Negro mothers.* (Doctoral dissertation, University of Michigan.) Ann Arbor, Mich.: University Microfilms, 1965.

Prothro, E. T. Socialization and social class in a transitional society. *Child Development,* 1966, **37,** 219–228.

Tulkin, S. R. Mother-infant interaction in the first year of life. Unpublished doctoral dissertation, Harvard University, 1970.

part II
separation of mother and child, and alternative care

There are two separate topics in this overall section, one on working mothers and one on day care. You might think that these two topics are inextricably tied, since virtually all children in day care have working mothers. But by no means are all children of working mothers in day care, and I thought it would be confusing in the long run to combine the two topics. There are really two questions involved: (1) What is the effect of the child's partial separation from the mother (or other caretaker) that occurs whenever the mother works? (2) Given that there is separation, what is the effect of the child's receiving *group* care, as opposed to individual care, while he or she is away from the mother? For the individual woman two separate decisions are involved: Should I work when I have young children (assuming she has a choice)? And if I work, what kind of care should I seek for my child? Because the two questions and decisions are separate, the discussions of them have been kept separate as well, although I suspect that in your own debates or discussions the two may merge somewhat.

Part II
Section 1
working mothers

the effect of maternal employment on the development of the child

HELEN L. BEE

Except for the period during World War II, when the labor of women was needed and there was fairly common approval of employment for women (even women with young children), we have had in this country a long history of opposition to having women work, particularly if the women have preschool children. (See Smuts, 1959, or Siegel and Haas, 1963, for a review of this history.) One of the assumptions underlying such opposition is that separation of mother and child, especially during the preschool years, is seriously detrimental to the child's welfare. This assumption was given great weight in 1951 by a review of studies of institutionalized children, prepared for the World Health Organization by John Bowlby. Bowlby concluded that children living in group care institutions (such as orphanages) suffered from severe "maternal deprivation," and that such deprivation was the cause of the cognitive deficits and emotional difficulties observed in such children. In fact, of course, children in the institutions studied suffered from a great many things besides a lack of a single mother figure. They also had very little contact with fathers or father figures (or any other adults), few toys, little contact with other children, and were in general "stimulus deprived" as well as "mother deprived." It was the emphasis on the importance of the single mother figure, however, that stood out in Bowlby's review. For many people, it was an easy step from there to the assertion that if a single mother figure is so important, obviously women with children should not work, since doing so would deprive the child of a single mother figure.

Hopefully, it is obvious that a conclusion about the ill effects of maternal employment does not necessarily follow from the data on institutionalized children. For one thing, most homes provide richer and more varied stimulation than was common in the institutions examined in Bowlby's review. For another, children of working mothers are not deprived of their mothers; rather they experience a condition that is best described as "partial separation," accompanied by "multiple mothering." So the questions we need to ask—and they are legitimate questions—have to do with the effects of partial separation versus no separation and of multiple mothering versus single mothering. Is it bad for the child to have more than one person caring for him? Does the mother's employment, and the partial separation that accompanies it, alter her relationship with the child? Does the age of the child when the separation and multiple mothering begins matter? Bowlby's review prompted a great deal of research on these and related questions (much of which is reviewed excellently and comprehensively by L. J. Yarrow, 1964). Our concern here is with the body of research that focuses on the effect of the partial separation of mother and child when the mother works.

Before we can go on to an examination of that research, there are two preliminary things we must explore. First, who are the women who work? How many of them are there? How old are their children? What kind of care is provided for their children? Second, how does one go about studying the problem? If you want to know the effect of maternal employment on the child, what kind of research strategy should you use?

WHO ARE THE WORKING MOTHERS?

According to the U.S. Department of Labor's Bureau of Labor statistics, in 1967 approximately two out of every five mothers of children 18 years old or younger were working at least part-time. That amounted to 10.6 million working mothers, of whom approximately 4 million had children under the age of 6. It is estimated that by 1980 there will be 5.3 million mothers with children under age 5 in the work force.

Who takes care of all these children? If the mother doesn't work

Table 1   Child Care Arrangements Made by Working Mothers

	Children under age 3	Children 3–5
Child cared for in the home by someone other than mother	45.9%	48.2%
Child cared for in another home by either a relative or a nonrelative	41.8%	34.3%
Child cared for in a group center of some kind	4.8%	9.7%
Child looked after him/herself[a]	0.2%	0.3%
Mother cared for the child while she was at work	6.4%	6.9%
Other	1.0%	0.8%

Source: Low and Spindler (1968).
[a]This is about 2,000 children under 3 and about 5,000 children from 3 to 5 years old.

full-time, she is likely to do much of the caretaking herself; about one-third of the children under age 6 whose mothers work part-time are cared for entirely by their mothers (Low and Spindler, 1968; United States Department of Labor, 1968). Of greater interest are the caretaking arrangements of women who work full-time, particularly those with children under age 6, since such women must arrange all-day care of some variety for their children. The Children's Bureau's analysis gives the figures in Table 1.

There are several clear conclusions that can be drawn from all the dry statistics. First, it is much more common for a mother of a school age child to work than it is for a mother of a preschooler, and among the mothers of preschoolers, the younger the child is, the less likely the mother is to work. But second, in actual numbers, there are vast numbers of infants and preschoolers with employed mothers; 4.5 million children 5 years old or younger have mothers who work. Third, most of the children of employed mothers are not in day care or in any kind of organized group care at all. Most are cared for by relatives, neighbors, or paid baby-sitters.

METHODOLOGICAL
CONSIDERATIONS

How would you go about discovering whether a mother's working has any effect on the child? The obvious procedure is to select a group of families in which the mother works and a group in which she does not, and then compare them in some way. One might compare the characteristics of the mother's relationship to the child, the type of child-rearing practices she uses, or the child's degree of dependency or emotional stability. This kind of research has been done extensively (see Stolz, 1960, for a review of a good deal of research of this kind), but it has not resulted in very clear conclusions. The reasons for the lack of clarity in the conclusions lie in the design itself. There are several major pitfalls in this sort of research procedure.

First, who is a working mother anyway? If you are picking a sample of working mothers, how long do they have to have worked before you are willing to classify them as "working"? One month? One year? Ten years? What about part-time work? Is that the same thing as full-time work? What about work in the home? Is that the same thing from the child's point of view? For example, I work in my "office" at home for two hours every day. Our youngest child (aged four) is cared for by her father during that time. As far as she is concerned, I "go away" for two hours, yet she knows exactly where I am, and that I could come to her in the case of an emergency. Is the psychological effect on the child the same as it would be if I went to an office in a distant place for two hours, or for a whole day?

And what about the group of nonworking mothers? How are they to be selected? Should you pick women who have never worked, even before the birth of their children? Is it okay to include women who have worked but are not working now? Ideally, if you want a proper contrast, you would have to compare women who have never worked, or at least not since the birth of the child, with women who have worked for some longish period and are away from the home while they work. Many of the studies of working mothers have not achieved this kind of contrast; they have included women in the nonworking group who have worked since the birth of the child but are not working now; and they have included women in the working group who have worked for very short periods. As a consequence, it's difficult to get anything very clear from the results.

Even if you are able to solve the problem of defining "working" and "nonworking" mothers, you have a second, more troublesome difficulty. Suppose you pick two groups with nicely contrasting work histories. They are also likely to differ in many other ways as well. The woman who chooses to work for her own satisfaction is undoubtedly different in many ways from the woman who chooses not to; and a woman who chooses to work for financial reasons comes from a family that is different from that of the woman who has no financial need to work. For example, mothers from intact families in which the husband earns less than $7,000 a year are more likely to work than mothers from families in which the husband earns more; and mothers without husbands are still more likely to be employed. Unless you take these differences into account when you select your samples, you can't be sure that any differences you find in the children, or in the mother-child relationships, are due to the fact that the mother works. They could be due to the fact that fathers are less likely to be present in homes with working mothers, to lower income, or to any one of the many other factors that differentiate the home in which the mother works from the home in which she does not.

There are several ways to solve these problems. One way is to choose very large samples of working and nonworking mothers so that you can look at subgroups as well as the groups as a whole. Marian Radke Yarrow, Phyllis Scott, Louise de Leeuw, and Christine Heinig use this strategy to some extent in their study, which is presented in the readings. Another way is to select matched pairs of working and non-working mothers. That is, you try to match each working woman with a nonworking woman on all the characteristics that you suspect will matter, so that as nearly as possible the two groups differ only in the employment status of the mother. There are precious few studies of this kind, simply because such matching is extremely difficult, but there are some. (See Siegel, Stolz, Hitchcock, and Adamson, 1959.)

A third methodological issue has to do with the way in which one locates the sample of working mothers in the first place. There are several studies mentioned in the review by Elva Poznanski, Annette Maxey, and Gerald Marsden, for example, in which families were selected from among those whose children had been referred to child guidance clinics. Researchers using this strategy typically select, from among children who are already showing difficulties, a group whose mothers are working and compare them to a group whose mothers are not working. If, then, the children of the working mothers have some common sort of disturbance, the conclusion is drawn that this sort of disturbance is a typical result of maternal employment. (See, for example, the Rouman paper discussed in Poznanski, Maxey, and Marsden's article.) You should keep in mind that research of this type does *not* tell you anything about the majority of the children of working mothers. It doesn't even tell you what percentage of children of working mothers wind up in child guidance clinics with difficulties of any kind. What it may tell you is that *when* children of working mothers have emotional or cognitive difficulties, those difficulties tend to be of a particular kind, compared to the emotional or cognitive difficulties that may be characteristic of disturbed children from homes in which the mother does not work.

The point to remember, after all these cautions about method-ological problems have been given, is that it is difficult to do good research in this area. It's not impossible, as shown by some of the research discussed by Poznanski, Maxey, and Marsden and by the two other papers included in the selections. But you should keep the various pitfalls in mind as you review the literature.

THE EVIDENCE

Since much of the evidence is reviewed carefully from a psycho-analytic viewpoint by Poznanski, Maxey and Marsden, I needn't go into enormous detail here. What I can do is sort out some of the major trends and indicate those areas in which my own interpretation of the results differs from theirs.

First, let's take a look at the effects on the child or the family when a mother works. Only two findings seem to hold up widely: (1) Mothers who work have fewer children, and (2) children of working mothers show higher school achievement than do children of non-working mothers. Poznanski et al. suggest three further possible effects of having a working mother, namely that the children in such families may be more dependent, have more sexual identity problems, and perhaps have a pattern of more delinquency. But the data they review can also be interpreted easily, I think, as showing that these three conditions occur primarily when there is family instability or unstable alternate care; they are not inevitable consequences of having a mother work. In particular, the evidence on the relationship of delinquency to maternal employment illustrates that it is the family's overall characteristics that are crucial, not the mother's work history (McCord and Thurber, 1963; Gleuck and Gleuck, 1957). When the mothers in unstable families work, the sons are more likely to be delinquent, but when the mothers in stable families from the same general kind of background and environment work, the higher rate of delinquency among the sons does not result. So the mother's working per se is not the crucial variable.

A variable that does seem to matter is the mother's enjoyment of her role, whether that role is working or homemaking. The paper by Yarrow, Scott, de Leeuw, and Heinig is the very best example available of work on this question. Their results indicate that the mother's satisfaction with her role, whichever it is, is more important than whether or not she works.

The nature of the substitute care provided for the child of the working mother is an additional important factor. Poznanski et al.'s review again gives data here. In particular, note the discussion of the study by Moore (1964), who found that the children who had working mothers and had had unstable substitute care were the ones showing greater dependency, greater attention seeking, and more anxiety about being separated from the mother. When the children of working mothers had had stable substitute care they did not show these anxious, dependent behaviors; in fact they were more assertive than were mother-reared children. Also relevant here is the study by Caldwell, Wright, Honig, and Tannenbaum, which is included in the next section. They studied a group of children who had been continuously enrolled in a day-care center from about one year of age to about two and a half. The alternative care was thus very stable. This group was compared to a group of children from similar backgrounds who had been reared at home for the same period. When the relationship of the child to the mother in the two groups was compared, essentially no differences were found. So it looks very much as if stable, adequate substitute care is functionally equivalent to (or even better than) having good home rearing, at least in terms of the effects measured in these studies. Inadequate or unstable substitute care, however, may have potentially disruptive effects, probably particularly for very young children.

The one factor that you would think would have received a great deal of attention, and has not, is the age of the child at the time of the mother's employment. The emphasis on "maternal deprivation," based on Bowlby's study of institutionalized children, focused attention on the importance of the first two or three years. The impression given was that it was essential for the child to have an exclusive relationship with a single mother figure during those first few years; after that time a separation was seen as potentially less damaging. Probably as a result of such assumptions, there is considerable pressure on mothers of very young children to stay at home. And as we have seen from the statistics, they *are* more likely to stay at home.[1] But do we know that these assumptions are valid? Is it a fact that there is more difficulty for the child and the mother-child relationship if the mother begins work when the child is very young? If anything, what evidence we have on this question suggests that the age of the child makes little difference. The studies of children reared in kibbutzim (Israeli collective settlements), where the children are reared in groups from the very earliest weeks, do not indicate any long-term deficits in, or damage to, the children (Rabin, 1958). The data from the study by Caldwell et al. also show that detrimental effects are not the necessary result of nonmaternal care for the very young infant. What is needed, of course, is research in which the age of the child of working mothers is examined systematically, in conjunction with some of the other variables mentioned. It might well be, for example, that unstable substitute care is more detrimental to an infant than to an older child, but that stable substitute care has no detrimental effect at all on the infant or toddler; indeed in some cases it may have a positive effect. (Again see the study by Caldwell et al.)

A quite different question has to do with the long-term effects of having had a mother who worked. As adults, are the children of work-

---

[1]This is changing, however. In 1959, 20 percent of the mothers with children under age six were working. In 1969, 30 percent were working.

ing mothers different from the children of nonworking mothers? One of the few studies to examine this question, by Susan R. Vogel, Inge K. Broverman, Donald M. Broverman, Frank E. Clarkson, and Paul S. Rosenkrantz, is included in the selections. Their particular concern is with the degree to which young adult men and women have stereotypes about the appropriate characteristics and roles for men and women. They found that college students whose mothers are working or had worked had less stereotyped views of male and female roles than students with nonworking mothers. Students with working mothers saw women as more competent and capable than is usual or saw men as warmer and more affectionate than is usual. Put another way, having a working mother appears to be associated with a perception of the male and female roles as being more similar. But there is a word of caution about this result: The samples of working and nonworking mothers in this study are not matched on other dimensions, so it is quite possible that the result comes from the fact that in those families in which the mother chooses to work, there *is* greater equality of roles. We simply can't tell from this result whether the mother's going to work would alter the stereotypes in a family that started out with clearly stereotyped roles.

If we look at all the available evidence, the following conclusion seems reasonable to me: When the mother is satisfied with her role and adequate alternative care is arranged, the separation of the mother from her child that accompanies maternal employment has no demonstrable negative effect. Indeed, in some cases positive effects are noted. (See Caldwell's paper and the material in the day-care section.) When the children of working mothers have developmental difficulties, they seem to be associated more with family instability or inadequate alternate care than with working per se.

QUESTION FOR DEBATE AND DISCUSSION

1. Assume that you are the mother of a one-year-old infant. An opportunity for a job you are interested in comes along. Should you take it? What factors enter into your decision?

ADDITIONAL REFERENCES USEFUL IN PREPARATION
FOR DEBATE OR DISCUSSION

Siegel, A. E., and Haas, M. B. The working mother: A review of research. *Child Development*, 1963, **34**, 513–542.
    This review focuses on the woman who works, rather than on her child or her relationship to her child. Who are the women

who work? How are they affected by the attitude of husband or family? How is the household labor distributed in families where the women work? An excellent review.

Yarrow, L. J. Separation from parents during early childhood. In M. L. Hoffman and L. W. Hoffman (Eds.), *Review of child development research.* Vol. 1. New York: Russell Sage Foundation, 1964, pp. 89–136.

This is an excellent overall review of the literature on all aspects of parent-child separation, including the question of maternal employment.

Yarrow, M. R. Maternal employment and child rearing. *Children.* 1961, **8,** 223–228.

This paper focuses on the effect of maternal employment on the child and the mother-child relationship, but it covers literature up to 1960 only. It's worth reading, though, as a supplement to the Poznanski paper, since it gives more detail on the earlier studies and because it gives a different, nonpsychoanalytic slant.

REFERENCES

Bowlby, J. *Maternal care and mental health.* Monograph Series, No. 2. Geneva: World Health Organization, 1951.

Caldwell, B. M., Wright, C. M., Honig, A. S., and Tannenbaum, J. Infant day care and attachment. *American Journal of Orthopsychiatry,* 1970, **40,** 397–412.

Glueck, S., and Glueck, E. Working mothers and delinquency. *Mental Hygiene,* 1957, **41,** 327–352.

Low, S., and Spindler, P. G. *Child care arrangements of working mothers in the United States.* Children's Bureau publication 461. Washington, D.C.: United States Government Printing Office, 1968.

McCord, J., and Thurber, E. Effects of maternal employment on lower-class boys. *Journal of Abnormal and Social Psychology,* 1963, **67,** 177–182.

Moore, T. Children of full-time and part-time mothers. *International Journal of Social Psychiatry,* 1964, **2,** 1–10.

Rabin, A. I. Infants and children under conditions of intermittent mothering in the kibbutz. *American Journal of Orthopsychiatry,* 1958, **28,** 577–584.

Siegel, A. E., and Haas, M. B. The working mother: A review of research. *Child Development,* 1963, **34,** 513–542.

Siegel, A. E., Stolz, L. M., Hitchcock, E. A., and Adamson, J. M. Dependence and independence in the children of working mothers. *Child Development,* 1959, **30,** 533–546.

Smuts, R. W. *Women and work in America.* New York: Columbia University Press, 1959.

Stolz, L. M. Effects of maternal employment on children: Evidence from research. *Child Development,* 1960, **31,** 741–782.

United States Department of Labor, Wage and Labor Standards Administration. *Working mothers and the need for child care services.* Washington, D.C.: United States Government Printing Office, June, 1968.

Yarrow, L. J. Separation from parents during early childhood. In M. L. Hoffman and L. W. Hoffman (Eds.), *Review of child development research.* Vol. 1. New York: Russell Sage Foundation, 1964, pp. 89–136.

child-rearing in families of working and nonworking mothers*

MARIAN RADKE YARROW   National Institute of Mental Health
PHYLLIS SCOTT   University of Queensland
LOUISE DE LEEUW   National Institute of Mental Health
CHRISTINE HEINIG   American Association of University Women

In the history of research on child development and child rearing, social concerns have often stimulated particular areas of inquiry. An instance is the work of the 1930's and 1940's on the influence of early institutionalization upon children. Society's concerns about the impact of hospitalization, orphanage placement and the like posed empirical questions which research recast and redefined as basic problems in socialization. In similar fashion the rapidly increasing employment of mothers has currently prodded investigation of the effects of this changed mother role on the rearing of children. Judged by frequency of occurrence in American family structure, maternal employment is a significant socialization variable: two out of five mothers of school age children were reported in the labor force in the 1957 survey.[1]

Reprinted from *Sociometry*, 1962, **25**(2). By permission.
*A grant from the Elizabeth McCormick Memorial Fund to the American Association of University Women made possible the work of Miss Christine Heinig and Miss Phyllis Scott.

[1]National Manpower Council, *Womanpower*, New York: Columbia University Press, 1957.

The initial questions directed to research on this problem, motivated from the social welfare concerns, were broad and atheoretical: "what happens to children whose mothers work?" The questions were framed with the strong suggestion that the working mother was a "problem," creating conditions of child neglect, juvenile delinquency, disorganized family life, etc. The studies resulting from the practical orientation produced a confusion of findings. In her review of the research literature on maternal employment, Stolz[2] suggests that the inconclusive nature of findings may be laid to the failure of investigators to specify the circumstances surrounding mothers' employment (whether in broken or intact families, motivated from economic stress or personal satisfactions in work, with young or older children, with or without good substitute care) and to the failure of investigators to include adequate control groups.

The inconclusive results can also be explained by the fact that most studies have failed to conceptualize maternal employment in terms of theoretically relevant variables. For example, inherent in the situation of a mother's work outside the home are mother-child separation, multiple mothering and changed mother-father roles, all of which are familiar variables of developmental research. It is apparent that maternal employment is not a single condition or variable of mothering; it is rather a set of conditions which may vary greatly from case to case.

The research questions in the present investigation are two: (1) When structural variables of the family environment (such as family class and composition, presence of mother, father, and supplemental mother figures) are controlled, do working and nonworking mothers provide different child-rearing environments? (2) Do working and nonworking mothers who differ in their attitudes and feeling about their adult roles differ in their maternal roles?

Personal variables which characterize the mother as an individual have generally been ignored in studies of child rearing. It is hypothesized that the mother's gratifications and frustrations in her other adult (nonmother) roles, her achievement needs, and her feelings of self-fulfillment influence her functioning as a mother and affect what is mediated to the child by her child-rearing practices. Since employment status may be intimately bound up with the mother's self attitudes and values, the study of employed and nonemployed mothers who differ in attitudes offers an opportunity for an initial test of the more general hypothesis concerning the significance of this class of variables in socialization studies. The

[2]Lois M. Stolz, Effects of Maternal Employment on Children: Evidence from Research, *Child Development*, **31** (December 1960), pp. 749–782.

particular personal factors studied are those relating to the meaning of working or not working, i.e., the woman's sex role ideology, her basic preferences regarding working or not, the motivations supporting her present work status, and her motivations in her role as mother.

Choice of dependent variables was made on the basis of existing opinion and theory concerning the possible consequences of maternal employment for the rearing of children. Working is presumed to result in "deficiencies" in mothering: less dedication and less effectiveness, deviations in supervision and control of the child, exaggeration of the child's dependency needs, greater stress on achievement, altered sex role training, and decreased participation of mother with child[3] Mothers' reports of practices and philosophies constitute the data on child rearing.

SAMPLE

The subjects of this study are 50 employed and 50 nonemployed mothers. The classification of *working* required at least 28 hours of work per week in steady employment extending over the past year. To be classed in the *nonworking* group, the mother could not have engaged in any paid employment over the past year. Unfortunately the two groups have similar work histories: all having worked at some time. Half of the nonworking mothers had worked after marriage, before the birth of a child.

Subjects of the employed and nonemployed groups were matched in family characteristics. Families were white, intact, with a male wage earner present. There were one to four children per family, with at least one child (about whom the mother was interviewed) between four and eleven years of age.

PROCEDURES

In selecting the sample it was the objective to choose social class groups in which employment is not a traditional role for married women, but in which both a traditional woman's role and a changed role exist and are tolerated, and in which differing values and sentiments about women's employment are held. We wished to have groups in which working or not working is more likely to be a matter of individual choice than of dire economic necessity. Narrowing the class range should also reduce variations in child-rearing values and practices, leaving remaining variations more clearly attributable to personal maternal factors or the maternal work role.

3 *Ibid.*

Middle and upper middle class families and upper working class families living in middle class neighborhoods were included in the sample (Groups I, II, III, IV on the Hollingshead Index of Social Position).

Family structural variations associated with maternal employment (separation of mother from child, substitute "mothers," changes in father and mother roles) were greatly reduced in range. Substitute care was primarily for the out-of-school hours, when, for the great majority, paid help or a relative (grandmother, aunt, occasionally an older sibling) cared for the children. Fathers retained wage earner roles in the homes of both groups.

The subjects were located in the Greater Washington area, in twelve public schools selected in terms of social class criteria. The location of eligible families in eight of the schools was facilitated by data on family characteristics from another study.[4] For these families, a letter, followed by a telephone call, determined willingness to cooperate in the study. For the other schools, it was necessary to canvass each home (with knowledge only of the age of the children) to enlist interest and determine eligibility. After preliminary screening on race and social class, approximately 650 families were further screened on family characteristics, using a brief set of polling-type questions. An eligible mother who did not consent to an interview after she had been informed of the nature of the study was counted as a refusal. Twenty-one per cent of the working mothers and 17 per cent of the mothers not employed did not consent to participate. Illness, imminent moving and the like, accounted for a few of the refusals. The other women indicated they preferred not to be research subjects. The social characteristics of the 100 interviewed mothers are presented in Table 1.

INTERVIEW PROCEDURE

The subjects were interviewed in their homes. A schedule was followed as closely as was consistent with the responses of the subject. The interview dealt, in sequence, with the mother's past and present employment status, her motives for working or not working, and her attitudes concerning role differences of men and women as these relate to dependency and achievement needs and to primary responsibility to the home. Interview questions about child rearing included the kind of substitute care provided for the children in the mother's absence, mother's opinions about her own employment or nonemployment in relation to the rearing of her children, and

[4]Thomas L. Gillette, "The Working Mother: A Study of the Relationship Between Maternal Employment and Family Structure As Influenced by Social Class and Race," unpublished doctoral dissertation, University of North Carolina, 1961.

Table 1 Characteristics of Employed and Nonemployed Mothers

Characteristics		Working mothers $N = 50$	Nonworking mothers $N = 50$
Index of social position	I	16	13
	II	14	16
	III	8	14
	IV	12	7
Number of children in family	Mean	2.14	2.36
Sex of children	Girls	27	27
	Boys	37	37
Age of children[a]	9–11 years	36	38
	6–8 years	21	19
	4–5 years	7	7
Age of mother	29–39	28	24
	40–50	22	26
Education of mother			
Some college or college graduate		30	26
Some high school or high school graduate		20	24
Mother's occupation			
Professional		13	—
Semiprofessional or managerial		12	—
Clerical or secretarial		19	—
Service trades		6	—

[a]Mothers were interviewed with regard to the children who met the criteria of the sample; i.e., keeping the age between 4 and 11 years, and having age and sex comparable in working and nonworking samples.

mother's philosophy and practices in the areas of discipline, and control, dependency and independency training, warmth and involvement with the child and sex role training.

INDEPENDENT VARIABLES

Analyses of child-rearing variables were made in terms of the following group comparisons: (1) working and nonworking mothers of similar social and family circumstances, (2) working and nonworking mothers who *preferred* and those who *did not prefer* their present work or nonwork status, (3) working mothers whose *motives* for *working* differed, (4) nonworking mothers whose *attitudes toward the mother role* differed, and (5) working and nonworking mothers who differed in *academic achievement*.

The sixth variable of sex role ideology was not used because there was little variation among the subjects. It was reasoned in designing the study that ideology concerning masculine and feminine roles might be relevant to the mother's career choice and her functioning in the mother role. Therefore, subjects were asked how they felt about the ideological position that "woman's place is in the home," about the relative achievement needs of men and women, and about the acceptability of either sex showing dependency on the other. Responses were rated as predominantly equalitarian or traditional. Only 15 per cent of the mothers were rated traditional on two or three of the dimensions, 44 per cent were rated traditional in one dimension, and 41 per cent were traditional in none of the dimensions. The decision to work or not seems, for the vast majority of the sample, to be outside of this area of ideological consideration, in spite of a rare expression or two, such as, "It is God's will that woman does what man wants."

Independent and dependent variables of child rearing are described in more detail in the presentation of the findings and in the Appendix. Group differences in child rearing were evaluated using Chi squares for qualitative data and "t" tests for quantitative data. A sample of 26 interviews was coded by two raters working independently. A few codes were dropped which did not reach an arbitrary minimum of 80 per cent coder agreement. Forty-seven per cent of coded categories used in the report were between 80 per cent and 89 per cent in inter-rater agreement; 53 per cent of the coded categories were 90 per cent or above in agreement.

DEPENDENT VARIABLES

Several aspects of the child-rearing relationship were explored in the interview. Relative to areas of discipline and control the interviewer attempted to draw out the general tone of control in the home: how strict was the mother and how did mother and father compare on strictness? Both a direct question to the mother and a rating based on answers to all interview questions on control were obtained. Since the two scores were highly correlated, only the mother's direct statement was used in analysis. The mother was questioned about techniques of discipline used more than occasionally with her child. She was questioned in more detail about the child's display of aggressive behavior and her handling of his aggression. An over-all evaluation was made of the degree to which discipline and control seemed to be a contested issue between mother and child. The interview questions forming the basis for ratings and the nature of the rating scales are given in the Appendix for each of the dependent variables.

The nature of dependency-independency relations between mother and child is not easily tapped by interview questions. Questions were asked about the areas in which the child was granted freedom of decision and action and in which he was given responsibility, and the kinds and amount of attention and help which the child sought from his mother. The child's age was taken into consideration in judging the degree to which these factors signified dependence of child and independency training by the mother.

The mother's sensitivity, emotional satisfaction and involvement with her children and her confidence in her mother role were judged by criteria applied to the total interview or sections of questioning rather than to specific questions.

The underlying philosophy and operation of rearing were appraised in the following terms: Did the mother have clearly formulated principles regarding child rearing or did she proceed in a kind of haphazard performance of child care-taking acts as the needs arose? How did principles of rearing carry over into practice? Were the limits set for the child clear or unclear in practice?

Working might make a difference in household schedule, therefore the amount of time pressure or close scheduling was rated. Because of possible differences between working and nonworking women in attitudes toward sex roles, the mother's philosophy about the rearing of boys and girls, and the practices of the family in carrying out household duties, whether according to traditional sex-typed patterns or not, were obtained.

Finally, prior to data analysis, a model of "good" mothering was constructed which combined a set of variables of philosophy and practice. The "good" mother is described in terms of eight variables measured by the interview. (1) At a cognitive level, the "good" mother gives evidence of some formulated principles that guide her rearing practices. (2) She recognizes the importance of supporting the individual potentialities and the growing independence of the child. (3) She shows reasonable consistency between her principles and reported practices. (4) The "good" mother's practices provide clear limits for her child. (5) She establishes controls which are accepted without continuing conflict between parent and child. (6) The "good" mother shows sensitivity to the individual child's needs. (7) She has a feeling of confidence about her child rearing (though she is not necessarily without problems) and (8) she expresses warmth and emotional satisfaction in her relationship with her child. A summary score (0 to 8) of "adequacy of mothering" was derived from ratings on these eight variables.

FINDINGS

WORK STATUS

As indicated in Table 2, the classification of mothers by whether or not they are employed is almost unrelated to child-rearing patterns. These working and nonworking mothers, who are of similar cultural background and family circumstances, are very much alike in philosophy, practices and apparent relationships with their children. In only one comparison is the difference between the groups statistically significant at the 5 per cent level. This difference is in the

Table 2 Parent-Child Relationships by Work Status and Satisfaction of Mother[a]

Parent-child variables	Working vs. nonworking mothers			Satisfied vs. dissatisfied	
	All mothers	Satisfied	Dissatisfied	Working	Nonworking
Discipline					
1. Mother's strictness	—	—	—	—	—
2. Father stricter than mother	—	—	—	S < D (.05)	—
3. Disciplinary techniques	—	—	—	—	—
4. Mother's permissiveness of aggression	—	—	—	—	—
5. Child's rebellious behavior	W < NW (.10)	—	W < NW (.05)	—	—
6. Control an issue between mother and child	—	—	W < NW (.01)	S < D (.10)	S < D (.05)
Independence training					
1. Nurturing independence	—	—	—	S < D (.10)	—
2. Household responsibilities	—	—	—	S < D (.10)	—
3. Child's dependence on mother	—	—	—	S < D (.02)	—
Emotional relationships					
1. Sensitivity to child's needs	W < NW (.10)	W < NW (.05)	—	—	—
2. Emotional satisfaction in relationships with child	—	—	W > NW (.10)	—	S > D (.02)

3. Planned activities with child:					
by mother	—	—	—	—	—
by father	—	—	—	—	—
4. Confidence in child rearing	W < NW (.05)	—	W > NW (.10)	—	D < S (.01)
Rearing environment					
1. Formulated principles of rearing	—	—	—	—	—
2. Clarity of limits set for child	—	—	W > NW (.10)	S < D (.05)	S > D (.05)
3. Consistency between principles and practices	—	—	—	—	S > D (.01)
4. Scheduling	W > NW (.10)	—	—	—	—
5. Traditional philosophy re sex role training	—	—	—	—	—
6. Traditional sex-typed household functions	—	—	—	—	—
7. Adequacy of mothering (summary rating)	—	W < NW (.10)	W > NW (.02)	—	S > D (.01)

aThe probability that an observed relationship could have occurred by chance is indicated in parentheses.

mother's confidence about her role as mother. Working mothers (42%) more frequently than nonworking mothers (24%) express misgivings and anxious concern about their role, often by explicit questioning and worry as to whether working is interfering with their relationships and the rearing of their children.

Absence of differences in certain of the variables is particularly interesting. The working and nonworking mothers do not express differing points of view on sex role training. About 40 per cent of the total sample present opinions or philosophies which emphasize differences in the rearing of boys and girls in such respects as handling of aggression, activity, social relationships; 40 per cent reject the idea of rearing differences; the others are uncertain. Using household responsibilities that are assigned to boys and girls as a measure of sex role typing, families of working and nonworking mothers again do not differ (40 per cent in the working group, 42 per cent in the nonworking assign tasks in terms of traditional sex roles). It may seem reasonable to expect that a working mother will have greater need to schedule time carefully and may, therefore, inject more time-tension into family routines. There is only a suggestive difference in the expected direction; pressured scheduling is prominent among 26 per cent of the working and 12 per cent of the nonworking group. Working and nonworking mothers do not differ on the summary measure of adequacy of mothering.

ROLE PREFERENCE

More important in differentiating mothers according to child-rearing practices than the fact of working or not working is how the work variable is combined with other maternal characteristic (Table 2). When work (or nonwork) is analyzed according to whether it is a goal in itself or a means to certain goal attainments, associations with child rearing take on more meaningful patternings. The mothers clearly differed in their desire to work or not to work outside the home. Replies to two questions determined their classification as preferring or not preferring their present status: (1) if given the choice, would the mother want to work, and (2) how would she rank a number of alternatives involving job, marriage and children. Seventy-six per cent of the working mothers and 82 per cent of the nonworking mothers indicated preference for their present situations. The resulting four subgroups were compared in their child-rearing characteristics.

The questions about these groups can be asked in two ways: (1) Do working and nonworking mothers who are similarly satisfied (or dissatisfied) with present status differ in child rearing? How do working mothers who prefer to work and those who do not prefer to work compare, and, likewise, how do nonworking mothers who prefer to work and those who do not prefer to work compare on child rearing?

Dissatisfaction with present role appears to contribute to mothering functions, and especially among mothers who are not employed. The subgroups differ as follows. If mothers are in their *preferred* work or nonwork *roles,* working or not working makes little difference in their child rearing. There are only two suggestive differences: Thirty-four per cent of satisfied nonworking mothers and 11 per cent of satisfied working mothers are rated as showing high sensitivity to children's needs. There is a difference of border-line significance giving the nonworking satisfied mothers higher scores on adequacy of mothering. When *dissatisfied* working and nonworking mothers are compared, differences appear in areas of control, emotional satisfaction, confidence in child rearing and on scores on adequacy of mothering, favoring the dissatisfied working mothers. For example 67 per cent of dissatisfied nonworking mothers and 18 per cent of dissatisfied working mothers report a more or less continuing "battle" for control between mother and child. High ratings in confidence in the mother role occur more often among the working than the nonworking dissatisfied mothers (50 per cent and 11 per cent, respectively). In the closely related measure of emotional satisfaction in relationship with the child there are similar differences favoring the working over the nonworking dissatisfied mothers. The sum of ratings shows significantly lower scores on adequacy of mothering for the dissatisfied nonworking mothers than for the dissatisfied working mothers.

The same data may be examined with work status controlled. Among *working* mothers there is some support for the idea that there are more internal inconsistencies in child rearing among the dissatisfied than among the satisfied mothers. Three-fourths of the dissatisfied mothers compared with two-fifths of the satisfied mothers report clear limit setting for the child. At the same time, however, control is more often rated a continuing issue in the family for the dissatisfied than for the satisfied mothers. More dissatisfied working mothers describe their children as dependent while at the same time tending to exert more verbal pressure toward independent behavior and to assign more responsibilities to their children than do the satisfied mothers.

Among *nonworking* mothers, several dimensions of child-rearing behavior are clearly related to role preference. Clarity in limit setting is more characteristic of the satisfied mothers (61 per cent of this group as compared with 22 per cent in the dissatisfied group). A significantly higher proportion of dissatisfied mothers show extreme inconsistency between principles and practices (57 per cent of the dissatisfied mothers as compared with 6 per cent of the satisfied mothers). Control remains a continuing "issue" between mother and child for 67 per cent of the dissatisfied and 32 per cent of the satisfied mothers. Lack of emotional satisfaction in relationships with her child is more frequent among dissatisfied than satisfied mothers (78 per cent and 35 per cent, respectively). Similarly, high confidence in the mother role, expressed in 90 per cent of the satisfied group, is rare (11%) among the dissatisfied mothers. The generally inferior mothering by the dissatisfied nonworking group is reflected in significantly lower summary scores on adequacy of mothering.

MOTIVES FOR WORKING AND NOT WORKING

Although it is understandable that a woman's career dissatisfactions may enter into her relationships with her child, it is not so clear why this should be more the case in the nonworking than in the working group. A possible explanation may lie in understanding why the women were working or not working, regardless of their expressed preference. The mothers in this sample were working either primarily as a means of achieving certain *family and child-rearing goals* that were not available without the mother's working, or as a means of *self-fulfillment*. Mothers (52%) who spoke of family goals were interested in cultural advantages, social status, educational and health goals for the family. They included both mothers who preferred and those who did not prefer to work. Mothers (48%) who found self-fulfillment through working referred to use of their educational training, feelings of contributing to society, needing to be with people, etc. These mothers preferred to work.

Since working but preferring not to is related to valued family benefits, the situation for these reluctant working mothers does not appear to represent great frustration. Certainly one would expect these mothers to be less frustrated than women who have reason to resent the necessity for their working as a circumstance forced upon them by their husbands' failures or as a circumstance in which the work itself involves personal hardship. The absence of differences in child rearing associated with family motivations and self-fulfillment motivation is, therefore, not surprising (Table 3).

Among nonworking women reasons for not working reflect either a *love of mothering* (48%), a *duty of mothering* (36%), or a desire for "freedom," or an "easier" life (15%). "Freedom" is for avocations and "volunteer" work but also, on the less noble side, it is freedom regarded selfishly. As one woman said, she "had it made"; now that husband and children could get their own breakfasts and get off to work and school, the day was for herself. Because of the heterogeneity of motives in the "freedom" group, it was not used in further analyses.

Mothers classified by "love" and by "duty" express different feelings toward the mother role. The "love" mothers are oriented entirely toward mothering; the "duty" mothers speak of child rearing as a responsibility that carries with it various hardships and deprivations. The classification of "love" and "duty" in general parallels the classification of satisfied and dissatisfied nonworking mothers, although "duty" mothers appear in both the satisfied and dissatisfied groups. Differences in child rearing are similar in both classifications; the less favorable qualities appearing in the "duty" and the dissatisfied mothers.

The data on the nonworking mothers support the position that the mother's motivations and fulfillments in nonmother roles are related to her behavior in the child-rearing role. It is necessary, in a sense, first to look at maternal employment and nonemployment as dependent variables before making predictions concerning associated child-rearing variables.

MOTHERS' EDUCATION

If work status is ignored, college-trained and high school-trained mothers (within the class range of our sample) do not differ on child-rearing measures. But, when work status and educational level and child rearing are considered together, suggestive interactions appear (Table 3). *Nonworking* college mothers and nonworking high school mothers appear to differ in more ways in child rearing than do *working* college mothers and working high school mothers. In the *nonworking* groups, college mothers are significantly more often rated high in independence training (30 per cent and 8 per cent for college and high school, respectively), in sensitivity (50% and 8%), in consistency between principles and practice (85% and 54%), and in clarity in limit setting (69% and 39%). The higher mean scores for college mothers on the "adequacy of mothering" summary score reflect the differences on the individual items. The *working* groups differ only on ratings of sensitivity to child's needs (40 per cent and 10 per cent of high school and college mothers, respectively, are rated low on sensitivity), and on the father's being the stricter parent (70 per cent and 34 per cent of high school and college groups are so rated). The data suggest that employment may be selective of certain kinds of mothers, or that working has the effect of "leveling" social class differences in child rearing. The mothers of high school background who are using working as a means of social mobility (more lessons, education, travel for family) may also be altering their child-rearing practices.

When working and nonworking mothers are compared within each educational group, it appears that families of different social class backgrounds make different types of adaptations to the mother's working. Mothers of high school background more often

Table 3   Parent-Child Relationships by Work Status, Motivation, and Education of Mother[a]

Parent-child variables	Family vs. self motives: working mother only	Love vs. duty motives: nonworking mothers only	Working vs. nonworking mothers		High school vs. college attendance	
			High school attendance	College attendance	Working mothers	Nonworking mothers
Discipline						
1. Mother's strictness	—	—	—	—	—	—
2. Father stricter than mother	F > S (.10)	—	W > NW (.05)	—	H > C (.02)	—
3. Disciplinary techniques	—	—	—	—	—	—
4. Mother's permissiveness of aggression	F > S (.10)	—	—	—	—	—
5. Child's rebellious behavior	—	L < D (.10)	W < NW (.01)	—	—	—
6. Control an issue between mother and child	—	L < D (.10)	—	—	—	—
Independence training						
1. Nurturing independence	—	L > D (.05)	W > NW (.05)	—	—	H < C (.05)
2. Household responsibilities	—	—	W > NW (.10)	—	—	—
3. Child's dependence on mother	—	—	—	—	—	—
Emotional relationships						
1. Sensitivity to child's needs	—	L > D (.02)	—	W < NW (.10)	H < C (.02)	H < C (.05)
2. Emotional satisfaction in relationships with child	—	L > D (.05)	—	—	H < C (.01)	—

3. Planned activities with child:				
by mother	—	—	W > NW (.10)	—
by father	—	—	W > NW (.02)	—
4. Confidence in child rearing	—	L > D (.02)	—	—
Rearing environment				
1. Formulated principles of rearing	—	—	—	—
2. Clarity of limits set for child	—	—	—	H < C (.05)
3. Consistency between principles and practices	—	—	W < NW (.02)	H < C (.02)
4. Scheduling	—	—	—	—
5. Traditional philosophy re sex role training	F < S (.05)	—	—	—
6. Traditional sex-typed household functions	—	—	—	—
7. Adequacy of mothering (summary rating)	—	L > D (.05)	—	H < C (.05)

aThe probability that an observed relationship could have occurred by chance is indicated in parentheses.

report the father as the stricter parent when these mothers work (70%) than when they do not work (33%). Children are less likely to be reported as rebellious by working mothers (10%) than by nonworking mothers (46%) in the high school group. Similarly, they are more likely to be assigned a heavy load of household responsibilities (30 per cent as compared with 8 per cent). The working mothers are more likely to stress independence training (80 per cent as compared with 54 per cent). In other words, children of the working mothers with *high school* backgrounds are under firmer control and are called upon to perform with more responsibility and independence.

The picture for the college-trained group is not the same. The college working mother compared with her nonworking peers is not more likely to describe the father as the stricter parent; there is instead a tendency in the opposite direction (the father is the stricter parent in 30 per cent and 50 per cent of the working and nonworking groups, respectively). Assignment of responsibilities and nurturance of independence are not stressed by the college-trained working mothers as they are by the working mothers with high school background. (The differences, though not significant, are in the opposite direction from the high school group.)

A variable which has not shown differences in any other comparisons but which appears in the working-nonworking comparisons of college-trained women is that of planned shared time and activities with the child. In the families of college working mothers both parents apparently attempt to compensate for out-of-the-home time by planned time together with the child. Forty per cent of the college working mothers report giving planned time to the child. It is reported for 38 per cent of the fathers. The nonworking college group have 16 per cent and 8 per cent in the comparable categories. In families of high school background there is no difference in this variable between working and nonworking groups.

Subcultural or social class analyses may be extremely important in attempting to pin down the kinds of influences that the widespread employment of mothers may have on the socialization of large populations of children. The present data suggest that rearing influences cannot be predicted across class and cultural boundaries (any more than they can be predicted across motivational differences among mothers), and that the nature of influences for different social groups will vary and will grow out of the values and needs of the particular groups.

SUMMARY AND CONCLUSIONS

Qualities of child rearing by mothers who are employed and those who are not employed outside the home have been studied. One hundred mothers of intact families, of the middle and upper middle class white urban population were interviewed. Families of working and nonworking mothers were matched on family composition and social class.

Mothers' employment status is not related to child-rearing characteristics. The data, however, support the hypothesis that mothers' fulfillments or frustrations in nonmother roles are related to child rearing. When mothers' motivations regarding working are taken into account, the nonworking mothers who are dissatisfied with not working (who want to work but, out of a feeling of "duty," do not work) show the greatest problems in child rearing. They describe more difficulties in the area of control, less emotional satisfaction in relationships with their children, and less confidence in their functioning as mothers. They have lower summary scores on "adequacy of mothering." Working mothers who prefer to work and those who do not wish to work show few group differences in child-rearing practices, probably because the working mothers (of this sample) who prefer not to work are nonetheless achieving certain valued family goals by means of their employment.

Among high school-trained mothers, differences between working and nonworking mothers appear in the following areas of rearing: firmer control over children, assignment of greater responsibilities to children, and delegation of the stricter disciplinary role to the father appear more frequently in families of working than nonworking mothers. In the college-trained working and nonworking group, these differences do not appear. The college working parents tend to compensate for time away from children by more planned, shared activities with their children than is found in the college nonworking group. The data on educational groups suggest that maternal employment brings different kinds of familial adaptations depending on the value systems of the particular cultural subgroups in which the mother is combining mother and worker roles.

The findings of the present study confirm and elaborate observations by other investigators[5] of the importance of social, familial and personal factors in determining the kind of success the mother achieves in her dual roles. The specific differences in child-rearing practices reported in the present study are perhaps less important in our conclusions (until they are replicated) than is the general

[5]Ibid.; Ruth E. Hartley, What Aspects of Child Behavior Should be Studied in Relation to Maternal Employment? In Alberta E. Siegel, editor, Research Issues Related to the Effects of Maternal Employment on Children, University Park, Pennsylvania: Social Science Research Center, 1961; Lois Hoffman, "Effects of Maternal Employment on the Child," Child Development, 32 (March 1961), pp. 187–197; Alberta E. Siegel "Characteristics of the Mother Related to the Impact of Maternal Employment or Non-employment," in Alberta E. Siegel, editor, op. cit.

pattern of significant subgroupings of mothers in relation to child rearing.

The findings of this study have relevance for studies of child rearing more generally in pointing to the interplay of rearing practices (as they are usually defined) and maternal motivations within differing subcultures. These variables need further scrutiny in studies of child-rearing antecedents of child behavior and personality.

clinical implications of maternal employment: a review of research

ELVA POZNANSKI University of Michigan, Children's Psychiatric
Hospital
ANNETTE MAXEY Georgia Mental Health Institute
GERALD MARSDEN University of Michigan, Children's Psychiatric
Hospital

Behind the cries of women's liberation and day-care centers for
lower-class working mothers is the very real issue of the effects on
the children of maternal employment. The debate about working
mothers has raged for at least two decades. One response has been
to produce research. Professionals in many disciplines have attempted to assess the correlates and effects of maternal employment,
and the fruits of their efforts have appeared in journals of education,
social work, sociology, psychology, and psychiatry. The dispersion
across disciplines has made it difficult for workers in any single field
to acquire an integrated sense of the findings. Several comprehensive reviews of the maternal employment literature, notably those
of Stolz (1960), Maccoby (1958) and Hartley (1961a), have summarized the field up to 1960. But like the research on which they
were based, these reviews tended to assume a sociological orienta-

From *Journal of the American Academy of Child Psychiatry*, 1970, **9**. Reprinted
with the permission of the authors and of the American Academy of Child Psychiatry, copyright 1970.

tion and, thus, failed to address themselves to questions of interest to clinicians.

We here review work in this area published since 1960, with, in the interest of completeness, some reference to the earlier period. Our purpose is to consolidate research findings from the several disciplines and to highlight issues relevant to clinical work with children and families. The paper's headings are loosely arranged in developmental sequence: the problems of the preschooler are presented first, followed by difficulties seen in the latency years and finally those of delinquency, which is chiefly an adolescent problem at the time of its recognition. Maternal-role implications are dealt with last, since they span all age groups. Under each heading, the research material is arranged according to age, allowing the reader to relate material to the development of the child.

DIRECT EFFECTS OF MATERNAL EMPLOYMENT

MOTHER-CHILD SEPARATION

Typically, research on maternal employment has sought evidence for a direct effect on the children of the mother's working. One of the oldest bodies of research in this tradition has dealt with the issue of the child's separation from his mother.

Following the brilliant demonstrations by Spitz (1945, 1946) and Bowlby (1951, 1953) that certain forms of infant-mother separation could produce shattering effects on personality development, many came to view maternal employment as dangerous to children. Much of the research in the 1940's and 1950's attempted to prove or disprove that maternal employment was or was not synonymous with maternal deprivation. The findings of these studies usually did not indicate adverse effects on the children of employed mothers in such broad areas as general adjustment, school achievement, or delinquency. However, these findings were inconsistent and thus inconclusive. While it was clear that maternal employment did not constitute maternal deprivation in any simple way, this early work suggested that its effects on the children were complex and subtly entangled with other factors. Studies conducted since 1960 have far more frequently considered maternal employment in the context of such variables as social class and family stability.

Recent studies of infant and child development lead one to expect that the effects on a child of his working mother's absence from home would vary considerably from one developmental phase to another. For example, we know that under conditions of extreme maternal absence, amounting to clear deprivation, during infancy, we can expect severe distortions in the development of object relations. But we know less about whether there are subtler distortions under the more usual circumstances of maternal employment. Among three- to five-year-old children, we would expect fewer difficulties in the development of object relations, but would anticipate an increase in symptoms of separation anxiety. Careful delineation of the developmental implications of maternal employment is hard to achieve because groups of preschool children[1] whose mothers are employed away from home are difficult to find, since most mothers wait until children are in school before resuming or seeking work. Some studies, however, are available.

Caldwell et al. (1970) studied lower-class working mothers and their children in an attempt to determine whether even optimal day-care services would inevitably distort socioemotional developmental processes, despite their possibly making a contribution to intellectual growth. Caldwell et al. compared the strength of attachment between mother and child in 23 home-reared children and 18 children enrolled in a day-care program. Day-care children entered the program at an average age of one year (minimum age: six months) and had attended for approximately 18 months at the time data were gathered. Caldwell found no evidence of socioemotional damage attributable to the mother-child separation necessitated by the day-care program. There was evidence, however, that the day-care attendance forestalled the now well-documented decline in developmental quotient with increasing age among young disadvantaged children.

Heinicke (1956) studied the effects of maternal absence on two years olds. One group of children attended a day nursery while their mothers were at their jobs. Another group lived temporarily at a residential nursery, while their mothers gave birth or were hospitalized due to illness. This study permits comparison of the effects of maternal employment with those of another more extreme form of maternal absence. The children in both groups came from intact families without parental rejection. Data for the study consisted of patterned observations in the nurseries and fantasy material produced during doll play. As expected, with the passage of time, children in the residential nursery exhibited an increasing number of symptoms, including intense hostility, loss of sphincter control, and more frequent illness. The day-nursery children did not show any global distortions of development, although they tended to avoid doll play, perhaps in an effort to avoid fantasies of family life. Un-

---

[1]We use the term preschool for children under age five, unless the context indicates a more limited group.

fortunately for the purposes of the present paper, Heinicke included no comparison with children who remained at home while their mothers were away.

In Moore's (1964) longitudinal study of children under age six, a small group of children exclusively cared for by their mothers was available for comparison with a group of children in substitute care while the mothers worked. The children in substitute care were divided into those with unstable and those with stable substitute-care groups. The groups with constant maternal care and stable substitute care were more similar to each other than to the group with unstable substitute care. The group with stable substitute care differed significantly from the group with constant maternal care in being more self-assertive, less conforming, and less fastidious. The differences between the stable and unstable substitute-care groups were more marked. Children in unstable substitute care were more dependent, attention seeking, and anxious when the mother had to leave, or was herself irritable. The investigators mentioned that they attempted to assess parental attitudes. They felt this did, indeed, account for some but not all of the differences.

Another opportunity to study the effects of mother-child separation within the context of maternal employment is offered by the radically different cultural setting of the Israeli kibbutzim. One aspect of the philosophy under which these collective settlements were founded and continue to operate is the universal employment of women. Hence, all kibbutzim mothers work prior to the birth of a child and return to work six weeks afterward. From birth, the children are raised in "Children's Houses" run by professional child-care workers. The parents live in separate buildings with a living-sitting room for themselves, where the children visit two hours each evening and all day Saturday and holidays. Bowel and bladder training, discipline, and education are all functions of the child-care workers. The role of the parents is more nearly comparable to that of the indulgent grandparent in American society. Although most studies of the kibbutzim are impressionistic, they do convey some information concerning the emotional reactions and behavior of children in this type of environment.

Most observers from America thought that the preschool children showed more thumbsucking, temper tantrums, lack of control, overt aggression, and enuresis than the preschoolers they had seen in the United States (Caplan, 1954). This impression has been related partially to the structure of the "Children's Houses," the number of child-care workers for the toddlers, as well as the more total or complete mother-child separation from that generally experienced in our culture. Frustrated maternal feelings and attitudes have caused the mothers to force some kibbutzim to increase mother-child contact, especially in early years (Irvine, 1952), and there have been numerous changes in recent years to correct these deficiencies.

Psychological testing of the kibbutz children compared with a control group of home-reared children from the Israeli community revealed that by age ten, the kibbutz children showed "more accurate perception of reality, more breadth of interest and cultural background, better emotional control, and greater overall maturity" (Rabin, 1957–1959, p. 152). The kibbutz children also showed a solid sexual identification, with homosexuality virtually nonexistent. Sexual identification was more diffuse in that the boys identified with several male figures, rather than solely with their fathers. Sibling rivalry was less marked. Strong family ties were still very evident. The fantasy life of these children, as revealed by Sentence Completion Form studies, showed a great deal of emotional involvement with their parents. Peer-group ties became very strong, particularly during adolescence, and kibbutz teenagers were noted for self-reliance and self-respect, and for having less emotional disturbances than adolescents in our culture (Rabin, 1957, 1957–1959, 1958a, 1958b, 1959). Of interest was the finding that adults raised in a kibbutz married individuals from kibbutzim other than their own, indicating that the kibbutz operates in some ways as a family, and is therefore subject to incest taboos (Caplan, 1954).

In the preschool years the children of the Caldwell, Heinicke, Moore and kibbutzim studies were able to tolerate mother-child separations with minimal difficulties. However, the preschool children in some of these studies demonstrated certain vulnerabilities. The stability and quality of the substitute care appears highly important. Among the studies reviewed, the day-care center studied by Caldwell provided the highest quality of substitute care and the children involved showed no developmental distortions. Follow-up, however, will not be available for some time. Moore's group, followed to age six, appeared to lag in conforming to parental standards and exhibited more aggressive behavior. A follow-up study of the kibbutz children indicated that by ten years of age they were functioning appropriately. Indeed, evidence of personality strengths not typically present in American children of the same age was found.

We lack information concerning the types of children who best tolerate multiple mothering. More studies are obviously needed which consider the age of the child, personality variables, home stability, and type of substitute care. With regard to group substitute care, we need information on the ratio of adults to children to facilitate comparisons between studies. Ultimately, longitudinal studies from birth to puberty will provide the only conclusive answer to possible long-term effects.

DEPENDENCY BEHAVIOR

Many attempts have been made to correlate certain personality characteristics of children with maternal employment. As one might expect, the large number of variables within one family assumes more importance than maternal employment per se. The behavioral characteristic of dependency may be one exception. Several studies showed trends toward increased dependency in the children of employed mothers.

Siegel et al. (1959) focused their investigation on children of kindergarten age. They studied the dependency behavior of children of working and nonworking mothers by means of a questionnaire and observation. They carefully matched their samples by age, sex, socioeconomic status, birth order, and family size. They found no difference in dependent and independent behavioral patterns between children of working and nonworking mothers. Possible explanations for these results, which differ from those discussed below, may be the social class of the sample (Siegel et al. included more upper- and middle-class families), different operational definitions of what constituted dependency behavior, the limits imposed by the study on observing dependency only within the kindergarten environment, or the greater methodological strengths of this study.

Studies of dependency in somewhat older children have yielded different results. Rouman (1957) investigated the child-guidance-clinic records of children between the ages of five and 16. Within each of three age ranges, each child whose mother was employed was matched in age with a child whose mother did not work. Rouman found that at all age levels children of employed mothers showed trends toward increased dependency. They had greater difficulty feeling independent of other people, less certainty of being liked, more withdrawing behavior, while in general demonstrating higher academic success.

Hoffman (1960) found that the sons of working mothers (third through sixth graders) showed greater dependency. This correlation was one of the strongest in her study. McCord et al. (1962) divided their group (ages 10 to 15 years) on the basis both of whether the mothers worked or not and of family stability. They found that strengthened dependent behavior was significant and striking when maternal employment was combined with an unstable family. However, "Encouragement of dependency was, indeed, related to maternal employment in stable homes . . ." (p. 180).

The etiology of the trend toward greater dependent behavior in children of employed mothers tempts speculation. Anxiety, regardless of its origin, can stimulate dependent behavior in children. McCord et al. (1962), in a study on dependency behavior in children, conclude that the parental rejection, over- and undercontrol of the child, and punishment for dependent behavior, all encourage dependency. Certainly these factors could easily operate in the children of employed mothers. Subtle to overt rejection of children by employed mothers may occur both in response to the intrapsychic needs of the mother, as well as to the external realities of reduced free time. Data on over- and undercontrol of the child appear fleetingly in the literature incidental to other hypotheses. For example, in a study of the dissatisfied working-mother group (Yarrow et al. 1962), marked inconsistencies of discipline appeared. The nonworking mother has greater opportunity both to express and to follow through on limit setting. Moore's study (1964) reflected this fact. In his group of preschool children in substitute care (because of mother's employment), the children showed less inclination to conform to rules and were less upset by parental discipline, regardless of the type of substitute care so long as it was stable. A study which came to opposite conclusions simply underscores the speculative nature of these comments. Von Mering (1955) found support for the hypothesis that working mothers from college backgrounds emphasized discipline more than nonworking mothers of similar backgrounds.

Many studies suggest that employed mothers tend to want early independent behavior in their children—perhaps to such an extent that the reverse effect is produced (Yarrow et al., 1962; von Mering, 1955). The Rouman (1956) study discussed above found that among employed mothers the child most frequently referred to the clinic was the youngest in the family, in contrast to the rest of the child-guidance-clinic population, where the oldest child was the most frequently referred. Possible difficulties in tolerating dependent behavior in the child could account for this finding.

Another contributor to the tendency toward dependent behavior could be the personality of employed mothers. As previously suggested, assertive and aggressive maternal behavioral characteristics could easily be relevant. Such characteristics in the mother could, in turn, provoke dependency in the child by not allowing appropriate and progressive independence.

SIBLING RIVALRY

Sibling rivalry except for the previously discussed kibbutz studies has been studied only within one social-class context, namely, lower-class boys (McCord et al., 1963). In these lower-class boys, sibling rivalry decreased with maternal employment and increased with family instability. Sibling rivalry was greatest in boys with nonworking mothers in unstable homes, whereas it occurred least in stable homes with working mothers. This finding can be correlated with the decrease in sibling rivalry observed during parental absence (Freud and Dann, 1951). Perhaps the children have more impetus to band together when the mother is not available or when there is less emotional investment by the mother. The importance of family stability should be emphasized, inasmuch as its relation to sibling rivalry is in inverse ratio to that of maternal employment. Within this study (McCord et al., 1963), peer relationships were unaffected by maternal employment, suggesting that if anxiety and insecurity existed, it did not exend to this area of functioning.

PROBLEMS IN SEXUAL IDENTIFICATION

Many maternal employment studies suggest difficulties in sexual identification, particularly in boys, although girls, too, seem to have difficulties in this area. The impact of the mother's work is clearly not the same for boys as for girls, neither in intensity nor in psychological meaning. Hartley (1961a), in referring to the identification problems of the boy with an employed mother, stated, "It might be easier if the boy could reject all his mother did or was without need to discriminate in his effort to defend his own identity" (p. 44).

In France, Dits and Combier (1966) studied working-class boys between six and eight years of age from intact families. The group whose mothers worked showed difficulties in sexual identification, as compared to the group from families where the mothers stayed home. For example, sons of employed mothers, in their drawings of male figures, more often added anxiety features and accentuated masculine symbols. At the same time, female figures were poorly drawn.

A study of lower-class boys (McCord et al., 1963) was made by means of a review of case-recorded material collected in the 1930's. While changed cultural factors limit this study's relevance, it is none the less of interest because of the care taken in its design. McCord et al. related both home instability and maternal employment to increased father-son difficulties. There were no reported changes in the mother-son relationships. However, during adolescence this same group of boys was rated as to its degree of sexual anxiety, based on spontaneous communications to school counsellors. The authors found that maternal employment did increase sexual anxiety in adolescent boys; however, instability in the home markedly escalated these difficulties. The highest incidence of anxiety (41 per cent) occurred in boys in unstable homes where the mothers worked, dropping to 17 per cent in stable homes where the mothers stayed home. It was 37 per cent in unstable homes where the mother was at home. The mother herself was checked for her degree of sexual anxiety in all groups and, except in unstable homes where sexual anxiety was frequent, there was no difference between working mothers and the control group. McCord et al. hypothesized that increased sexual anxiety, as well as increased father-son difficulties, in boys from stable homes of employed mothers stemmed from the boys' perception that the fathers occupied an insignificant role. Inasmuch as these boys came from lower-class families, the discrepancy between the role the boy (and perhaps mother too) thought the father should play and the role he actually played would be greater than that of their friends whose fathers were sole wage earners.

Hartley's (1961b) study of latency-age girls showed that whereas 98 per cent cf the girls identified with their mothers as mothers, only a portion of these girls identified with the working role of the mother. Furthermore, with increasing age from eight to 11 years, there was a decrease in acceptance of the mother's working. These same girls, in contrast to girls whose mothers stayed home, indicated that women liked a wider variety of tasks, i.e., household activities, work role, and recreation. Essig and Morgan's study (1946) suggested that adolescent girls of working mothers may have difficulties in their relationships with their fathers as well as with their mothers.

Undoubtedly, lower-class boys have been studied more extensively in the belief that they would demonstrate the greatest difficulty with sexual identification. Compared to the middle-class boy, a lower-class boy has a sharper image of what constitutes masculine and feminine behavior (Kagan, 1964). Hence, he finds it culturally more deviant when the mother works outside the home. Unfortunately, there is insufficient information on corresponding attitudes among middle- and upper-class boys. Because social class is a powerful factor in maternal employment, it would be hazardous to extend these findings to other social classes.

Girls appear to benefit in some ways from maternal employment, which seems to encourage them to a broader range of interests and activities. Intrafamily difficulties, however, suggest that girls, too, have sex-role difficulties.

While cultural factors may well be significant in accounting for the above findings, psychological factors have been ignored in these studies. One wonders about the personality contributions of the mother, the possible characteristics of husbands of working mothers and the attitudes within the family toward sexual, work, and provider roles. Problems in sexual identity could as easily arise from such factors as from cultural deviance. The clinician must still look for clues in the dynamics of the individual family.

Future studies need to explore the nature and extent of cultural factors. Both boys and girls react to their parents' working, simply because it's different from the patterns in the families of their friends. How comfortable the parents feel in their roles, how the children perceive the parental roles, both for themselves and in contrast to the expectations of friends, neighborhood, and school, are all questions which have been ignored, and they appear to have significance in assessing the effects of maternal employment.

SCHOOL ACHIEVEMENT

The majority of studies of school achievement tend to favor the children of employed mothers over children · of nonemployed mothers (Stolz, 1960; Nye, 1959); however, this seems to be more a trend than a solid fact.

In a reading study among sixth-grade children of professionally-employed mothers, significantly higher scores on reading achievement were demonstrated, in contrast to those obtained by the children whose mothers were solely housewives (Jones, Fundstein and Michael, 1957). This study corroborated previous work which indicated that the greatest difference in school achievement between employed and nonemployed groups was in the area of reading (Stolz, 1960). Of interest was the peripheral discovery that the professionally-employed mothers had home libraries averaging 392 books, compared with 198 in the home libraries of the control groups. While the study did control for socioeconomic differences, it failed to adequately acknowledge cultural values which may account, at least in part, for the findings.

A questionnaire study of 3,014 high school seniors (Banducci, 1967) concluded, "The fact that mothers were employed full-time appeared to have little, if any, detrimental effect on children in regard to educational aspirations, expectations and achievement" (p. 263). The children were divided into three socioeconomic groups (laborer, skilled worker, and professional) on the basis of the child's stated occupation of the father. Girls' grade point-averages consistently improved with the level of social class, regardless of maternal employment. Sons of employed mothers had higher grade point-averages in the skilled-worker and laborer groups than the boys whose mothers stayed home. The boys of employed mothers from the professional group had lower grade point-averages and educational aspirations than the nonemployed group. Hence, this finding is an exception to the general trend and needs further investigation. The potency of social class as a variable is again demonstrated in that the sons of professionally-employed mothers whose grades were lower than the sons of the nonemployed group still showed higher grade point-averages than the sons of the next social-class level, i.e., the skilled-worker group.

The enhanced school achievement of children of employed mothers suggests several possibilities. These children could be identifying with an achievement-oriented household. Anxiety may also be a factor, particularly with the high scores obtained in reading, where mild anxiety may have stimulated reading performance (Rabinovitch, 1959). Greater parental desire to have the children do well in school may also have been present, perhaps partially based on guilt and on the parental personality. In Jones' study (1957) of reading, working mothers not only spent more time at home reading with the children than nonemployed mothers, but induced their husbands to spend additional time as well! Von Mering (1955) concluded that professionally-active mothers differed from other mothers in the same socioeconomic group in that expectations were higher. This could account for the lower school-grades of the highest socioeconomic group of boys in Banducci's study. In the higher socioeconomic group, the pressure to achieve may be too great, while in the skilled-worker and laborer groups, the message given the boys from the working-mothers' homes may well have been, "Do better than your father."

DELINQUENCY

An association between delinquency and maternal employment has long been sought in an attempt to find a link between delinquency and inadequate supervision. These studies have been confined mainly to adolescents. Glueck and Glueck's (1957) classic work on delinquent boys showed that delinquency was associated with maternal employment when employment was sporadic, but not when employment was steady. The conclusion was that the mother's sporadic employment represented periodic "crisis" events in a disorganized family and that the inherent family structure was the more important issue. McCord et al. (1963), in his study of lower-class boys, confirmed this finding. Despite lower-class neighborhoods with higher delinquency rates, the employment of mothers from stable homes was not significantly associated with the percentage of sons' court convictions. In unstable homes, however, maternal employment did tend to increase the number of sons' court convictions. Once again, the crucial issue was the stability of the family and the relationships between family members. However, both studies dealt with lower-class families.

Nye's (1959a) study of high school students, without assessing family stability, suggested that maternal employment was associated with increased though undetected delinquency. More adolescents of employed mothers admitted to such acts as petty thefts, truancy, vandalism, driving without a license, and alcoholic and sexual offenses. When family size, socioeconomic status, rural-urban residence, and sex of the adolescent were taken into account, differences in the incidence of delinquent behavior were not statistically significant. However, there was a trend toward higher delinquency and maternal employment, the major portion coming from the middle class, suggesting that an association between delinquency and maternal employment may be valid for the middle-class family and invalid for the lower-class family.

These studies have two important implications. As previously noted, social class is a strong influence on child-rearing, and its importance cannot be underestimated. Perhaps social class is so powerful because it roughly determines parental expectations (and children do respond to parental expectations!). Another factor, however, is apparent in the two different definitions of delinquency used in the above studies. A more profitable approach for the clinician would be the assessment of the adolescent's ego development. Longitudinal studies would here be most helpful.

THE MATERNAL ROLE AND EMPLOYMENT

Parental attitudes toward maternal employment and the influence of these attitudes on how children experience their mothers' working are of obvious importance. Does the mother work from necessity or from choice? Does the mother who chooses to work have different personality characteristics, and are these, in turn, modified by employment? What is the role of the father's attitudes? Indeed, the area of attitudes has been largely neglected.

Important aspects of the impact of maternal employment on children are certainly mediated by the attitudes of both the mother and father toward mother's work role. For example, the way a child experiences his mother's routinized departure for and return from work, her absences during significant portions of his waking life, must be affected by the attitudes of the parents themselves. These, in turn, are undoubtedly influenced by parental personality characteristics interacting with the circumstances of their lives, i.e., the family's financial situation, the mores of the neighbors, relatives, and friends, their own prior attitudes concerning maternal employment, characteristics of the children themselves, such as their number, ages, health status, and so on. While this brief analysis only hints at the complex influences which determine how maternal employment will be experienced within a family, it serves to put the researcher on notice that to enter this field of research is to take on a bewildering network of reciprocating influences. Indeed, research reported to date has only scratched the surface. For example, the authors were able to find no studies which examined the father's attitude toward his wife's working, or which focused on the problems and typical patterns of the resolution which parents had to work out in adapting to maternal employment.

It is only logical to assume that the age of a child whose mother works influences the maternal attitude toward both the child and her job. This area is largely unexplored. Most of the studies dealing with the maternal role have focused on mothers with elementary-school-age children. It would be hazardous to extend the limited findings of these investigations to families in which the mother has preschool or adolescent children.

Some of the studies seem to hint at more activity and aggressivity in working mothers. Working mothers tend to have a higher education, husbands in a lower socioeconomic group than themselves, increased incidence of being widowed, divorced, or separated, and smaller families. Perhaps the higher educational attainment of working mothers demonstrates a greater need for achievement. One could easily speculate that highly-educated women would more easily find suitable employment. Nevertheless, the percentage of women in executive and professional jobs is lower than it was 40 years ago, while the total number of women working has steadily increased (Parrish, 1961). The tendency of working mothers to marry men from a lower socioeconomic class probably represents a statistical combination of several factors. Perhaps the wife's work represents a temporary effort to help the husband move ahead; perhaps there are fewer men available for marriage in the higher socioeconomic classes; perhaps the women have a greater need for power and dominance. Actually all these possibilities could be directly or indirectly related to assertiveness. The increased incidence of widows, divorced, or separated women among employed mothers suggest reality factors and personality instability of which assertiveness may be one facet. (It is the cultural expectations that a woman sues for divorce.)

The tendency of working mothers to have smaller families again suggests realistic factors. It is easier for the mother with fewer children to work. Stolz (1960) found, by means of a large sample questionnaire study, that "in small families, employed mothers are more likely to be well-adjusted to children than non-employed mothers, but the reverse is true in families of four or more children" (p. 753). However, a mother who makes a decision to limit her family in favor of working, partially repudiates the maternal role in favor of satisfactions gained outside the home.

Several investigators have begun to explore aspects of mothers' attitudes toward their work and the relation of these to various characteristics of their children. However, few have focused explicitly on these problems, and then only tangentially. For example, Peterson (1961) noted high absenteeism among women workers and observed that the role of wife and mother took precedence over the role of employee. Hartley (1960) found that working mothers more frequently express misgivings and anxious concerns about their maternal role and that these concerns are noticed by their children, who during latency more often report that their mothers feel uncomfortable about leaving home to work.

Yarrow et al. (1962) attempted to relate maternal attitudes toward children with maternal employment. The largest group of women involved were middle class with children ranging from nine to 11, although the study included children ranging in age from four to 11. The working and nonworking mothers were divided into two groups: those who wished to work and those who did not. All mothers were rated on adequacy of mothering, defined by eight variables including sensitivity, warmth, consistency, discipline, and confidence in the maternal role. Nonworking mothers who did not wish to work were rated somewhat higher on adequacy of mothering than the others, although this finding was of borderline significance. More important, working mothers who did not wish to work were rated significantly higher than nonworking mothers who wished to work. Thus, it would appear that if a woman is unhappy in her role at home, it does not make her a better mother and homemaker simply to stay at home. On the other hand, the mothers who stayed home and enjoyed this role included women with high maternal attributes. In this study, the working mother who preferred to work and the working mother who did not want to work differed little in child-rearing practices.

Hoffman (1961), too, included the mother's attitude toward work as a variable. She found that children of working mothers who did not like to work showed more assertive behavior toward the mother, more aggressiveness toward peers, and a higher general level of rebelliousness than children of mothers who were nonemployed. Unfortunately, the mothers with positive attitudes toward their work were not also subdivided into those who enjoyed the maternal role and those whose work could be viewed as an escape from that role. Perhaps studies employing this high degree of differentiation would throw light on Nye's (1959b) finding that the children of employed mothers tend to feel either more fully accepted or more completely rejected than the children of nonemployed mothers, and Peterson's (1961) finding that working mothers as a group contain the extremes of interest and lack of interest in their daughters' lives (when compared with a group of nonworking mothers).

Mothers who work, as well as those who stay home, but wish they worked, all tend to reveal some degree of anxiety and guilt. A critical issue is whether their anxiety is based solely on the implicit conflict with the cultural expectations that they will remain happily at home, or whether it exists in combination with neurotic or situational anxieties. Working mothers who liked to work, in contrast to those who did not, showed least difficulties in the maternal role. Evidence for this statement comes primarily from studies of middle- and upper-class women, and its relevance to the lower-class situation is unknown. There appears to be some evidence that the relationship between some mothers and their children improves when the mother finds herself a job. One may speculate on the reasons for this. Perhaps the narcissistic gratification gained from working, or the need to establish an identity separate from that of "mother" or "wife," explains the phenomenon.

Some of the positive value of mother's work, when done by choice, may simply be the effect of allowing her to shift scenes. By changing from home to work and home again, mothers encounter different environments with different problems which increase her zest in life and effectiveness in both. Other reasons may have to do with her broadened social contacts.

DYNAMICS AND DEVELOPMENTAL CONSIDERATIONS

Dynamic factors within the family have been relatively unexplored in maternal employment research to date, although many studies include references in that direction. It is becoming increasingly clear that emotional factors within each family are of central importance in evaluating the impact of a mother's working outside her home. The mother's motivation for seeking employment, the underlying personalities of both the mother and father, the ages and number of children, as well as the way each family member views maternal employment are the core features of the clinical considerations. Whether the child views maternal employment as a rejection, an economic necessity, or a normal family style would largely depend on the parents' attitudes. In any event, the child should be prepared for the mother's working and understand why the family has embarked on this course.

It is only natural that a child's response to his mother's employment would vary according to his age. Similarly, her employment throughout the child's development would have different meanings at different ages. No research has been directed squarely at these issues, and there has been little investigation of the effect of commencing maternal employment at different stages of development. Inferences as to the effects of maternal employment at different age levels can now be made only from a general knowledge of child development and from piecemeal integration of data available.

The major concern of the preschooler would probably center around the ease or discomfort engendered by daily separations. Instability in the substitute care very much aggravates these concerns and contributes to a breakdown in desirable behavior. But those children who suffered unstable substitute care often came from unstable homes, i.e., the provisions made for the child reflected the personality of the parents. Under conditions of stable care, Moore's (1964) comments seem especially applicable: "it tends to toughen the child, strengthening the ego perhaps at the expense of the superego" (p. 9). That more information about substitute care is not available is indeed unfortunate. Perhaps multiple mothering dilutes the disciplinarian role, working both advantageously or disadvantageously for the individual child, depending on family style.

During latency, other problems come into focus, although some obviously have had their origins earlier. The latency-child begins to have an understanding of what the parents are actually doing when they are away at work. Hartley (1960) stated that children do not adequately conceive the parental work-role status until eight years of age. Because mastery and achievement are some of the ego resources from which the latency-age child derives pleasure, it may be somewhat easier for the child to persist and master skills if he is able to identify with parents who strongly emphasize this type of activity. On the other hand, during the elementary-school years, children compare their families with others and are more susceptible to peer attitudes and school influences. Cultural attitudes within the neighborhood, classmates, and school teachers all have a tremendous influence. Hence, new anxieties around old problems manifested by dependency and sexual identification may surface again, fostered by the increased awareness of the child.

Adolescents generally showed least difficulty in having an employed mother. Hints at unresolved earlier difficulties did appear, e.g., academic underachievement among boys from the highest socioeconomic group, increased delinquency in the middle-class boys. Sexual anxiety is normally present in the adolescent; however, it could become exacerbated if the perception of the mother's and father's role is unclear, unhappy, or critically different from that of their friends'. The adolescent's increased strivings for independence are well known. Maternal employment could lessen the mother's involvement with the teenage activities. This might be interpreted positively only if the involvement prior to adolescence had been mutually satisfying and the child had a good ego development. Otherwise, the adolescent could seize upon the mother's employment as another manifestation of her lack of interest and use it as license to act out.

SUMMARY

Our attempt to arrange sequence in developmental research findings in maternal employment demonstrates that only rarely has developmental staging been given priority in this body of research. Studies in the area of maternal employment have produced provocative questions, but few hard facts. Working mothers obviously encompass a sizable group of women, with a variety of motives concerning employment and child raising. The effects of maternal employment probably depend on the developmental stage of the child and on its ego maturity. In broad outline, an increase in dependency behavior and in sexual identity problems (particularly among boys) may accompany maternal employment. But these effects are clearest among lower-class children. In general, school achievement, particularly reading, is enhanced by maternal employment. Whereas maternal employment places stress on the family, it can be tolerated, and in some situations even appears beneficial, if the family itself is stable. Under adverse conditions of intrafamilial strife, maternal employment escalated many undesirable behavior problems in children, including delinquency. The inherent family stability is more important than maternal employment.

On glancing at our list of references for this article, we noticed that most of the writers contributing to this area of research have been women. One may infer that many are themselves working mothers. We wonder if the assumptions underlying these studies and their findings are influenced by the sex of the investigator. Women's motivation to study this problem may possibly spring from guilt as well as genuine concern with children, and perhaps a degree of feminism.

REFERENCES

Banducci, R. (1967), The effect of mother's employment on the achievement, aspirations and expectations of the child. *Personnel & Guid. J.*, **46**:263–267.

Bowlby, J. (1951), *Maternal Care and Mental Health*. Geneva: World Health Organization, Monogr. 2.

————— (1953), Some pathological problems engendered by early mother-child separation. In: *Problems of Infancy and Childhood*, ed. M. J. E. Senn. New York: Josiah Macy, Jr. Foundation, pp. 38–90.

Caldwell, B. M., Wright, C. M., Honig, A. S., and Tannenbaum, J. (1970), Infant day care and attachment. *Amer. J. Orthopsychiat.*, **40**:397–412.

Caplan, G. (1954), Clinical observations in the emotional life of children in the communal settlements of Israel. In: *Problems of Infancy and Childhood*, ed. M. J. E. Senn. New York: Josiah Macy, Jr. Foundation, pp. 91–120.

Dits, A. and Combier, A. (1966), L'absence de la mère tors du retour de l'enfant de l'école. *Enfance*, **1**:99–111.

Essig, M. and Morgan, D. H. (1946), Adjustment of adolescent daughters of employed women to family life. *J. Educ. Psychol.*, **37**:219–233.

Freud, A. and Dann, S. (1951), An experience in group upbringing. *The Psychoanalytic Study of the Child*, **6**:127–168. New York: International Universities Press.

Glueck, S. and Glueck, E. (1957), Working mothers and delinquency. *Ment. Hyg.*, **41**:327–352.

Goldfarb, W. (1944), Effects of early institutional care on adolescent personality: Rorschach data. *Amer. J. Orthopsychiat.*, **14**:441–447.

Hartley, R. F. (1960), Children's concepts of male and female roles. *Merrill-Palmer Quart.*, **6**:83–97.

———— (1961a), What aspects of child behavior should be studied in relation to maternal employment. In: *Research Issues Related to Effects of Maternal Employment on Children*, eds., A. Siegel and L. Stolz. Penn. State University, Social Science Research Center.

———— (1961b), Current patterns of sex roles: children's perspectives. *J. Natl. Assn. Women Deans & Councilors*, **25**:3–13.

Heinicke, C. M. (1956), Some effects of separating two-year-old children from their mothers: a comparative study. *Hum. Rel.*, **9**:102–176.

Hoffman, L. W. (1960), Effects of the employment of mothers on parental power relations in the division of household tasks. *Marriage & Family Living*, **22**:27–35.

———— (1961), Effects of maternal employment on the child. *Child Devel.*, **32**:187–197.

———— (1963), The decision to work. In: *The Employed Mother in America*, ed., F. I. Nye and L. W. Hoffman. Chicago: Rand-McNally, pp. 18–39.

———— and Wyatt, F. (1960), Social change and motivations for having larger families: some theoretical considerations. *Merrill-Palmer Quart.*, **6**:235–244.

Irvine, F. F. (1952), Observations on the aims and methods of child-rearing in communal settlements in Israel. *Hum. Rel.*, **5**:247–275.

Jones, J., Fundstein, S. and Michael, W. (1957), The relationship of the professional employment status of mothers to reading achievement of 6th grade children. *Calif. J. Educ. Res.*, **18**:102–108.

Kagan, J. (1964), Acquisition and significance of sex typing and sex role identity. *Review of Child Development Research*, vol. 1, ed., M. L. Hoffman and L. W. Hoffman. New York: Russell Sage Foundation.

Maccoby, E. E. (1958), Effects upon children of their mothers' outside employment. In: *Work in the Lives of Married Women*. New York: Columbia University Press, pp. 150–172.

McCord, J., McCord, W. and Verden, P. (1962), Familial correlates of dependency. *Child Develop.*, **33**:313–326.

——— ——— and Thurber, E. (1963), Effects of maternal employment on lower-class boys. *J. Abnor. Soc. Psychol.*, **67**:177–182.

Moore, T. (1964), Children of full-time and part-time mothers. *Internat. J. Soc. Psychiat.*, **2**:1–10.

Nye, F. I. (1959a), Employment status and recreational behavior of mothers. *Pacific Sociol. Rev.*, **1**:69–72.

——— (1959b), Employment status of mothers and adjustment of adolescent children. *Marriage and Family Living*, **21**:240–244.

Parrish, J. B. (1961), Professional womanpower as a national resource. *Quart. Rev. Econ. & Business*, **1**:54–63.

Peterson, E. T. (1961), The impact of maternal employment on the mother-daughter relationship. *Marriage and Family Living*, **22–23**:355–361.

Rabin, A. I. (1957), Personality material of kibbutz and non-kibbutz children as reflected in Rorschach findings. *J. Proj. Tech.*, **21**:148–153.

——— (1957–1959), The Israeli kibbutz (collective settlement) as a laboratory for testing: psychodynamic hypothesis. *Psychol. Res.*, **7–9**:111–115.

——— (1958a), Some psychosexual differences between kibbutz and non-kibbutz Israeli boys. *J. Proj. Tech.*, **22**:328–332.

——— (1958b), Infants and children under conditions of intermittent mothering in the kibbutz. *Amer. J. Orthopsychiat.*, **28**:577–584.

——— (1959), Attitudes of kibbutz children to family and parents. *Amer. J. Orthopsychiat.*, **29**:172–179.

Rabinovitch, R. (1959), Reading and learning disabilities. In: *Handbook of Psychiatry*, 1st ed., S. Arieti. New York: Basic Books, pp. 857–869.

Rouman, J. (1957), School children's problems as related to parental factors. *J. Educ. Res.*, **50**:105–112.

Siegel, A., Stolz, L., Adamson, J. and Hitchcock, E. (1959), Dependence and independence in the children of working mothers. *Child. Devel.*, **30**:533–546.

Spitz, R. A. (1945), Hospitalism, an inquiry into the genesis of psychiatric conditions in early childhood. *The Psychoanalytic Study of the Child*, **1**:53–74. New York: International Universities Press.

——— (1946), Hospitalism, a follow-up report. *The Psychoanalytic Study of the Child*, **2**:113–117. New York: International Universities Press.

Stolz, L. M. (1960), Effect of maternal employment on children: evidence from research. *Child. Devel.*, **31**:749–782.

Von Mering, F. H. (1955), Professional and non-professional women as mothers. *J. Soc. Psychol.*, **42**:21–34.

Yarrow, M. R., Scott, P., De Leeuw, L. and Heinig, C. (1962), Child-rearing in families of working and non-working mothers. *Sociometry*, **25**:122–140.

maternal employment and perception of sex roles among college students*

SUSAN R. VOGEL   Mental Health Center, Brandeis University
INGE K. BROVERMAN
DONALD M. BROVERMAN
FRANK E. CLARKSON
Worcester State Hospital, Worcester, Massachusetts
PAUL S. ROSENKRANTZ   College of the Holy Cross

Numerous investigators have noted the existence of sex-role stereo-types, that is, consensual beliefs about the differing characteristics of men and women. These sex-role stereotypes are widely held (Lunneborg, 1968; Rosenkrantz, Vogel, Bee, Broverman, and Brover-man, 1968; Seward, 1946), persistent (Fernberger, 1948), and highly traditional (Komarovsky, 1950; McKee and Sherriffs, 1957). Sex-role stereotypes also ascribe greater social value to masculine than to feminine characteristics (Broverman, Broverman, Clarkson, Ro-senkrantz, and Vogel, 1970; Goldberg, 1967; Kitay, 1940; McKee and Sherriffs, 1959; Rosenkrantz et al., 1968; Sherriffs and Jarrett, 1953).

Susan R. Vogel, Inge K. Broverman, Donald M. Broverman, Frank E. Clarkson, and Paul S. Rosenkrantz. Maternal employment and perception of sex roles among college students. *Developmental Psychology*, **3**, 1970, 384–391. Copyright 1970 by the American Psychological Association, and reproduced by permission.
*Requests for reprints should be sent to Susan R. Vogel, Psychology Department, Worcester State Hospital, Box 57, Worcester, Massachusetts 01604.

Stereotypic sex-role perceptions may be influenced by the degree of actual sex-role differentiation in a given family or society, that is, the greater the actual sex-role differentiation, the greater the perception of sex-role stereotypes. Maternal employment status, in turn, may be a key factor in determining the degree of role differentiation that occurs between parents. If the father is employed outside the home, while the mother remains a full-time homemaker, their roles are clearly polarized for the child. On the other hand, if both parents are employed outside the home, their roles are more likely to be perceived as similar. A child growing up in a family with a working mother, therefore, should experience less parental sex-role differentiation than would a child with a nonworking mother.

Hartley (1964) reported that the mother's employment status does, in fact, influence a child's perception of sex-role characteristics. Daughters of working mothers see adult men and women as sharing more in their activities than do daughters of nonworking mothers.

In the present study the authors explored the generality and persistence of this effect by examining the stereotypic sex-role perceptions of college-aged men and women with working versus nonworking mothers. It is hypothesized that individuals whose mothers have been employed perceive less difference between the masculine and feminine roles than those individuals with homemaker mothers.

METHOD

SUBJECTS

One hundred and twenty college students were used as subjects in this study; these subjects were selected from a pool of 154 subjects used in an earlier study (Rosenkrantz et al., 1968). The subjects had been asked to indicate their mother's current occupation, or, if the mother was currently unemployed, when and at what job she had previously worked. Of the original 154 subjects, there were 24 men and 23 women whose mothers had never been employed during the subject's life time (homemaker mothers). Another 35 men and 38 women had mothers who were currently employed (employed mothers). The occupations of these mothers were rated according to Hollingshead (1957) and were found to be distributed in the following manner: Levels 1 and 2 (predominantly teachers, social workers, and nurses), 27 mothers; Levels 3 and 4 (predominantly secretaries, clerks, and sales women), 37 mothers; Levels 5, 6, and 7 (skilled and unskilled workers), 9 mothers. Information about the length of employment was not available. Subjects who could not be clearly classified into the homemaker or employed mother groups were eliminated from the present study.

No significant differences were found between the 47 subjects with homemaker mothers and the 73 subjects with employed mothers with respect to mother's current age and education and father's education and occupational level (Hollingshead, 1957).

ASSESSMENT OF SEX-ROLE STEREOTYPES HELD BY SUBJECTS

Instrument. Sex-role perceptions of the subjects were assessed by means of a Stereotype Questionnaire developed by the authors (Rosenkrantz et al., 1968). Briefly the instrument consists of 122 short phrases arranged in bipolar fashion with the poles separated by 60 points:

Not at all aggressive   Very aggressive
1....2....3....4....5....6....7

Subjects were instructed to mark the point along each dimension that characterized the typical adult male, that is, masculinity response. The instructions stressed that subjects should not use themselves as anchor points for the descriptions of other people. After completing the 122 items, subjects were instructed to mark the questionnaire a second time according to what they would expect the characteristics of an adult woman to be, that is, femininity response. Finally, subjects were asked to mark the questionnaire a third time describing themselves. Approximately half of the subjects were given the masculinity instruction first; the remaining subjects were given the femininity instruction first. Self instruction was always given last, in order to permit these ratings to occur explicitly within a masculine-feminine context.

Stereotypic Items. The concept of sex-role stereotype implies extensive agreement among individuals as to the characteristic differences between men and women. In the earlier study (Rosenkrantz et al., 1968), the authors found 41 items about which 75% or more of the subjects of each sex agreed as to the direction of the masculine-feminine difference. These items have been termed stereotypic items, since they represent those characteristics about which the most extreme consensus exists. For each of these stereotypic items, the difference between the means of the masculinity responses and the femininity responses was statistically significant beyond the .001 level of probability.

Differentiating Items. These are 48 items about which less than 75% of subjects of each sex agreed as to the direction of the masculine-feminine difference. However, the difference between the means of the masculinity and the femininity responses of each of these items was significant beyond the .05 level of probability.

The 33 remaining items were nondifferentiating; that is, the mean masculinity and femininity scores did not differ significantly.

MALE-VALUED AND FEMALE-VALUED ITEMS

In an earlier study (Rosenkrantz et al., 1968), a different sample of college men and women was asked to indicate which pole of each item represented the more socially desirable behavior or characteristic. These ratings allowed the authors to break down both the stereotypic and the differentiating items into those items for which the masculine pole was more socially desirable (male-valued items) and those items for which the feminine pole was more socially desirable (female-valued items). There were 29 stereotypic and 25 differentiating male-valued items; the great majority of these items reflect effectiveness and competence. The remaining 12 stereotypic items and 23 differentiating items were female valued; in general, these items are concerned with emotional warmth and expressiveness.

RESULTS

Analyses of the differences between students whose mothers had been employed and those whose mothers were primarily homemakers were made separately for the stereotypic items, and for the differentiating items. Nondifferentiating items were not examined. Possible unrelated response biases of the subjects were controlled for in the following manner: For slightly more than half of the items a high score indicated the masculine pole, while for the remaining items a high score indicated the feminine pole. These latter items were reflected so that a high score indicated the masculine pole for all items. For each subject, the mean and sigma of his 366 responses (masculine, feminine, and self responses for the 122 items) were computed, and his 366 responses were then converted to sigma scores. The average masculine, feminine, and self responses were then computed for each subject across the 41 stereotypic items and across the 48 differentiating items. This resulted in 6 scores for each subject: a masculinity score (m), a femininity score (f), and a self score (s) for the stereotypic items and for the differentiating items.

Difference scores were also computed between each subject's m and f scores $(m-f)$ for the stereotypic items and the differentiating items. These difference scores provide for a direct test of the major hypothesis of this study, that children of employed mothers perceive less *difference* between the roles of men and women than children of homemaker mothers.

MASCULINITY AND FEMININITY RESPONSES

The mean $m-f$ scores, mean m scores, and the mean f scores for the subjects with working mothers were compared, using t tests, to the mean scores for subjects with homemaker mothers, separately for stereotypic and for differentiating items (see Table 1). As can be seen in Table 1, the major hypothesis dealing with the perception of difference between the two sex roles receives substantial support. Three of the four $m-f$ difference comparisons yield significance levels of .05 or better, while the fourth $m-f$ difference (men on stereotypic items) has a p value of .06. Thus, both men and women who are children of employed mothers perceive significantly less difference between the masculine and feminine roles, on both the stereotypic and differentiating items, than do men and women who are the children of homemaker mothers.

The expectations for the differences between groups with respect to the separate perception of the masculine and feminine roles are also largely confirmed by the data. The daughters of working mothers perceive both the masculine role and the feminine role as significantly less extreme on both the stereotypic and differentiating items than do the daughters of homemaker mothers (see Table 1). These results indicate that women whose mothers have worked perceive the masculine role as significantly less masculine, and the feminine role as significantly less feminine, than do women whose mothers have not been employed. Thus, not only is the perceived gap between masculinity and femininity significantly smaller for women whose mothers have worked, but so, too, are both the masculine and feminine poles themselves defined differently by the two groups.

The comparable results for men are less consistent, but those differences that do occur are in the predicted direction, and parallel to the significant differences for women. The mean masculinity score for men with employed mothers on the stereotypic items is significantly lower than the comparable score for men with homemaker mothers, indicating that men whose mothers have worked perceive the masculine role as significantly less masculine (see Table 1). The difference is not significant, however, between the mean masculinity scores of the two groups for the differentiating items; the mother's employment influences only the stereotypic characteristics. Just the reverse is true for the men's perception of the feminine role. Mean femininity scores for the two groups do not differ significantly on the stereotypic items but do on the differentiating items. Sons of employed mothers perceive the feminine role as less feminine than do sons of homemaker mothers (see Table 1).

In order to assess the possible differential influence of the moth-

Table 1 Average Masculinity and Femininity Scores for Men and Women with Employed Versus Homemaker Mothers

Score	Men with			Women with		
	Employed mothers (N = 35)	Homemaker mothers (N = 24)	t	Employed mothers (N = 38)	Homemaker mothers (N = 23)	t
Stereotypic items						
Masculinity	.394	.504	2.327[a]	.482	.649	2.626[a]
Femininity	−.698	−.794	1.316	−.423	−.626	2.727[b]
Masculinity-femininity	1.092	1.298	1.990	.905	1.275	3.158[b]
Differentiating items						
Masculinity	.182	.231	1.568	.256	.369	2.026[a]
Femininity	−.261	−.379	2.667[b]	−.196	−.292	2.388[a]
Masculinity-femininity	.443	.610	2.581[b]	.452	.661	2.383[a]

NOTE. A high score indicates that the response is closer to the masculine pole, while a low score indicates that the response is closer to the feminine pole.
[a] p < .05.
[b] p < .01.

er's work history on the male-valued and female-valued characteristics, the comparisons described previously were repeated separately for these two dimensions within the stereotypic items and
within the differentiating items. The results of these analyses for
the male-valued items (competency) are presented in Table 2 and
for the female-valued items (warmth and expressiveness) in Table 3.

Inspection of Table 2 reveals a striking sex difference in the
perception of the competency dimension as a function of the mother's work history. For men, the mother's employment has no influence whatsoever on their perception of this dimension of the sex
role. However, women with employed mothers perceive less difference between the masculine and feminine roles with respect to
competency, and perceive the feminine role itself as entailing
greater competency than do women with homemaker mothers.
These relationships reach significance in both the stereotypic and
the differentiating items (see Table 2). Women's perception of the
competency dimension of the masculine role is less strongly influenced by the mother's work history. Although women with working
mothers perceive the masculine role as entailing somewhat less
competency than do women with homemaker mothers, this difference fails to reach the .05 level of significance (significant at the
.06 level for the differentiating items; see Table 2).

Men and women also differ in their perception of the warmth-
expressiveness dimension of the sex roles as a function of the
mother's employment, although here it is men whose perception is
more strongly influenced. Men whose mothers are employed perceive significantly less difference between the masculine and feminine roles with respect to warmth-expressiveness, on both the stereotypic and differentiating items (see Table 3). The feminine role itself
is perceived as entailing somewhat less warmth-expressiveness by
men with employed mothers than by men with homemaker mothers
(this difference reaches the .05 level of significance for the differentiating items, but falls slightly short of the .05 level for the
stereotypic items; see Table 3). The masculine role is perceived as
entailing somewhat more warmth and expressiveness by sons of
working mothers than by sons of homemaker mothers on the stereotypic items only (see Table 3).

Turning to the women's perception of the warmth dimension
on the stereotypic items, the influence of the mother's work history
is similar but less pronounced. On the stereotypic items, women
with employed mothers perceive less of a difference bètween the
maculine and feminine roles with respect to warmth-expressiveness,
and perceive the masculine role itself as entailing a greater degree
of warmth-expressiveness than do women with homemaker mothers
(see Table 3). No differences occur between the groups (daughters

Table 2 Male-valued Items: Average Masculinity and Femininity Scores for Men and Women with Employed Versus Homemaker Mothers

Score	Men with			Women with		
	Employed mothers (N = 35)	Homemaker mothers (N = 24)	t	Employed mothers (N = 38)	Homemaker mothers (N = 23)	t
			Stereotypic items			
Masculinity	.638	.723	1.451	.740	.877	1.991
Femininity	−.537	−.607	.828	−.204	−.468	2.641[a]
Masculinity-femininity	1.175	1.330	1.377	.944	1.345	3.070[b]
			Differentiating items			
Masculinity	.595	.609	.223	.689	.790	1.521
Femininity	.086	.019	.955	.279	.063	2.682[b]
Masculinity-femininity	.509	.590	1.159	.410	.727	3.826[b]

NOTE. A high score indicates that the response is closer to the masculine pole, while a low score indicates that the response is closer to the feminine pole.

[a] $p < .05$.
[b] $p < .01$.

Table 3 Female-valued Items: Average Masculinity and Femininity Scores for Men and Women with Employed Versus Homemaker Mothers

Score	Men with			Women with		
	Employed mothers (N = 35)	Homemaker mothers (N = 24)	t	Employed mothers (N = 38)	Homemaker mothers (N = 23)	t
Stereotypic items						
Masculinity	−.195	−.021	1.887	−.128	.099	1.987
Femininity	−1.088	−1.246	1.777	−.966	−1.006	.584
Masculinity-femininity	.893	1.255	2.729[b]	.838	1.105	2.003[a]
Differentiating items						
Masculinity	−.265	−.179	1.102	−.214	−.087	1.054
Femininity	−.640	−.806	2.211[a]	−.716	−.674	.645
Masculinity-femininity	.375	.627	2.827[b]	.502	.587	.663

NOTE. A high score indicates that the response is closer to the masculine pole, while a low score indicates that the response is closer to the feminine pole.
[a] p < .05.
[b] p < .01.

of employed mothers versus daughters of homemaker mothers) for the differentiating items. Perception of the feminine role with respect to warmth-expressiveness does not differ significantly for the two groups.

SELF RESPONSES

No significant differences were found between the self responses of subjects with employed mothers compared to like responses of subjects with homemaker mothers, either for the stereotypic and differentiating items taken as a whole, or for the male-valued and female-valued items considered separately. For all cases, the self response fell between the masculinity and the femininity responses. However, since the $m-f$ distance is relatively small in subjects with employed mothers, the s response of these subjects is closer to the opposite sex response than the s response of subjects with homemaker mothers, where the distance between m and f responses is significantly larger. Thus, although the self responses, as such, do not differ in these two groups, it is possible that the meaning of the self-concepts differs as a function of the different contexts in which they occur.

DISCUSSION

The results support the hypothesis that sex-role perceptions are affected by actual parental role behaviors to which children are exposed. College students whose parents have both been employed outside the home perceive significantly smaller differences between masculine and feminine sex roles than do students whose fathers have worked and whose mothers have remained at home, unemployed. Moreover, maternal employment affects perceptions of the masculine sex role, as well as the feminine role, even though the fathers of both groups were uniformly employed outside the home. Perhaps the similarity of the roles of the two groups of fathers is more apparent than real. Hoffman (1963) found that in families where the mother is employed, the father participates significantly more in household tasks than in families where the mother is a full-time homemaker. This suggests that children of working mothers are exposed to the father in a somewhat different role, and possibly have closer contact with him, than children of homemaker mothers.

SEX DIFFERENCES IN RESPONSE TO MATERNAL EMPLOYMENT

Women's perceptions of the sex roles appear, in general, to be more strongly influenced by the mother's employment than are men's perceptions. Because of greater commonality of activity in the mother-daughter relationship compared to the mother-son relationship, the fact that a mother works may impinge more on girls than on boys. It is also possible that the identification process by which a girl models herself after her mother intensifies the significance of the mother's sex-role behaviors for a daughter, but not for a son.

Another sex difference appears when the effects of maternal employment on the male-valued items and female-valued items are examined separately. For each sex, maternal employment tends to "upgrade" the perception of their own sex with respect to those characteristics that are seen as socially desirable for the opposite sex. Thus, sons of employed mothers perceive men as being somewhat more warm and women less warm, as compared to sons of homemaker mothers. On the other hand, daughters of employed mothers perceive women as more competent and men as less competent as compared to daughters of homemaker mothers. It appears, then, that maternal employment exerts a positive influence on the child's perception of his own sex, by augmenting competency for girls, and emotional warmth and expressiveness for boys. Evidently the perception of those positive characteristics traditionally associated with one's own sex is much less affected by the mother's working. Boys with working mothers do not relinquish any of their own sex's positive characteristics in the area of competency, nor do they perceive women as increasing in these positive characteristics. Although girls with working mothers perceive the sexes more nearly alike with respect to emotional warmth and expressiveness, they achieve this not by sacrificing their own positive attributes (perception of the feminine role is unchanged), but by increasing the male's perceived warmth-expressiveness.

CHANGING SEX-ROLE PERCEPTIONS IN SOCIETY

The most important implication of the obtained results is the evidence they provide that the traditional conceptions of sex roles are not immutable. If individual perceptions of sex roles are subject to variation as a function of individual experience, then societal sex-role stereotypes are subject to eventual change.

That such change is called for has become increasingly clear. Rossi (1964), in her proposal for equality between the sexes, makes the claim that the traditional conceptions of masculinity and femininity are no longer either necessary or appropriate in the latter half of the twentieth-century. As these traditional conceptions now stand, they not only reflect the unequal status of the sexes, but serve to perpetuate this differential status by negatively reinforcing many socially valued behaviors for women, and a lesser number for men. For example, assertiveness, constructive aggression, and striving for achievement and excellence, all characteristics considered desirable in adults in this society, are discouraged for women; while tenderness, emotional warmth, and expressiveness, equally valued in the abstract, are not encouraged for men.

Rossi (1964) proposed a socially "androgynous" conception of sex roles, by which she means that each sex cultivates those highly valued qualities traditionally limited to the other. Sex-role conceptions held by the children of working mothers are androgynous in just this sense, that is, sons and daughters of employed mothers each perceive their own sex as sharing the positive characteristics traditionally limited to the opposite sex to a greater degree than do the children of homemaker mothers.

Presumably, the less restrictive and more congruent definitions of sex roles held by children of working mothers influence role behavior, so that the children of working mothers feel even freer than their parents to engage in overlapping role behaviors, and so achieve in their own lives a greater degree of sex-role equality.

REFERENCES

Broverman, I. K., Broverman, D. M., Clarkson, F. E., Rosenkrantz, P. S., and Vogel, S. R. Sex-role stereotypes and clinical judgments of mental health. *Journal of Consulting and Clinical Psychology,* 1970, **34,** 1–7.

Fernberger, S. W. Persistence of stereotypes concerning sex differences. *Journal of Abnormal and Social Psychology,* 1948, **43,** 97–101.

Goldberg, P. A. Misogyny and the college girl. Paper presented at the meeting of the Eastern Psychological Association, Boston, April 1967.

Hartley, R. E. A developmental view of female sex-role definition and identification. *Merrill-Palmer Quarterly,* 1964, **10,** 3–16.

Hoffman, L. W. Parental power relations and the division of household tasks. In F. I. Nye and L. W. Hoffman (Eds.), *The employed mother in America.* Chicago: Rand McNally, 1963.

Hollingshead, A. B. Two factor index of social position. New Haven, Conn.: Author, 1957. (Mimeo)

Kitay, P. M. A comparison of the sexes in their attitudes and beliefs about women. *Sociometry,* 1940, **34,** 399–407.

Komarovsky, M. Functional analysis of sex roles. *American Sociological Review,* 1950, **15,** 508–516.

Lunneborg, P. W. Stereotypic aspect in masculinity-femininity measurement. Paper presented at the meeting of the American Psychological Association, San Francisco, September 1968.

McKee, J. P., and Sherriffs, A. C. The differential evaluation of males and females. *Journal of Personality*, 1957, **25**, 356–371.

McKee, J. P., and Sherriffs, A. C. Men's and women's beliefs, ideas, and self-concepts. *American Journal of Sociology*, 1959, **64**, 356–363.

Rosenkrantz, P. S., Vogel, S. R., Bee, H., Broverman, I. K., and Broverman, D. M. Sex-role stereotypes and self-concepts in college students. *Journal of Consulting and Clinical Psychology*, 1968, **32**, 287–295.

Rossi, A. S. Equality between the sexes. In R. J. Lifton (Ed.), *The woman in America*. Boston, Mass.: Houghton Mifflin, 1964.

Seward, G. H. *Sex and the social order*. New York: McGraw-Hill, 1946.

Sherriffs, A. C., and Jarrett, R. F. Sex differences in attitudes about sex differences. *Journal of Psychology*, 1953, **35**, 161–168.

Part II
Section 2
day
care

day care

HELEN L. BEE

For some, the phrase "day care" is a rallying cry for social change. Women's groups see day care for their children as an essential step in the freeing of women from the roles of homemaker and child rearer. Welfare groups see day care as a necessary adjunct to the elimination of the poverty cycle; if women who are heads of households are to be able to work and thus to support themselves, they must have some kind of (good, inexpensive) care for their children. Student groups demand that day care be provided for their children so as to enable mothers to attend school on an equal basis with fathers or to do so with less difficulty than has been present in the past.

For others, the phrase "day care" calls up a frightening image of vast numbers of babies cared for in institutional settings by people other than mothers. President Nixon, in vetoing the 1971 Child Care bill, which included a federally funded child-care program, indicated that one of his reasons for vetoing was that "the child development program appears to endanger the family structure."

Although members of student groups or women's liberation groups may wish to ignore these fears about day care or call them foolish, they are real and must be discussed. The fears appear to center around several major issues: (1) First, to place a child in day care means to separate that child from his family and may weaken his attachment to his family. I've already discussed this question in some detail in the section on working mothers, since this general concern is voiced about any situation in which the child and the mother are separated. (2) If the mother is going to work anyway, day care may be worse than other kinds of care because it is institutional group care, and we know from research on other kinds of institutions that institutional care can and often does result in intellectual retardation and emotional "stunting." As I mentioned in the preceding section, Bowlby's paper for the World Health Organization on institutionally reared infants and children placed great emphasis on the dire consequences of "maternal deprivation" for the child. But he also placed emphasis on the harmfulness of the institutional setting; any setting in which the child did not have a one-to-one relationship with a single adult was seen as potentially damaging to the child. Obviously, day care does not include a one-to-one relationship between a child and a single adult. There are many children and comparatively few adults; hence the fear that day care will result in some of the same effects as were seen by Bowlby and others. The paper by Dale R. Meers in the selections deals with this issue at some length. (3) When children are in groups for protracted periods, as they are in day-care settings, the danger of infectious diseases being transmitted may be increased.

These fears cannot simply be rejected as old-fashioned. They are based on past experience and past analyses of research, as well as on old cultural traditions and biases. If day care is to become a major part of our services to families, it is important that these questions be discussed and dealt with honestly. Is group care necessarily bad for a child? If not, what conditions are needed in a group care arrangement in order to prevent ill effects and foster good effects? Does group care necessarily result in higher rates of infection? How can the effect be avoided or ameliorated? Is the child's relationship with his or her family altered by a group care experience? Is the family "weakened" as Nixon suggested?

Before looking at the data relevant to these questions, let's look— as usual—at some facts and figures about day-care programs that are in existence, their goals and organizational features.

KINDS OF DAY-CARE PROGRAMS
AND THEIR PURPOSES

The Office of Child Development, using estimates prepared by several organizations, comes up with the following figures for children in day-care programs (Grotberg, 1971):

Children under age six in some kind of day care for a full day	1,300,000
In day-care centers	575,000
In family day-care homes	712,000

What's the difference between a day-care center and a family day-care home? The day-care center is what you probably think of when the phrase "day care" is mentioned. It's a school-like place, usually with at least 15 infants or children and often with many more. Ordinarily, for a group of 15 children there is a highly qualified teacher and 3 or 4 aides with varying degrees of training. The center may contain many units of 15 to 20 children each, with 4 or 5 adults in each unit, or it may contain only one. Some centers are in buildings especially built for that purpose, but it is much more common to find day-care centers in basements of churches, in old stores, or in any building that can be made suitable. A family day-care home, on the other hand, is a private house or apartment. The family (usually just the mother) takes in 3 to 5 children in addition to the children in the family and cares for them for part or all of the day.

As you can tell from the figures from the Office of Child Development, family day care is more common than day-care centers, but much less is known about family day care, since almost all the research currently available has been done on centers.

One other fact you should know: Unlike the situation in other countries, only 10 percent of the day-care centers or homes are run for research purposes or to provide a service, and even those are not free. Most day care (90 percent) is provided by private individuals or organizations and is operated for profit.

What are the goals and purposes of day care? Two kinds of purposes have emerged in recent discussions of the problem. On the one hand, there is a need to provide a service for families in which all the adults work. What such families want is a stable, reliable caretaking arrangement for their children, which will provide the equivalent of good home care. In a sense, this kind of day care is the all-day analogue to the middle-class "traditional" nursery school so prevalent over the past 40 years. Alternatively, day care is seen by some (such as Bettye M. Caldwell and her co-workers, and Halbert B. and Nancy M. Robinson) as a potential vehicle for providing educational benefits to the enrolled children, particularly children from poverty environments. For these researchers, day care is envisaged as an early, intensive, compensatory education program, which has the potential not just to ameliorate problems that already exist, but to prevent the development of problems in the first place.

The two goals are not necessarily incompatible; few parents who are looking for a reliable service would object to having their child in a day-care center that offered extensive enrichment experiences. The distinction between the two sorts of goals, or the two sorts of programs, is important however, for two reasons. First, enriched educational day care is vastly more expensive than the "good baby-sitting" kind of care, and second, virtually all the research on day care done in this country has been done on very intensively educational centers. You should keep this in mind when you look at the papers by Bettye M. Caldwell, Charlene M. Wright, Alice H. Honig, and Jordan Tannenbaum and by Halbert B. Robinson and Nancy M. Robinson. The centers they describe are not necessarily typical of the day-care facilities you would find in your own community, although they are reasonably typical of the experimental day-care centers that are found in university settings.

SOURCES OF EVIDENCE ABOUT
THE EFFECTS OF DAY CARE

As I've indicated, nearly all the research in this country on day care comes from a handful of experimental, highly intensive programs carried out at university-based centers (The Frank Porter Child Development Center, in Chapel Hill, North Carolina; Group Care of Infants Demonstration Project, Greensboro, North Carolina; Howard University Nursery School Demonstration Project, Washington, D.C.: Children's Center, Syracuse, New York, and one or two others). These programs all began fairly recently, and comparatively little data have come out of them as yet.

An alternative source of evidence is the several analyses of the long-standing day-care programs in Europe and the kibbutz group-rearing system in Israel. As you probably know, day-care centers are much more common in Eastern Europe and Scandinavia than they are here. For example, in 1964 in the USSR approximately 10 percent of *all* children under the age of seven were in some kind of day care, either all-day centers or 24-hour residential centers. By 1967 approximately 30 percent of preschoolers were said to be enrolled, and that figure is also typical of other Eastern European countries, such as Hungary, Czechoslovakia, East Germany, Poland, and Yugoslavia. Among the Scandinavian countries, Denmark and Sweden have the most extensive programs, although in both countries the current enrollment in day care is quite small, and there is great demand for more services. (In all of these cases, again unlike the United States, the day-care centers are financed almost entirely by state funds.)

In many of the European countries with extensive programs, the development of day care dates from World War II, or shortly thereafter, when the labor of women was badly needed. With these many years of experience with day-care programs, you would think that there would be a great deal of data about the effects on the children and the family. Unfortunately, there isn't. There is a handful of studies, mostly done by Americans and mostly focusing on children older than the preschool age we're concerned with (Bronfenbrenner, 1970;

Wolins, 1969a, 1969b). In Israel the situation is somewhat better, since extensive research has been done on children reared in the kibbutzim.

As I am sure you know, on a kibbutz children are reared in groups from their very earliest weeks, although during the first six months or so the mother is present a good deal of the time and is responsible for feeding the child. The infants are ordinarily in a group of four, with a single caretaker; older children are in larger groups. Parents, grand-parents, siblings, and friends and other relatives see the children often during the day, and all the children spend the late afternoon and all day Saturday with their families, so there is a good deal of contact between the child and his family, as well as between the child and his caretaker. Kibbutz rearing is obviously not like anything we are familiar with; it is not like day care in our sense, but it is group care and does involve, to some extent, the same kind of multiple mothering as in day care in this country. So it seems useful to look at the evidence from research on the kibbutz-reared children.

EFFECTS OF DAY CARE
ON FAMILY RELATIONSHIPS

The best information we have on the effects of day care on family rela-tionships comes from the single study by Caldwell, Wright, Honig, and Tannenbaum, which is included in the selections. As you will see, they found that children reared in their day-care center from before age one did not differ from home-reared peers on measures of attachment to their mother. Since one of the great fears about day care is that it will somehow dilute or destroy the relationship between the child and his natural mother, Caldwell et al.'s study is of particular importance. They found that it was the nature of the relationship between the child and the mother when they *were* together that was crucial, which suggests that day care per se did not modify the mother-infant rela-tionship. Obviously, other research of this kind is needed, along with investigations that examine the impact of day-care attendance on a child's relationships with his father and siblings.

EFFECTS OF DAY CARE ON THE CHILD'S
EMOTIONAL AND SOCIAL DEVELOPMENT

What about the child's emotional development, aside from his attach-ment to his mother? Dale R. Meers, in the section of his paper ex-cerpted here, raises some serious questions about the effects of pro-grams in other countries. Perhaps, as Meers intimates, early group rearing has long-term effects on the child's later emotional health. Data relevant to this possibility are hard to come by. There are no figures from Eastern European countries to tell us whether there has been an increase in mental health problems since the inception of day-care programs, and there are no long-term follow-ups comparing children who have been in group care with those who have not. Studies of kibbutz-reared children, however, do not indicate that as adults a greater number emerge from the group-rearing situation with emotional problems, compared with children from comparable backgrounds but reared in the home (Kaffman, 1965). In fact, in Israel adults who were kibbutz-reared are considered to be among the most responsible and stable, and are disproportionately chosen for leadership positions in the government and military. There is evidence from some studies that kibbutz infants and young children show a higher rate of thumb-sucking than non-kibbutz children (Kaffman, 1961), but this seems to be related to the caretakers' permissiveness about thumb-sucking rather than a reflection of any deep-seated difficulties. Other investigators have suggested that kibbutz children have some difficulty in interpersonal relationships as young children, but that any early difficulty has disappeared by age ten (Rabin, 1958).

A study by Wolins (1969a, 1969b) of adolescent children reared in group settings in several countries underlines the same overall conclusions. Wolins could find no evidence of any widespread emotional disturbance resulting from the group rearing. In those instances where emotional difficulties seemed to be present, they could be attributed to the disrupted family conditions that led to the placement of the child in a group-rearing situation in the first place.

All of this does not mean that we should not be interested in the long-term effects of group rearing, but to me the meager data available do not give cause for as much concern as Meers has expressed.

EFFECTS OF DAY CARE ON THE CHILD'S INTELLECTUAL DEVELOPMENT

The data on the child's intellectual development are quite clear. In virtually every study done in this country and in most studies done abroad, group care children are superior to their home-reared comparison group in intellectual development. This effect is illustrated in Robinson and Robinson's paper, but their findings are by no means unique. Caldwell (1971) examined the intellectual status of the children in the Syracuse center and found that center infants showed an increase in IQ of about 17 points, whereas the matched controls showed a decrease of about 6 points. Children in the Greensboro program were also significantly higher than those in the control group on IQ tests (Keister, 1970), as were the children in the Howard University experimental program (Cisin, 1970).

In general, the greatest gains have been made by infants or children from poverty-level families. Middle-class children have shown either smaller gains or no gains at all compared to the control group (Keister, 1970).

Studies in Europe and Israel provide similar evidence. Kibbutz-reared children score higher than home-reared counterparts in most studies (Rabin, 1958). In Wolin's study of five different group-rearing settings, three of the five groups were higher in cognitive functioning than their controls, and two were no different.

EFFECTS OF DAY CARE
ON THE CHILD'S HEALTH

What little evidence we have on the effects of day care on the child's health comes from the experimental programs in this country. The Robinsons' program in Chapel Hill included detailed analyses of health problems, and the first findings from those analyses have been published by Glezen, Loda, Clyde, Senior, Schaeffer, Conley, and Denny (1971). They found that the children who had attended the center, particularly those who had been in the center as infants, showed slightly higher rates of respiratory illnesses than was typical for the metropolitan area in which the center was located. Keister (1970) has reported somewhat similar findings from the Greensboro project; she found that the center children had more diaper rash and more colds or runny noses than did the control group of home-reared children.

If these findings hold for other centers, then provision must be made for appropriately increased medical surveillance and care of any children in group care settings.

CONCLUSIONS

Although the research is scanty, the evidence points—at least to me—to a relatively clear conclusion: Group care *need not* have detrimental effects, and for some children it can be positively beneficial. There are two things you should understand about this conclusion, however. First, it is based very heavily on findings from very expensive, well-planned experimental programs. These are not run-of-the-mill local day-care programs; they are all funded as research projects by governmental agencies, and they have money for large staffs, extensive play equipment, and medical care. They are all run by psychologists who have applied all their knowledge about normal infant development to the design of daily programs. What this research tells us is that under conditions that we presume to be reasonably optimum, day care can be beneficial over the short run. At the other end of the continuum, we also know from all the old research on institutionalized infants (Bowlby, 1951; Provence and Lipton, 1962) that group institutional care can be harmful when there is inadequate stimulation and inadequate contact between the child and caretakers. What we don't know is the break-even point on this continuum. What are the necessary minimums for good care? And how many nonexperimental day-care programs meet those minimums?

Second, most of the research is short term. The benefits observed are over a few years of involvement in the program, and we don't know whether difficulties are to be expected later. The evidence from abroad, what little there is of it, leads me to be optimistic. I don't think we are going to find lots of long-term emotional or intellectual difficulties traceable to group care. But by no means does everyone agree with me; for example, witness Meers' paper.

Laying to rest the old saw that *all* group care is inherently detrimental to the child and to the family is no mean achievement. But we are now in need of more information about the minimum conditions necessary for adequate day care. Research evidence from Eastern European countries is beginning to be forthcoming, and that will be of considerable help, as will further research in this country on more "typical" day-care centers.

QUESTIONS FOR DEBATE AND DISCUSSION

1. a. If you were the person in the federal government who had to decide whether to fund day-care programs on a nationwide basis, would you say, Yes, No, or Maybe? Why?
b. What standards do you think you would need to set, if any?
c. What evidence would you like to have before making any decision?
2. Assume you are a parent with a year-old child. Some alternative care for your child is needed, since the adults in the family work. Would you choose day care? If so, why? If not, why not? What information would you want to have about a day-care center before placing your child in it?

ADDITIONAL REFERENCES USEFUL IN PREPARATION
FOR DEBATE OR DISCUSSION

Dittman, L. L. (Ed.) *Early child care. The new perspectives.* New York: Atherton, 1968.

A paper by Meers and Marans is included, which parallels much of Meers' comments in the selection included in this book, but *also includes a description of programs abroad. There are also papers in which Robinson, Caldwell, and Provence describe their respective day-care centers in some detail.*

Grotberg, E. (Ed.) *Day care: Resources for decisions.* Office of Economic Opportunity, Office of Planning, Research and Evaluation, 1972.

An excellent overview of research on day care and various theoretical perspectives on day care. It is available from Day Care and Child Development Council of America, Inc. (1401 K St., N.W., Washington, D.C., 20005) for $4.50. Not available elsewhere as far as I know.

Provence, S., and Lipton, R. *Infants in institutions.* New York: International Universities Press, 1962.

A description of orphanage-reared children, which highlights some of the potential difficulties of being so reared.

Robinson, N. M., and Robinson, H. B. A cross-cultural view of early education. In I. J. Gordon (Ed.), *Early childhood education,* 71st Yearbook of the National Society for the Study of Education. Chicago: University of Chicago Press, 1972, pp. 291–316.

In this paper the Robinsons outline some of the factors that lead to different kinds of early child-care programs in various countries. The chapter includes a discussion of programs other than day care, but it should give a good overall perspective.

REFERENCES

Bowlby, J. Maternal care and mental health. Monograph Series, No. 2. Geneva: World Health Organization, 1951.

Bronfenbrenner, U. *Two worlds of childhood: U.S. and U.S.S.R.* New York: Russell Sage Foundation, 1970.

Caldwell, B. M. Impact of interest in early cognitive stimulation. In H. E. Rie (Ed.), *Perspectives in child psychopathology.* New York: Aldine-Atherton, 1971.

Cisin, I. A group day care program for culturally deprived children and parents. George Washington University, Washington, D.C.: Progress Report, Office of Child Development, U.S. Department of Health, Education and Welfare, 1970.

Glezen, W. P., Loda, F. A., Clyde, W. A., Jr., Senior, R. J., Schaeffer, C. I., Conley, W. G., and Denny, F. W. Epidemiological patterns of acute lower respiratory diseases of children in a pediatric group practice. *Journal of Pediatrics,* 1971, **78,** 397–406.

Grotberg, E. A review of the present status and future needs in day care research. A working paper. Prepared for the interagency panel on early childhood research and development, Office of Child Development, Department of Health, Education and Welfare, 1971.

Kaffman, M. Inquiry into the behavior of 403 kibbutz children. *American Journal of Psychiatry*, 1961, **117,** 732–738.

Kaffman, M. Comparative psychopathology of kibbutz and urban children. In P. Neubauer (Ed.), *Children in collectives*. Springfield, Ill.: Charles C Thomas, 1965, pp. 261–269.

Keister, M. W. *"The good life" for infants and toddlers*. Washington, D.C.: National Association for the Education of Young Children, 1970.

Provence, S., and Lipton, R. *Infants in institutions*. New York: International Universities Press, 1962.

Rabin, A. I. Infants and children under conditions of intermittent mothering in the kibbutz. *American Journal of Orthopsychiatry*, 1958, **28,** 577.

Wolins, M. Group care: Friend or foe? *Social Work,* 1969, **14,** 35–53. (a)

Wolins, M. Young children in institutions: Some additional evidence. *Developmental Psychology*, 1969, **2,** 99–109. (b)

infant day care and attachment*

BETTYE M. CALDWELL, Ph.D.
CHARLENE M. WRIGHT, M.A.
ALICE S. HONIG, M.A.
JORDAN TANNENBAUM, B.S.
College of Home Economics, Syracuse University, Syracuse, New York

Day care for infants has had a slow crawl toward social respectability. Boosted on the one hand by zealots who see in it an antidote for many of today's social ills, it has been denounced on the other hand as destructive of a child's potential for normal social and emotional development. Such partisanship has made it somewhat difficult to operate innovative programs with sufficient objectivity to permit collection of the data needed to establish guidelines for current and future programs.

The authors and their colleagues have been engaged in operating a day care program for infants and preschoolers for four years. The broad aim of the program was to create an environment which would foster optimal cognitive, social, and emotional development

Bettye M. Caldwell, Charlene M. Wright, Alice S. Honig, and Jordan Tannenbaum. Infant day care and attachment. *American Journal of Orthopsychiatry*, 1970, **40**(3). Copyright © 1970, the American Orthopsychiatric Association, Inc. Reproduced by permission.
*Presented at the 1969 meeting of the American Orthopsychiatric Association, New York, N.Y.
This work was supported by Grant D-156 from the Children's Bureau, Social and Rehabilitation Services, Department of Health, Education and Welfare.

in young children from disadvantaged families. As data from other studies suggested that by age 3 such children already showed cognitive deficits, the logic of the Syracuse program was to devise a delivery procedure which could get certain types of critical environmental experiences to the children prior to age 3 and thus hopefully circumvent the process of gradual decline. As there are few if any facilities through which large numbers of very young children in this society can be reached, it seemed necessary to devise a new kind of facility. The pressing clamor from working mothers for better child care facilities for their children presented the opportunity to set up a delivery process, and in 1964 the Children's Center, a day care center for infants and preschoolers, was established.

At that time the developers of the program (see Caldwell and Richmond) were acutely aware that there might be certain inherent risks in group day care for infants. For one thing, little was known about the health consequences of bringing substantial numbers of infants into daily contact. For another, there was concern stemming from an awareness of the consistent findings that experiences which diluted the normal mother-infant relationship were likely to produce (be associated with) serious emotional, social, and cognitive impairment. When the plan to offer group day care for infants was announced, many persons expressed alarm that such an arrangement would surely produce deleterious social and emotional consequences, regardless of what benefits it might foster in the cognitive domain. Particularly it was feared that exposure of an infant to large numbers of adults might weaken his primary maternal attachment. If this were to happen, what price gains in any other area?

The question of whether such dilution actually occurs as a consequence of infant day care cannot be answered overnight. It is much easier to report gains or losses in the cognitive area because they can be measured more precisely (though not necessarily more meaningfully) and because they might register at least temporary effects more quickly. However, a certain passage of time is required before one can examine data for the relatively long-term effects upon the basic mother-child relationship of group day care for infants.

Informal checks have been made from the beginning, partly through the use of outside consultants who were experts in early development and objective and unbiased about possible effects of infant day care. Such impartial evaluations have on occasion identified areas of concern, yet offered reassurance that social and emotional development was not suffering. However, none of the outside consultants had the opportunity to observe the children interacting with their own mothers, seeing them instead with the day care staff.

Accordingly, the Center staff members who were on duty at arrival and departure times were alerted to signs of healthy attachment. For example, resistance to separation upon being brought to the Center, calling for the mother during times of distress during the day, positive emotional responses shown upon sighting a returning parent, and scampering to gain proximity when the mother comes upon the scene have all been looked for and noted in the day care children. However, it still appeared necessary to conduct a formal evaluation to determine whether there were basic differences in the strength of attachment in a group of day care and a comparable group of home-reared infants.

WHAT IS ATTACHMENT?

Attachment is a term which is somewhat elusive of a conceptual definition and one about which there is not unanimity of opinion as to appropriate definition. Ainsworth has attempted to distinguish among the terms *object relations, dependency,* and *attachment.* She suggests that attachment refers to an affectional tie to a specific person which may wax and wane as a function of the situation but which has an enduring quality which can survive even adverse socio-emotional circumstances. Attachment is characterized essentially by maintenance of proximity, by mutual pleasure in a relationship, and by reciprocal need gratification.

The importance of maternal attachment for healthy development has been perhaps more inferred than demonstrated. That is, some infants reared in circumstances which did not permit the formation of an exclusive child-mother attachment have developed deviant patterns of affective relationships with other people (see Goldfarb, Provence and Lipton, and summaries by Bowlby, Yarrow, and Ainsworth). From such findings the inference has been drawn that the absence of a one-to-one relationship is the causative factor which explains the deviance. This inference has been challenged by Casler and others, who proposed the alternative interpretation that the deficits shown in nonattached children are more the product of inadequate environmental stimulation than of maternal deprivation per se. The findings of Freud and Dann that mother-separated children who have had prolonged contact with one another show intense peer attachment have been interpreted as indicating that reciprocal peer attachments can possibly substitute for maternal attachment. Also on the basis of his studies of nonhuman primates, Harlow has suggested that peer attachments are actually more critical for subsequent species-normal social and sexual behavior than is maternal attachment. Mead, referring to the need of children in today's world to be able to go many places without fear and to interact with many people, questions the advocacy of a very close tie b'etween mother and child, suggesting that perhaps wider experiences "in the arms of many individuals in different degrees of intimacy, if possible of different races," might represent the more adaptive experience for young children.

Empirical studies of attachment are scarce in the literature. Schaffer and Emerson studied longitudinally 60 infants ranging in age from 21 to 78 weeks of age. They found indiscriminate attachment behavior during the second quarter and specific attachments during the third quarter of the first year of life. Mothers whose interaction with their children was more intense tended to have infants who were more intensely attached to them. Attachment was unrelated to whether the attachment object had had major responsibility for the child's physical care. Maternal availability to child did not differentiate significantly infants who formed exclusive attachments from those who attached to more than one object. Children who had extensive contacts with other people, independent of the nature of the mother-child relationship, tended to show broader attachment patterns than did children who had limited contacts with other people.

By far the greatest amount of empirical work on the topic of attachment has been carried out by Ainsworth and her associates. In a group of 28 Uganda babies she categorized 15-month-old infants in terms of strength and security of attachment as: unattached, insecure-attached, and secure-attached. She then compared the infants in these groups on certain maternal variables. Warmth of the mother, care by people in addition to the mother, and use of scheduled versus demand feeding bore no relationship to strength of attachment. The only variables that showed a clear relationship were total amount of care given by the mother, mother's excellence as an informant, and positive attitudes toward breast feeding. Whether the mother had an ample milk supply was marginally related to attachment. In regard to the multiple caretaker variable, Ainsworth concluded that "there is no evidence that care by several people necessarily interferes with the development of healthy attachment." In a sample of American babies and mothers studied throughout the first year of life, Ainsworth and Wittig found that sensitivity of the mother in responding to the baby's signals and the amount and nature of the interaction between the mother and the infant were additional variables which bore a relationship to strength of attachment.

Attachment during the preschool years, at which time the primary child-mother attachment should weaken somewhat and new attachments form, has been studied to only a very limited extent.

OBJECTIVES OF THIS STUDY

The main question asked by the present study was: are there differences in child-mother attachment and mother-child attachment between a sample of home-reared children and a sample of children who have participated in a group day care program since infancy. Stated in the null version, the formal hypothesis would be that there are no differences between the groups. Additional questions addressed to the data related to whether there are associations between attachment and sex, race, and developmental level of child, and between attachment and stimulation and support available for development within the home.

SUBJECTS

Subjects for the study were 41 children who had been followed since early infancy in a longitudinal study relating infant and child development to the social and physical environment. Data for this study were collected as close to each child's 30-month birthday as possible. Twenty-three of the children had received their primary care from their mothers from birth until the time of data collection, except for brief periods during which the mother might have had temporary work or might have been out of the home because of illness. Eighteen of the children had been enrolled in the Children's Center from the time they were about a year old, with all but two of the children having been enrolled prior to 15 months of age. At the time data were collected for this study, the mean duration of day care attendance was 18.8 months, with a range of 5 to 24 months.

Demographic characteristics of the sample can be seen in Table 1. Most of the subjects were from lower-class families, with 25% being from one-parent families. As enrollment in the day care program was limited to children whose parents requested the service, certain desirable touches of methodological elegance—such as matching for sex and ethnicity—could not be achieved. The Home group contained a disproportionate number of males and Caucasian children.

On a gestalt of home characteristics the two groups were, at the time of the present analysis, quite comparable. This is perhaps best supported by current scores on the Inventory of Home Stimulation. The Home sample had a mean of 52.8 and the Day Care sample a mean of 54.7 ($t = .98$, $p = $ NS). However, Stimulation Inventory scores of 53.4 and 49.5 for the Home and Day Care samples when

Table 1 Demographic Characteristics of the Sample

	Home	Day care	Total
Sex			
Boys	14	4	18
Girls	9	14	23
Race			
White	19	9	28
Nonwhite	4	9	13
Parents in household			
1 parent	3	7	10
2 parent	20	11	31
No. of siblings			
None	6	6	12
One	11	6	17
Two	4	1	5
Three or more	2	5	7
Mother's education			
Some high school	9	12	21
High school graduate	12	2	14
Some college	2	4	6
Father's education			
Some high school	10	7	17
High school graduate	8	3	11
Some college	2	1	3
Not applicable	3	7	10
Social class			
Lower social class	20	14	34
Middle social class	3	4	7
IQ (current mean)	107.2	108.8	
Stim score (current mean)	52.8	54.7	

the study children were 12 months of age indicated a marginal difference ($t = 1.87$, $p = .10$) in favor of the Home sample at that time. The closer contact between the parents of the Day Care sample and staff of the project, plus continued exposure to the philosophy of the day care program, presumably (and hopefully) accounted for the higher Home Stimulation scores that were earned by the Day Care families at the current assessment. Objectively the Day Care group would be described as having been somewhat more "disadvantaged" in the customary connotation of that term at the time their children entered the day care program; clinically and subjectively, there was no doubt but that they were.

THE DAY CARE PROGRAM

The generalizability of results from any scientific study is limited by the fidelity with which the sample represents the characteristics of the population from which it was drawn and by the replicability of the experimental procedures. At the outset it should be stated that the experimental procedure of the present study—the infant day care program—is not duplicated in every facility that advertises itself as a day care center. It is a very special day care center. A technical description of the program may be found in Caldwell and Richmond, but at least a few descriptive sentences must be offered here.

The establishment of the Center effected a rather unique blend of social concern for the welfare of young children with the challenge of an intellectual idea—that disadvantaged children will benefit maximally if environmental supports are made available during the first three years of life. "Enrichment" in this carefully planned environment is not merely cognitive enrichment but is an atmosphere in which people and objects give proper levels and quantities of stimulation to young children in a context of emotional warmth, trust, and enjoyment. Teachers, research staff, and office personnel alike are selected partly on the basis of such personal characteristics as warmth and affection for children, empathy for (and often experience with) the problems of the poor, understanding of the complexities and difficulties of family life, and personal convictions about the importance of early experience. Visitors have repeatedly, over the years, commented on such things as the large number of rocking chairs (almost always containing an assortment of adults and children) in the Center, the fact that everybody seems to know everybody else's name, the apparent confidence in adults shown by the children, and the zest for their task displayed by all adults working in the program.

Vital statistics include an average daily attendance of 65 to 70 children ranging in age from 6 months to 5 years, with group assignment based roughly on developmental age. The largest group (the older children) contains 16 children, and the adult-child ratio is approximately one to four. The total group is racially balanced, but the goal of having approximately equal numbers of boys and girls is seldom achieved. Although some middle-class children are accepted into the program, preference for all openings is always given to socially and economically needy families.

The daily schedule is arranged to permit alternating cycles of action and rest, of adult-initiated and child-initiated activity, of group activities and pursuit of individualized interests, of playing for fun and working to learn. One cannot walk into a classroom without thinking, "This is a place where children will be happy." The authors are justified in offering this seemingly immodest and somewhat emotional description, as they are only peripherally involved in the daily programming and can take no credit for the creation of this special milieu for the children. It is hoped that the reader can forgive the immodesty, for knowledge about the program is essential to a correct interpretation of the material to follow.

PROCEDURE

Primary data for the study were obtained from three sources: (1) an intensive semistructured interview; (2) a home visit; and (3) developmental testing. All procedures were scheduled as close together in time as possible, with an interview and the developmental test usually administered on the same day. Also used in the data analysis was the developmental test administered to the subjects when they were one year of age.

INTERVIEWS AND RATINGS

Most of the assessment procedures employed in this project were designed to cover some specific and relatively circumscribed aspect of child and/or family functioning. The interview conducted for the present study was deliberately planned to achieve the opposite purpose—namely, to obtain a broad picture of the mother-child interaction and of child behavior in settings not ordinarily open to observation by the research staff. All interviews were conducted by a research-oriented social worker (CMW) in a room at the Children's Center comfortably furnished to encourage a relaxed atmosphere. The mothers were told simply, "We want to talk with you about your child's activities and about some of the things you and he (she) are doing now." The study child was present during the interview, and ratings were based on both maternal report and maternal and child behavior. The interview was observed through a one-way vision mirror by a second staff member, and immediately after the session the interviewer and the observer independently rated both mother and child.

Although the interview deliberately covered a broad array of topics, ratings made from the interviews mainly dealt with clusters of behavior representing attachment and achievement. For the present analysis only those concerned with attachment were used.

Each variable was defined as ranging along a 9-point continuum, with all odd-numbered points described and behaviorally anchored in terms of either maternal or child behavior. The mothers were rated on all variables in terms of their behavior toward the study child, not toward other persons. For example, a mother might be very close to her husband but very distant and remote from the study child; only the latter behavior entered into the ratings used for this data analysis. Each child was rated on the attachment variables twice, once in terms of his relationship with his mother and once in terms of his behavior toward other people. These latter ratings were, of course, based entirely upon maternal report.

Both the interviewer and the observer rated the children and the mothers on these scales immediately following the interview and then, within a few hours, held a discussion and arrived at a rating consensus. Identical ratings were recorded on the final data sheet and were not discussed. Differences of one point were resolved in the direction of the more extreme rating (away from the midpoint of the scale), and differences of two points were reconciled by recording the intermediate rating. When the ratings differed by more than two points, the two raters reassessed the interview and defended their ratings until a consensus emerged. Although this form of rating obviates the need for conventional inter-rater reliability figures, a check was made on the extent of agreement between the raters. On four protocols across all scales the two raters agreed within two points on the maternal ratings on an average of 87% of the ratings (range 80% to 93%). On the child ratings the average agreement was 91% (range 83% to 96%).

It should be noted here that both the interviewer and the rater knew whether a particular mother-child dyad belonged in the Home or the Day Care sample. In a project like the present one, such knowledge will be unavoidable until a fiscal millennium is reached which permits the luxury of completely blind assessment by impartial assessors. However, the analytic strategy was not discussed with the interviewer until all the interviews had been completed and the ratings filed. She was not told at the outset that the interviews would be used for a comparison between the responses of the Home and Day Care samples. She knew only that the children's age ($2\frac{1}{2}$ years) had been designated as a major assessment point at the time the longitudinal study of the Home babies began. The interviewer's assignment was identical to that communicated to the mothers: to get a broad picture of the mother-child relationships and the development of the children, not to look for "strength of attachment." Furthermore, one of her major functions in the total project was to maintain rapport with the Home families. Therefore, she was actually closer to and friendlier to the Home than to the Day Care mothers, and any bias might have been in their favor. Thus it is the honest conviction of the authors that as much objectivity was maintained as is possible under such circumstances.

INVENTORY OF HOME STIMULATION

This is an experimental procedure developed within the research program of which the present study is a component. It represents an attempt to assess those qualities of the home environment impinging directly upon the young child which have the potential to inhibit or support development. The Inventory contains 72 binary items, about one-half of which depend entirely upon observation of home conditions for their score. It is scored on the basis of a home visit which usually lasts about two hours. Inter-observer reliability in terms of percent of agreement has been found to average around 95% for persons trained in the administration of the Inventory.

DEVELOPMENTAL EXAMINATIONS

The instrument used was the Stanford-Binet Intelligence Scale unless the child was somewhat slow and did not attain the basal age of two years. In such instances, and in all assessments of children younger than two, the Cattell Infant Intelligence Scale was used. Most of the examinations were given by the same person (ASH).

OPERATIONAL DEFINITION OF ATTACHMENT

For this study attachment was defined operationally as involving the behavior characteristics sampled in the maternal interviews and rated on seven scales. The variables defined in terms of the behavior considered descriptive of the most intense manifestation for both mothers and children are as follows:

Affiliation. Mother: actively responsive to child; initiates non-routine contacts; likes to be with child. Child: initiates contacts with mother with high frequency; protests being left alone; follows mother around; resists separation.

Nurturance. Mother: initiates support of child; tries to gratify needs; extremely helpful. Child: highly responsive to mother's activities; child's behavior reinforcement for mother's actions; is helpful.

Hostility. Mother: openly hostile; disapproves of much of child's behavior; imposes own schedule upon child; perceives child negatively. Child: expresses anger toward mother; demanding; negativistic, uncooperative; resists manipulation.

Permissiveness. Mother: lets child have own way much of time; invites manipulation and control by child. Child: extremely submissive to maternal control; yields to mother's wishes.

Dependency. Mother: hates to separate from child; extreme emotional involvement with this child to the exclusion of other persons; activities exclusively child-centered; enjoys company of child. Child: strong attachment to mother; is dependent upon mother; maintains proximity; resists separation when proximity is possible; likes to be with or near mother.

Happiness. Mother: expresses great happiness and pleasure in relation to child; child is the emotional high spot in mother's life. Child: extremely happy in interaction with mother; laughs, smiles, shows positive affect.

Emotionality. Mother: persistent extreme overt emotional expression displayed to child; frequently laughs or cries or becomes upset in interactive sessions. Child: persistent extreme overt emotional expression displayed to mother; interaction characterized by high affect rather than apathy and lack of involvement.

All scales except Hostility were expected to co-vary positively with attachment; low ratings on the Hostility scale were interpreted as indicative of strong attachment.

DATA ANALYSIS

For data analyses involving the behavior ratings, a distribution-free statistic was needed, and chi square and Fisher's exact test were used. When the developmental tests and the Inventory of Home Stimulation were examined internally, the t test for independent samples was used. For this type of study, it was felt that t Type II decision error (accepting the null hypothesis when it was actually false—i.e., inferring no difference when actually there were differences between the groups) carried greater interpretive risks. Therefore, it was decided to report and discuss p-values of .10.

ATTACHMENT AND EARLY CHILD CARE

CHILD-MOTHER ATTACHMENT

The major hypothesis tested by the present study was that there would be no significant difference between child-mother attachment patterns shown by a sample of children who had been home-reared since birth and a sample who had been enrolled in a group day care program since roughly one year of age. The hypothesis was tested by dichotomizing the behavior ratings (above and below the median for the total sample of 41) and examining the obtained distributions for disproportionality related to membership in the Home or the Day Care samples by means of chi square. Results of this analysis are summarized in Table 2. From the first column it can be seen that there were no significant differences between the Home and Day Care samples on any of the ratings of the child's relationship with his mother. This failure to disconfirm the null hypothesis

Table 2   Summary of Chi Square Analyses of Distribution of Ratings
(Above and Below Median) for Home and Day Care Children*

	Child-mother	Child-other	Mother-child
1. Affiliation	.24	.05	.00
2. Nurturance	.40	.20	.03
3. Hostility	.00	.96	.24
4. Permissiveness	.50	.17	5.49[b](H)
5. Dependency	1.45	3.39[a](DC)	.24
6. Happiness	1.04	.59	.96
7. Emotionality	.59	1.62	.09

[a]Significant at .10 level.
[b]Significant at .05 level.
*All chi squares have df = 1 and represent 4-cell tables enumerating numbers of
persons in Home (H) and Day Care (DC) samples rated above or below the median
of the total sample on the behavior ratings. Letters in parentheses (H, DC) after
significant chi squares identify the group excessively represented in the above-
median cell.

indicates that such group experience as that provided in our Center
can occur without producing deviant child-mother relationship.

CHILD-OTHER RELATIONSHIPS

In Column 2 of Table 2 are presented data on the way the children
in the Home and Day Care samples relate to other people in their
environment. These data were gathered and analyzed in order to
determine whether children who see a larger number of people in
an emotionally supportive context might not relate more positively
to other people. Schaffer and Emerson's finding that infants who
had more contact with persons other than the mother formed
broader attachment patterns would lead to this prediction, as would
Rheingold's finding that infants in an experimentally mothered
group were more socially responsive than the controls to a neutral
person in the environment as well as to the person who had
supplied the extra mothering. In the present study there was only
one scale on which a difference significant at the .10 level was
found. This was on the Dependency scale, on which the Day Care
children were found to have higher ratings than the Home children.
As defined in the present scales, dependency connotes proximity-
seeking more than help-seeking and perhaps indicates an enjoyment
of interaction with others more than anything else. Although the
difference is of marginal statistical significance, it offers some con-
firmation of previous findings relating to the breadth of interest in
other people shown by children who have extensive nonfamily
contacts.*

*In reacting to an earlier version of this paper, Dr. John Bowlby (personal com-
munication) suggested that the slightly higher ratings of the day care children on
the dependency scale in terms of their interactions with persons other than the

MOTHER-CHILD ATTACHMENT

Of perhaps equal relevance to the child's attachment to the mother is the mother's attachment to the child. If early day care in any way diminishes the intensity of the emotion which the mother brings to the relationship with her baby, then this might also have negative consequences for the child no matter how normally the child's own attachment pattern might develop. The data in Column 3 of Table 2 indicate that this does not appear to be a valid threat. On six out of the seven ratings, there were no significant differences between the mothers of the Home and the Day Care samples. On the remaining scale, permissiveness, the Day Care mothers were rated lower than were the Home mothers. Whether this reflects a general concern with achievement, "looking good" as a parent, or a basic personality characteristic of early Day Care mothers cannot be determined. It may reflect the fact that the Day Care mothers are more attuned to parent education literature and perceive permissiveness as being currently out of favor.

SEX AND RACE DIFFERENCES

If the samples for the two groups had been more perfectly matched in terms of all possibly influential variables, the finding of only one significant difference as a function of group membership (Home or Day Care) could be interpreted more unequivocally. It will be recalled from Table 1 that girls were overrepresented in the Day Care sample and that Negroes were underrepresented in the Home group. Differences in either of these variables might conceivably mask differences related to early child care experience. As so many recent research studies have reported sex differences in behavioral characteristics measured during early childhood, an analysis by sex was considered relevant.

In order to determine whether there were differences in ratings as a function of sex or race, the same kind of analysis described above and summarized in Table 2 for infant care pattern was carried out for sex and then for race. In the child-mother and child-other ratings, there was only one significant disproportion. That was on the Nurturance scale in the child's relationships with his mother (see definition under Method). On this scale girls were found

---

mother might indicate that these children show an "overanxious" attachment. One manifestation of this would be apprehension about breaking contact with an adult and a tendency to maintain constant proximity with the adult at the expense of exploration. Experimental tests of this would have been desirable and will indeed be made in future studies.

(chi square = 3.81, p. = .10) to be more responsive and helpful to their mothers—a difference which certainly fits the cultural sterotype for sex-typed behavior. There were no significant differences as a function of sex in the child-other ratings or in the mother-child ratings.

On the racial variable there were no significant differences between the groups on the child-mother or child-other variables. On the mother-child attachment variables, however, there were three that attained significance: Affiliation (whites high: chi square = 3.35, p = .10), Permissiveness (whites high: chi square = 3.69, p = .10), and Emotionality (whites high: chi square = 10.81, p = .001). This appearance of a fairly consistent pattern on three out of the seven maternal attachment scales suggests that in this particular sample the Negro infants received slightly less intense affective responses from their mothers. These relationships also suggest that the earlier reported findings of relatively greater concern with control (low permissiveness) on the part of the Day Care mothers (see Table 2, Column 3) may be confounded by the fact that Negro infants are slightly overrepresented in the Day Care sample in relation to the Home sample.

In general these data strengthen the interpretation of no major differences in attachment patterns associated with Home or Day Care group membership. Unbalanced sex distribution made essentially no contribution, and racial differences in the mothers, if anything, should have increased the likelihood of significant differences as a function of group membership. Thus the unbalanced representation in the two infant care groups of sex and race cannot be cited as obscuring differences that might have existed as a function of child care group membership.

DEVELOPMENTAL LEVEL AND ATTACHMENT

Although the major task of this project was to ascertain whether there were differences in attachment patterns of mothers and children as a function of child care history, the research program of which this project is but one part is concerned with broader aspects of child development. As stated previously, a major orientation of the program has been an attempt to develop a model of infant care that would support a child's development and provide certain critical experiences necessary to normalize development. It was conceivable that the child-mother and the mother-child attachment systems might in some way interact with the rate of development shown by the child.

Ratings on the attachment variables were examined for an

Table 3 Summary of Chi Square Analyses of Attachment
and Child's Developmental Level

	Child-mother	Mother-child
Affiliation	.59	.00
Nurturance	3.69a(HH)*	2.81a(HH)
Hostility	3.69a(HL)	.02
Permissiveness	1.77	.15
Dependency	1.77	1.95
Happiness	7.00b(HH)	.12
Emotionality	.02	.33

aSignificant at .10 level.
bSignificant at .01 level.
*H (High) and L (Low) in parentheses indicate patterns of significant dispropor-
tionalities on the two variables.

association with child's developmental level at 30 months, with the
results shown in Table 3. Only one of the maternal variables, Nurturance, achieved marginal significance, thus suggesting that in this
sample child's developmental level bore little or no relation to
strength of maternal attachment. In terms of child-mother attachment, however, there is a definite suggestion that the better developed infants tend to be more strongly attached to their mothers.
This finding should be especially reassuring to those who are concerned that cognitive enrichment might be fostered at the expense
of social and emotional development. These obtained associations
suggest quite the contrary, namely, that rate of development and
strength of attachment co-vary positively.

In view of the fact that cognitive enrichment was one of the
goals of the research program, it appeared valid to examine the developmental quotients of the children in order to determine whether
there were demonstrable differences between the Home and Day
Care samples on this variable both in terms of current functioning
and in terms of development prior to entering day care. The results
of the analysis are shown in Figure 1. Data in Figure 1 show that the
two groups were not comparable with respect to developmental
level at 12 months of age (another situation that one must live with
in research where random assignment of subjects is not possible).
The difference between the DQ's obtained on the children at that
time is significant at the .01 level of confidence. The Home children
show the decline in DQ over time that has been consistently reported for disadvantaged children. The Day Care children, while not
showing any astronomical rise in developmental level, have managed to avoid decline and have, in fact, shown a slight rise. The
difference between the groups at 30 months is not statistically significant. This finding, coupled with the above results pointing to
comparable attachment patterns in the two groups, demonstrates

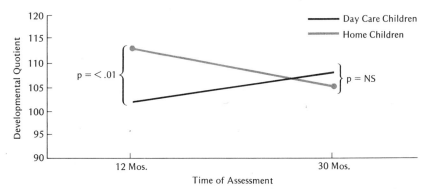

Figure 1 Time trends in developmental quotients for home and day care children at 12 and 30 months.

the feasibility of devising programs which circumvent developmental decline without damaging the child's capacity to relate to his mother or her capacity to relate to him.

HOME CHARACTERISTICS AND ATTACHMENT

The remaining assessment procedure used for this study was the Inventory of Home Stimulation. The score obtained by a given mother on this Inventory should provide some information about whether the verbal report and behavior which formed the basis for the attachment ratings were at all representative of child and maternal behavior. Accordingly, scores on the Inventory were dichotomized and related to dichotomized ratings on the attachment variables for the total sample of 41 children. Data from this analysis are presented in Table 4.

Table 4 Summary of Chi Square Analyses of Home Stimulation and Attachment Behavior (Above and Below Median on STIM, Above and Below Median on Attachment Scales)

	Child-mother*	Mother-child*
Affiliation	7.06[c]	3.38[a]
Nurturance	10.51[c]	5.11[b]
Hostility	1.71	.09
Permissiveness	.00	.85
Dependency	.00	7.06[c]
Happiness	.20	4.89[b]
Emotionality	1.95	6.93[c]

[a]Significant at .10 level.
[b]Significant at .05 level.
[c]Significant at .01 level.
*Significant disproportionalities were consistently of the High-High pattern.

From Column 2 of Table 4 it is obvious that the mother-child ratings were rather consistently related to independent data about mother and child gathered during a visit to the home. On five of the seven attachment variables, high ratings on the interview data were associated with high scores on the Home Stimulation Inventory. Similarly, on two of the child-mother ratings, there was an association between amount of stimulation available in the home and the intensity of the child's attachment to his mother. These data give support to the reliability of the behaviors sampled in the rating scales and also provide clues as to factors in the home situation which can be expected to correlate with strength of attachment.

HOME CHARACTERISTICS AND DEVELOPMENT

So far in this paper we have shown that child-mother and mother-child attachment were not adversely affected by the kind of early day care experience provided in this setting. We have further shown that attachment patterns are to some extent associated with developmental level of the child and are rather strongly associated with amount and quality of stimulation available to the child within the home. The data collected for this study also lent themselves to an examination of the relationship between home stimulation, pattern of early child care, and development. Results of this analysis are presented in Table 5. Here the association between child's developmental level (above or below a quotient of 100 at 30 months) and family score on the Home Stimulation Inventory (above or below the median) is examined separately for the Home sample, the Day Care sample, and the total group of children and families. The results of this analysis are again quite reassuring from the standpoint of the contribution that early day care can make to the total welfare of the developing child. In the Home sample, there is a statistically significant association (Fisher's exact test) between score on the Home Stimulation Inventory and developmental level—that is, children from homes low in stimulation tend to score below the median on the intelligence test. A similar association exists for the total

Table 5 Distribution of Home Stimulation Scores and Developmental Quotients for Home, Day Care, and Total Samples

	Home		Day care		Total	
	Hi Stim	Lo Stim	Hi Stim	Lo Stim	Hi Stim	Lo Stim
Above 100	9	3	7	4	16	7
Below 100	3	8	4	3	7	11
	p = .05		NS		p = .05	

sample. However, for the Day Care sample the distribution of scores on the variables of home stimulation and developmental level is random. Thus it appears that infant day care intrudes into the relationship between home stimulation and developmental level; it can, in effect, offer at least some of the resources and some of the influence of a "second home." It is clearly not the absence of a home.

DISCUSSION AND CONCLUSIONS

At the time the project of which this study is a part was introduced to the scientific literature, the following statement of goals was made:

> This paper describes a recently initiated program which has as its aim the development of a day care program for children three years of age and under to foster their subsequent educability. In order to accomplish this aim, an attempt will be made to program an environment which will foster healthy social and emotional development as well as provide stimulation for cognitive growth during a developmental period that is critical for its priming. . . . The basic hypothesis to be tested is that an appropriate environment can be programmed which will offset any developmental detriment associated with maternal separation and possibly add a degree of environmental enrichment frequently not available in families of limited social, economic, and cultural resources.

The data reported in this paper demonstrate that at least with respect to the social-emotional variables of child-mother and mother-child attachment, we can claim some success at this point. We *have* offered environmental enrichment, and we *have* shown that it is possible to do this without producing the classical picture of maternal deprivation. It is our hope that these findings will offer encouragement and reassurance to all persons interested in obtaining for children the benefits of high quality infant day care but cautious about jumping into premature programming lest the welfare of the children be forgotten. We ourselves are reassured.

These findings do not guarantee that a socio-emotional deficit would never be associated with infant day care. In the strict statistical sense, we can generalize only to samples participating in similar programs. As such programs are so scarce in America, the generalizability of the findings is sharply restricted. What they do show is that one *can* have infants in quality day care without having jeopardized the child's primary emotional attachment to his mother. In the present program, great pains were taken to avoid this jeopardy. For example, no infants were taken into the program prior to the age of six months, by which time rudimentary forms of attachment have developed. In point of fact, most children who enter the program during infancy do so around one year of age. Also the program is one which offers a generous adult-child ratio and which features in abundance the kinds of behavior shown to be associated with strength of attachment (intensity of response, sensitivity to child's needs, and general competence as adults).

Results of this study provide some extremely valuable information about the range of acceptable variability in patterns of social care for young infants which can be tolerated without damaging the developing children. The implicit equation of infant day care with institutionalization should be put to rest. Infant day care *may* be like institutionalization, but it does not have to be. Day care and institutional care have only one major feature in common: children in groups. Characteristics of institutional children that day care children do not share—prolonged family separation, a sameness of experience, absence of identity, isolation from the outside world, often *no* significant interpersonal relationship—undoubtedly far outweigh the one characteristic that the groups have in common.

The group with which we are working offers sufficient variation on both child and maternal dimensions to permit further investigations of factors influencing attachment and other important types of social and emotional development. For example, second in importance only to the development of child-mother and mother-child attachments is the development of peer attachments and other types of child-adult and adult-child attachments. One of the findings of the Schaffer and Emerson study referred to earlier was that exclusivity of maternal care was not related to strength of child-mother attachment, but its opposite, wide child care experiences, bore a slight relationship to the tendency of the infant to develop broader attachment patterns. In this study our concern has been primarily with the influence of infant day care upon the basic child-mother attachment; only incidentally did we address ourselves to the influence of such an infant care experience upon attachment to others. We are currently designing new research strategies to determine whether infant day care tends to be associated with strong attachments to more than one person without weakening the basic child-mother attachment.

When we talk about "group care for infants," it is easy to sound as though we are proposing something radically deviant for the children. In the Western world of today with its tract houses, Dick and Jane and mother and dad readers, and our carefully nurtured concern for territoriality and for "mine" and "yours," it is easy to forget that until very recent times isolation of the nuclear family from relatives and friends was rare. Many children living and developing in a small amount of space was the rule, not the exception.

Furthermore, the prevalence of extended family living arrangements made for interpersonal environmental settings not unlike that which exists in our infant day care setting: that is, a small group of infants cared for by several friendly and supportive adults but with never a question about who belongs to whom. Our teachers and nurses no more wish to usurp the maternal and paternal role than did relatives and friends who still help perform the child care functions in non-literate societies and did so in our own country until some 60–70 years ago. We would like to claim that our program is truly innovative, but we must at least consider the possibility that it represents a return toward a pattern that is normal and adaptive for the species. At the same time, we fervently hope that it represents progression toward the goal of more complete utilization of society's resources to foster optimal development for its children.

REFERENCES

Ainsworth, M. 1962. Reversible and irreversible effects of maternal deprivation on intellectual development. Child Welfare League of America: 42–62.

Ainsworth, M. 1967. Infancy in Uganda. Johns Hopkins Press, Baltimore.

Ainsworth, M. 1969. Object relations, dependency, and attachment: a theoretical review. Child Devel. **40**:969–1026.

Ainsworth, M., and Wittig, B. 1968. Attachment and exploratory behavior of one-year-olds in a strange situation. In Determinants of Infant Behavior IV, B. M. Foss, ed. Methuen, London and John Wiley & Sons, New York.

Bowlby, J. 1951. Maternal Care and Mental Health. World Health Organization, Geneva, Switzerland.

Caldwell, B., and Richmond, J. 1964. Programmed day care for the very young child—a preliminary report. J. Mar. and Fam. **26**:481–488.

Caldwell, B., Heider, J., and Kaplan, B. 1966. The Inventory of Home Stimulation. Paper presented at meeting of Amer. Psychol. Assn., Sept. 1966.

Caldwell, B., and Richmond, J. 1968. The Children's Center in Syracuse, New York. In Early Child Care: The New Perspectives, L. L. Dittmann, ed. Atherton Press, New York: 326–358.

Casler, L. 1961. Maternal deprivation: a critical review of the literature. Monographs of the Society for Research in Child Development, **26**(2).

Freud, A. and Dann, S. 1951. An experiment in group upbringing. Psychoanal. Study of Child, **6**:127–168.

Goldfarb, W. 1955. Emotional and intellectual consequences of psychologic deprivation in infancy: a revaluation. *In* Psychopathology of Childhood, P. H. Hoch and J. Zubin, eds. Grune and Stratton, New York: 105–119.

Harlow, H., and Harlow, M. 1966. Social deprivation in monkeys. *In* Human Development, M. L. Haimowitz and N. R. Haimowitz, eds. Thomas Crowell, New York: 230–235.

Mead, M. 1957. Changing patterns of parent-child relations in an urban culture. Int. J. Psychoanal. **38**(6):1–10.

Provence, S., and Lipton, R. 1962. Infants in Institutions. International Universities Press, New York.

Rheingold, H. 1956. The modification of social responsiveness in institutional babies. Monograph of the Society for Research in Child Development, **21**(2).

Schaffer, H., and Emerson, P. 1964. The development of social attachments in infancy. Monograph of the Society for Research in Child Development, **29**(3).

Yarrow, L. 1964. Separation from parents during early childhood. *In* Review of Child Development Research, Vol. I, M. L. Hoffman and L. W. Hoffman, eds. Russell Sage Foundation, New York: 89–130.

longitudinal development of very young children in a comprehensive day care program: the first two years*

HALBERT B. ROBINSON
NANCY M. ROBINSON
University of North Carolina

In September 1966 the Frank Porter Graham Child Development Center of the University of North Carolina at Chapel Hill opened a day care center offering comprehensive services to a small number of infants and very young children. This center was established as a pilot facility for a much larger multidisciplinary research project. The latter was to be devoted in part to a longitudinal intervention study of a sizable cohort of children ranging in age from birth to 13

From *Child Development*, 1971, **42.** Copyright © 1972 by the Society for Research in Child Development, Inc. By permission.
*Support for this research and for the facility was furnished by the U.S. Children's Bureau, MCH and CC research grant H-79; by the National Institute of Child Health and Human Development, grant 2P01-HD-03110, by a grant from the Carnegie Corporation of New York, and by the University of North Carolina. Our sincere thanks to Harriet Rheingold and to Carol Eckerman, who carried out most of the infant testing; to Barbara Semonche, who carried out the special language assessment; and to Frances Campbell, who completed some of the final tests. Special debts are acknowledged to the center staff and in particular to Ann Peters, a cofounder of the center, whose sustained determination and compassion profoundly influenced its operation during this period. Authors' address: Developmental Psychology Laboratory, University of Washington, Seattle, Washington 98105.

years given education and comprehensive day care under conditions as optimal as could reasonably be devised (Robinson 1969). This study presents the assessment of the development of the 11 children admitted in 1966 and the 20 enrolled in 1967 and 1968. The data reflect the results of a complex experimental plan which combined several rather unusual characteristics:

1. Almost all Ss admitted as infants were selected before their birth, with the conditions only that the sample be roughly balanced for sex and race and that no gross anomalies be detected during the neonatal period. They entered day care when the mother returned to work, which ranged from 4 weeks to 6 months after the birth of the child.

2. The sample was broadly representative of the community's socioeconomic spectrum of Caucasian and Negro children of working mothers.

3. Comprehensive daytime care was given, including complete health care; children attended the center whether sick or well.

4. A carefully structured educational program, beginning in early infancy, constituted a strong focus of the center. Pilot curricula were developed in language, sensorimotor skills, perception and reading, scientific and numerical concepts, music, art, and French.

5. The basic organizational pattern consisted of two cottages of up to 16 children of all ages represented in the center for basic activities such as eating, sleeping, and free play. All center children in the same family were housed together. Grouping by developmental level for instruction and play occurred for approximately 3 hours each day, children ages $2\frac{1}{2}$–$4\frac{1}{2}$ going from their cottage to an educational unit.

6. Child-focused work with parents occurred through daily conversations with staff, frequent contact with the pediatrician, and home visits by the public health nurse. There were also occasional newsletters, parent meetings, and parties.

SUBJECTS

CENTER SAMPLE

During this pilot phase of the study, infants and 2-year-olds were admitted in order to provide for some heterogeneity. Most infants were selected through routine interviewing of all employed women receiving prenatal care in the university hospital, the only hospital in Chapel Hill. A few infants, and all older children, were admitted after applications by families not initially contacted prior to the birth of the child. Four infant siblings born to families already having a child in the center were automatically admitted. Efforts were made to keep each of the three annual waves (1966, 1967, 1968) as varied and balanced as possible in race, sex, and socioeconomic status.

During the fall of 1966 four children were admitted between the ages of 2.0 months and 5.5 months (mean age, 3.8 months) and seven others between 26 and 36 months (mean age, 28.7 months). In the fall of 1967, seven infants between 1.5 and 5.5 months old were admitted (mean age, 2.7 months), and five children who were 23–28 months of age (mean age, 25.6 months). In 1968, all eight new Ss were infants, 1.1–4.0 months (mean age, 2.1 months). Of the 31 children, 12 (7 Caucasian and 5 Negro) were admitted at age 2; 19 (8 Caucasian and 11 Negro) were admitted as young infants. One additional child, however, was a congenital athyreotic admitted before his condition was diagnosed at age 3 months. Borderline retarded, he is omitted from this report. One boy admitted at age 2 was withdrawn when his family moved 18 months later. He is included in the comparison with community controls, but not in the longitudinal analysis. By the end of the 2½-year period covered by this report, the 31 Ss ranged in age from a few weeks to 4½ years.

Twenty-four families were represented. Total incomes of the 12 Caucasian families (i.e., all adults with legal responsibility for child) ranged from $4,500 to above $40,000, the median family income for the 15 children being $10,976. Incomes of the 12 Negro families ranged from zero (unmarried student mothers) to $10,000, the median for the 16 children being $3,519. Median education for the Caucasian mothers was 14.5 years and for the Caucasian fathers, 16.5 years. Median education of the Negro mothers was 12.0 years, and of the Negro fathers, 11.0 years. One Caucasian child and four Negro children had no father in the home.

The dramatic differences between the Caucasian and Negro families in the sample are, in large part, a reflection of the disparities in this community. Its Caucasian wage earners are largely university staff and merchants, while its Negro population has traditionally performed supportive services. Community acceptance was also an issue, however. The early appeal of the center was to the poorer Negro parents, attracted by the low cost, and to the more affluent Caucasian parents, attracted by the potential benefits for their children. Eventually, however, the center's reputation began to attract blue-collar Caucasian parents and middle-class Negro parents. Included in the 1968 sample are, for example, the infant sons of a white policeman and of a Negro social worker.

CONTROL GROUPS

Two separate control groups were studied. One was followed from early infancy onward and is compared with center infants; the other was tested only once and was compared with center children who were at that time $2\frac{1}{2}$–$4\frac{1}{2}$ years old.

From 1967, when pediatric services became available as part of the center's program, control groups of infants were selected by the same prenatal interviewing methods as center infants, an attempt being made to equate the annual waves as closely as possible on sex, race, number of siblings, education and occupation of parents, and number of rooms in the house. These groups were evaluated medically and psychologically on the same schedule as the center population, and additional health records were kept in conjunction with medical studies being carried out in the center. Complete medical supervision was given to the control children, in part to enlist the families' cooperation, but more important, to attempt to equalize medical care, the better to evaluate the effects of the enriched daily experience of the center children. Eleven control group infants were followed during the period of this report.

By 1968, the 16 oldest center Ss were $2\frac{1}{2}$–$4\frac{1}{2}$. Four of these children had entered in 1966 as infants; 12 had entered in 1966 or 1967 at age 2. None had attended less than 1 year. As a rough comparison, a completely different group of noncenter children was matched with them individually on the basis of race, sex, parents' education and occupation, and the age at which the center child had last been given the Stanford-Binet and PPVT (see below). The controls were chosen from applicants to the center for whom there had not been space $(N = 5)$, from friends of the family of the child for whom matching was sought $(N = 9)$, and from another local day care center $(N = 2)$. Mean CA of each group was 41 months, the mean within-pair age difference being 1.8 months. Exceedingly close matching on occupation and education of both parents was achieved, except that six control mothers were not currently employed.

BEHAVIORAL MEASURES

The data reported here represent only the results of standardized testing over the period being considered. Tests were scheduled every 3 months to age 18 months, the Bayley mental scale, the Bayley motor scale, and the Bayley behavior profile (Bayley 1961) being completed on each occasion. Table 2 lists most of the subsequent tests administered to age $4\frac{1}{2}$. In addition, several language-assessment measures were administered in June 1968 to the 14 oldest children (ages 2–7 to 4–3) and three additional tests (WPSSI, Frostig, Caldwell preschool inventory) were given at age 4.

Testing through age 18 months was conducted by the staff of the University of North Carolina Laboratory of Infant Behavior to which the infants were transported by a caretaker from the center or by the mothers of the control infants. Testing of center children 2 and over was conducted at the center by a member of its staff. The control children for the special one-time comparison with the older Ss were seen in their own homes or regular day care settings by the same examiner who tested the older center children. The Stanford-Binet and Peabody Picture Vocabulary Test (PPVT) were administered. Effort was made to establish rapport through an initial period of play and the presence, when apparently desirable, of a trusted adult. For almost all of the Negro children, whose homes had no telephones, the testing visit constituted the second to the fourth contact with the examiner, who had played with the child during each previous visit. Nevertheless, these comparison data suffer the obvious drawbacks of the greater familiarity of the examiner with the center Ss and the unknown practice effects of their previous testing.

TEST RESULTS

SUBJECTS ADMITTED AS INFANTS

Test results for all children admitted as infants are shown in Table 1, together with those for the control infants. A 2 × 5 analysis of variance (Dixon 1965) nested on treatments (center-control) with repeated measures on comparisons over time and using a general linear hypothesis to handle missing data values was applied to the infant test scores. Analysis of the Bayley mental scale scores yielded a between-groups F ratio of 7.99 (df 1/116, $p = .01$) for the treatments, an F ratio of 2.72 (df 4/116, $p = .05$) for the comparisons over time, and a nonsignificant interaction ($F = 1.45$, df 4/116). For the Bayley motor scale, the only significant F ratio (4.75, df 1/109, $p = .05$) occurred in the comparison of center and control groups. A t test of the mental scale scores at 18 months was significant at the .01 level, but a t test of motor scale scores at that age failed to reach significance at the .05 level. A t test of the small samples tested on the Stanford-Binet at 24 months also failed to reach significance.

In other words, scores for center and control Ss were significantly different on both tests, but a significant trend over time was found only on the mental scale, consisting of an initial rise for both groups, and a drop for the control group at the 18-month level. The suddenness of that drop probably accounts for the lack of significance in the interaction. The scores on the Bayley motor scale favored the center group but were less consistently different over time.

Table 1 Test Results for Ss Admitted as Infants and Controls

Group	Bayley mental scale					Bayley motor scale					Stanford-Binet	
	6 Mo	9 Mo	12 Mo	15 Mo	18 Mo	6 Mo	9 Mo	12 Mo	15 Mo	18 Mo	24 Mo	30 Mo
Center:												
N	17	18	19	10	11	17	18	18	8	7	4	4
X	108.00	115.94	112.16	116.60	115.18	110.94	109.22	99.61	107.62	107.29	116.25	117.25
SD	8.95	14.71	9.91	9.19	8.95	14.06	11.90	14.45	9.29	16.71	8.67	4.76
Control:												
N	11	11	11	10	8	11	11	11	10	8	4	—
X	105.90	113.27	110.91	110.70	99.75	103.82	105.00	101.09	103.60	94.00	99.75	—
SD	10.15	12.23	9.97	8.79	11.61	13.11	11.45	14.96	10.95	7.17	11.23	—

SUBJECTS ADMITTED AT AGE 2

The test results for children admitted to the center at age 2 are described in Table 2. Additional tests administered to the 1966 group at age 4–0 yielded the following mean scores and standard deviations: Wechsler primary and Preschool Inventory full scale IQ 124.6 (SD 12.4), verbal IQ 126.0 (8.8), performance IQ 117.7 (14.5); Frostig test of visual perception IQ 100.0 (20.9) and Caldwell preschool inventory, median percentile 90 (middle-class norms).

Scores on most primarily verbal measures were high, as shown by the Stanford-Binet (Terman and Merrill 1960), the verbal scale of the WPPSI (Wechsler 1967), the Caldwell preschool inventory (Caldwell 1967), and, as an exception, the nonverbal Arthur Adaptation of the Leiter scale (Arthur 1952). Peabody Picture Vocabulary Test (Dunn 1959) scores were consistently lower than the other measures.

On the nonverbal measures, most of the children's scores fell below their verbal scores. On the Frostig test of visual perception (Frostig, Lefever, and Whittlesey 1964), the draw-a-man test (Harris 1963), and portions of the Illinois Test of Psycholinguistic Abilities (McCarthy and Kirk 1961), this lower performance was evident. Sensorimotor items (motor encoding, visual-motor sequential) were consistently the lowest of the mean ITPA scores, with the exception of the visual-motor association test, which is "motor" only to the extent that a pointing response is required. Similarly, on the WPPSI,

Table 2 Test Scores of Children Admitted at Age 2

Test	Admitted 1966 (N = 6)					Admitted 1967 (N = 5)	
	2–6	3–0	3–6	4–0	4–6	2–6	3–0
Stanford-Binet							
$\overline{X}$	112.3	124.5	132.7	—	127.2	118.4	123.8
SD	23.5	20.2	17.5	—	13.4	23.1	13.9
PPVT							
$\overline{X}$	93.8	100.8	114.0	111.5	108.5	111.4	107.2
SD	15.5	19.7	7.2	6.9	6.9	17.9	10.8
ITPA							
$\overline{X}$	104.3	124.5	122.2	—	—	––	115.0
SD	14.0	17.0	12.8	—	—	—	15.0
Leiter							
$\overline{X}$	—	128.0	128.3	—	126.8	106.6	130.0
SD	—	19.6	16.4	—	8.7	26.1	14.9
Draw-a-Man							
$\overline{X}$	—	—	96.8	—	98.5	––	—
SD	—	—	15.3	—	9.9	—	––

the mean subscale scores for the seven children tested at age 4 ranged from a high of 16.43 on arithmetic to a low of 12.29 on geometric designs, the single exception being a mean score of 9.71 on the highly motoric mazes. The WPPSI performance IQ was approximately ½ SD below the mean verbal IQ.

The language assessment in June 1968 likewise revealed advanced verbal behavior. Of the 12 children given the Templin-Darley scale (Templin and Darley 1960), the score of each S was at or above CA level, the mean speech age exceeding the mean CA (42 months) by approximately 22 months. On the action-agent test (Gesell 1940), 10 of the 12 scored at age level or better, three Ss exceeding the CA by at least 6 months. On the Michigan Picture Language Inventory (Lerea 1958; Walski 1962) given to the seven oldest children, mean standard score of expression was +.96, while the mean comprehension standard score was +.65.

Test results for the 16 older center children and 16 matched controls are shown in Figures 1 and 2. The most striking findings on both tests are the differences, on the order of two standard deviations, between the center Negro children and their controls. Mean Stanford-Binet IQs were 119.7 for these seven center children and 86.1 for their controls; both groups showed a marked clustering of scores (SDs 8.16 and 6.59, respectively). On the PPVT, center Negro children attained a mean IQ of 107.4 (SD 10.03) while that of the control Negro children was only 77.6 (SD 13.75). There was no overlap of scores between these groups on either test.

Differences between the nine Caucasian center children and their controls appeared on the Stanford-Binet but not on the PPVT. Mean IQs on the Stanford-Binet were 129.7 (SD 17.00) and 116.9 (SD 11.71), respectively. On the PPVT, mean IQ of the center Caucasian group was actually lower (108.1, SD 12.42) than that of the controls (110.2, SD 12.81).

According to an analysis of variance (Dixon 1965) of Stanford-Binet scores, F ratios were highly significant for the comparisons of racial groups ($F = 22.27$, df 1/28, $p < .001$) and center control groups ($F = 28.89$, df 1/28, $p < .001$), the significant interaction ($F = 5.81$, df 1/28, $p = .05$) highlighting the much greater magnitude of the difference between the Negro groups. In the analysis of scores on the PPVT, there were also significant effects of race ($F = 14.29$, df 1/28, $p = .001$) and of the center/control variable ($F = 9.90$, df 1/28, $p = .01$). The interaction term ($F = 13.14$, df 1/28, $p < .01$) demonstrated that the significant differences were limited to the Negro groups. Center Ss who were 3–6 and older attained somewhat higher scores on both tests than did center Ss 3–0 and younger (mean Stanford-Binet IQs 129.1 and 121.5, respectively; mean PPVT IQs 113.5 and 102.1), but a t test of these Stanford-Binet differences was not sig-

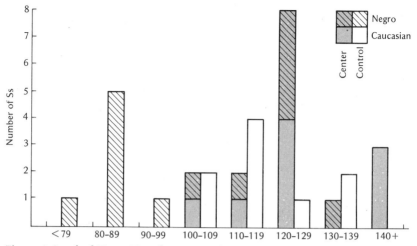

Figure 1 Stanford-Binet IQs of center and control children ages 2½–4½.

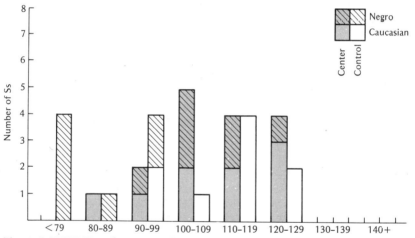

Figure 2 PPVT IQs of center and control children ages 2½–4½.

nificant, and the PPVT difference ($t = 2.346$, df 14) was significant at only the .05 level. The control group showed no such age trends. Practice effects cannot be ruled out. Sex differences were not significant.

DISCUSSION

Within the serious limitations which characterize the data, a number of tentative suggestions emerge:

1. Enriched group care of the young infant, when carefully designed and fully staffed, may enhance cognitive development, espe-

cially during the time when verbal abilities are beginning to emerge. The differences between experimental and control groups which were apparent at the 18-month level suggest that the period before this may be a crucial one. Earlier concern about the possibility of detrimental cognitive effects of "institutionalization" (i.e., any form of group care) is apparently unjustified. On the contrary, a decline in scores was found for the control group, while the center's group maintained its status on cognitive measures at about 1 SD above the mean of the national normative sample.

2. High quality group care combined with educational efforts during ages 2–4 years may have its major impact upon culturally disadvantaged children. Although the center Caucasian (more advantaged) children in the study obtained higher scores on the Stanford-Binet than the control Caucasian children, the really dramatic differences occurred between the center Negro (less advantaged) children and their controls. Indeed, the center Negro children attained a mean Stanford-Binet of approximately 120, as opposed to the control Negro mean IQ of approximately 86. The crucial variables of the day care, educational, and health programs cannot be identified in this pilot study, but that the "package" made a difference in the lives of the children is unmistakable.

3. The major impact of the program was in verbal rather than motoric areas. The nonverbal scores of the center children were "normal" but not particularly advanced.

The lack of well-standardized instruments to assess social-emotional functioning of young children is a major handicap to a study of this nature. A series of attempts to devise a problem-behavior checklist or interview with the mothers was unsuccessful because of the inability of some poorly educated mothers, even with considerable prompting, to think in differentiated terms about their children's behavior. Overall evaluation by a team of psychoanalytically-oriented clinicians yielded interesting individual assessments which were based on limited observations of center children and did not yield useful research data. Similarly, detailed behavioral ratings by the staff, useful in many ways for longitudinal research, are not reported here because they yielded only within-group comparisons. There was unanimous agreement among all the staff, who were of diverse cultural and educational backgrounds, that as a group the children were extremely amicable, stable, and outgoing, and that none exhibited behavior deviant from the normal range of childhood behavior patterns.

A study such as the present one raises many more questions than it can answer. What are the long-range residuals of a program such as that provided by the center? In the long run, will the development of children who enter as infants differ significantly from that of children admitted at age 2, later, or not at all? What elements within the program are most effective? Can these elements be packaged and delivered more economically than through comprehensive full-day programs? What positive impact may the availability of reliable day care have on the stability of families, and on the mother's employment and personal adjustment? What are the immediate and delayed effects on the children's relationships with their parents? Major longitudinal research efforts will be required to answer these compelling questions.

REFERENCES

Arthur, G. A. *The Arthur adaptation of the Leiter international performance scale.* Washington, D.C.: Psychological Service Center Press, 1952.

Bayley, N. Manual of directions for infant scales of development (temporary standardization). (Mimeographed.) Bethesda, Md.: National Institute of Neurological Diseases and Blindness, Colloborative Research Project, 1961.

Caldwell, B. M. *The preschool inventory.* Princeton, N.J.: Educational Testing Service, 1967.

Dixon, W. J. (Ed.) General linear hypothesis (BMDO5V). Biomedical Computer Program. Los Angeles, UCLA Health Sciences Computing Facility, 1965.

Dunn, L. M. *Peabody Picture Vocabulary Test manual.* Minneapolis: American Guidance Service, 1959.

Frostig, M.; Lefever, D. W.; and Whittlesey, J. R. B. A development test of visual perception for evaluating normal and neurologically handicapped children. *Perceptual and Motor Skills,* 1964, **12,** 383–394.

Gesell, A. *The first five years of life.* New York: Harper & Row, 1940.

Harris, D. B. *Measuring the psychological maturity of children: a revision and extension of the Goodenough draw-a-man test.* New York: Harcourt, Brace & World, 1963.

Lerea, L. Assessing language development. *Journal of Speech and Hearing Research,* 1958, **1,** 75–85.

McCarthy, J. J., and Kirk, S. A. *Illinois test of psycholinguistic abilities.* (Exp. ed.) Urbana: University of Illinois, Institute of Research on Exceptional Children, 1961.

Robinson, H. B. From infancy through school. *Children,* 1969, **16,** 61–62.

Templin, M. C., and Darley, F. L. *The Templin-Darley tests of articulation.* Iowa City: University of Iowa Bureau of Education Research and Service, 1960.

Terman, L. M., and Merrill, M. A. *Stanford-Binet intelligence scale.* Boston: Houghton Mifflin, 1960.

Walski, W. Language development of normal children, four, five, and six years of age as measured by the Michigan Picture Language Inventory. Unpublished doctoral dissertation, University of Michigan, 1962.

Wechsler, D. A. *A manual for the Wechsler preschool and primary scale of intelligence.* New York: Psychological Corp., 1967.

international day care: a selective review and psychoanalytic critique*

DALE R. MEERS

CONCLUSIONS: A CRITICAL OVERVIEW

This less than complete review of some international child care programs permits a number of conservative conclusions that are relevant to present U.S. interests in Day Care. As a first consideration, one may review assumptions about Day Care that are either irrelevant or demonstrably untrue; secondly, there are lessons that derive from organizational experiences abroad; and thirdly, there are highly significant questions relating to the psychiatric dangers of early Day Care.

It is easiest to start with those assumptions that are irrelevant or untrue. Analogies made between proposed Day Care in the U.S.

*The excerpts included here are taken from Edith Grotberg (Ed.), *Day care: Resources for decisions,* published by the Office of Economic Opportunity, Office of Planning, Research and Evaluation. The paper is, however, a revision of an earlier manuscript by Dr. Meers and his colleague Allen D. Marans.
In abridging the paper for inclusion in this volume I have omitted all of Dr. Meers' excellent (but lengthy) descriptions of day-care systems in other countries and retained only his conclusions and concerns. Readers who are interested in having more detail about foreign systems are urged to read Meers and Marans' paper in Laura Dittman (Ed.), *Early child care,* Atherton Press, 1968, or to obtain a copy of the Grotberg volume from the Office of Economic Opportunity. [Ed.]

and the systems of Kibbutzim child care are simply illogical since the Kibbutzim are typically a unique configuration of self-selected families who are deeply committed to an experiment in social living that is almost totally unlike anything in the U.S. (other than our few rural, religious settlements). The Kibbutz child programs are an organic part of life, and not an ancillary service for distressed or underprivileged families.

It has been argued that U.S. federal funding of Day Care would eventually lead to a decrease in spending for welfare, via the training and subsequent employment of welfare mothers whose children would be placed in Day Care. That Day Care could lead to economies in government expenditures seems contradicted by the evidence of the Communist nations. The capital investments of these nations for adequate centers approximate a quarter of a million dollars per center, and the operating expenses have equaled one-quarter to one-third of the earnings of the mothers of each child, with the state typically funding 85% of operating expenses. Where government support and authority have been given, this has been understood as an assurance of the adequacy and desirability of Day Care. Under such circumstances, Day Care has become "socially acceptable" and the public has pressed for ever greater expansion and expenditure, even in Czechoslovakia at the very time that research evidence was leading to a reversal in national policy (for the under-threes).

We sometimes assume that recruitment, staffing and training of Day Care personnel should be elementary. The assumption is most questionable. The status of mothers, and their substitutes (whether babysitters or caregivers), is minimal in the hierarchy of U.S. social conventions. Since we lack the emotional zest of the Kibbutzim or the ideological thrust of the Communist world, it appears singularly unlikely that U.S. recruitment of caregivers could be maintained at a level much beyond that of France or East Germany. One might expect that the principle of lesser employability would determine the caregiver's self-selection and that, in lieu of high pay or high status, mobility of caregivers would be considerable.

Motives that were persuasive in the establishment of Day Care in Communist countries appear much less relevant in the U.S. The Communist nations have been hard pressed in their industrial development and have needed the labor skills that working mothers provide. The U.S. appears to have a diametrically opposite problem since our technological revolution has made many jobs obsolete and gives promise of an eventual reduction in the work week. Given the U.S. "generation gap," and ever increasing crime, drug and delinquency rates, a powerful argument can be offered in the opposite direction, that is, that there is a profound need for increasing direct maternal/parental involvement with children, particularly in the early years when social attitudes and conscience are formed.

The philosophical rationale that Day Care provides women with equal rights with men (to work) appears at first blush persuasive and reasonable. The psychoanalytic clinician would certainly be among the first to concur that some women would greatly relieve themselves and their children by the use of Day Care, when such mothers are miserable or distraught in the normal course of "mothering" and homemaking. This, however, does not solve the problem of the right of infants to proper nurture and care. The problems inherent in group care have profound developmental implications and it is anything but clear that men of intellect and determination can provide programs that nurture half so adequately as even the uneducated, unconflicted mother. Nor does the provision for equal rights to work take into account sufficiently the right of a mother to independently provide nurture and love to her own infant, in her own home, if she so chooses. There are many women who prefer to care for their own children at home, and yet find themselves unable to do so for economic reasons. The social planner must ask, therefore, if the psycho-biological process of gestation and maternity confer special rights on mothers, namely, for optimal social support in the nurture of our young—a right that has never been realized under existing welfare programs. Planners also need to ask whether such support ought not to extend to direct assistance to the family as well as to public programs such as Day Care.

It is argued that provision of state supported Day Care could be of immediate benefit to many disadvantaged mothers who are overburdened with large families and excessive responsibilities in the absence of a husband. If Congressional concern, however, is to extend programmatic supports to the stability of disadvantaged families, then one may question whether Day Care should be the solution of choice. Day Care may free a woman to work, but it does not follow that it enhances her authority or her availability to her children, or her acceptability in marriage. Income maintenance programs, when analyzed in terms of costs and benefits, might be a more logical alternative than Day Care.

There are a number of uncontroversial findings that seem clear in the assessment of organization, administrative and staffing experience of international programs. Medical regimes have appeared inappropriate, wanting, and often damaging. The traditional educational model is equally inappropriate to the nursery and the "pedagogical" label of the Communist departments proves somewhat of a misnomer. Although these programs are increasingly administered in educational departments, these administrative units appear to be a new and continuing synthesis of professional ideas and practices that derive from pediatrics, nursing, education, and psychology, and this synthesis is far from complete.

The ineffectiveness of French supervising authority in maintaining minimal standards clearly illustrates a major administrative problem. Bureaucracies are hardly well known for their intrepid enforcement of even important regulations, and their dilatory action presents critical hazards in child-rearing programs that are less consequential elsewhere. Those who are familiar with the plight of other populations who suffer state care and supervision, such as the mentally ill, would urge that every Day Care center should have its Ombudsman.

If Day Care is to be used widely and beneficially, the "recognition" of the value of the caregiver must be extended in clear terms of status and income. Otherwise, the child in care remains the helpless victim of the lesser-employables. Physical characteristics of the Day Care centers and particular staff ratios, moreover, are as important to the staff as to the children. Empathic, sensitively tuned-in women do not continue in employment when the conditions of care leave children chronically upset or passively miserable.

In its selection of caregivers, Metera opted for the empathic-intuitive, (nominally) maternalistic woman. Pikler's benevolently paternalistic "professionals" appear as the polar opposite of a continuum on which caregiving qualities may be described. Metera may have erred in its screening policy that demanded a choice between marriage, with the prospects of biological motherhood, and the substitute of nursing care. Woman who can opt for a profession to the exclusion of marital intimacy may prove unprepared for the emotional intimacy and intuitive spontaneity that provide a communication bridge for the infant and preverbal child. Moreover, if economics dictate staff ratios of ten babies per adult, as occurs commonly elsewhere, it is doubtful that empathic staff can endure the consequent depersonalization of babies and the pain the babies will manifest. Under these circumstances, staff may seek a solution in the alternative emphasis on professionalization and technical management of routines.

The most consequential and controversial question of early Day Care is that of potential danger and damage to the very children for whom the centers are designed. From a psychoanalytic viewpoint, the dangers of psychiatric damage are inversely related to chronological age: the younger the child, the more vulnerable he is to genetically determined, involuntary, automated adaptations.

Marasmus is a rarity today in the U.S., the U.S.S.R. and other modern states. Hospitalism, a childhood debility first described and defined by Brenneman (1932), however, can usually be found in the lesser of contemporary institutions of any nation. The phenomenon merits further comment since it is too often assumed that, in the absence of gross symptomatology, children are not otherwise affected. Hospitalism is an omnibus descriptive label that has had a varied professional usage, one more recently used as a synonym for *anaclitic depression* (e.g., Hinsie and Campbell, 1970). The latter term, however, has a regressive clinical history that is relatively explicit as to age of onset. The range of developmental failures and arrests of early childhood that are subsumed under the term *hospitalism* are not well studied and psychiatric nomenclature lacks appropriate diagnostic labels for them (Sachs, 1970). Irrespective of whether the dysfunction is a developmental failure or a regressive process, some measures of retardation and depression are typical (see Joffee and Sandler, 1965). The term *hospitalism* is a professional invention, a misnomer in its semantic, guilt reducing implications. The physical structure of hospitals or residential institutions have, in fact, little bearing on the pathology. Children who live with their families within the physical structure of an institution simply do not suffer from this malady. The significant causal variable appears to be the depersonalization of human relationships that are vital to the child's healthy maturation.

Other professions have seen psychiatry as the *bête noire* of the hospital and institution since its clinicians, of necessity, challenge the anonymity and professional detachment that proves so necessary, for example, to medical staff who individually and collectively (via routines) defend their own psychological equilibria from empathic responsiveness to the pains so constantly in evidence in their patients. Depersonalization can readily take place in institutions; it is demonstrable in private homes; and it is a chronic potentiality in group care of children. The typical concatenation of variables include (1) a multiplicity of caregivers who (2) are interchangeable, a problem that becomes greater where the dispersion of caregiving interests is to groups (rather than individual babies) who are (3) so young that they make spontaneous psychological adaptations that may not be totally reversible. Maturational adaptations that may be pathological, it should be noted, are not necessarily evidenced as developmental failures, e.g., Kanner (1949) and James (1960) have described exceptionally precocious skills that reflect such severe pathological illnesses as autism.

The early years from birth through three appear developmentally as the time of maximum psychiatric risk, and failures of psycho-biological adaptation are manifest in a progression that includes marasmus, autism, childhood schizophrenia, and an extended range of poorly understood pathologies, e.g., impulse disorders, noncongenital retardation, psychopathic and schizoid personality disorders, etc. Since these severe pathologies are not directly evident in present Day Care populations of the Communist world, or in the experimental nurseries of the U.S., many academically oriented child development researchers presume that mental change is an all or nothing phenomenon. Yet one may confidently, dogmatically assert that no one knows enough about childhood developmental deficits to be completely certain of their presence or their remediation. However, clinical experience does provide dramatic evidence of the apparent irreversibility of psychological damage incurred in early and prolonged institutional care. Further, psychiatric and psychoanalytic experience constantly reaffirm the enormity of pain and effort necessary to modify even the more benign psychoneurotic disturbances. The clinician is less fearful of gross pathology that might derive from Day Care than of incipient, developmental impediments that would be evident in later character structure, such as flattened feelings (schizoid personality), a-social attitudes (psychopathic tendencies), defense against emotional intimacy (fear of marriage), etc.

Anaclitic depression is a universal phenomenon that toddlers suffer when separated from mothers for any appreciable length of time (Spitz, 1946). The Soviets have recognized the greater difficulties of accommodation after seven months of age and place many babies earlier. The adaptational, psychiatric consequences of early placement can prove extreme, though the process is subtle. Where a baby's aggressive hurt and anger in response to separation is not mitigated, and his anger is afforded little option for external expression, such recriminations may be internalized and "turned back on the self" and thus provide a base for clinical depression in later years. In time, the Communist nations will inevitably provide epidemiological evidence of the behavioral and emotional effects of group care.

In emphasizing the potential damage of early Day Care, there is a danger of implying that there is little risk for the three to five year olds. From the psychoanalytic viewpoint, the maturational vulnerabilities of that age span include (only) the risk of phobic, hysteric and obsessional neuroses and these risks certainly should be taken into account. Nevertheless, the child who is emotionally secure in his third year exudes intellectual curiosity and evidences a hunger for experience with his contemporaries and, in this instance, part-time Day Care offers delight and a momentous learning experience, i.e., so long as the option for daily attendance remains, more or less, with the child.

Child care by experts seems to have found a ready audience in both Congress and the general public. With Moynihan (1969) one may comfortably state that science is at its best as a critical tool, and that the scientist has lost his perspective when he commends modifications of such complex social-cultural-psycho-biological processes as child-rearing. Given the present state of our ignorance about psychiatric damage, massive Day Care programs appear all too much like Pandora's box. Those who would convey the idea that Day Care is unproblematic should review the programmatic, compensatory routines of Soviet texts (Tur, 1954; Schelovanova and Aksarina, 1960; Schelovanova, 1964) and the U.S. literature of child development research (e.g., Escalona and Leitch, 1952; Skeels, 1964; McV. Hunt, 1964; Bloom, Davis and Hess, 1965; A. Freud, 1965).

In specifying the apparent dangers of early Day Care, one cannot ignore that some alternatives present even greater hazards. A range of studies of existing child care methods documents that disadvantaged children are too often left unattended for hours, or are cared for by older siblings of five and six years, or by ill and senile adults. The inadequacies of child care for some of our most disadvantaged mothers quite outweigh professional reservations and concerns about Day Care. Yet the danger in recommending Day Care, however conditionally, may be likened to the medical use of morphine. The pain of the symptom may be relieved without cure, and addiction may follow.

Some clinicians and child development researchers, such as this author, are presently in an anomalous position. They have long and fervently recommended and supported the establishment of Day Care centers for special cases for the very young; yet, it now appears that a conditional recommendation may be misunderstood as a general endorsement. Professionals have previously carried partial responsibility for the oversale of institutional care, for foster care, and more recently for Head Start. Group Day Care entails far greater risks and these should be taken only where the alternatives are patently worse.

BIBLIOGRAPHY

Administration Generale de l'Assistance Publique a Paris, Department de la Seine. *Nouvelles Realisations de Protection Maternelle et Infantile*, 1956–60.
Barkoczi, I. Development of infant's manipulative activity. *Pszichologiai Tanulmanyok*, 1964, **6**, pp. 65–80.
Bloom, B. S., Davis, A. and Hess, R. *Compensatory Education for Cultural Deprivation*. New York: Holt, 1965.
Brenneman, J. The infant ward. *American Journal of Diseases of Children*, 1932, **43**, pp. 577 ff.

Bronfenbrenner, U. The making of the new Soviet man; A report of institutional upbringing in the U.S.S.R. Ithaca, New York: Cornell University, 1963a. (Mimeographed)

———. Soviet methods for character education: Some implications for research. Ithaca, New York: Cornell University, 1963b. (Mimeographed)

———. In Colloquium on maternal deprivation, II, Excerpta Medica Foundation, New York, 1964.

Centre International de L'Enfance. Paris, *Seminaire sur les Creches,* 1960.

Davidson, F. Day Care centers in Paris and its suburbs, Working Paper No. 13, World Health Organization. Joint UN/WHO Committee on the care of well children in day-care centers and institutions, Geneva, 1962.

Egeszsegugyi Miniszterium, Budapest, *Egeszsegugyi Terygyujtemenye,* EM Kosepule Hervezo Vallalat, 1957.

Escalona, S. K. and Leitch, M. *Earliest Phases of Personality Development: A Non-normative Study of Infant Behavior.* Monographs of the Society for Research in Child Development, 1952, Vol. 17 (Serial no. 54), No. 1, Evanston, Ill.: Child Development Publications.

Freud, A. *Normalcy and Pathology of Childhood, Assessment of Development,* New York: International Universities Press, 1965.

Gerson, M. The family and other socializing agents in the Kibbuts, (sic). Oranim, Israel, 1970. (Unpublished)

Hinsie, L. E. and Campbell, R. J. *Psychiatric Dictionary,* Fourth edition, New York: Oxford University Press, 1970.

Hunt, J. McV. How children develop intellectually. *Children,* May–June, 1964, **11**(3), pp. 83–91.

James, M. Premature ego development: some observations upon disturbances in the first three years of life. *International Journal of Psycho-Analysis,* 1960. **41,** pp. 288–94.

Joffee, W. G. and Sandler, J. Notes on pain, depression and individuation. *The Psychoanalytic Study of the Child,* Vol. 20, New York: International Universities Press, 1965.

Kanner, L. Problems of nosology and psychodynamics of early infantile autism. *American Journal of Orthopsychiatry,* July 1949, Vol. XIX (3).

Koltsova, N. A. Pavlov Institute of Physiology, Leningrad. Personal Communication, 1967.

Langmeier, J. New observations on psychological deprivation in institutional children in Czechoslovakia, 1965. (Unpublished)

Langmeier, J. and Matejcek, Z. *Psychical Deprivation in Childhood.* Prague: Statni Zdravotnicke Nakladetelstvi, 1963.

————. Psychological aspects of the collective care for children. *Social Science and Medicine*, UNESCO, 1970. (In press)

Laslow, M. Personal communication, 1965.

Lourie, R. S. Report from the viewpoint of child psychiatry on mission to U.S.S.R. for the President's Panel on mental retardation, 1962. (Unpublished)

Makarenko, A. S. *A Book for Parents*. Moscow: Foreign Languages Publishing House, 1954.

Marans, A. D. Personal observation, 1963, cited in Meers, D. R. and Marans, A. D. Group care of infants in other countries. In L. L. Dittman (Ed.) *Early Child Care*. New York: Atherton Press, Inc., 1968.

Marburg, H. M. Changes in the education of the Kibbutz children. Giuataim, Israel, 1970. (Unpublished)

Matejcek, Z. Personal Correspondence, 1970.

Matejcek, Z. and Langmeier, J. Die Zeitweilige Gemeinschaftserziehung im hinblick ouf Die Psychische Deprivation, *Paedagogica Europaea*, 1968.

Meers, D. R. and Marans, A. D. Group care of infants in other countries. In L. L. Dittman (Ed.) *Early Child Care*. New York: Atherton Press, Inc., 1968.

Ministerium fur Gesundheitswesen, Kinderpflegerin, *Ausbildungsunterlagen fur die sozialisticahe*, Berufssusbildung, Berlin, August, 1963a.

Ministerium fur Gesundheitswesen, Kinderpflegerin, *Rahmenlehrplane fur die Ausbildung der Werktatigen Qualifizierungsabachnitt*, A 1–A 5, Fachrichtung Kinderpflege, Berlin, September, 1963b.

————. Arbeitsordnung fur Kinderkippen, May, 1964.

Moynihan, D. P. *Maximum Feasible Misunderstanding*. New York: The Free Press, 1969.

Neubauer, P. (Ed.) *Children in Collective*. Springfield, Ill.: Charles C. Thomas, 1965.

Pikler, E. Some principles concerning supervision of creches and residential nurseries. *Nepegeszsegugy*, 1964, **46,** pp. 33–6.

————. Personal Communication, 1965.

Powell, G. F., Brasel, J. A., Raiti, S. and Blizzard, R. M. Emotional deprivation and growth retardation simulating idiopathic hypopituitarism. *The New England Journal of Medicine*, **276**(23), pp. 1279–83.

The President's Panel on Mental Retardation. Report of the Mission to the U.S.S.R., August, 1962. Washington, D.C.: U.S. Government Printing Office, 1964.

Report of the Medical Exchange Mission to the U.S.S.R. *Maternal and Child Care*. U.S. Department of Health, Education, and Welfare, Public Health Service Publication No. 954. Washington, D.C.: U.S. Government Printing Office, 1962.

Ribble, M. A. Infantile experience in relation to personality development. In J. McV. Hunt (Ed.) *Personality and the Behavior Disorders,* Vol. II. New York: Ronald Press Co., 1944.

Robinson, J. B. Day care for infants and young children in Russia. (Working paper presented at Conference on Early Child Care Reexamined, National Institute of Mental Health, Bethesda, Maryland, 1965.)

Sachs, L. J. Emotional acrescentism, *Journal of the American Academy of Child Psychiatry,* 1970, **8,** pp. 636–55.

Schelovanova, N. M. Studies in the development and physiology of the central nervous system from birth through three years of age, 1964. (Described in personal communication from A. V. Zaporozhets.)

Schelovanova N. M. and Aksarina, N. M. *The Upbringing of Young Children in Children's Establishments,* Fourth edition. Moscow: Medgiz, 1960. (Translation by the Center for Studies on Children and Youth, National Institute of Mental Health, Bethesda, Maryland.)

Schmidt-Kolmer, E. Personal Correspondence, 1970.

Schmidt-Kolmer, E. and Hecht, S. Die Entwicklung 1-bix-6-jahriger kinder in gemischten Gruppen im Vollheim. *Padagogische Forschung,* Wissenschaftliche Nachrichten des Deutschen Padagogischen Zentralinstituts, Jahragant, No. 2, 1964.

Segal, M. Theory and aims of Kibbutz education. In P. Neubauer (Ed.) *Children in Collectives.* Springfield, Ill.: Charles C. Thomas, 1965.

Silver, H. K. and Finkelstein, M. Deprivation dwarfism. *The Journal of Pediatrics,* **70**(3), pp. 317–24.

Silverman, M. The happy orphans of Metera. *Saturday Evening Post,* March 19, 1960.

Skeels, H. M. An interim brief on the NIMH-Iowa follow-up studies relative to mental retardation, dependency and maternal deprivation, 1964. (Mimeographed)

Spitz, R. Hospitalism. *The Psychoanalytic Study of the Child,* 1954, **1,** pp. 53–74.

———. Anaclitic depression. *The Psychoanalytic Study of the Child,* 1946, **2,** pp. 313–42.

Tardos, A. Effect of environmental change on infants' play activity. *Pszichologiai Tanulmanyok,* 1964, **6,** pp. 273–87.

Tur, A. F. *The Care of the Young Infant,* Leningrad: Medgiz, 1954.

Zaporozhets, A. V. Research on Child Development and Its Application in the U.S.S.R. (Address presented at Children's Hospital of Washington, Washington, D.C., 1964.)

ACKNOWLEDGMENTS

This paper derives from research that was made possible by the administrative support of Children's Hospital of the District of Columbia. Particular thanks are due both the National Institute of Mental Health and the Edgar Stern Fund for financial support (of research previously titled "The Prevention of Culturally Determined Retardation").

The observations and conclusions of this section express the views of this author, and the acknowledgments that follow are an expression of appreciation and gratitude, only. It is clear that some conclusions will be disputed by one's domestic and international colleagues. In anticipation of that probability, one may express the hope that continued clarification of scientific differences may turn argument into effective research.

The researchers and administrators who have been helpful, and often graciously accommodating to this author, and to Dr. Allen D. Marans, are many, and for reasons of space this list must remain incomplete:

Czechoslovakia: Dr. Z. Matajcek, Institute for Post Graduate Medical Education, Prague. Special acknowledgments are extended for a range of courtesies in making available present Day Care data, plus a number of research papers, some of them in English, and others in Czechoslovakian and German.

France: Dr. F. Davidson, Chief Medical Inspector of Health, Mme. Hermant, Chief of Social Service, and Dr. Clair Vesin, Creche Pediatrician, Medical-Social Service for National and Infant Protection, Paris.

German Democratic Republic: Professor Dr. E. Schmidt-Kolmer, Zentralstelle fur Hygiene des Kindes-und Jugendalters, Berlin. Special acknowledgments are extended for a range of professional courtesies in making available present and projected Day Care data, plus a wealth of literature concerning programming and staff training.

Greece: Dr. S. Doxiadis, Medical Director of the Metera Babies Center, Medical Director of the Aghia Sophia Children's Hospital, and Miss L. Alexandraki, Special Advisor on Child Care to the Greek Ministry of Social Welfare.

Hungary: Dr. E. Peter-Pikler, Medical Director, the National Methodological Institute for Infant Care and Education, and Mrs. M. Laszlow, the Hungarian Ministry of Health, Budapest. Special acknowledgments are extended for making available a number of English translators of staff research publications and architectural designs of contemporary child care centers.

Israel: M. Segal, the Seminar Hakibutzim Oranim. Special acknowledgments are extended for sharing and translating the curriculum for Metapelet Training.

U.S.S.R.: Professor H. M. Aksarina, Moscow Institute for Post Graduate Training; Professor A. V. Zaphorozhets, Institute for the Study of Pre-School Children; and Dr. D. A. Orloff, Director, Foreign Relations Department, U.S.S.R. Minister of Health, Moscow; Dr. M. V. Ivanova, Director of the Children's Division, City Health Department; Professor N. A. Koltsova, Chief of Laboratory of Higher Nervous Activity of Children, Pavlov Institute of Physiology, Leningrad; and Dr. V. V. Kanep, Ministry of Public Health, Latvian S.S.R., Reiga. Indebtedness to other Soviet dignitaries and researchers needs expression but magnetic tape records have proved undecipherable.

U.S.A.: Verne G. Robinson, Coordinator, U.S. Soviet Health Exchange, Office of International Health, U.S. Department of Health, Education, and Welfare, Public Health Service, Washington, D.C. Particular thanks are due Dr. Robinson for his counsel of patience and his continuing support in the extended negotiations that led to the Soviet research tour. Dr. Allen D. Marans, Pediatrician, Child Psychiatrist, Psychoanalyst, former research colleague and co-author, benevolent critic and friend, who was instrumental in introducing this author to child development research. Particular indebtedness now derives from Dr. Maran's review and helpful criticism of this paper.

part III
the effects
of poverty

the effects
of poverty

HELEN L. BEE

A few years ago this introductory chapter would have been very easy to write, not because we then had a clearer understanding of the mechanisms by which poverty had the effects it did, but because there was some agreement at least about what those effects were. Clearly, children from poverty circumstances did poorly in school, and clearly such children had lower scores on standard measures of intelligence. Further, there was quite good agreement that the poor school performance and lowered IQ scores were the result of generally "deficient" cognitive development, particularly in the areas of verbal skills, concept development, and some kinds of perceptual skills. (See, for example, Klaus and Gray, 1968). Thus the assumption was not that poor school performance resulted because the child from a poverty environment was being asked to cope with a middle-class school; rather the difficulty was seen as being more fundamental than that, as a basic deficit in learning skills. Overall, although there was no good agreement on precisely what it was about the poverty environment that produced such "deficits," there was agreement at least that the child from poverty had low IQ, poor language, poor conceptual abilities, poor ability to focus attention, and low probability of success in school.

There are still many who agree with this description, but it is far from unanimous, as you will see. Low IQ and poor school performance are not disputed by anyone, to my knowledge, although these facts are interpreted very differently by some. The other features of the "deficit" description have been disputed by many. Most notably writers such as Labov (1970) and Baratz (1969) have disputed the presumed language deficit, and Ginsburg (1972) has disputed the presumed deficit in general conceptual abilities.

Because of the fundamental disagreement about the characteristics of children reared in poverty environments, it is not possible in this section to focus only on explanations of the effects of poverty. Instead, we must first ask the prior question: What *are* the effects of poverty? Or, more precisely, what are the opposing views of the effects of poverty, and what is the evidence for each view? Then we can turn to some of the various theories that have been offered to explain why poverty has the effects it does.

So that we know who we are talking about, let's begin with a brief description of the nature of the population of the poor in the United States.

WHO ARE THE POOR CHILDREN?

According to data presented to the 1970 White House Conference on Children and Youth, roughly 10 million children in the United States were being raised in conditions that could be described as poverty-stricken. In other words, approximately 14 percent of all American children under age 18 were living in families whose yearly income was less than $3000. The common assumption seems to be that most poverty-stricken families are nonwhite. Not true. Of the 10 million poor children, 6 million were white, 4 million were nonwhite. But a higher *percentage* of the nonwhite are poor: About 40 percent of all nonwhite children in 1969 were in families with earnings below the poverty line, and only about 10 percent of the white children were in poor families. Thus more of the poor are white, but more of the non-white are poor. Another common misconception is that the vast majority of the poor live in cities. Again, not quite true. In 1969 about two-fifths were in rural areas, and about three-fifths were in urban environments. Bear these facts in mind as we discuss the characteristics of the poor child. We are not just talking about urban, ghetto-reared minority group children. We are also talking about rural kids, suburban kids, white kids in the Appalachian Mountains, Indians on reservations, and many other groups.

CHARACTERISTICS
OF POOR CHILDREN

THE TRADITIONAL EVIDENCE

General intellectual ability. Virtually every study ever done that included IQ or other standard intellectual measures of middle-class and poor children shows middle-class children with significantly higher average IQ (Lesser, Fifer, and Clark, 1965; Kennedy, Van de Reit, and White, 1963; Whiteman and Deutsch, 1968). Furthermore, there is evidence from several studies that these same differences hold *within* ethnic groups. That is, the overall social-class difference is not just the result of some kind of test bias against blacks or other minority groups who make up a large portion of the poor; within each minority group the middle-class children score higher than do the poor children. For example, Kennedy, Van de Reit, and White (1963), in a study of black children selected from all elementary school age children in five Southern states, found that the average IQ of the middle-class black children was 105 (above average), and the mean IQ of the poverty-level black children was 79 (considerably below average). In a more impressive study, Lesser and his associates (Lesser et al., 1965) tested groups of middle-class and poor first-grade children from Chinese, Jewish, black, and Puerto Rican families in New York City. The test used was one that yielded separate scores for verbal, reasoning, numerical, and spatial abilities. Their results are clear: On every scale, for every ethnic group, there was a difference in favor of the middle-class children of the ethnic group. That is, middle-class Chinese children were higher on verbal, higher on reasoning, higher on numerical and higher on spatial abilities than were lower-class Chinese, and the same was true of blacks, Puerto Ricans, and Jews.

There is also evidence from a number of sources that prolonged living under conditions of poverty results in a steady *lowering* of the IQ score. In a large number of studies done in the Appalachian Mountain region during the 1930s and 1940s, the consistent finding was that the older children in a community had lower IQs than did the younger children in the same community. (This evidence is reviewed in Jones, 1954.) Similar findings were obtained more recently by Kennedy et al. (1963) in their study of black children in the South. They found that the 5 years olds in their sample had a mean IQ of 86, whereas the 13 year olds had a mean IQ of 65.

Overall, then, there is strong evidence that on *standard measures* such as an IQ test, poverty-level children score lower. It is important to note, however, that in studies in which children below approximately two years of age have been examined, social-class differences in IQ have *not* been found. Bayley (1965), in a monumental study including 1400 children from all racial and economic backgrounds, found no social-class or racial differences on any of the Infant Scales up to 15 months of age—except that black children were somewhat more advanced in motor development. Mark Golden, Beverly Birns, and Abigail Moss in the paper included in this section, report similar findings: Their all-black samples from middle-class and poverty environments showed no differences on "infant IQ" tests or in performance on Piaget-style tests up to age two. By the time the children were three, however, there were significant social-class differences. Middle-class black children at age three had an average IQ of approximately 112, but the poorest children in the sample had an average IQ of only 93.5.

School performance.   Again there is good agreement: Poor children do not do as well in school. One study involving children in western Pennsylvania, for example (Hill and Giammateo, 1963), showed that by grade three, children from middle-class families, compared to children from poor families, were 8 months ahead in vocabulary, 9 months ahead in reading comprehension, 6 months ahead in arithmetic skills, and 11 months ahead in problem solving. The same sort of findings are reported in Coleman's nationwide study of school performance (Coleman, 1966).

Verbal ability.   Measures of verbal ability have been almost exclusively measures of vocabulary, and on such measures poor children appear to be clearly lower (Stodolsky, 1965; Templin, 1957). John and Goldstein (1964), in an effort to discover just what kinds of words the poverty child is less likely to know, analyzed the performance of urban ghetto children and middle-class children on a vocabulary test and found that vocabulary differences did not apply just to nouns with which the ghetto child might reasonably be unfamiliar (such words as "leaf," "bush," or "kangaroo"). Poor children did not know such words, but neither did they know action words such as "digging," "tying," "pouring," and "building"—words with which one might expect them to be familiar.

Lesser et al. (1965), in their study of ethnic differences in cognitive functioning, demonstrated that the vocabulary differences hold up even when the child is tested in his native language or dialect, and when all words that show an initial social-class bias are eliminated from the test. That is, if all the words that the middle-class child is more likely to know merely because he is middle class (like "sonata") and all the words that the poor child is more likely to know because he is from a poor environment (such as, perhaps, "welfare" or "stickball") are eliminated, there is still a difference between the two groups. What this seems to mean is that the poor child appears simply to know fewer of the words to which both groups have access.

Problem solving.   A number of studies indicate that the problem-solving strategies used by poor children differ qualitatively from the strategies used by middle-class children, and further, that the middle-class strategies are the developmentally more mature form. For example, if children are given a group of objects or pictures and asked to pick out "those that go together," and to say why they go together, there are a number of possible strategies. The child may select a grouping and give reasons that are superordinate, that is, involve his using a category that deals with the objects as wholes, such as "they are all fruit, or they are animals." A second kind of grouping is based on the objects' relationships, such as "the boy and the dog play together." A third alternative is an analytic grouping, based on some similar parts of the objects, such as "these two have arms." The available data indicate that with increasing age, there is an increase in analytic responses and a large increase in superordinate groupings, along with a decrease in relational groupings (Kagan, Rosman, Day, Albert, and Phillips, 1964). But this age trend seems to take place more slowly in poor children than in middle-class children (Sigel, Anderson, and Shapiro, 1966; Sigel and McBane, 1967).

Cognitive impulsivity.   Children differ from one another in problem-solving situations in their tendency to pause and "reflect" on the answer or to choose an answer impulsively. Kagan and his associates have devised a number of tests of this dimension (Kagan et al., 1964), and have some evidence that the tendency to be reflective or impulsive is a relatively enduring individual characteristic. Further, they have demonstrated that among first graders, children who are relatively more reflective learn to read more readily than do more impulsive children (Kagan, 1965). In research of my own several years ago (Bee, Nyman, Pytkowicz, Sarason, and Van Egeren, 1968) involving poor and middle-class four-year-old children, we found that the poor children were more likely to be impulsive, and the middle-class children were more likely to be reflective. This piece of data provides the missing link in this particular chain, suggesting that the impulsive style may be more common among poverty-level children; if Kagan's findings are generally correct, the impulsiveness may in turn affect the poor child's ability to learn to read during the early school years.

Emotional and social characteristics.   As you have no doubt gathered from all the detail I've already given, much of the research attention has been given to the question of differences in the cognitive development of poor and middle-class children. We have much less information about any differences in personality characteristics, and the data that we do have are in less agreement. The clearest finding is that children from poverty environments are less likely to have a good opinion of themselves and their skills, and that this becomes more and more true the more "deprived" the environment. For example, Whiteman and Deutsch (1968) rated the home situation of each child in a group of first- and fifth-grade ghetto children on a "deprivation index," on which "more deprived" was scored when the housing was dilapidated, the parents had low educational aspirations for the child, there were many children in the home, there was no conversation at the dinner table, there were few "cultural experiences" outside the home, and the child had not attended kindergarten. Whiteman and Deutsch found that many more of the children from the most deprived home situations had a very poor self-concept. Since children with a poor self-concept also do poorly on the various tests of cognitive functioning, one can't tell whether they think poorly of themselves because they do poorly or the reverse, but it's likely that the two interact to create a vicious circle: The child thinks of himself as incompetent; this gives him a "set" to fail, which he then does, which in turn reinforces his belief that he's not capable.

There are other less well replicated findings about personality or social differences between poor and middle-class children: (a) Poor children are more likely to see responsibility for their actions as lying outside themselves, rather than seeing themselves as responsible for their own behavior (Battle and Rotter, 1963). (b) Lower-class children tend to be lower in "achievement motivation," that is, the desire to compete successfully with a standard of excellence (Rosen, 1956). (c) Poor children seem to be somewhat more sensitive to both disapproval and approval. That is, in at least one study in which approval or disapproval was given for performance of a simple task, Rosenhan (1966) found that the poverty children's performance declined more when they were given disapproval and improved more when they were given approval than did the performance of the middle-class children. (d) Poor children learn experimental tasks more rapidly when they are working for material rewards (such as candy) than when they are working for nonmaterial rewards (such as knowledge of results). (Terrel, Durkin, and Wiesley, 1959; Zigler and deLabry, 1962).

Health differences. The subject of health differences is well covered in the excellent paper by Herbert G. Birch included in the selections. It is quite clear that the poorer the family is, the poorer is the health status of the child and the mother. In particular, one notes that poverty conditions are accompanied by a substantial increase in complications surrounding pregnancy and birth and by poorer diet (Knobloch and Pasamanick, 1963).

THE COUNTERARGUMENT AND COUNTER EVIDENCE

It might appear that the weight of the evidence I've already given leads one inevitably to the conclusion that the poor child is in fact slowed down in cognitive development, that he does indeed have some specific "deficits" that will affect his ability to perform in school or to learn in other situations. But by no means does everyone agree that the evidence requires such a conclusion. In fact, one can argue that the poor child is basically no different from his middle-class peer in most important characteristics. Among the several spokesmen for this position, the most articulate is Herbert Ginsburg, whose book *The Myth of the Deprived Child* is well argued and carefully documented. An excerpt from this book has been included in the selections, so you can read for yourselves some of what he says. I will try here only to summarize his positions very briefly and to suggest the kind of evidence that can be offered to support his argument.

Ginsburg grants that children from poverty environments score lower on standard tests and that they do badly in school, but he does not take this as evidence that they are fundamentally less skilled or less competent. Instead, he takes it as evidence that the tests have not really measured the poor child's competence. The essence of his position is that there is a fundamental difference between competence and performance. (See Glick, 1968, for an extensive discussion of this distinction.)

The tests measure performance, and the schools measure performance; they do not necessarily tap the child's fundamental ability. Most people who have worked with poor children have looked at the vast amount of evidence showing that poverty-level children perform poorly and have concluded that the poor performance results from less competence. Ginsburg starts from the other end. He assumes, essentially, that all children are basically equal in competence, that they all begin life with the same kinds of abilities to deal with their world, and that they proceed to do so, developing in the process a fixed sequence of kinds of logical abilities. Following Piaget, he emphasizes that the active, exploring child utilizes his particular environment to make cognitive progress, and that the specific characteristics of the environment do not matter very much, so long as there is sufficient variety of experience to provide the needed input. Given this overall assumption about the nature of cognitive development, it obviously follows that any differences we observe between the poor child and the middle-class child are merely surface differences; they do not reflect what Ginsburg assumes to be fundamental equality of competence. Why, then, doesn't the poor child perform as well? Presumably for several reasons. First, the tests have been designed to test middle-class children and may demand specific information that is more readily available to them. Second, and more importantly, with most measures of performance, it is assumed that the child is motivated to do his best and that he understands the test is in fact something to be taken seriously. If poor children are less motivated to perform in standard assessment situations or if they do not understand the demands of the situation, they may not perform as well. Thus one could have low performance without low competence.

There is a good deal of support for Ginsburg's general position. Let's look at some of the evidence.

Motivation. We do know that the child's motivation and his attitude about standard testing situations affect his test scores. An often-cited study by Zigler and Butterfield (1968) demonstrates this clearly. They tested preschool age children under normal, standard IQ-testing conditions, and then tested them again two weeks later, with half the children again being tested under standard conditions and the other half being tested under what was called optimizing conditions. The optimizing conditions were designed to maintain a high positive motivation in the child, and included such things as giving a great deal of encouragement to the child, allowing more time for the child to answer, and rearranging the order in which the items were presented so that easy items were interspersed with the hard ones, thus giving the child repeated successes. Under these conditions the poor children's performance on the IQ test showed an increase of about 10 points, compared to an increase of about five points for the children who were tested the second time with the standard procedure. What this suggests is that we may consistently underestimate the poor child's performance ability, since our standard testing conditions involve assumptions about the child's motivation and perseverance that simply may not hold for the poor child.

Language. You probably noticed in the presentation of the traditional data on language that the only language measure mentioned was vocabulary. There's a very good reason: Other measures of language, such as measures of sentence complexity or rate of development of grammar, do not show social-class differences. (There are several good reviews of this research. See Dale, 1972, or Ginsburg, 1972.) One can suggest from this that although the specific experiential part of language, namely the vocabulary, does differ as a function of social class, the *logical* part, namely the grammar, does not. Or, put another way, one can perhaps argue that grammatical skills reflect competence more directly than do vocabulary skills, and since poor children apparently do not differ from middle-class children in grammar development, this is evidence that their developing logical competencies are equivalent.

Piagetian tests.   If the preceding argument holds, then the closer we can get to measuring important competencies in other areas, the less difference we ought to find between the poor child and the middle-class child. Ginsburg presents evidence in support of this contention, citing studies that use tests based on Piaget's theory. The research he reviews seems to show fairly clearly that when Piagetian measures are used, the *sequence* of development is the same for children from widely divergent cultures. Since Ginsburg's analysis of this evidence is included in the selection from his book, I won't go into his arguments further here.

Lack of difference on infant tests.   As I mentioned earlier, the consistent finding is that there are no measured differences between the poor and the middle-class child until about age two and a half or three. Prior to that time, the two groups seem to be equivalent in performance. There are several possible interpretations of this finding, but one obvious one is that the tests of performance in the infant and very young child are primarily nonverbal, whereas the tests for older children, beginning at about age two and a half or three, are heavily verbal. If the poor child often appears to be less competent because he has a smaller vocabulary, then one might expect to find performance differences starting at the point at which language becomes dominant in the testing procedures.

THE THIRD ALTERNATIVE: GENETIC DIFFERENCES

A word, however brief, must be said about a third possible alternative, namely that children from poverty environments show poor performance on various kinds of tests and in school because they are simply genetically less bright. Arthur Jensen (1969), in his highly controversial article, has suggested something like this. As comment, let me make only three points.

First, no one that I know of disputes the assertion that a good portion of what is measured with a standard IQ test is genetically determined. Jensen suggests that about 80 percent of the variance is accounted for by heredity; Jencks (1972) gives a more conservative estimate of 45 percent, but virtually everyone agrees that the contribution is substantial.

Second, it is not legitimate to go from statements about heritability of IQ of individuals to statements about groups or group differences. The tendency is to say, "Well if IQ is inherited that much, inheritance must explain the difference between the poor and the affluent or between blacks and whites." But the argument *simply does not follow*. It is entirely possible for IQ to have as high a degree of heritability as Jensen suggests and still have differences between *groups* that are entirely the result of environment.[1]

Third, the available evidence gives us every reason to suppose that the observed social-class (and/or racial) differences in observed test performance *are* a product of environment or test motivation or test construction bias and not heredity. Martin Deutsch, in replying to Jensen's suggestions about genetically based racial differences in IQ, makes this point very well and his argument is equally good for the differences between social-class groups.

> He [Jensen] explicitly states that the median IQ difference between Negro and White samples is 15 to 20 points. If we add the 8 or 10 points attributable to the test situation, the few points which Jensen concedes can be gained in compensatory education, and the additional 5 points which he is willing to attribute to poor environments, we find that all statistically significant differences have been obliterated. Jensen thereby leaves himself with no argument [Deutsch, 1969, p. 77].

To be sure, we cannot logically rule out the possibility that some of the differences in performance that we observe may be due to heredity, but since the demonstrable environmental influences appear to account for virtually all the variance, there is little reason to emphasize a genetic explanation.

---

[1]Because this is a difficult concept to grasp, let me give two examples. In small villages in the rural areas of Mexico, the people are quite a bit shorter than the people in the larger cities, such as Mexico City. Height, as you probably know, is a highly heritable trait; it is influenced by environment, but a very heavy dose of heredity is involved in one's height. This is true within the Mexican villages—where the tallest children are born to the tallest parents—and within the city. So there is high heritability within each group. But what about the difference between the groups? Is that difference the result of hereditary differences between the village and city people? No. It is mostly the result of diet. When the diet of the village people is improved, they too grow as tall as the city people. So you have a situation in which there is high heritability within each group, but the difference between the two groups is largely, if not totally, environmental.

Another delightful example of the same thing was given by Ken Kaye in his review of Eysenck's book, *The IQ Argument*. Kaye says:

> Imagine, for example, that we test all white Americans, but just before the test we give away some of the answers to everyone whose name begins with a letter from A to M. Suppose we give away just enough answers so that each person in the A–M group gets a score 15 points higher than he would have otherwise. This raises their average score 15 points above that of the N–Z group. The heritability will still be just as high within each group—because we will have done nothing to increase the variance within either group—but the 15 point difference between the two groups will have nothing to do with heritability [Kaye, 1972].

SYNTHESIS

Excluding the genetic argument for now, how do we put the first two alternative positions together? There's good evidence on each side, and it's obviously impossible to choose one or the other as completely "true." In fact, I suspect we will find, as is often the case in such debates, that the truth lies somewhere in the middle. It is my own belief that there are some fundamental differences in competencies, but that the degree of difference may be exaggerated by our too-frequent use of such tests as the IQ. Let me give some support for this notion. First, Lesser et al. (1965), in one of the best studies around, found performance differences even when optimizing test conditions were used. They not only tested the child in his native language; they also used as many testing sessions as were necessary, did not start the testing until the child was thoroughly familiar with the testing situation and the materials, set no time limits on the tests, and rewrote the tests themselves to include only items with which all groups might reasonably be familiar. Even under these unusually careful methodological conditions, differences between poor and middle-class children were obtained. They also made an effort to measure the child's motivation and his responsiveness to the tester, and found that these factors could not account for the social-class differences they found. To be sure, these are still measures of perhaps "surface performance," but the differences do not go away when one is careful and fair about the measurement procedures and attempts to equalize motivational factors.

Second, in some recent studies of social-class differences on Piagetian measures, differences have been found that are of the same magnitude as measures on other sorts of tests. Gil Gaudia's paper, included in the selections, is a good example of such a study. (See also Wei, Lavatelli, and Jones, 1971; Overton, Wagner, and Dolinsky, 1971.) The recent evidence on this question persuades me that although the sequence of development may be the same for groups from different cultural backgrounds, the rate of development through that sequence is not, and that in fact poor children in this country appear to be moving more slowly through the sequences Piaget has described. What this suggests, if true, is that although the poor child may have the same potential competencies, he may not have the same actual competencies as does the more affluent child at a given moment in time.

Third, there are several other possible interpretations of the fact that one does not find differences between poor and middle-class children until about age two and a half. For example, one might assume that the effects of the poverty environment simply take time to accumulate to the point where they are measured by traditional tests. Alternatively, one could argue that the sensorimotor and perceptual skills measured in infants' tests are not affected adversely by the characteristics of a poverty environment, but that the "preoperational" skills (to borrow Piaget's term), which become dominant at about age two and a half, are affected adversely. Piaget has emphasized the fact that not until about age two does the child have internal representation of objects and events; until that age he does not have what most of us would call thought. Perhaps it is only at this stage that the effects of the poverty environment come into play. (In fact, I suspect that the effects of poverty begin immediately at birth, if not before, but that we just don't pick up the effects until later.)

Fourth, we cannot ignore the differences in health described in Birch's paper. Not only do we know that poor children are more likely to have experienced trauma in utero and during birth, but we know that they are more likely to have a poor diet. And there is now quite good evidence that poor diet is associated with cognitive deficits. Most of the research justifying this conclusion has been done with animals (see Scrimshaw, 1969, or Birch, 1972, for a review), but there is a recent accumulation of evidence indicating that the same thing holds for children (Brockman and Ricciuti, 1971; Chase and Martin, 1970). In particular, protein-calorie malnutrition appears to have a fairly direct effect on intellectual development, resulting in retardation of development and perhaps a lower final level of development.

For all of these reasons, I think it is reasonable to assume that there is some difference in level of competence, as well as in performance, between the poor and the more advantaged child. But I also think that we must be careful not to exaggerate that difference by emphasizing too heavily such measures as vocabulary. To be sure, differences in vocabulary are going to have implications for the child in school, where he is likely to be confronted with a middle-class teacher using a middle-class vocabulary, but such vocabulary differences should not be taken as irrefutable evidence that the child is incompetent or incapable of learning. On the contrary, as Ginsburg has so cogently argued, all children are capable of learning.

EXPLANATIONS OF THE EFFECTS OF POVERTY

Obviously, if you have taken the position that poverty-level children are essentially the same as nonpoverty-level children, there is nothing further to explain. But if you have taken the position, as I have and as others have, that some kinds of deficits or a slowing down of cognitive development is associated with poverty circumstances, it becomes important to try to specify what it is about the typical poverty environment that has this effect. Clearly, to talk about a "poverty environment" as having "caused" intellectual retardation is a gross oversimplification. Poverty environments are not all alike, and the children who come out of them are not all alike. What we need are some explanations that suggest much more precisely what kinds of early environmental experiences may produce the observed effects.[2]

Essentially, three varieties of explanation have been offered, all focusing on different aspects of the environment.

HEALTH DIFFERENCES AS CAUSE

In recent years increasing attention has been paid to health factors as possible causes of the observed cognitive deficits in children from poverty environments. As research on animals accumulated showing clearly that dietary deficiency produced slower development and slower learning in offspring, there was increasing concern that the same relationship might hold with children. The evidence available certaintly indicates that it does, at least for fairly extreme forms of malnutrition. (See Birch's 1972 paper for a more detailed analysis of this question than the one he gives in the paper included in the selections.) Two important questions remain: (1) How widespread is severe malnutrition in this country? In the paper included in this section, Birch reviews some of the evidence relating to this question and concludes that moderate forms of malnutrition are quite common among the poor and particularly among minority groups. (See also Chase, Kumar, Dodds, Sauberlich, Hunter, Burton, and Spalding, 1971; Christakis, Miridjianian, Nath, Khurana, Cowell, Archer, Frank, Ziffer, Baker, and James, 1968; Owen and Kram, 1969). In general, the lower the income of the family, the greater the likelihood of poor nutrition, particularly inadequate iron intake—which leads to iron deficiency anemia—and inadequate total caloric intake. Most of the malnutrition noted in the studies on this question is moderate to mild; it is not severe enough to require hospitalization of the child, which leads to the second question. (2) What is the effect of more moderate levels of malnutrition? Are they the same, only milder, as the effects of severe malnutrition? We do not have the research evidence to answer this at the moment, although what evidence there is suggests that there are measurable negative consequences of more moderate malnutrition. For example, in his 1972 review Birch describes a recent study by Hertzig, Tizard, Birch, and Richardson, in which a group of children who were hospitalized for severe malnutrition were compared, on a variety of tests of cognitive development, to a sibling and

---

[2]Incidentally, you will find in the discussion to follow that virtually all work has been done to explain the origin of cognitive deficits in poverty-level children; no equivalent work that I know of has dealt with the personality or social variables described earlier.

to a group of classmates. Test results showed that the hospitalized children, presumably those with the most severe malnutrition, showed the lowest scores, but their siblings were also lower than the classmates. If one assumes that the siblings suffer from some more moderate forms of malnutrition, the results make sense; the less severely malnourished sibling does better, but still shows some intellectual retardation compared to classmates from similar backgrounds who were not apparently malnourished. Obviously, such research is only the first step; there is a great deal more work to be done in this area. But the current data indicate, to me at least, that one of the major sources of intellectual deficits among poor children may well be their diet. Evidence from work with animals suggests that malnutrition, if it occurs early in the infant's life, has a permanent debilitating effect. If that is true for humans—and it appears to be—this is an area that should be given major attention, both in research and in public policy.

INSUFFICIENT ENVIRONMENTAL STIMULATION AS CAUSE

A second view of the causal factors in poverty environments focuses primarily on the inanimate environment surrounding the child. What kind of toys are available? What opportunities for play? We know from research on institutionalized infants that one of the necessary ingredients for normal development is the opportunity to move around, to play with objects, to explore the environment. (See, for example, Dennis, 1960.) It seems logical to extrapolate from the institutional environment to the poverty environment, and look to the characteristics of the stimulation available to the infant as a primary cause. The "deprivation index" that Whiteman and Deutsch developed in the study discussed earlier is an example of one effort to specify some kinds of stimulation variables more precisely, although they also include some interpersonal variables in their index. In support of the notion that the amount or variety of stimulation may make a difference, they report that children who are high on the deprivation index show a deterioration in school performance between grades one and five, and children from the same neighborhood who are not high on the deprivation index do not show this decline in performance over time.

Further, there is evidence showing that poverty homes and middle-class homes differ on some dimensions of amount and variety of stimulation. Tulkin (1970), for example, examined ten-month-old infants from working-class and professional families. The working-class infants in his sample had fewer objects to play with and spent less time in free exploration without barriers than middle-class infants. Middle-class mothers more often gave their infants objects to play with, and the infants played more often.

Finally, there is very recent evidence (Yarrow, Rubenstein, Pederson, and Jankowski, 1972) that differences in the variety, complexity, and "responsiveness" of the inanimate environment surrounding the baby predicts the infants development of various early cognitive and motivational skills. Yarrow and his associates, studying five-month-old infants in their homes, differentiated carefully between inanimate stimulation (such as toys and objects surrounding the child) and animate stimulation (such as the interactions with the mother). They found that the complexity and variety of inanimate stimulation was related to the infants' exploratory behavior and to their goal-directed behaviors. That is, infants who were surrounded with a wider variety of objects and toys and with objects that were more complex and more "responsive" (i.e., objects that changed as a result of the infant's action) showed more exploratory behavior when presented with novel objects and more persistence in trying to reach goals.

Although the Yarrow et al. research did not include any poverty-level infants, it highlights the fact that aspects of the inanimate environment may indeed be crucial in some areas of cognitive development.

STYLE OF SOCIAL INTERACTION AS CAUSE

Another way to look at the environment is to emphasize the interpersonal interactions between the infant and his or her caretakers as the primary origin of the observed deficits in the poverty child.

A number of sources provide good evidence indicating that middle-class mothers and poverty-level mothers differ in the amount they talk to their children, starting when the child is a tiny infant. Kilbride, Johnson, and Streissguth (1971) found such differences in mothers of two-week-old infants; Tulkin (1970) found the same thing in mothers of ten-month-old infants. There is similarly consistent evidence that mothers from poverty environments are more critical of their children; they tell the child more often when he has done something wrong, and praise him less often when he has done something right (Bee, Van Egeren, Streissguth, Nyman, and Leckie, 1969; Streissguth and Bee, 1972; Hess and Shipman, 1965, 1967). So we know there are differences in interpersonal interaction patterns. But do we know whether these differences are related to the child's cognitive development? There are several lines of evidence here.

Hess's work on this problem is the best known. He has called attention in particular to the "mother's strategies for orienting the child toward selected cues in the environment, the types of regulatory or control techniques she uses, and her patterning of stimuli to organize information for the child" (Hess, 1970, p. 515). Does the mother emphasize that the child should do something "because I say so" (that is, because it is a rule), or does she emphasize that the child should do something because if he doesn't someone's feelings will be hurt, or because the consequences of the action will be beneficial to the child, or because of some other "rational" or "social-emotional" reason? Hess and Shipman (1967) have reported that mothers from poverty environments are much more likely to resort to appeals to status or rules; middle-class mothers more often use the rational or social-emotional approach. Further, Hess and his associates have found that these differences in maternal style not only predicted the child's concurrent cognitive functioning, with status and rule orientations on the part of the mother being associated with poorer intellectual performance in the child, but that they also predicted the child's later performance in school (Hess, Shipman, Brophy, and Bear, 1969).

A second piece of evidence comes from the Yarrow et al. study (1972). They found that the *animate* stimulation (primarily stimulation from the caretaker) was related to the child's general mental development and to his language development. That is, mothers who provided a greater variety and a greater amount of stimulation to their infants (talking, holding, etc.) had infants who scored higher on the standard infant scales and who showed more vocalization in test situations. The same highly stimulated infants also showed greater development of goal-directed behavior. A similar finding was apparent in the case of what they called "positive affect," a measure of the mother's level of affectionate demonstrativeness. The more demonstrative mothers had infants who were higher on overall developmental scales, were more socially responsive, and talked more.

Obviously, we are a long way from being able to specify the precise characteristics of any environment that promote or impede normal intellectual development. It is clear however, that some aspects of both the animate and inanimate early environment do appear to be important, and that these aspects differ from poor to nonpoor families. What is needed now is a greater number of studies like Yarrow et al.'s, in which the characteristics of the environment are carefully specified and measured, and the child's competence is assessed in a variety of ways.

QUESTIONS FOR DISCUSSION AND DEBATE

1. Given all that you have read, what do you think is the validity of a "deficit" description of the poverty child? Are you persuaded by Ginsburg's argument? If so, why? If not, why not?
2. How would each of the explanations discussed in the last section affect public policy? What sorts of federal or local program would be appropriate, given the assumptions in each case?

ADDITIONAL REFERENCES USEFUL AS PREPARATION FOR DEBATE OR DISCUSSION

Deutsch, M. (Ed.) *The disadvantaged child*. New York: Basic Books, 1967.
Another reasonably good collection of papers.
Frost, J. L., and Hawkes, G. R. (Eds.) *The disadvantaged child: Issues and innovations*. Boston: Houghton Mifflin, 1966.
A collection of papers on the disadvantaged, many of them worth looking at.
Ginsburg, H. *The myth of the deprived child*. Englewood Cliffs, N.J.: Prentice-Hall, 1972.
The whole book should be read by anyone proposing to debate on that side of the issue.
Lesser, G. S., Fifer, G., and Clark, D. H. Mental abilities of children from different social-class and cultural groups. *Monographs of the Society for Research in Child Development*, 1965, **30**(4, Whole No. 102).
I've mentioned this study frequently. It should be read in its entirety by anyone planning to participate in a debate.
Riessman, F. The overlooked positives of disadvantaged groups. *Journal of Negro Education*, Summer 1964, 225–231.
An argument in favor of the notion that there are many things the poor do better than the middle class.
Scrimshaw, N. Early malnutrition and CNS function. *Merrill-Palmer Quarterly*, 1969, **15**, 375–388.
A clear and readable presentation of much of the animal research on the effects of malnutrition. A good supplement to the material in Birch's paper.

REFERENCES

Baratz, J. C. A bi-dialectal task for determining language proficiency in economically disadvantaged Negro children. *Child Development*, 1969, **40**, 889–901.
Battle, E. S., and Rotter, J. E. Children's feeling of personal control as related to social class and ethnic groups. *Journal of Personality*, 1963, **31**, 482–490.
Bayley, N. Comparisons of mental and motor test scores for ages 1–15 months by sex, birth order, race, and geographical location, and education of parents. *Child Development*, 1965, **36**, 379–411.
Bee, H. L., Nyman, B. A., Pytkowicz, A. R., Sarason, I. G., and Van Egeren, L. *A Study of cognitive and motivational variables in lower and middle class preschool children: An approach to the evaluation*

of the impact of Head Start. Vol. 1. University of Washington Social Change Evaluation Project, Contract 1375, Office of Economic Opportunity, 1968.

Bee, H. L., Van Egeren, L. F., Streissguth, A. P., Nyman, B. A., and Leckie, M. S. Social class differences in maternal teaching strategies and speech patterns. *Developmental Psychology,* 1969, **1,** 726–734.

Birch, H. G. Malnutrition, learning and intelligence. *American Journal of Public Health,* 1972, **62,** 773–784.

Brockman, L. M., and Ricciuti, H. N. Severe protein-calorie malnutrition and cognitive development in infancy and early childhood. *Developmental Psychology,* 1971, **4,** 312–319.

Chase, H. P., Kumar, V., Dodds, J. M., Sauberlich, H. E., Hunter, R. M., Burton R. S., and Spalding, V. Nutritional status of preschool Mexican-American migrant farm children. *American Journal of Diseases of Children,* 1971, **122,** 316–324.

Chase, H. P., and Martin, H. P. Undernutrition and child development. *New England Journal of Medicine,* 1970, **282,** 933–939.

Christakis, G., Miridjanian, A., Nath, L., Khurana, H. S., Cowell, C., Archer, M., Frank, O., Ziffer, H., Baker, H., and James, C. A nutritional epidemiologic investigation of 642 New York City children. *American Journal of Clinical Nutrition,* 1968, **21,** 107–126.

Coleman, J. S. *Equality of educational opportunity.* Washington, D.C.: United States Government Printing Office, 1966.

Dale, P. S. *Language development: Structure and Function.* Hinsdale, Ill.: Dryden Press, 1972.

Dennis, W. Causes of retardation among institutional children: Iran. *Journal of Genetic Psychology,* 1960, **96,** 47–59.

Deutsch, M. Happenings on the way back to the forum: Social science, IQ, and race differences revisited. *Harvard Educational Review,* 1969, **39,** 523–557.

Ginsburg, H. *The myth of the deprived child.* Englewood Cliffs, N.J.: Prentice-Hall, 1972.

Glick, J. Some problems in the evaluation of pre-school intervention programs. In R. Hess and R. Bear (Eds.), *Early education.* Chicago: Aldine, 1968.

Golden, M., Birns, B., Bridger, W., and Moss, A. Social-class differentiation in cognitive development among black preschool children. *Child Development,* 1971, **42,** 37–45.

Hess, R. D. Social class and ethnic influences on socialization. In P. H. Mussen (Ed.), *Carmichael's manual of child psychology.* (3rd ed.) Vol. 2. New York: Wiley, 1970, pp. 457–557.

Hess, R. D., and Shipman, V. C. Early experience and the socialization of cognitive modes in children. *Child Development,* 1965, **34,** 869–886.

Hess, R. D., and Shipman, V. C. Cognitive elements in maternal behavior. In J. P. Hill (Ed.), *Minnesota symposia on child psychology.* Vol. 1. Minneapolis: University of Minnesota Press, 1967.

Hess, R. D., Shipman, V. C., Brophy, J. E., and Bear, R. M. *The cognitive environments of urban preschool children: Follow-up phase.* Chicago: The Graduate School of Education, The University of Chicago, 1969.

Hill, E. H., and Giammateo, M. C. Socioeconomic status and its relationship to school achievement in the elementary school. *Elementary English,* 1963, **50,** 265–270.

Jencks, C., et al., *Inequality: A reassessment of the effect of family and schooling in America.* New York: Basic Books, 1972.

Jensen, A. R. How much can we boost IQ and scholastic achievement? *Harvard Educational Review,* 1969, **39,** 1–123.

John, V. P., and Goldstein, L. S. The social context of language acquisition. *Merrill-Palmer Quarterly,* 1964, **10,** 266–275.

Jones, H. E. The environment and mental development. In L. Carmichael (Ed.), *Manual of child psychology.* (2nd ed.) New York: Wiley, 1954, pp. 631–696.

Kagan, J. Reflection-impulsivity and reading ability in primary grade children. *Child Development,* 1965, **36,** 609–628.

Kagan, J., Rosman, B. L., Day, D., Albert, J., and Phillips, W. Information processing in the child: Significance of analytic and reflective attitudes. *Psychological Monographs,* 1964, **78**(1, Whole No. 578).

Kaye, K. Review of H. J. Eysenck, *The IQ argument: Race, intelligence and education. Adult Education,* 1972, **22,** 229–233.

Kennedy, W. Z., Van de Reit, V., and White, J. C., Jr. A normative sample of intelligence and achievement of Negro elementary school children in the southeastern United States. *Monographs of the Society for Research in Child Development,* 1963, **28**(6).

Kilbride, H., Johnson, D., and Streissguth, A. P. Early home experience of newborns as a function of social class, infant sex, and birth order. Unpublished manuscript, University of Washington, 1971.

Klaus, R., and Gray, S. The early training project for disadvantaged children: A report after five years. *Monographs of the Society for Research in Child Development,* 1968, **33**(4).

Knobloch, H., and Pasamanick, B. Predicting intellectual potential in infancy. *American Journal of Diseases of Children,* 1963, **106,** 43–51.

Labov, W. The logic of nonstandard English. In J. E. Alatis (Ed.), *20th annual round table.* Washington, D.C.: Georgetown University Press, 1970, pp. 1–39.

Lesser, G. S., Fifer, G., and Clark, D. H. Mental abilities of children from different social class and cultural groups. *Monograph of the Society for Research in Child Development,* 1965, **30**(4).

Overton, W. F., Wagner, J., and Dolinsky, H. Social-class differences and task variables in the development of multiplicative classification. *Child Development,* 1971, **42,** 1951–1958.

Owen, G. M., and Kram, K. M. Nutritional status of preschool children in Mississippi: Food sources of nutrients in the diets. *Journal of the American Dietary Association,* 1969, **54,** 490–494.

Profiles of Children. (1970 White House Conference on Children) Washington, D.C.: United States Government Printing Office, 1970.

Rosen, B. C. The achievement syndrome: A psychocultural dimension of social stratification. *American Sociological Review,* 1956, **21,** 203–211.

Rosenhan, D. L. Effects of social class and race on responsiveness to approval and disapproval. *Journal of Personality and Social Psychology,* 1966, **4,** 253–259.

Scrimshaw, N. Early malnutrition and CNS function. *Merrill-Palmer Quarterly,* 1969, **15,** 375–388.

Sigel, I. E., Anderson, L. M., and Shapiro, H. Categorization behavior of lower- and middle-class Negro preschool children: Differences in dealing with representation of familiar objects. *Journal of Negro Education,* 1966, **35,** 218–29.

Sigel, I. E., and McBane, B. Cognitive competence and level of symbolization among five-year-old children. In J. Hellmuth (Ed.), *Disadvantaged child.* Vol. 1. Seattle: Special Child Publications, 1967.

Stodolsky, S. Maternal behavior and language and concept formation in Negro preschool children: An inquiry into process. Unpublished doctoral dissertation, Department of Psychology, University of Chicago, 1965.

Streissguth, A. P., and Bee, H. L. Mother-child interactions and cognitive development in children. In W. W. Hartup (Ed.), *The young child: Reviews of research.* Vol. 2. Washington, D.C.: National Association for the Education of Young Children, 1972, pp. 158–183.

Templin, M. C. *Certain language skills in children: Their development and interrelationships.* Minneapolis: University of Minnesota Press, 1957.

Terrel, G., Jr., Durkin, K., and Wiesley, M. Social class and the nature of the incentive in discrimination learning. *Journal of Abnormal and Social Psychology,* 1959, **59,** 270–272.

Tulkin, S. R. Mother-infant interaction: Social class differences in the first year of life. Paper presented to the American Psychological Association, Miami, Fla., September 1970.

Wei, T. T. D., Lavatelli, C. B., and Jones, R. S. Piaget's concept of classification: A comparative study of socially disadvantaged and middle-class young children. *Child Development,* 1971, **42,** 919–927.

Whiteman, M., and Deutsch, M. Social disadvantage as related to intellective and language development. In M. Deutsch, I. Katz, and A. R.

Jensen (Eds.), *Social class, race and psychological development.* New York: Holt, Rinehart, and Winston, 1968.

Yarrow, L. J., Rubenstein, J. L., Pederson, F. A., and Jankowski, J. J. Dimension of early stimulation and their differential effects on infant development. *Merrill-Palmer Quarterly,* 1972, **18,** 205–218.

Zigler, E., and Butterfield, E. C. Motivational aspects of changes in IQ test performance of culturally deprived nursery school children. *Child Development,* 1968, **39,** 1–14.

Zigler, E., and deLabry, J. Concept-switching in middle-class, lower-class and retarded children. *Journal of Abnormal and Social Psychology,* 1962, **56,** 267–273.

social-class differentiation in cognitive development among black preschool children*

MARK GOLDEN
BEVERLY BIRNS
WAGNER BRIDGER
ABIGAIL MOSS
Albert Einstein College of Medicine, Yeshiva University

It is of theoretical and practical importance to determine when so-cial-class differences in intellectual performance first emerge and to identify the specific deficiencies which prevent many lower-class children from achieving academically. It might then be possible to discover the causal mechanisms or factors which account for social-class differences in cognitive development. Only on the basis of such information can optimally timed and really effective compensatory education programs be designed.

In a cross-sectional study reported previously (Golden and Birns 1968), we compared 192 black children of 12, 18, and 24 months of

From *Child Development*, 1971, **42.** Copyright ©1971 by the Society for Research in Child Development, Inc. By permission.

*Revised for publication from a paper presented at the 1969 meeting of the Society for Research in Child Development, Santa Monica, California. The study was supported by grant HDMH-01926 from the National Institute of Child Health and Human Development and by grant MH15458 from the National Institute of Mental Health. Author Golden's address: Department of Psychiatry, Albert Einstein College of Medicine of the Yeshiva University, 1300 Morris Park Avenue, Bronx, New York 10461.

age from three socioeconomic-status (SES) groups on the Cattell Infant Intelligence Scale and the Piaget Object Scale. Children from the following SES groups were studied:

A. Welfare families: Neither mother nor father was employed or going to school; family on welfare.

B. Lower-educational-achievement families: Neither parent had any schooling beyond high school.

C. Higher-educational-achievement families: Either mother or father had some schooling beyond high school (from a few months of secretarial school to completion of medical training).

Ninety-three percent of the Group A children were from fatherless families, in contrast to 5 percent of the B and 0 percent of the C children. Contrary to our expectations, we did not find any social-class differences in either the Cattell or the Object Scale scores during the first 2 years of life.

The present paper is a report of a longitudinal follow-up study in which children in the 18- and 24-month samples of the cross-sectional study were retested on the Stanford-Binet at 3 years of age. The purpose of the follow-up study was to see whether the same pattern of social-class differentiation in cognitive development, emerging during the third year of life, reported for white children was also present in black children (Hindley 1962; Terman and Merrill 1937; Willerman, Sledge, and Fiedler 1969).

In the present study, only black children from different social-class groups were compared. In this respect, it differs from other studies (Knobloch and Pasamanick 1960; Wachs, Uzgiris, and Hunt 1967) which include both black and white children, where race and social class may be confounded.

METHOD

Eighty-nine of the original 126 A, B, and C children in the 18- and 24-month samples were retested on the 1960 revision (form L-M) of the Stanford-Binet Intelligence Scale at approximately 3 years of age. Most of the children were retested between 3 and 3½ years of age. A few were a month or so under 3 years or over 4 years of age. The mean chronological ages (CAs in years and months) for the A, B, and C children at the time they were tested on the Binet were 3.2, 3.5, and 3.4 years. The Peabody Picture Vocabulary Test was administered to the mothers in order to see at what age the children's IQ scores began to correlate with mothers' intellectual performance.

Every effort was made to retest as many of the 18- and 24-month children as possible. This included a payment of $10 to the mothers, several letters, and numerous telephone calls. We succeeded in retesting about 70 percent of the children in all three SES groups for both age samples combined. The follow-up rates for Groups A, B, and C were 53, 70, and 80 percent. We were unable to obtain the rest of the children for a variety of reasons, the principal one being that the families had moved and the new address was unknown. Comparisons were made, using the t test, between the Cattell scores of children who were retested and those who did not return. There were no significant differences in this respect.

As in the original cross-sectional study, every effort was made to obtain each child's optimal intellectual performance. This included taking as much time as necessary to establish rapport and to elicit responses. Children were seen a second time if the examiner felt that they were not doing their best. It was only necessary to see four out of 89 children twice.

The children in the original cross-sectional study were recruited from well-baby clinics, child health stations, and private pediatricians and through mothers who had participated in the study. Where records were available, children were screened to include only normal healthy children who had no histories of serious prolonged illness, birth complications, or prematurity (birth weight less than 5½ pounds). Where records were not available, this information was obtained from the mothers.

RESULTS

Whereas there were no significant social-class differences on the Cattell at 18 and 24 months of age, when the same children were tested on the Stanford-Binet at 3 years of age, there were highly significant SES differences in intellectual performance (see Table 1). Two independent samples of children, one originally tested at 18 months and the other originally tested at 24 months, showed similar patterns of social-class differences on the Stanford-Binet at 3

Table 1   Mean IQ Scores of Children in the 18- and 24-Month Samples Retested at 3 Years of Age Classified by ABC SES System

| | | 18-month sample | | | 24-month sample | |
Social class	N	18 months	36 months	N	24 months	36 months
C (>high school)	16	110	112	21	102	113
B (≤high school)	10	113	104	21	99	101
A (welfare)	10	110	94	11	96	93

NOTE. The 18- and 24-month scores are based on the Cattell, and the 36-month scores are based on the Stanford-Binet.

years of age. The fact that the same results were obtained at age 3 on two independent samples strengthens the validity of the findings.

The 3-year Binet scores for the 18- and 24-month samples were combined for purposes of data analysis. The combined Binet mean IQs for the A, B, and C Groups were 94, 103, and 112, respectively. A one-way analysis of variance resulted in highly significant SES differences in IQ $(F = 13.25, df = 2, 86, p < .0005)$. Scheffe tests, involving all possible comparisons, yielded the following results: C > A, $p < .01$; C > B, $p < .05$; and B > A, $p < .10$ [Edwards 1965]. Children from middle-income families obtained significantly higher Stanford-Binet IQ scores than children from poor stable families and those from fatherless welfare families. Children from poor stable families obtained higher IQ scores than those from fatherless welfare families, but this difference fell short of the .05 level of significance.

In the original cross-sectional study, we did not employ a more widely used SES measure, such as Hollingshead's Index of Social Status, because it is based on the educational-occupational achievement of the head of the household, which in most cases is the father. In many black families, the mother's achievements in these respects may be higher than the father's. For this reason, we had assumed that the Hollingshead Index would not adequately reflect important differences in social status among blacks. We had also assumed that, by classifying the black children in our sample in terms of Hollingshead's Index, there would be a range in mean IQ scores narrower than the range obtained on the basis of our ABC classification system. Both of these assumptions proved to be quite erroneous.

The children in our sample were classified on the basis of the following modification of Hollinghead's Index of Social Status: (1) middle class or higher, (2) working class, (3) lower class/nonwelfare, and (4) lower class/welfare (Hollingshead 1957). Group 1 corresponds to Hollingshead's Classes I, II, and III combined; Group 2 corresponds to Hollingshead's Class IV; and Groups 3 and 4 represent subclasses of Hollingshead's Class V. In terms of the original ABC classification system, all of the children in Group 1 were in Group C; Group 2 is about equally divided between B and C children; Group 3 children were in Group B, with the exception of one child from Group C; and all of the children in Group 4 were in Group A.

When the same children were classified in terms of the modified Hollingshead Index, there were still no significant SES differences on the Cattell at 18 and 24 months of age, but there was a somewhat greater range in mean Stanford-Binet IQ scores than was obtained on the basis of the original ABC classification system. The mean IQ

Table 2 Mean IQ Scores of Children in the 18- and 24-Month Samples Retested at 3 Years of Age Classified by Modified Hollingshead SES System

| Social class | (N) | 18-month sample | | (N) | 24-month sample | |
		18 months	36 months		24 months	36 months
1 (middle class)	(5)	106	115	(11)	102	115
2 (working class)	(15)	113	110	(23)	101	106
3 (lower class/ nonwelfare)	(5)	114	102	(8)	98	101
4 (lower class/ welfare)	(10)	110	94	(11)	96	93

scores for Groups 1, 2, 3, and 4 were 116, 107, 100, and 93, respectively, a spread of 23 IQ points (see Table 2). A one-way analysis of variance resulted in highly significant SES differences in IQ ($F = 8.85$, $df = 2, 85$, $p < .0005$). The range in mean IQ scores obtained on the basis of the modified Hollingshead Index in the present longitudinal study of black children was almost identical to that reported by Terman and Merrill (1937) for 831 white children between $2\frac{1}{2}$ and 5 years of age in their standardization sample, classified into seven SES groups on the basis of the fathers' occupations. Children in Class I (professionals) obtained a mean IQ score of 116, and children in Class VII (laborers) obtained a mean IQ score of 94 (see Table 3). The unique and perhaps significant contribution of the present longitudinal study is that the same pattern and degree of social-class differentiation in intellectual performance, emerging during the third year of life, previously reported for white children have now been demonstrated for black children.

Pearson r's were computed between mothers' Peabody Picture Vocabulary scores and children's IQ scores at 18, 24, and 36 months of age. The correlation between the Peabody and 18-month Cattell scores was .10, which is not significant. The correlation between the Peabody and the 24-month Cattell scores was .28, which is significant at the .05 level. The correlation between the Peabody and 3-year Stanford-Binet scores was .32, which is significant at the .01 level. The pattern of increasing correlations of children's IQ scores with those of their mothers in our sample of black families was similar to the pattern previously reported for white families. Bayley (1965) and Honzik (1957) found that children's IQ scores do not correlate at all with their mothers' intelligence or education during the first 18 months of life, but after 18 months the correlations gradually increase, reaching an asymptote of about .50 by 5 years of age.

Social-class influences on cognitive development already appear to be operating between 18 and 24 months of age. These are reflected in low but significant correlations between children's IQ scores after

Table 3 Comparisons of Stanford-Binet IQ Scores of Black Children in Longitudinal Study Classified by ABC System and Hollingshead's Modified System, and White Children from Terman and Merrill's Standardization Sample

Social class	N	IQ
Black children in longitudinal study classified by ABC system[a]		
C (>high school)	37	112
B (≤high school)	31	102
A (welfare)	21	93
Black children in longitudinal study classified by modified Hollingshead system[b]		
1 (middle class)	16	116
2 (working class)	38	107
3 (lower class/nonwelfare)	13	100
4 (lower class/welfare)	21	93
Terman and Merrill's white children classified by father's occupation[c]		
I (professional)		116
II (semiprofessional managerial)		112
III (clerical, skilled trades, retails)		108
IV (rural owners)		99
V (semiskilled, minor clerical, small business)		104
VI (semiskilled laborers)		95
VII (unskilled laborers)		94

[a]$N = 89$; $p > .0005$.
[b]$N = 88$; $p > .0005$. One child was excluded because there was not enough information to classify him in terms of Hollingshead's Index.
[c]$N = 831$.

18 months of age and mothers' intelligence and education. In the present study, the rank order of the mean IQ scores at 24 months of age corresponds perfectly with social class (see Tables 1 and 2), whereas at 18 months of age this is not the case. However, the differences in the mean IQ scores at 24 months are not great enough to produce a significant F. Low significant correlations between social-class factors, such as mother's intelligence and education, reflect a relatively *weak effect*, whereas mean IQ differences between SES groups reflect a relatively *strong effect*. The process of social-class differentiation in cognitive development appears to begin somewhere between 18 and 24 months of age, but the divergence in intellectual ability only becomes great enough to be reflected in statistically significant SES differences in mean IQ scores by about 3 years of age.

DISCUSSION

The results of the present longitudinal study of black children confirm the findings of other investigators (Bayley 1965; Hindley 1962;

Knobloch and Pasamanick 1960). When such factors as birth complications and poor nutrition and health are ruled out, social-class differences in intellectual performance have not been demonstrated until the third year of life.

Why should social-class differences in intellectual performance first manifest themselves during the third year of life and not earlier? Since SES differences in cognitive development emerge during a period of rapid language growth, it seems reasonable to assume that these differences may be due to language. There is reason to believe that between 18 and 36 months of age there is a shift from the preverbal or sensorimotor to the verbal or symbolic level of intelligence and that different environmental conditions facilitate or retard development on these two qualitatively different levels of intelligence.

Given an average expectable environment with an opportunity to explore and manipulate objects and a sufficient amount of attention or handling by parents or care-taking adults, children reared under a variety of social conditions can acquire on their own the kinds of perceptual-motor skills measured by infant tests or Piaget-type scales. On the sensorimotor level, the child's construction of reality, to borrow Piaget's terminology (1954), for the most part may not be socially transmitted but, rather, acquired through his own direct experience or activity. To be sure, during the first 18 to 24 months of life, children in New York City learn something about elevators and automobiles while children in a rural village in India learn about elephants and tigers. In this respect, the knowledge which they acquire is different. But children in different cultures, or in black ghettos and middle-class suburbs, learn that objects exist when they are no longer in the perceptual field, that objects fall down and not up, and so forth. The basic knowledge which children acquire about the world on the sensorimotor level—in terms of the dimensions which Piaget has described, such as object permanence and spatial, causal, and temporal relations—may be acquired largely through their own direct experience and hence may be universal. While language may be present, very little of what children learn during the first 2 years of life is acquired from other people through language. Their ability to understand and express ideas verbally is fairly limited. Their capacity to use language as a tool for symbolic or representational thinking is probably not present to any significant degree during the first 2 years. During the third year of life, as children become increasingly capable of using language for these purposes, social class—and, in particular, the intellectual, verbal, and educational level of the parents—begins to make a difference in terms of facilitating a child's cognitive development.

In regard to the question of why social-class differences in intellectual performance were not found during the first 2 years of life, it is possible that social-class differences are present but that infant tests, such as the Cattell, which largely seem to measure perceptual-motor skills, may not be sensitive enough to detect them. Operating on this assumption, we included in the original cross-sectional study (Golden and Birns 1968) the Object Scale, a new measure of cognitive development based on Piaget. The Object Scale seemed more related to cognitive development, and therefore we had expected to find social-class differences. However, we did not find SES differences on the Object Scale among black children between 12 and 24 months of age. It is possible, of course, that other measures may be more sensitive to social-class influences. There are two recent unpublished studies which report SES differences in cognitive development much earlier than other investigators have found. One of these is a report by Kagan (1966) in which social-class differences in perceptual discrimination, attention, and persistence were observed in infants of about 1 year of age. In another study, Wachs et al. (1967) obtained SES differences as early as the first year of life on several new cognitive measures based on Piaget. More specific details of these studies and replication of the results are necessary, however, before the findings can be properly evaluated.

In the original cross-sectional study, while we did not find social-class differences in the Cattell or Object Scale scores, children in the fatherless welfare families (Group A) seemed more difficult to test and more effort was required to get them to perform at their optimal intellectual level. This was reflected in the fact that significantly more of the welfare children had to be seen on more than one occasion to obtain a valid estimate of their intellectual ability. However, in a subsequent study to be reported more fully elsewhere, when children were tested on the Cattell and the Piaget Object Scale under identical conditions, including number of testing sessions, we did not find any differences in intellectual performance in children between 18 and 24 months of age from black welfare (Group A), black middle-income (Group C), and white middle-income families.

To summarize, in a longitudinal follow-up study of 89 black children from different social classes, there were no significant social-class differences on the Cattell or Piaget Object Scale at 18 or 24 months of age. When the same children were retested on the Stanford-Binet at approximately 3 years of age, there was a highly significant 23-point mean IQ difference between children from black welfare and middle-income families. The range in the mean IQ scores of the black children from the two extreme SES groups (93–116) was almost identical to that reported by Terman and Merrill (1937) for 831 white children between 2½ and 5 years of age in their standardization sample. The unique contribution of the present study is that the same pattern of social-class differentiation in cognitive development, emerging during the third year of life, previously reported for white children has now been demonstrated for black children.

REFERENCES

Bayley, N. Comparisons of mental and motor test scores for ages 1–15 months by sex, birth order, race, geographical location, and education of parents. *Child Development*, 1965, **36**, 379–411.

Edwards, A. L. *Experimental design in psychological research*. New York: Holt, Rinehart & Winston, 1965.

Golden, M., and Birns, B. Social class and cognitive development in infancy. *Merrill-Palmer Quarterly of Behavior and Development*, 1968, **14**, 139–149.

Hindley, C. B. Social class influences on the development of ability in the first five years. In *Child and Education: Proceedings of the XIV International Congress of Applied Psychology*. Copenhagen: Munksgaard, 1962.

Hollingshead, A. B. Two factor index of social position. Mimeographed, A. B. Hollingshead, New Haven, Conn., 1957.

Honzik, M. P. Developmental studies of parent-child resemblance in intelligence. *Child Development*, 1957, **28**, 215–228.

Kagan, J. A developmental approach to conceptual growth. In H. J. Klausmeier and C. W. Harris (Eds.), *Analyses of concept learning*. New York: Academic, 1966.

Knobloch, H., and Pasamanick, B. Environmental factors affecting human development after birth. *Pediatrics*, 1960, **26**, 210–218.

Piaget, J. *The construction of reality in the child*. New York: Basic, 1954.

Terman, L. M., and Merrill, M. A. *Measuring intelligence: a guide to the administration of the new revised Stanford-Binet tests*. Boston: Houghton-Mifflin, 1937.

Wachs, T. D.; Uzgiris, I.; and Hunt, J. McV. Cognitive development in infants of different age levels and from different environmental backgrounds. Paper presented at the biennial meeting of the Society for Research in Child Development, New York, 1967.

Willerman, L.; Sledge, S. H.; and Fiedler, M. Infant development, Binet IQ and social class. Paper presented at meeting of the Society for Research in Child Development, Santa Monica, California, 1969.

health and the education of socially disadvantaged children*

HERBERT G. BIRCH
Albert Einstein College of Medicine, Yeshiva University

INTRODUCTION

Recent interest in the effect of social and cultural factors upon educational achievement could lead us to neglect certain bio-social factors which through a direct or indirect influence on the developing child affect his primary characteristics as a learner. Such a danger is exaggerated when health and education are administered sep-

From *Developmental Medicine and Child Neurology*, 1968, **10.** By permission.

*A working paper presented at the Conference on 'Bio-Social Factors in the Development and Learning of Disadvantaged Children' held in Syracuse, New York, April 19–21, 1967.

Acknowledgments: The research reported was supported in part by the National Institutes of Health, National Institute of Child Health and Human Development (HD-00719); the Association for the Aid of Crippled Children; and the National Association for Retarded Children.

The background examination of the literature and the detailed spelling out of many problems was carried out in conjunction with Mrs. Joan Gussow and Mrs. Ronni Sandroff Franklin.

This paper was commissioned under United States Office of Education Contract #6-10-240 (ERIC). It was also used at the Conference on 'Bio-Social Factors in the Development and Learning of Disadvantaged Children,' held in Syracuse in April 1967 under the terms of United States Office of Education Contract #6-10-243.

arately. The educator and the sociologist may concentrate quite properly on features of curriculum, familial environment, motivation, cultural aspects of language organisation, and the patterning of preschool experiences. Such concentration, while entirely fitting, becomes one-sided and potentially self-defeating when it takes place independently of, and without detailed consideration of, the child as a biological organism. To be concerned with the child's biology is not to ignore the cultural and environmental opportunities which may affect him. Clearly, to regard organic factors as a substitute for environmental opportunity (Hunt 1966) is to ignore the intimate interrelation between the biology of the child and his environment in defining his functional capacities. However, it is equally dangerous to treat cultural influences as though they were acting upon an inert organism. Effective environment (Birch 1954) is the product of the interaction of organic characteristics with the objective opportunities for experience. The child who is apathetic because of malnutrition, whose experiences may have been modified by acute or chronic illness, or whose learning abilities may have been affected by some 'insult' to the central nervous system cannot be expected to respond to opportunities for learning in the same way as does a child who has not been exposed to such conditions. Increasing opportunity for learning, though entirely admirable in itself, will not overcome such biologic disadvantages (Birch 1964, Cravioto et al. 1966).

There are two considerations with children who have been at risk of a biologic insult. First, such children must be identified and not merely additional but *special* educational opportunities effective for them must be provided. As no socially deprived group can be considered to be homogeneous for any particular disability, groups of children from such backgrounds must be differentiated into meaningful subgroups for purposes of remedial, supplemental and habilitative education. Secondly, if conditions of risk to the organism can be identified, principles of public health and of current bio-social knowledge should be utilized to reduce learning handicap in future generations.

Concern for the socially disadvantaged cannot in good conscience restrict itself to the provision of either equal or special educational and preschool opportunities for learning. It must concern itself with all factors contributing to educational failure, among which the health of the child is a variable of primary importance.

Such an argument is not new. The basic relationship between poverty, illness and educational failure has long been known, as has the fact expressed by James (1965) that 'poverty begets poverty, is a cause of poverty and a result of poverty.' What is new is the nature of the society in which such an interaction occurs. As Galbraith (1958) has put it, to secure each family a minimum standard, as a normal function of society, would help insure that the misfortunes of parents, discerned or otherwise, were not visited on their children. It would help insure that poverty was not self-perpetuating. Most of the reaction, which no doubt would be almost universally adverse, is based on obsolete attitudes. When poverty was a majority phenomenon, such action could not be afforded. . . . An affluent society has no similar excuse for such rigor. It can use the forthright remedy of providing for those in want. Nothing requires it to be compassionate. But it has no high philosophical justification for callousness.

The pertinence of Galbraith's concern as it applies to the health of children, particularly those in the non-white segments of our population, is underscored by the fact that, according to the Surgeon General Stewart (1967), the United States standing with respect to infant mortality has been steadily declining with respect to other countries. Though we are the richest country our 1964 mortality rate of 24.8 per 1,000 live births causes us to rank fifteenth in world standing. Had we had Sweden's rate, the world's lowest, approximately 43,000 fewer infants would have died in that year. Of particular pertinence to the problem of social disadvantage is the fact that the mortality rate for non-white infants is twice as high as that for whites, with the highest rates for the country as a whole in the east south central states, Kentucky, Tennessee, Alabama and Mississippi. Wegman (1966) notes that 'Mississippi again has the dubious distinction of having the highest rate (infant mortality) . . . more than twice that of the lowest state.' Most of this difference could be related to the higher Negro population of Mississippi.

The data on infant mortality have been extended to other features of child health by Baumgartner (1965) and by Densen and Haynes (1967), who have pointed out that although detailed and careful documentation of the 'degree and magnitude of the health problems' of the Negro, Puerto Rican and Indian groups are not readily available, a strikingly dangerous picture may be pieced together as a montage from various public health statistics, research studies and occasional articles. The picture is striking, not merely because it shows these minority groups to be at a significant health disadvantage with respect to the white segment of the population, but because it indicates that the disparity between white and non-white groups is increasing. Thus, while in 1930 twice as many non-white mothers died in childbirth, in 1960 'for every white mother who lost her life in childbirth, four non-white mothers died' (Baumgartner 1965). In 1940 the number of non-white mothers delivered by poorly trained midwives was 14 times that for white mothers, a discrepancy that rose to 23 times as great by 1960. Gold (1962) pointed out that while the overall death-rate for mothers in child-birth had reached an all-time low of 3.7 per 10,000 live births, this change was largely due to the reduction of the mortality rate among white mothers to 2.6. Non-white mothers had a death-rate four times as great, 10.3, a rate characteristic of white mothers two decades earlier. In generalizing these findings Baumgartner believes 'that the most advantaged non-white family has a poorer chance of having a live and healthy baby than the least advantaged white family.'

In our concern with educational disadvantage we must therefore recognize the excessive risk of ill-health relevant to educational handicap that exists in the children with whose welfare and education we are concerned. To this end I shall discuss some selected features of health and how far they differentiate the population of socially disadvantaged children from other children in the U.S.A.

PREMATURITY AND OBSTETRIC COMPLICATIONS

Few factors in the health history of the child have been as strongly associated with later intellectual and educational deficiencies as prematurity at birth and complications in the pregnancy from which he derives (McMahon and Sowa 1959). Although a variety of specific infections, explicit biochemical disorders, or trauma may result in more clearly identified and dramatic alterations in brain function, prematurity, together with pre- and perinatal complications, are probably factors which most broadly contribute to disorders of neurologic development (Lilienfeld et al. 1955, Pasamanick and Lilienfeld 1955).

A detailed consideration of health factors which may contribute to educational failure must start with an examination of prematurity and the factors associated with it.

Prematurity has been variously defined either by the weight of the child at birth, by the maturity of certain of his physiologic functions, or by gestational age (Coiner 1960). Independently of the nature of the definition in any society in which it has been studied, prematurity has an excessive representation in the lower social strata and among the most significantly socially disadvantaged. Prematurity in any social group is simultaneously indicative of two separate conditions of risk. In the first place fetuses that are primarily abnormal and characterized by a variety of congenital anomalies are more likely to be born before term than are normal fetuses. Second, infants who are born prematurely, even when no congenital abnormality may be noted, are more likely to develop abnormally than are infants born at term. Thus, Baumgartner (1962) has noted that follow-up studies have 'indicated that malformation and handicapping disorders (neurological, mental and sensory) are more likely to be found among the prematurely born than those born at term. Thus, the premature infant not only has a poorer chance of surviving than the infant born at term, but if he does survive he has a higher risk of having a handicapping condition.' One consequence of this association between prematurity and neurological, mental, sensory and other handicapping conditions is the excessive representation of the prematures among the mentally subnormal and educationally backward children at school age (Drillien 1964).

Baumgartner (1962) has presented the distribution of live births by birthweight for white and non-white groups in the United States for 1957 (Table 1). For the country as a whole 7.6 per cent of all live births weighed 2,500 g. or less. In the white segment of the population 6.8 per cent of the babies fell in this category, while 12.5 per cent of the non-white infants weighed 2,500 g. or less. The frequency at all levels of low birthweight was twice as great in non-white infants. Baumgartner attributed the high incidence of prematurity among non-whites to the greater poverty of this group. The studies of Donnelly *et al.* (1964) in North Carolina, of Thomson (1963) in Aberdeen, Scotland, and of Shapiro *et al.* (1960) in New York suggest that many factors, including nutritional practices, maternal health, the mother's own growth achievements as a child, as well as deficiencies in prenatal care and birth spacing and grand multiparity, interact to produce group differences between the socially disadvantaged and more advantageously situated segments of the population.

It has sometimes been argued that the excess of low birthweight

Table 1 Percentage Distribution of 4,254,784 Live Births by Birthweight and Ethnic Group, USA 1957

Birth weight (g.)	Total	White	Non-white
1,000 or less	0.5	0.4	0.9
1,001–1,500	0.6	0.5	1.1
1,501–2,000	1.4	1.3	2.4
2,001–2,500	5.1	4.5	8.1
2,501–3,000	18.5	17.5	24.5
3,001–3,500	38.2	38.4	37.2
3,501–4,000	26.8	28.0	19.6
4,001–4,500	7.3	7.8	4.8
4,501–5,000	1.3	1.3	1.3
5,001 or more	0.2	0.2	0.2
Total	100	100	100
Percentage under 2,501 g.	7.6	6.8	12.5
Median weight (g.)	3,310	3,330	3,170
Number of live births	4,254,784	3,621,456	633,328

From Baumgartner 1962.

babies among the socially disadvantaged is largely a consequence of ethnic differences (i.e., Negroes 'naturally' give birth to smaller babies). However, the high association of prematurity with social class in an ethnically homogeneous population such as that in Aberdeen, the finding of Donnelly et al. that within the Negro group higher social status was associated with reduced frequency of prematurity, the findings of Pakter et al. (1961) that illegitimacy adds to the risk of prematurity within the non-white ethnic group, and the suggestion made by Shapiro et al. that a change for the better in the pattern of medical care reduces the prevalence of prematurity, all make the ethnically based hypothesis of 'natural difference' difficult to retain.

If gestational age is used instead of birthweight as an indication of prematurity, the non-whites are at an even greater risk than when birthweight is used. In 1958–1959 (Baumgartner 1962) 18.1 per cent of non-white babies born in New York City had a gestational age of 36 weeks or less, in contrast to 8.5 per cent for live-born white babies.

Both the data on birthweight and the data on gestational age leaves little doubt that prematurity and its attendant risks are excessively represented in the non-white segment of the population. Moreover, an examination in detail of regional data such as that provided by Donnelly et al. for hospital births in university hospitals in North Carolina indicate clearly that in that community the most advantaged non-white has a significantly greater risk of producing a premature infant than the least advantaged segment of the white population.

For equal degrees of prematurity, non-white infants have a somewhat better chance for survival during the first month of life (Erhardt 1964). However, during the remainder of infancy this likelihood is reversed, particularly for infants weighing between 1,500 and 2,500 g. at birth. Baumgartner, reviewing these data, concludes,

> this observation strongly suggests that inadequate medical care, inadequate maternal supervision, inadequate housing and associated socioeconomic deprivations are exerting unfavorable influences on the later survival of those non-white babies who initially appear the more favored. It is apparent that socio-economic factors not only influence the incidence of low birthweight in all ethnic groups, but greatly influence survival after the neonatal period.

If the low birthweight and survival data are considered distributively rather than categorically, it appears that the non-white infant is subject to an excessive continuum of risk reflected at its extremes by perinatal, neonatal, and infant death, and in the survivors by a reduced functional potential.

THE BACKGROUND OF PERINATAL RISK

Clearly, the risk of having a premature baby or a complicated pregnancy and delivery begins long before the time of the pregnancy itself. A series of studies carried out in Aberdeen, Scotland, on the total population of births of that city (Thomson 1963, Walker 1954, Thomson and Billewicz 1963) indicate that prematurity as well as pregnancy complications are significantly correlated with the mother's nutritional status, height, weight, concurrent illnesses, and the social class of her father and husband. Although the relation among these variables is complex, it is clear that the women born in the lowest socio-economic class and who have remained in this class at marriage were themselves more stunted in growth than other women in the population, had less adequate dietary and health habits, were in less good general health, and tended to be at excessive risk of producing premature infants. The mother's stature as well as her habits were determined during her childhood, tended to be associated with contraction of the bony pelvis, and appeared systematically related to her risk condition as a reproducer. In analyzing the relation between maternal health and physique to a number of obstetrical abnormalities such as prematurity, caesarean section and perinatal death, Thomson (1959) (Table 2) has shown each of these to be excessively represented in the mothers of least good physical grade.

The finding of a relation between the mother's physical status and pregnancy outcome is not restricted to Scotland. Donnelly et al., in their study of North Carolina University Hospital births, [have] shown a clear distribution of height with social class. In Class I (the

Table 2   Incidence of Obstetric Abnormalities in Aberdeen Primigravidae by Maternal Health and Physique As Assessed at the First Antenatal Examination. (Twin Pregnancies Have Been Excluded.)

	Health and physique			
	Very good	Good	Fair	Poor; very poor
Prematurity[a] (%)	5.1	6.4	10.4	12.1
Cesarean section (%)	2.7	3.5	4.2	5.4
Perinatal deaths per 1,000 births	26.9	29.2	44.8	62.8
No. of subjects	707	2,088	1,294	223
Percentage tall (5 ft. 4 in. or more)	42	29	18	13
Percentage short (under 5 ft. 1 in.)	10	20	30	48

[a]Birthweight of baby 2,500 g. or less (From Thomson 1961).

most advantaged whites) 52 per cent of the women were less than 5 ft. 5 in. tall. In contrast in social class IV (the least advantaged non-whites) 75 per cent of the women were under 5 ft. 5 in. in height. The proportion of shorter women increased consistently from Classes I to IV and within each class the incidence of prematurity was higher for women who were less than 5 ft. 3 in. tall. Moreover, within any height range the least advantaged whites had lower prematurity rates than the most advantaged non-whites. Thus in the least advantaged whites less than 5 ft. 3 in. tall the prematurity rate was 12.1 per cent as contrasted with a rate of 19.6 per cent for the non-whites in the same height range. In the tallest of the most disadvantaged whites the rate was 5.6 per cent whereas in non-whites of the same height range who were least disadvantaged the prematurity rate was 10.1 per cent.

DIETARY FACTORS—PRE-WAR AND WARTIME EXPERIENCE

The physical characteristics of the mother which affect her efficiency as a reproducer are not restricted to height and physical grade. As early as 1933, Mellanby, while recognizing that 'direct and accurate knowledge of this subject in human beings is meagre,' asserted that nutrition was undoubtedly 'the most important of all environmental factors in childbearing, whether the problem be considered from the point of view of the mother or that of the offspring.' It was his conviction that the reduction of a high perinatal mortality rate as well as of the incidence of maternal ill health accompanying pregnancy could effectively be achieved by improving the quality of the diet. Acting upon these views he attempted to supplement the diets of women attending London antenatal clinics and reported a significant reduction in morbidity rates during the puerperium.

Although Mellanby's own study is difficult to interpret for a number of methodologic reasons, indirect evidence rapidly came into being in support of his views. Perhaps the most important of these was the classical inquiry directed by Sir John Boyd-Orr and reported in *Food, Health and Income* (1936). This study demonstrated conclusively that the long recognised social differential in perinatal death rate was correlated with a dietary differential, and that in all respects the average diet of the lower income groups in Britain was inadequate for good health. Two years later McCance et al. (1938) confirmed the Boyd-Orr findings in a meticulous study of the individual diets of 120 pregnant women representing a range of economic groups ranging from the wives of unemployed miners in South Wales and Tyneside to the wives of prefessionals. The diet survey technique which they used and which has, unfortunately, been rarely imitated since, was designed to minimize misreport. The results showed that there was wide individual variation in the intake of all foods which related consistently neither to income nor to intake per kilogram of body weight. But when the women were divided into six groups according to the income available for each person per week, the poorer women proved to be shorter and heavier and to have lower hemoglobin counts. Moreover, though economic status had little effect on the total intake of calories, fats and carbohydrates, 'intake of protein, animal protein, phosphorus, iron and Vitamin B_1 rose convincingly with income.' The authors of the study offered no conclusions about the possible outcome of the pregnancies involved, but the poorer reproductive performance of the lower class women was clearly at issue. For as they stated, 'optimum nutrition in an adult implies and postulates optimum nutrition of that person as a child, that child as a fetus, and that fetus of its mother.'

A second body of indirect data supporting Mellanby's hypothesis derived from animal studies on the relation of diet to reproduction. Warkany (1944), for example, demonstrated that pregnant animals maintained on diets deficient in certain dietary ingredients produced offspring suffering from malformation. A diet which was adequate to maintain maternal life and reproductive capacity could be inadequate for normal fetal development. The fetus was not a perfect parasite and at least for some features of growth and differentiation could have requirements different from those of the maternal host.

It would divert us from the main line of our inquiry to consider the many subsequent studies in detail. However, Duncan et al. (1952), in surveying these studies, as well as the wartime experiences in Britain, have argued convincingly that the fall in stillbirth and neonatal death rate could only be attributed to a reduction in poverty accompanied by a scientific food rationing policy. Certainly there was no real improvement in prenatal care during the war when so many medical personnal were siphoned off to the armed forces. Furthermore, the improvement took place chiefly among those deaths attributed to 'ill defined or unknown' causes—that is among those cases when low fetal vitality seems to be a major factor in influencing survival—and these types of death 'are among the most difficult to influence by routine antenatal practice.' Of all the possible factors then, nutrition was the only one which improved during the war years (Garry and Wood 1945). Thomson (1959) commented that the result was 'as a nutritional effect' all the more convincing 'because it was achieved in the context of a society where most of the conditions of living other than the nutritional were deteriorating.'

While this National 'feeding experiment' was going on in the British Isles, a more controlled experiment was being carried out on the continent of Europe (Toverud 1950). In 1939 Dr. Toverud set up a health station in the Sagene district of Oslo to serve pregnant and nursing mothers and their babies. Though war broke out shortly after the station was opened, and it became progressively more difficult to get certain protective foods, an attempt was made to insure that every woman being supervised had the recommended amounts of every essential nutrient, through the utilization of supplementary or synthetic sources when necessary. In spite of food restrictions which became increasingly severe, the prematurity rate among the the 728 women who were supervised at the station never went above the 1943 high of 3.4 per cent, averaging 2.2 per cent for the period 1939–1944. Among the unsupervised mothers the 1943 rate was 6.3 per cent and the average for the period 4.6 per cent. In addition, the stillbirth rate of 14.2/1,000 for all women attending the health station was half that of the women in the surrounding districts.

Meanwhile, even as the British and Norwegian feeding experiments were in progress, there were some hopefully never-to-be repeated starvation 'experiments' going on elsewhere. When they were reported after the war, the childbearing experiencs of various populations of women under conditions of severe nutritional restriction were to provide evidence of the ways in which deprivation could negatively affect the product of conception, just as dietary improvement appeared able to affect it positively.

Smith (1947), for example, studying infants born in Rotterdam and the Hague during a delimited period of extreme hunger brought on by a transportation strike, found that the infants were shorter and lighter (by about 240 g.) than those born both before and after the period of deprivation. Significantly enough Smith also found that those babies who were five to six month fetuses when the hunger period began appeared to have been reduced in weight as much as those who had spent a full nine months in the uterus of a malnourished mother. He was led to conclude from this that reduced maternal caloric intake had its major effect on fetal weight beginning around the sixth month of gestation. Antonov's study of babies born during the siege of Leningrad (1947) confirmed the fact of weight reduction as well as Smith's observations that very severe deprivation was likely to prevent conception altogether rather than reduce the birthweight. Antonov found that during a six month period which began four months after the start of the siege, there was an enormous increase in prematurity as judged by birth length

—41.2 per cent of all the babies born during this period were less than 47 cm. long and fully 49.1 per cent weighed under 2,500 g. The babies were also of very low vitality—30.8 per cent of the prematures and 9 per cent of the full-term babies died during the period. Abruptly, during the latter half of the year, the birthrate plummeted—along with the prematurity rate. Thus, while 161 prematures and 230 term babies were born between January and June, 1942, five prematures and 72 term babies were born between July and December. Where information was available it suggested that the women who managed to conceive during the latter part of the year, when amenorrhea was widespread, were better fed than the majority, being employed in food industries or working in professional or manual occupations which had food priorities. Antonov concluded that while the fetus might behave for the most part like a parasite, 'the condition of the host, the mother's body, is of great consequence to the fetus, and that severe quantitative and qualitative hunger of the mother decidedly affects the development of the fetus and the vitality of the newborn child.'

Long after the war, Dean (1951) was able to confirm the Smith and Antonov results with a careful analysis of a series of 22,000 consecutive births at the Landesfrauenklinik, Wuppertal, Germany, during 1937–1948. It was apparent from this series that the small reduction in the average duration of gestation recorded was insufficient to account for the degree of weight reduction observed. The study demonstrated, even more clearly than before, that severe hunger did not merely reduce the mother's ability to maintain the pregnancy to term, but could act directly through the placenta to reduce the growth of the infant.

POST-WAR STUDIES

These wartime and post-war analyses leave little doubt of an association between maternal diet and the growth and development of the child in utero. Moreover, they suggest that the nature of the diet is significantly associated with pregnancy course and complications.

It is unfortunate that most of the more recent studies of the relation of maternal nutrition to pregnancy course and outcome have tended to obscure rather than to clarify the issue. Most of these studies, such as the excellently conducted Vanderbilt Cooperative Study of Maternal and Infant Nutrition (Darby et al. 1953 a and b, McGanity 1954) have produced confusing and equivocal findings because of patient selection. Since the women included for study have tended to be those who registered for obstetrical care early in pregnancy the lowest class women were markedly unrepresentative of their social group. As a result, these studies have failed to include the very women who are most central to our concern. What is sorely needed is a detailed study of nutrition and pregnancy course in socially disadvantaged women who come to obstetrical notice far too late to be included in the usual dietary surveys in obstetrical services. The design of such a study and its conduct would not be easy. However, if conducted, it would have one virtue absent in most extant studies—pertinence.

. . .

POST-NATAL CONDITIONS FOR DEVELOPMENT

Densen and Haynes (1967) have indicated that many types of illness are excessively represented in the non-white segments of the population at all age levels. I have selected one, nutritional status, as the model variable for consideration. A considerable body of evidence from animal experimentation as well as field studies of populations at nutritional risk (Cravioto et al. 1966) have suggested a systematic relation between nutritional inadequacy and both neurologic maturation and competence in learning.

At birth the brain of a full-term infant has achieved about one quarter of its adult weight. The bulk of subsequent weight gain will derive from the laying down of lipids, particularly myelin, and cellular growth. Animal experiments on the the rat (Davison and Dobbing 1966), the pig (Dickerson et al. 1967, McCance 1960) and the dog (Platt et al. 1964) have all demonstrated a significant interference in brain growth and differentiation associated with severe dietary restriction, particularly of protein, during the first months of life. In these animals the behavioral effects have been dramatic with abnormalities in some cases persisting after dietary rehabilitation.

The relation of these data to the human situation is made difficult by the extreme severity of the dietary restrictions. More modest restrictions have been imposed by Widdowson (1965) and Barnes et al. (1966) and the latter experiments indicated some tendency for poorer learning in the nutritionally deprived animals. Cowley and Griesel's work (1963) suggests a cumulative effect of malnutrition on adaptive behavior across generations.

The animal findings as a whole can be interpreted either as suggesting a direct influence of malnutrition on brain growth and development, or as resulting in interference with learning at critical points in development. In either case the competence of the organism as a learner appears to be influenced by his history as an eater. These considerations add cogency to an already strongly held belief that good nutrition is important for children and links our general concerns on the relation of nutrition to health to our concerns with education and the child's functioning as a learner.

Incidents of severe malnutrition appear rarely in the United States today, but there is evidence to suggest that the low income segments of the population suffer from subtle, sub-clinical forms of malnutrition which may be partially responsible for the higher rates of morbidity and mortality of children in this group. Brock (1961) suggests that 'dietary sub-nutrition can be defined as any impairment of functional efficiency or body systems which can be corrected by better feeding.' Since 'constitution is determined in part by habitual diet . . . diet must be considered in discussing the aetiology of a large group of diseases of uncertain and multiple aetiology. . . .' The relationship between nutrition and constitution is demonstrated by the fact that the populations of developed nations are taller and heavier than those of technically underdeveloped nations and that 'within a given developed nation children from economically favoured areas are taller and heavier than children from economically under-privileged areas.'

In comparison to the vast body of data available on the diets of peoples in tropical countries, very little research has been done in recent years on the nutritional status of various economic groups in the United States. The effects of long term sub-clinical malnutrition on the health of the individual are not yet known, and little research has been directed at this problem since 1939. However, it is instructive to review the studies comparing the diets of low income people with the rest of the population since these lay the basis for hypothesizing that nutritional differences may have some effect on the overall differences in health and learning ability between groups.

The nutritional differences between lower and higher income individuals begin before birth and continue thereafter. In a study of maternal and child health care in upper New York State, Walter Boek et al. (1957) found that babies from low income families were breast fed less often and kept on only milk diets longer than upper income infants. In a study of breast feeding in Boston, Salber and Feinleib (1960) confirmed Boek's results and, 'social class was found to be the most important variable affecting incidence of breast-feeding.'

Social class differences in feeding patterns continue after weaning. Filer and Martinez (1964) studied 4,642 six month old infants from a nationally representative sample and found that 'infants of mothers with least formal education and in families with lowest incomes are fed more milk formula . . .' and less solid foods at six months old than those from higher educational and economic groups. Class differences in the intake of most nutrients varied primarily according to the amount of milk formula consumed.

The researchers found that for 'almost all nutrients studied, the mean intakes were well above recommended levels. The single exception was iron; more than half of infants do not get the lowest recommended provision—a finding that corroborates the results reported by a number of other investigators.' Iron deficiency was most prevalent among infants of mothers with low educational and income levels. Infants whose mothers attained no more than a grade school education received a mean intake of only 6.7 mg. of iron a day, as compared to the 9.1 mg. mean intake of infants whose mothers had attended high school. Since 'nutritional iron deficiency is widespread and most prevalent in infants in the low socioeconomic group,' and iron deficiency is the most common cause of anemia in infants during the first two years of life, malnutrition at least with respect to this nutrient is widely prevalent in lower class infants.

A study of Negro, low income infants in South Carolina (Jones and Schendel 1966) uncovered more extensive areas of malnutrition in this group; the death-rate for Negro infants in South Carolina was twice the national rate. Thirty-six Negro infants from low income families were tested when they visited a Well-Baby Clinic for routine examinations. The subjects ranged in age from four to ten months. 'The bodyweights of 66 per cent of the infants were below the 50th percentile in the Harvard growth charts, 34 per cent below the 10th percentile and 9 per cent below the 3rd percentile.' Twenty-nine per cent of the subjects had 'serum albumin concentrations which have been associated with marginal protein nutrition' and serum globin concentrations below normal range. Sixty-one per cent had total protein concentrations below normal and 33 per cent had 'serum ascorbic acid concentrations which have been associated with a sub-optimal intake of vitamin C.' One infant's albumin concentration showed severe protein deficiency and 'eight . . . infants had concentrations of serum ascorbic acid reflecting a severely limited dietary intake of vitamin C.' The researchers concluded that 'it would appear possible that malnutrition may be one of the many underlying causes for the high rate of Negro infant mortality in South Carolina.' Since Greenville County, where the study was conducted, has a relatively small number of infant deaths, 'it is possible that malnutrition may be even more severe and/or prevalent in many other counties of the state.'

Since the sample used in this study is small (36 infants), the results must be viewed as suggestive rather than conclusive. But taken together with the findings on iron intake, a New York study which shows that anemia is common among Negro and Puerto Rican infants (James 1966) and the recent finding of Arneil (1965) that 'some anemia was present in 59 per cent of Glasgow slum children,' the suggestion is strengthened that poor diet may be partly responsible for the poor health of lower socio-economic class children.

The studies so far reviewed have dealt with populations that are in some way representative of the nutritional status of large groups of children. Since these studies are few in number and limited in approach, they cannot give a complete picture of the nutritional status of lower class Americans. Hints about areas of malnutrition which have not been thoroughly investigated can be drawn from studies of special groups within the American population. In a survey of the 'Dietary and Nutritional Problems of Crippled Children in Five Rural Counties of North Carolina,' Bryan and Anderson (1965) found that the diets of 73 per cent of the 164 subject sample were less than adequate. The cause for the malnourishment of nine out of ten of the poorly fed children was poor family diet and in only one of ten cases was the malnutrition related to the physical handicap of the child.

Although all the children were from families in the low income group, the researchers found certain significant differentiations between the Negro and white families studied. Seventy-one per cent of the Negro children and 35 per cent of the white children's diets were rated as probably or obviously inadequate. Only a limited number of food items were used and 'in many of the families . . . only one food was cooked for a meal and this would be eaten with biscuits and water, tea or Kool-Aid. . . . For the most part, the diet of our low income families contained few foods that are not soft or that require much chewing.' Suggestions of poor nutrition in infancy and childhood can also be drawn from studies of constitutional differences as well as from measurements of food intake.

A study of the nutritional status of junior high school children in Onondaga County, New York (Dibble et al. 1965) compared subjects from broadly different economic groups. School 'M' was 94 per cent Negro, while Schools 'L' and 'J' were overwhelmingly white. The schools were also differentiated on the basis of the occupation of the students' fathers: '. . . of the 58 per cent of the employed fathers from school M, 52 per cent were laborers, whereas only 10 per cent from school L and 38 per cent from school J were in this category.' When the heights and weights of the subjects were compared, a greater percentage of students from the lower socio-economic class school fell in the short stature and low weight zones. There was also a tendency for students from the predominantly Negro school to have less subcutaneous fat by ranking of skinfold than students from other schools.

Blood and urine samples were taken for all the subjects and the researchers set up criteria to determine the level of adequacy for the various nutrients. 'Subjects from school M (the Negro school) had a slightly lower average hematocrit, largely due to the greater number of female subjects from that school in the low classification, [and] the average plasma ascorbic acid value for school M was about half as great as the average in school L. There was also a tendency for the Negro population to have low values for hexose and pentose when erythrocyte hemolysate transketolase activity was determined. Average urinary excretions of riboflavin and thiamine was above acceptable level in all groups, but data for folinic acid indicated lower levels of excretion for children from school M than for children in schools L and J.' The question [of] whether this observation was related to the lower ascorbic acid levels of these children indicates a need for further study in this area. The authors conclude that the differences between the schools show a relationship between nutrition and socio-economic status. These differences are greater than the differences between male and female students, and are related to each other on the various parameters of the study. 'There was a slight indication that the growth of the male subjects in . . . school [M] had not been as great as that of the subjects in the other schools with whom they were compared. This fact was supported by somewhat lower average levels in the other parameters. . . .'

Although the students at the predominantly Negro school in Onondaga County did not appear to suffer from gross nutritional deficiencies, their diets were significantly less adequate than the subjects from the white, middle-class schools. The investigators did not attempt to link dietary habits with health records, but the results of the study lead to speculations about the relationship between suboptimal diet, rates of infection, school absence and academic performance.

CONCLUSIONS

In this review I have examined certain selected conditions of health which may have consequences for education. Other factors such as acute and chronic illness, immunizations, dental care, the utilization of health services and a host of other phenomena, perhaps equally pertinent to those selected for consideration, have been dealt with either in passing or not at all, but in fact studies of these factors that do exist reflect the same picture that emerges from those variables which have been discussed. In brief, though much of the information is incomplete, and certain aspects of the data are sparse, a serious consideration of available health information leaves little or no doubt that children who are economically and socially disadvantaged, and in an ethnic group exposed to discrimination, are exposed to massively excessive risks for maldevelopment.

Such risks have direct and indirect consequences for the functioning of the child as a learner. Conditions of ill-health may directly affect the development of the nervous system and eventuate either in patterns of clinically definable malfunctioning in this system or in sub-clinical conditions. In either case the potentialities of the child as a learner cannot but be impaired. Such impairment, though it may in fact have reduced functional consequences under exceptionally optimal conditions for development and education, in any case represents a primary handicap which efforts at remediation may only partially correct.

The indirect effects of ill health or of conditions of sub-optimal health care on the learning processes may take many forms. Only two can be considered at this point. Children who are ill nourished are reduced in their responsiveness to the environment, distracted by their visceral state, and reduced in their ability to progress and endure in learning conditions. Consequently, given the same objective conditions for learning, the state of the organism modifies the effective environment and results in a reduction in the profit which a child may derive from exposure to opportunities for experience. Consequently, the provision of equal opportunities for learning in an objective sense is never met when only the school situation is made identical for advantaged and disadvantaged children. Though such a step is indeed necessary, proper and long overdue, a serious concern with the profitability of such improved objective opportunities for socially disadvantaged children demands a concern which goes beyond education and includes an intensive and directed consideration of the broader environment, the health and functional and physical well-being of the child.

Inadequacies in nutritional status as well as excessive amounts in intercurrent illness may interfere in indirect ways with the learning process. As Cravioto *et al.* (1966) have put it, at least

three possible indirect effects are readily apparent:

1. *Loss of learning time.* Since the child was less responsive to his environment when malnourished, at the very least he had less time in which to learn and had lost a certain number of months of experience. On the simplest basis, therefore, he would be expected to show some developmental lags.

2. *Interference with learning during critical periods of development.* Learning is by no means simply a cumulative process. A considerable body of evidence exists which indicates that interference with

the learning process at specific times during its course may result in disturbances in function that are both profound and of long term significance. Such disturbance is not merely a function of the length of time the organism is deprived of the opportunities for learning. Rather, what appears to be important is the correlation of the experiential opportunity with a given stage of development—the so-called critical periods of learning. Critical periods in human learning have not been definitively established, but in looking at the consequences associated with malnutrition at different ages one can derive some potentially useful hypotheses. The earlier report by Cravioto and Robles (1965) may be relevant to the relationship between the age at which malnutrition develops and learning. They have shown that, as contrasted with older patients, infants under six months recovering from kwashiorkor did not recoup their mental age deficit during the recovery period. In older children, ranging from 15 to 41 months of age, too, the rate of recovery from the initial mental deficit varied in direct relation to chronological age at time of admission. Similarly, the findings of Barrera Moncada (1963) in children, and those of Keys *et al.* (1950) in adults, indicated a strong association between the persistence of later effects on mental performance and the age at onset of malnutrition and its duration.

3. *Motivation and personality changes.* It should be recognized that the mother's response to the infant is to a considerable degree a function of the child's own characteristics of reactivity. One of the first effects of malnutrition is a reduction in the child's responsiveness to stimulation and the emergence of various degrees of apathy. Apathetic behavior in its turn can function to reduce the value of the child as a stimulus and to diminish the adults' responsiveness to him. Thus, apathy can provoke apathy and so contribute to a cumulative pattern of reduced adult-child interaction. If this occurs it can have consequences for stimulation, for learning, for maturation, and for interpersonal relations, the end result being significant backwardness in performance on later more complex learning tasks.

However, independently of the path through which bio-social pathology interferes with educational progress, there is little doubt that ill health is a significant variable for defining differentiation in the learning potential of the child. To intervene effectively with the learning problems of disadvantaged children it would be disastrous if we were either to ignore or to relegate the physical condition and health status of the child with whose welfare we are concerned to a place of unimportance. To do so would be to divorce education from health; a divorce which can only have disorganizing consequences for the child. Unless health and education go hand in hand we shall fail to break the twin curse of ignorance and poverty.

REFERENCES

Antonov, A. N. (1947) 'Children born during the siege of Leningrad in 1942.' *J. Pediat.*, **30**, 250.

Arneil, G. C., McKilligan, H. R., Lobo, E. (1965) 'Malnutrition in Glasgow children.' *Scot. med. J.*, **10**, 480.

Barnes, R. H., Cunnold, S. R., Zimmerman, R. R., Simmons, H., Mac-Leod, R., Krook, L. (1966) 'Influence of nutritional deprivations in early life on learning behaviour of rats as measured by performance in water maze.' *J. Nutr.*, **89**, 399.

Barrera-Moncada, G. (1963) Estudios sobre Alleraciones del Crecimiento y del Desarrollo Psicológico de Sindrome Pluricarencial Kwashiorkor. Caracas: Editoria Grafos.

Baumgartner, L. (1962) 'The public health significance of low birth weight in the U.S.A., with special reference to varying practices in providing special care to infants of low birth weights.' *Bull. Wld. Hlth. Org.*, **26**, 175.

———. (1965) 'Health and ethnic minorities in the sixties.' *Amer. J. publ. Hlth.*, **55**, 495.

Birch, H. G. (1954) 'Comparative psychology.' *In* Marcuse, F. A. (Ed.) Areas of Psychology. New York: Harper.

——— (Ed.) (1964) Brain Damage in Children: Biological, and Social Aspects. Baltimore: Williams & Wilkins.

Boek, W. E., Boek, J. K. (1956) Society and Health. New York: Putnam.

——— and co-worker (1957) Social Class, Maternal Health and Child Care. Albany, N.Y.: New York State Department of Health.

Brock, J. (1961) Recent Advances in Human Nutrition. London: Churchill.

Bryan, H., Anderson, E. L. (1965) 'Dietary and nutritional problems of crippled children in five rural counties of North Carolina.' *Amer. J. publ. Hlth.*, **55**, 1,545.

Corner, B. (1960) Prematurity. London: Cassell.

Cowley, J. J., Griesel, R. D. (1963) 'The development of second generation low-protein rats.' *J. genet. Psychol.*, **103**, 233.

Cravioto, J., DeLicardie, E. R., Birch, H. G. (1966) 'Nutrition, growth and neuro-integrative development: an experimental and ecologic study.' *Pediatrics*, **38**, 319.

———, Robles, B. (1965) 'Evolution of adaptive and motor behaviour during rehabilitation from kwashiorkor.' *Amer J. Orthopsychiat.*, **35**, 449.

Darby, W. J., Densen, P. M., Cannon, R. O., Bridgeforth, E., Martin, M. P., Kaser, M. M., Peterson, O., Christie, A., Frye, W. W., Justus, K., McClellan, G. S., Williams, C., Ogle, P. J., Hahn, P. F., Sheppard, C. W., Crothers, E. L., Newbill, J. A. (1953) 'The Vanderbilt co-operative study of maternal and infant nutrition. I. Background. II. Methods. III. Description of the sample data.' *J. Nutr.,* **51,** 539.

——, McGanity, W. J., Martin, M. P., Bridgeforth, E., Densen, P. M., Kaser, M. M., Ogle, P. J., Newbill, J. A., Stockell, A., Ferguson, E., Touster, O., McClellan, G. S., Williams, C., Cannon, R. O. (1953) 'The Vanderbilt co-operative study of maternal and infant nutrition. IV. Dietary, laboratory and physical findings in 2,129 delivered pregnancies.' *J. Nutr.,* **51,** 565.

Davison, A. N., Dobbing, J. (1966) 'Myelination as a vulnerable period in brain development.' *Brit. med. Bull.,* **22,** 40.

Dean, R. F. (1951) 'The size of the baby at birth and the yield of breast milk.' *In* Studies of Undernutrition, Wuppertall, 1946–49. M. C. R. Special Report Series, No. 275. London: H.M.S.O. Chap. 28.

Delgado, G., Brumback, C. L., Deaver, M. B. (1961) 'Eating patterns among migrant families.' *Publ. Hlth. Rep. (Wash.),* **76,** 349.

Densen, P. M., Haynes, A. (1967) 'Research and the major health problems of Negro Americans.' Paper presented at the Howard University Centennial Celebration, Washington. (Unpublished.)

Dibble, M. F., Brin, M., McMullen, E., Peel, A., Chen, N. (1965) 'Some preliminary biochemical findings in junior high school children in Syracuse and Onondaga County, New York.' *Amer. J. clin. Nutr.,* **17,** 218.

Dickerson, J. W., Dobbing, J., McCance, R. A. (1967) 'The effect of under nutrition on the postnatal development of the brain and cord in pigs.' *Proc. roy. Soc. B.,* **166,** 396.

Donnelly, J. F., Flowers, C. E., Creadick, R. N., Wells, H. B., Greenberg, B. G., Surles, K. B. (1964) 'Maternal, fetal and environmental factors in prematurity.' *Amer. J. Obstet. Gynec.,* **88,** 918.

Drillien, C. M. (1964) The Growth and Development of Prematurely Born Children. Edinburgh: Livingstone, Baltimore: Williams & Wilkins.

Duncan, E. H. L., Baird, D., Thomson, A. M. (1952) 'The causes and prevention of stillbirths and first week deaths. I. The evidence of vital statistics.' *J. Obstet. Gyncea. Brit. Emp.,* **59,** 183.

Erhardt, C. L., Joshi, G. B., Nelson, F. G., Kron, B. H., Weiner, L. (1964) 'Influence of weight and gestation on perinatal and neonatal mortality of ethnic group.' *Amer. J. publ. Hlth.,* **54,** 1,841.

Filer, L. J., Martinez, G. A. (1964) 'Intake of selected nutrients by infants in the United States: an evaluation of 4,000 representative six-year-olds.' *Clin. Pediat.,* **3,** 633.

Galbraith, J. K., (1958) The Affluent Society. Boston: Houghton Mifflin.

Garry, R. C., Wood, H. O. (1945–46) 'Dietary requirements in human pregnancy and lactation: a review of recent work.' *Nutr. Abstr. Rev.*, **15**, 591.

Gold, E. M. (1962) 'A broad view of maternity care.' *Children*, **9**, 52.

Hartman, E. E., Sayles, E. B. (1965) 'Some reflections on births and infant deaths among the low socioeconomic groups.' *Minn. Med.*, **48**, 1,711.

Hunt, E. E. (1966) 'Some new evidence on race and intelligence.' Paper read at the meeting of the New York Academy of Sciences —Anthropology Section, Oct. 24, 1966. (Unpublished.)

James, G. (1965) 'Poverty and public health—new outlooks. I. Poverty as an obstacle to health progress in our cities.' *Amer. J. publ. Hlth.*, **55**, 1,757.

—— (1966) 'New York City's Bureau of Nutrition.' *J. Amer. dietet. Ass.*, **48**, 301.

Jeans, P. C., Smith, M. B., Stearns, G. (1952) 'Dietary habits of pregnant women of low income in a rural state.' *J. Amer. dietet. Ass.*, **28**, 27.

Jones, R. E., Schendel, H. E. (1966) 'Nutritional status of selected Negro infants in Greenville County, South Carolina.' *Amer. J. clin. Nutr.*, **18**, 407.

Kass, E. H. (1960) 'Bacteriuria and the prevention of prematurity and perinatal death.' *In* Kowlessar, M. (Ed.) Transactions of the 5th Conference on the Physiology of Prematurity. Princeton, 1960.

Keys, A., Brožek, J., Henschel, A., Mikelsen, O., Taylor, H. (1950) The Biology of Starvation. Vol. 2. Minneapolis: University of Minnesota Press.

Lilienfeld, A. M., Pasamanik, B., Rogers, M. (1955) 'Relationship between pregnancy experience and the development of certain neuropsychiatric disorders in childhood.' *Amer. J. publ. Hlth.*, **45**, 637.

McCance, R. A. (1960) 'Severe undernutrition in growing and adult animals. I. Production and general effects.' *Brit. J. Nutr.*, **14**, 59.

——, Widdowson, E. M., Verdon-Roe, C. M. (1938) 'A study of English diets by the individual method. III. Pregnant women at different economic levels.' *J. Hyg. (Lond.)*, **38**, 596.

McGanity, W. J., Cannon, R. O., Bridgeforth, E. B., Martin, M. P., Densen, P. M., Newbill, J. A., McClellan, G. S., Christie, A., Peterson, J. O., Darby, W. J. (1954) 'The Vanderbilt co-operative study of maternal and infant nutrition. VI. Relationship of obstetric performance to nutrition.' *Amer. J. Obstet. Gynec.*, **67**, 501.

MacMahon, B., Sowa, J. M. (1961) 'Physical damage to the foetus.' *In* Causes of Mental Disorders: A Review of Epidemiological Knowledge, 1959. New York: Milbank Memorial Fund, p. 51.

Mayer, J. (1965) 'The nutritional status of American Negroes.' *Nutr. Rev.*, **23**, 161.

Mellanby, E. (1933) 'Nutrition and child bearing.' *Lancet*, **ii**, 1, 131.

Orr, J. B. (1936) Food, Health and Income. London: Macmillan.

Pakter, J., Rosner, H. J., Jacobziner, H., Greenstein, F. (1961) 'Out-of-wedlock births in New York City. II. Medical aspects.' *Amer. J. publ. Hlth.*, **51**, 846.

Pasamanik, B., Lilienfeld, A. M. (1955) 'Association of maternal and fetal factors with development of mental deficiency. I. Abnormalities in the prenatal and perinatal periods.' *J. Amer. med. Ass.*, **159**, 155.

Platt, B. S., Heard, R. C., Stewart, R. J. (1964) 'Experimental protein-calorie deficiency.' *In* Munro, H. N., Allison, J. B. (Eds.) Mammalian Protein Metabolism. New York: Academic Press. p. 446.

Salber, E. J., Feinleib, M. (1966) 'Breast feeding in Boston.' *Pediatrics*, **37**, 299.

Shapiro, S., Jacobziner, H., Densen, P. M., Weiner, L. (1960) 'Further observations on prematurity and perinatal mortality in a general population and in the population of a prepaid group practice medical care plan.' *Amer. J. publ. Hlth.*, **50**, 1,304.

Smith, C. A. (1947) 'Effects of maternal undernutrition upon the new born infant in Holland.' *J. Pediat.*, **30**, 229.

Stewart, W. H. (1957) 'The unmet needs of children.' *Pediatrics*, **39**, 157.

Thomson, A. M. (1959) 'Maternal stature and reproductive efficiency.' *Eugen. Rev.*, **51**, 157.

———. (1959) 'Diet in pregnancy. III. Diet in relation to the course and outcome of pregnancy.' *Brit. J. Nutr.*, **13**, 509.

———. (1963) 'Prematurity: socio-economic and nutritional factors.' *Bibl. paediat. (Basel),* **81**, 197.

———, Billewicz, W. Z. (1963) 'Nutritional status, physique and reproductive efficiency.' *Proc. nutr. Soc.*, **22**, 55.

Toverud, G. (1950) The influence of nutrition on the course of pregnancy.' *Milbank mem. Fd. Quart.*, **28**, 7.

U. S. Welfare Administration. Division of Research. (1966) Converging Social Trends—Emerging Social Problems. Welfare Administration Publication No. 6. Washington: U.S. Government.

Walker, J. (1954) 'Obstetrical complications, congenital malformations and social strata.' *In* Mechanisms of Congenital Malformations. New York: Association for the Aid of Crippled Children, p. 20.

Warkany, J. (1944) 'Congenital malformations induced by maternal nutritional deficiency.' *J. Pediat.*, **25**, 476.

Wegman, M. E. (1966) 'Annual summary of vital statistics, 1965.' *Pediatrics*, **39**, 1,067.

Widdowson, E. M. (1966) 'Nutritional deprivation in psychobiological development: studies in animals.' *In* Proceedings of the Special Session, 4th Meeting of the PAHO Advisory Committee on Medical Research, June, 1965. Washington: World Health Organization.

race, social class, and age of achievement of conservation on Piaget's task[*]

GIL GAUDIA   State University of New York College at Fredonia

Typical findings in studies of disadvantaged children support the contention that children from low socioeconomic status and minority groups perform poorly on intelligence tests. In general, studies of standardized test performance and social class status lead to conclusions of what Stodolsky and Lesser (1967, p. 547) have called a "*deficit* or less-than model." But, if as has been claimed (e.g., Hunt, 1961), standardized intelligence tests do not measure cognitive processes, then attempts to compare different cultural groups in intellectual performance are usually based upon inadequate criteria.

The traditional psychometric approach that has valued the predictive validity of IQ tests has resulted in a tendency to regard the measure as the construct when it would be more accurate to conceive of it as a best estimate or intervening variable. In a more theoretically oriented view of intelligence (Kohlberg, 1968, p. 1052), intelligence is defined and measured as an evolutionary advantage permitting superior adaptation to the environment and the ability

Gil Gaudia, Race, social class, and age of achievement of conservation on Piaget's tasks, *Developmental Psycholsky*, **6**, 1972, 158–165. Copyright © 1972 by the American Psychological Association and reproduced by permission.
[*]This study is based on a dissertation done under the direction of Aubrey Roden and submitted to the State University of New York at Buffalo in partial fulfillment of the requirements for the PhD degree in May of 1970.

to organize information about the real world. Within the context of this latter philosophy, Piaget has conceived of a model of intelligence in which the construct is a process that can be measured through behavior on various tasks such as the classification of objects and the understanding of certain invariances. One of these latter behaviors, conservation, has been the focus of extensive research, as well as the central construct underlying several attempts to derive measures of intellectual functioning which seem to be relatively free of cultural content (Goldschmid and Bentler, 1968; Hunt, 1961; Tuddenham, 1969). According to Piaget's theory, acquisition of conservation marks the transitional period in a child's development where his cognitive processes shift from preoperational to operational (or logical) thought. It is defined as the understanding that certain empirical properties such as quantity or weight remain invariant in the child's mind despite certain transformations such as displacing objects, sectioning an object into pieces, or changing its shape(Inhelder and Piaget, 1958, p. 32).

The primary purpose of this study was to investigate conservation acquisition across subcultural groups. If systematic cultural and racial differences in cognitive ability exist, then the age or rate at which children of different cultures or races acquire conservation should be measurably different (Hunt, 1961; Kohlberg, 1968). Several researchers have already shown some evidence that even on Piagetian tasks there are cultural influences in performance that are supportive of the hypothesis of differential performance across racial and social class groups (De Lemos, 1969; Tuddenham, 1969; Vernon, 1965). In addition, Ames and Ilg (1967) found Negro performance on other developmental tests such as the Rorschach to be surprisingly atypical regarding improvement and development with age.

De Lemos (1969) has shown that conservation performance of full-blooded Australian aboriginal children on Piagetian tasks is significantly lower than for part-blooded aborigines with an average admixture of white genes equivalent to having one white great-grandparent. De Lemos concluded that the significant differences found between the part and the full aboriginal children may be due to genetic factors which could have contributed to retarded development of conservation in these children, since he found no "apparent differences in the environment of the two groups [p. 265]." Tuddenham (1969) found that Negro children consistently did less well than whites and Orientals on a series of tasks that was being developed for use as a standardized instrument in measuring conservation. Vernon (1965), in finding a large g loading in Piagetian tasks, concluded that the performance of West Indian Negro children was substantially lower than a comparable group of English children.

Excellent treatment of conservation research can be found in

Sigel and Hooper (1968), and thorough reviews have been made by Flavell (1963), Hunt (1961), and Wallach (1963). The research results have supported the notion of invariance of the sequence of acquisition of conservation (mass, weight, and then volume), as well as the close relationship between CA and ability to conserve (Almy, Chittenden, and Miller, 1966; Goodnow, 1962; Hyde, 1959; Mermelstein and Shulman, 1967; Price-Williams, 1961).

Two of the most serious inadequacies of previous research into the concept of conservation and its relationship to cultural background have been the use of unsophisticated testing techniques (Goldschmid and Bentler, 1968) and sampling designs lacking in external validity (see, e.g., Campbell and Stanley, 1963). Uzgiris (1964) found that there were appreciable individual differences in ability to conserve when the tasks dealt with different materials, and that these differences were not constant across individuals and materials. Almy's (1966) study, otherwise an excellent cross-sectional and longitudinal investigation of conservation in lower- and middle-class children, exemplified the typical design failure in this type of research. Two schools were identified as a "middle-class" and a "lower-class" school, and performances of the children from the two schools were then compared for social class effects. The assumption that every child attending each of the schools was in the same social class was untenable and allowed for no meaningful social class comparisons (see Sigel and Perry, 1968, for further discussion of global measures of socioeconomic status). With both criterion measure and sampling weakness present, it is difficult to interpret the results of studies which, under more precise conditions, could have crucial implications for educational, psychological, and sociological problems.

Recently, Goldschmid and Bentler (1968) published a Conservation Concept Diagnostic Kit on which they established satisfactory interitem and test-retest reliability. Through the use of this standardized instrument, the restriction of inconsistent criterion measures was largely eliminated in the present study.

METHOD

EXPERIMENTAL DESIGN

Three groups of 42 children each, American Indians, Negroes, and whites comprised the sample of 126 subjects. Each group contained 7 boys and 7 girls from each of the first three grades. The Warner, Meeker, and Eells (1949) scale was used to insure that all children selected were members of the lowest social class. It was planned to examine the data for social class effects by comparing the performance of the total research sample with the norming group data obtained by the test's authors on large samples of children who represented all strata of society.

SUBJECTS

The area sampled includes four counties in western New York State, but excludes the largest metropolitan area because of the inability to identify Indians living there. The desire to control for cultural milieu left as a sample base a large rural area, several small cities, and many small villages and towns from which the names of virtually all (about 95%) of the Indian children and a great bulk (about 85%) of the Negro children of school age were obtained. These names formed the pool from which the samples were drawn, using either a table of random numbers or a computerized random selection procedure at a data processing center in one of the city schools. The names of white children of lower socioeconomic status were randomly selected from a pool of all children who were identified by the school principal and nurse as "living under conditions of extreme poverty." The final sample included Indian children from 7 schools, Negro children from 24 schools, and white children from 19 schools. In all cases, but one, children from at least two races came from the same school (12 Indian children came from an all Indian elementary school), so that the total number of schools involved was 33.

TESTS, PROCEDURES, AND ANALYSES

The Conservation Concept Diagnostic Kit Form A devised by Goldschmid and Bentler (1968) measures the child's understanding of conservation in six areas: two dimensional space, number, substance, continuous quantity, weight, and discontinuous quantity. There are two tasks within each area, one of which is termed behavioral, that is, the child indicates his judgment of equality or inequality, and the other is called explanatory, that is, the child gives a reason for his judgment. One point is given for each correct response, yielding a maximum possible score of 12 (6 for behavior and 6 for explanation). The protocol for administration is standardized so that the words and gestures of the questioner provide the same amount of information for each subject. The materials include Play-Doh, poker chips (red and white), wooden blocks, water, beakers, and corn seeds.

The criterion measure was designed to yield scores which were to be treated continuously, and in the initial analysis they were so treated. However, the implication from Piaget's theory is that the scores should be regarded primarily as discrete measures of three categories: nonconservers, children in transition, and conservers. Examination of the results clearly supports Piaget (Flavell, 1963, pp.

299–303). Mainly for this reason, Pearson's chi-square test of association was selected as the final method of analysis (Hays, 1963).

This three-way classification was accomplished as follows: Scores of 1 were included with 0 in the category of nonconservation because it was the only score other than 0 that precluded the possibility of a correct explanation by the subject. In short, a score of 1 was likely to have been a chance occurrence. On the other hand, scores of 10 and 11 were included with 12 in the category conservation, because in every case of a child who scored 10, the same item was missed (conservation of weight). This item was the most difficult one for both the sample and the norming groups (as measured by the rank order of difficulty of the items). This result is in close agreement with Piaget's prediction that the conservation of weight is acquired later than the conservation of mass. The conservation of weight task is actually more appropriate for use with an older group, since this concept is usually acquired between the ages of 10 and 12 (Flavell, 1963, p. 299).

The Peabody Picture Vocabulary Test (PPVT) was also administered to all subjects prior to the conservation tasks.

RESULTS

CONSERVATION SCORES

The conservation scores of the three research samples are summarized in Table 1, along with the results of the norming groups. All

Table 1   Summary of Raw Score Distribution for
Research Sample and Norming Group

Score	Indians	Negroes	Whites	Research sample	Norming group
0	17	14	15	46	97
1	0	3	2	5	12
Total nonconservation	17	17	17	51	109
2	1	3	2	6	28
3	1	2	0	3	6
4	1	2	0	3	20
5	1	1	1	3	3
6	2	4	0	6	16
7	0	2	1	3	3
8	0	4	1	5	25
9	1	1	1	3	5
Total transitional	7	19	6	32	106
10	2	2	7	11	24
11	3	2	1	6	7
12	13	2	11	26	64
Total conservation	18	6	19	43	95
	42	42	42	126	310

scores are recorded as total scores rather than separate behavior and explanation scores.

ANALYSIS OF COVARIANCE

Since the test developers assumed that the scores on the Conservation Concept Diagnostic Kit would be continuously distributed, a parametric analysis of the data was undertaken. Using race as the main effect and CA as a covariate, an analysis of covariance revealed significant differences between the racial group means on total conservation score ($F = 4.65$, $df = 2/122$, $p < .025$). The adjusted means are shown in Table 2 along with the PPVT raw scores.

CORRELATION BETWEEN CONSERVATION AND OTHER VARIABLES

The means and standard deviations for the scores on the Conservation Concept Diagnostic Kit, CA, and PPVT are reported in Table 2.

In the total sample the correlation (Pearson r) between CA and conservation scores is .43 ($p < .001$), and between the PPVT raw scores and conservation scores is .47 ($p < .001$) These correlations are in close agreement with those obtained by the test developers on middle-class children as well as with earlier findings by other investigators (Flavell, 1963, Ch. 11). These moderate positive correlations suggest that both traditional psychometric techniques and Piaget's tasks, at least in part, are tapping the same cognitive structures (Kohlberg, 1968, p. 1052). The degree of communality of the conservation tests and the psychometric test of intelligence is such that a covariance analysis using both CA and PPVT raw scores as control variables yields no significant differences between the ethnic groups' conservation scores.

CHI-SQUARE ANALYSIS

A chi-square test shows that the three racial samples do not represent the same population distributions on the criterion of total conservation score when the categories were: nonconservation scores = 0–1, transitional scores = 2–9, and conservation scores = 10–12 ($\chi^2 = 17.09$, $df = 4$, $p < .005$). Inspection of Table 3 reveals that the major differences between the groups are found between the transitional children and the conservers. A disproportionately large number of Negro children were in the transitional rather than the conservation cells in relation to the other two groups. When we disregard the category of *nonconservation*, there were significant differences between the racial groups ($\chi^2 = 17.09$, $df = 2$, $p < .001$). Thus, the significance level is increased when dealing only with the two categories of transitional and conservation. The reason is that the larger differences are found among the older children, as one

Table 2 Means, Standard Deviations, and Covariance Adjusted Means of Conservation Scores and Control Variables

| | Conservation score | | | | | | | | Controls | |
| | Raw mean | | SD | | Adjusted mean[a] | | Adjusted mean[b] | | | |
Group	Behavior	Explanation	Behavior	Explanation	Behavior	Explanation	Behavior	Explanation	CA	PPVT
Indian	3.024	2.786	2.361	2.360	3.006	2.755	2.591	2.378	7.673	63.07
Negro	2.286	1.833	1.766	1.638	2.317	1.889	2.904	2.421	8.063	55.86
White	3.071	2.833	2.228	2.217	3.057	2.809	2.886	2.653	7.700	61.19

NOTE. For CA and the Peabody Picture Vocabulary Test (PPVT) Raw Scores.
[a]CA controlled.
[b]CA and PPVT controlled.

Table 3 Summary of Chi-Square Analyses

Comparison	Category-conservation			
	Noncon-servation	Transi-tional	Conser-vation	χ^2
Race and 3 categories of conservation				
Indian	17	7	18	
Negro	17	19	6	
White	17	6	19	17.09[a]
Race and 2 categories of conservation				
Indian	—	7	18	
Negro	—	19	6	
White	—	6	19	17.09[b]
Sample and norming groups (all ages)				
Research sample	51	32	43	
Norming group	109	106	95	.513
Sample and norming groups (6.5–7.5 yr.)				
Research sample	25	7	8	
Norming group	16	36	36	24.8[b]
Race and 3 categories of conservation ($<$ 8.0 yr.)				
Indian	15	4	6	
Negro	12	6	2	
White	14	6	6	2.42
Race and 3 categories of conservation ($>$ 8.0 yr.)				
Indian	2	3	12	
Negro	5	13	4	
White	3	0	13	21.3[b]

[a] $p < .005.$
[b] $p < .001.$

would expect in the increasing divergence of negatively accelerated growth curves.

The most interesting finding of this study lies in a comparison of the frequency distributions of the conservation scores for the research sample and the norming group. Using the data in the test manual of instructions, which included means, standard deviations, and percentile ranks for each age level in the norming group, it was possible to compare the scores of these 310 children with the 126 children in the research sample. Upon inspection, the relative proportion of nonconservation, transitional, and conservation children in the two groups appeared to be about the same. However, there was an important difference between the groups. The research sample was made up of children whose ages ranged up to 2 years older than the norming group, with mean CA, respectively, of 7 years 10 months versus an estimated 6 years 7 months. It was reasoned that if it could be shown that there were no significant differences in performance between these two groups, then one conclusion could be that lower-class children of ages 6–10 were performing at about the same level as more advantaged children of ages $5\frac{1}{2}$–$7\frac{1}{2}$. No significant differences were found when the groups were compared in this way (see Table 2), lending support to a conclusion of a developmental lag in the lower social class sample.

In order to obtain some estimate of this effect, a comparison was made between the research sample and norming groups using only children who were in the same age ranges, the range between $6\frac{1}{2}$ and $7\frac{1}{2}$ years. Significant differences were found in this test, $\chi^2 = 24.8$, $df = 2$, $p < .001$ (see Table 3). Since the norming groups represented all strata of society, one would expect to find an even greater difference if the research sample were compared with a homogeneous middle-class group. In addition, this difference could be expected to be increased even further if a wider age range were to be compared, since the evidence shows the developmntal lag increasing with age. It is probable, then, that lower-class children make the transition from nonconserving to conserving behavior at a somewhat later age than has been found with other children, perhaps later than age 8. This assumption suggested two hypotheses: First, that there are no racial differences in conserving behavior among children in the research sample below age 8; second, there are racial differences among those children who are over 8 years of age.

A test of the first hypothesis revealed no significant differences among the three racial groups. However, when the older group of children was compared for racial differences, the chi-square test was significant ($\chi^2 = 21.3$, $df = 4$, $p < .001$).

A common interpretation of such findings is that environmental deprivation, operating differentially over time, is increasing the differences. Another possible interpretation is that children from low and high social class groups differ in intrinsic developmental rates. Of course, both environmental and developmental factors could be involved simultaneously. Since age of concept acquisition is correlated with CA, one can hypothesize that the significant differences shown in Table 2 emerge in the older rather than in the younger children.

DISCUSSION

The most general conclusion of this study is that there are major differences in rates of acquisition of conservation between children of different racial and social class backgrounds. Within the lower-class research sample, Negro children were behind Indian and white children in rate of acquisition and, specifically, older Negro children

seemed to be even further behind. This increasing difference between racial groups with increasing CA suggests that lower-class environments may be entirely different among different races. When
the lower-class children in the research sample were compared with
the more heterogeneous norming groups, the lower-class children
were later in acquiring conservation than the more advantaged social class groups. There was also a tendency for the Negro IQs, as
measured by the PPVT, to decrease with age, a trend that is consistent with findings in other studies of Negro intelligence (see Kennedy, 1969). The magnitude and direction of the differences on the
Conservation Concept Diagnostic Kit between Negroes on the one
hand and Indians and whites on the other were almost identical
with the reported summaries of studies of Negro-white differences
in mental test performance so widely discussed today (Jensen, 1969;
Kennedy, 1969; Lesser, Fifer, and Clark, 1965; Shuey, 1958). The
lower mean level of verbal ability for the Negroes as measured by
the PPVT and reported as raw scores may be closely related to their
lower performance on the conservation tasks, since the correlation
of IQ with conservation is moderate. It is possible that some lan-
guage-mediated variable is involved as an antecedent condition in
the development of both of these abilities. On the other hand, one
has difficulty in explaining the relative similarity of performance
between the Indians and whites, since many Indian families are bi-
lingual. The Seneca language is spoken by many adult Indians as a
second language, and a decided dialect is detectable when convers-
ing with many Indian children. However, their performance on the
PPVT did not reflect any substantial language inadequacy. This supports Coleman's (1966) finding that Indian children coming from
backgrounds with lower levels of deprivation than Negro children,
nevertheless, performed higher on verbal ability measures than did
the Negro children.

The differences between the racial groups are not as large as
those between the entire lower-class sample and the norming data
supplied by the test's authors. Here we found a very large gap in
performance between children of the same ages. By 8 years of age,
for example, the children in the norming group had reached a mean
score of almost 11, whereas of the entire 126 children tested in the
present study, only 32 achieved a score of 11 or 12, and at no place
in the distribution did the mean of any subset by age, race, or grade
level reach a value as high as 10, even if we considered the mean of
all children over the age of 8, which is only 7.9 $(N = 53)$. Social
class, then, seems to be more closely related to performance differences, in this study, than racial group membership.

Piaget (1964) claims that environment is a factor in cognitive
development, but a relatively minor one, and then only when the

cultures are widely divergent, for example, in climate or geography. He also maintains that nervous maturation is a necessary factor, and that there is evidence of racial and social class differences in rate of physical maturation (p. 10). If these are the factors separating the groups in the present study, and if they are cultural, rather than, or in addition to, intrinsic developmental factors, they have as yet to be identified specifically.

REFERENCES

Almy, M. E., Chittenden, E., and Miller, P. *Young children's thinking: Studies of some aspects of Piaget's theory.* New York: Teachers College, Columbia University Press, 1966.

Ames, L. B., and Ilg, F. L. Search for children showing academic progress in a predominantly Negro school. *The Journal of Genetic Psychology,* 1967, **110,** 217–231.

Campbell, D. T., and Stanley, J. C. Experimental and quasi-experimental designs for research on teaching. In N. L. Gage (Ed.), *Handbook for research on teaching.* Chicago: Rand McNally, 1963.

Coleman, J. S., et al. *Equality of educational opportunity.* Washington, D.C.: United States Government Printing Office, 1966.

De Lemos, M. M. Development of the concept of conservation in Australian Aborigine children. *International Journal of Educational Psychology,* 1969, **4,** 255–269.

Flavell, J. H. *The developmental psychology of Jean Piaget.* Princeton: Van Nostrand, 1963.

Goldschmid, M. L., and Bentler, P. M. The dimensions and measurement of conservation. *Child Development,* 1968, **39,** 787–802.

Goodnow, J. J. A test of milieu effects with some of Piaget's tasks. *Psychological Monographs,* 1962, **76**(36, Whole No. 555).

Hays, W. L. *Statistics for psychologists.* New York: Holt, Rinehart & Winston, 1963.

Hunt, J. McV. *Intelligence and experience.* New York: Ronald Press, 1961.

Hyde, D. M. An investigation of Piaget's theories of the development of the concept of number. Unpublished doctoral dissertation, University of London, 1959.

Inhelder, B., and Piaget, J. *The growth of logical thinking from childhood to adolescence.* New York: Basic Books, 1958.

Jensen, A. R. How much can we boost IQ and scholastic achievement? *Harvard Educational Review,* 1969, **39,** 1–123.

Kennedy, W. A. A follow up normative study of Negro intelligence and achievement. *Child Development Monographs,* 1969, **34**(3, Whole No. 126).

Kohlberg, L. Early education: A cognitive developmental view. *Child Development*, 1968, **39**, 1013–1062.

Lesser, G. S., Fifer, G., and Clark, D. H. Mental abilities of children from different social-class and cultural groups. *Monographs of the Society for Research in Child Development*, 1956, **30**(4, Serial No. 102).

Mermelstein, E., and Shulman, L. S. Lack of formal schooling and the acquisition of conservation. *Child Development*, 1967, **38**, 39–52.

Price-Williams, D. R. A study concerning concepts of conservation of quantities among primitive children. *Acta Psychologica*, 1961, **18**, 297–305.

Piaget, J. Cognitive development in children. In R. Ripple and V. Rockcastle (Eds.), *Piaget rediscovered. A report of the conference on cognitive studies and curriculum development*. Ithaca, New York: Cornell University Press, 1964.

Shuey, A. M. *The testing of Negro intelligence*. Lynchburg, Va.: Bell, 1958.

Sigel, I. E., and Hooper, F. H. *Logical thinking in children*. New York: Holt, Rinehart & Winston, 1968.

Sigel, I. E., and Perry, C. Psycholinguistic diversity among "culturally deprived" children. *American Journal of Orthopsychiatry*, 1968, **38**, 122–126.

Stodolsky, S. S., and Lesser, G. Learning patterns in the disadvantaged. *Harvard Educational Review*, 1967, **37**, 546–593.

Tuddenham, R. D. A Piagetian test of cognitive development. Symposium presented at the meeting of the Ontario Institute for Studies in Education, Toronto, May 1969.

Uzgiris, I. C. Situational generality of conservation. *Child Development*, 1964, **35**, 831–841.

Vernon, P. E. Environmental handicaps and intellectual development, Part 1. *British Journal of Educational Psychology*, 1965, **35**, 1–22.

Wallach, M. A. Research on children's thinking. *Yearbook of the National Society for the Study of Education*, 1963, **62**, Part 1.

Warner, W. L., Meeker, M., and Eells, K. *Social class in America*. Chicago: Science Research Associates, 1949.

the myth of the deprived child

HERBERT GINSBURG

The following selections are taken from an entire book of the same name by Dr. Ginsburg. The book is excellent and worth your further study. In order to give some flavor of Ginsburg's arguments in the short space available, I have selected two short sections, one from fairly early in the book, in which he gives his view of the "traditional" deficit hypothesis about poor children's intellect, and one from later in the book, in which he explains the application of Piaget's theory to the study of poor children's thinking. [Ed.]

POOR CHILDREN'S INTELLECT

Many psychologists believe—mistakenly, I think—that the poor child's intellect is deficient, although they disagree to some extent on the precise nature of the deficiency.

The *nativists* have traditionally asserted that poor children are characterized by inadequate "intelligence" as measured by the IQ test. Intelligence refers to a basic mental capacity which is at the root of the child's learning, his thinking, and his problem solving. Intelligence is the fundamental intellectual ability, the basic power

Herbert Ginsburg, *The myth of the deprived child: Poor children's intellect and education*, © 1972. Reprinted by permission of Prentice-Hall, Inc., Englewood Cliffs, N.J.

of the mind. Superior intelligence permits the child to cope with the environment and to profit from experience. Deficient intelligence hinders both adaptation and learning.

The *empiricists* generally place less emphasis on general intelligence and tend to stress the role of specific intellectual abilities. For example, many empiricists propose that poor children employ an impoverished mode of speech which in turn degrades thought. In this view, the poor child uses a "restricted code"—a language which is simple and terse, containing few abstractions. Lower-class speech is emotional, not intellectual; it is authoritarian, not reasonable; it is concrete, not abstract. Speech of this type is not a good vehicle for complex thinking, for logical reasoning, for considered judgments. Deficient speech produces deficient thought: the poor child's language produces an intellect which is overly concrete and illogical and which bases its judgments on emotion rather than reason. It should therefore come as no surprise that the poor child, burdened as he is with a restricted language and a deficient intellect, cannot succeed in academic endeavor.

At first the nativist and empiricist positions seem quite reasonable, either alone or in combination. Yet closer examination reveals serious flaws in each argument.

There is a great deal of confusion regarding the notion of intelligence as it is usually employed by the nativists. Try to define what "intelligence" is. When people do this, they generally succeed in producing two or three definitions which are at odds with one another or which at least seem to refer to different things. For example, is intelligence the ability to engage in abstract reasoning or to profit from experience? Is it the ability to adapt to the environment or to use verbal and symbolic skills? Confusion over the meaning of intelligence is not limited to the lay public. David Wechsler, a leading worker in the area of intelligence testing and the originator of the Wechsler Intelligence Scale, writes as follows:

> Some psychologists have come to doubt whether these laborious analyses have contributed anything fundamental to our understanding of intelligence while others have come to the equally disturbing conclusion that the term intelligence, as now employed, is so ambiguous that it ought to be discarded altogether. Psychology seems now to find itself in the paradoxical position of devising and advocating tests for measuring intelligence and then disclaiming responsibility for them by asserting "nobody knows what the word really means" [Quoted in Tuddenham, 1962, pp. 470–71].

This confusion is obviously quite damaging to the nativist position. How can intelligence be so fundamental, so basic, when after years of research "nobody knows what the word really means"? How can a presumably scientific psychology employ so ephemeral a concept as that of intelligence to explain poor children's academic failure? And if poor children's IQ is relatively low, what does that fact mean?

The empiricist view also suffers from serious deficiencies. For one thing, the research evidence is full of contradictions. Some studies seem to support the empiricist view. They show that poor children's intellectual performance on a variety of measures is inadequate to some degree. But other research efforts support a different conclusion. They show that poor children's language and thought are generally no different from middle-class children's abilities in these areas. Moreover, one can make the argument that the empiricist position suffers from the limits of a middle-class perspective. For example, some empiricists ask whether poor children are capable of the kind of speech that the middle class happens to consider congenial. The empiricists generally do not attempt to determine whether poor children use a language which is both distinctive and well suited to their own environment.

These considerations raise many questions. Chief among them is whether poor children's intellect is really deficient. If not deficient, is it at least different from that of middle-class children?

In Chapters 2, 3, and 4, I attempt to deal with many of these issues—with the nature of poor children's cognition, their intelligence, language, and thought. I try to probe the nativist and empiricist positions, to identify defects in their reasoning, and to evaluate both the evidence which supports their arguments and the evidence which contradicts them.

My conclusion, which I call the *developmental view*, is that in many fundamental ways poor children's cognition is quite similar to that of middle-class children. There are *cognitive universals*, modes of language and thought shared by all children (except the retarded and severely emotionally disturbed) regardless of culture or upbringing. At the same time, there do exist social-class differences in cognition. Yet the differences are relatively superficial, and one must not make the mistake of calling them deficiencies or considering them analogous to mental retardation.

· · ·

THE IMPORTANCE OF PIAGET

As I mentioned earlier, we have reviewed only a minute portion of Piaget's voluminous work. He has produced some forty books on different aspects of cognitive development, so that you have seen only a smattering of his theory in the last several pages.

Here I want to discuss why it is so important for us to study Piaget's ideas as they relate to poor children. You will recall that earlier I described aspects of Palmer's and Lesser's work as superficial. I said that it was not particularly important to know that a child can attach the label "ball" to the proper object or that he can remember that two and two are four. I maintained that other aspects of thought are more fundamental. Now I must answer this question: Why is Piaget's work more basic than the others?

I will give two arguments. The first can be approached through a simple example concerning arithmetic. According to Lesser *et al.*, the child shows a high degree of arithmetic ability when he can consistently solve problems such as finding the sum of three and four objects. What is the minimal set of skills needed to do something like this? First, the child must be able to count the objects properly so that he knows that there are three here and four there. Second, he must have some way of finding the sum. He can use a rote method, simply holding in memory the addition facts for small numbers. If the objects are all visible, he can use a counting procedure, simply combining the two sets and enumerating the elements.

Is all this fundamental? From one perspective, it is: The child cannot do arithmetic and succeed in school without being able to count and without remembering some basic number facts. So Lesser's work is important from this point of view. But from another perspective, counting and adding may be based on little understanding; arithmetic skills may function without the child's appreciating the underlying mathematical concepts which Piaget's work focuses on. For example, in one interview Piaget presented a child of 5 years with two sets of objects, arrayed as in A in Figure 4-4, and asked the child to count them. He did so and correctly maintained that each set had seven. Then, as the child watched, the examiner performed the classic conservation experiment, bunching up one of the sets. Again the child was asked to count the elements in the sets, and again he correctly reported the numbers: seven in each. Then the examiner asked whether the sets had the same number or whether one had more. The child maintained that the lower set had more because it was longer (Piaget 1952, p. 45)!

The example shows what nearly everyone who has been through school knows quite well: you can correctly execute various calculations without understanding the ideas involved. In this case, the child could count, but the results were meaningless to him.

Piaget's work attempts to focus on the basic concepts of various areas of knowledge. In dealing with number, for example, Piaget examines the concepts of equivalence and of a series: he largely ignores counting and mastery of the addition or subtraction facts. This, then, is the first reason that Piaget's work is fundamental: it

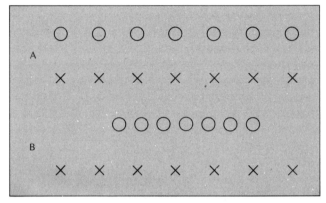

Figure 4-4 Conservation of number.

concentrates on the basic ideas of a discipline, not on the superficial aspects which schools often stress.

A second reason is that the mental operations which Piaget's theory describes underlie the child's thinking in a variety of areas. For example, Piaget has studied the "formal operations" which characterize adolescent and adult thought. Briefly, this kind of thinking involves the ability to imagine hypothetical possibilities, to consider in an exhaustive way the various combinations of events that may occur, to reason in a logical fashion, and so on. Piaget shows that the formal operations manifest themselves in several areas of endeavor. For example, when the adolescent acquires the formal operations, he can handle certain types of scientific problem solving (Inhelder and Piaget, 1958); he elaborates theories of society and of religion (1958), and he engages in advanced forms of moral judgment (Piaget, 1932). In brief, formal operations subsume many areas of content: they make possible scientific, social, religious, and moral thought. This, then, is the second reason for the importance of Piaget's theory: the mental activities it describes are central to many areas of intellectual endeavor.

Indeed, some of the mental activities which Piaget describes are almost essential for human survival. For example, some of Piaget's work deals with the development of basic categories of mind: concepts of space, time, causality. Without these, the child would have a difficult time surviving his first several years.

CROSS-CULTURAL STUDIES

Piaget's theory proposes, with a few minor qualifications, that the stages and order of cognitive development are universal. All children, regardless of culture, progress through the stages of the sensori-motor period, as in the case of object permanence, and proceed from there to pre-operational thought, then concrete operational thought, and finally, in all but the most primitive societies, to the stage of formal operations..

The cultures may differ in the ages at which the various stages are attained, but not in the basic course of development. For example, in one culture children may acquire the conservation of number at age 6 whereas in another they cannot conserve until age 8. But in both cultures, all children eventually acquire the mental operations which make conservation possible. Also, in both cultures children first must progress through pre-operational thinking before the concrete operations will appear. What evidence is there to support these claims, and what bearing does it have on problems of poor children's intellect?

Goodnow (1962) attempted to determine whether children in a non-Western culture show cognitive abilities similar to those of Western children. The subjects were a large number of boys, from 10 to 13 years of age, all of whom lived in Hong Kong. One group consisted of 148 Europeans, mainly English and mainly middle class. A second group involved 151 Chinese boys of middle-class origin. They attended exclusive schools where instruction was in English. A third group involved 80 lower-class Chinese boys, whose parents had unskilled or semi-skilled jobs and who attended schools in which Chinese was the language of instruction. A fourth group consisted of 80 Chinese boys of lower-class background who had a minimum of schooling, education not being compulsory in Hong Kong. Each group had approximately equal numbers of subjects at ages 10, 11, 12, and 13. To summarize, Goodnow's four major groups of subjects were Europeans, Westernized middle-class Chinese, lower-class Chinese attending school, and lower-class Chinese with a minimum of education. Presumably the last two groups represent a non-Western culture, whereas the first two groups are Western or at least Western influenced.

Each boy was given four Piagetian tasks: conservation of weight, volume, and area, and a test of combinatorial reasoning. . . . the conservation of weight involves showing the child two identical clay balls which are of the same weight. When the child accepts this fact, one of the balls is transformed into a different shape, for example, a sausage, and he is asked whether the weight remains the same. The conservation of volume involves the same materials. The child is first shown that the two identical balls, placed in two identical beakers of liquid, displace the same volumes. Then both balls are removed from the water, one is transformed in shape, and the child must predict whether it will still displace the same amount of liquid.

The conservation of area involves placing on two identical rectangular surfaces two identical arrays of objects (for example: houses arranged in the same way on two fields). After the child agrees that the objects cover up the same amount of surface, one set of objects is transformed so that it is arranged differently on the surface. The three conservation tasks are intended to assess the child's concrete operational thinking. The tasks are not of equal difficulty, however. Piaget has found that the conservation of area is mastered at about age 7 or 8, weight at about 10 years, and volume at about 12 years.

The fourth problem involved presenting each child with a collection of poker chips of six different colors. The task was to construct from the six colors all possible combinations of two colors at a time. There are 15 such combinations of elements. If we symbolize the six colors as A, B, C, D, E, and F, then the combinations are: AB, AC, AD, AE, AF, BC, BD, BE, BF, CD, CE, CF, DE, DF, EF. (Order does not count. Thus BA is not a legitimate combination since we already have AB.) Note that the sequence in which the combinations are listed is systematic. First, A was paired with each of the others, then B with each (except A), and so on. Without some system, it is easy to lose track of what has been paired with what. The test is intended to tap one aspect of formal operational thought, namely the ability to combine things in an exhaustive and systematic way. From the point of view of formal operations, the task is relatively simple, since it involves concrete objects. All four tasks were administered in a standard way, the questions being taken from published protocols of Piaget's clinical interviews.

The findings showed that on the conservation tasks there were only minor differences among the four groups. For example, in the conservation of weight, Europeans and Chinese children with a minimum of schooling received almost identical scores at all ages. Interestingly, the children who did most poorly, on the average, were not the Chinese children with a minimum of education, but the middle- and lower-class Chinese children who attended school: they tended to parrot "scientific" explanations referring to mysteries such as "center of gravity" which they did not understand and which were inappropriate. Further, the Chinese subjects' incorrect and correct answers generally took the form predicted by Piaget. A minor discrepancy with Piaget's results involved the sequence of mastery of the tasks. Piaget maintains that conservation of area is mastered first, then weight, then volume. Goodnow found, however, that area and weight were of about equal difficulty, and (in agreement with Piaget) that volume was hardest of all. Goodnow speculates, though, that the area task may have been presented in an especially difficult manner. In sum, the cultural and social-class differences on the three types of conservation are generally quite minor.

The results for the combinatorial task were much different. Europeans and Chinese boys of middle-class origin who attended Western type schools performed much better than did lower-class Chinese with or without schooling. Goodnow found, however, that lower-class Chinese, while doing poorly on the combinatorial task relative to the middle-class subjects, nevertheless improved with age. This suggests that in due course the lower-class Chinese acquire formal operations, too, albeit more slowly than the others. The lower-class boys lag behind but are not completely deficient in combinatorial thought.

To summarize, Goodnow finds that on the three conservation tasks, all cultural and social class groups perform at about the same level. On the combinations task, middle-class Chinese and European boys are superior to lower-class Chinese, although the latter show signs of improvement with age.

I wish to make several comments on these findings. First, while cultural and social-class factors have little effect on conservation, the meaning of the combinatorial reasoning results is not clear: several interpretations might account for them. One possibility is that success at the task depends on Westernization. The Europeans and the middle-class Chinese in Western type schools, both of which groups one might consider to be Westernized, performed at a higher level than the two non-Westernized groups, the lower-class Chinese. The difficulty with this interpretation is the postulate that the middle-class Chinese were Westernized. We do not know for a fact that they really were.

Another possibility is that social class is crucial. Those showing superior performance were middle class, and inferior performance, lower class. But is the middle class in Chinese culture really similar to the middle class in European culture? Does not cultural difference override class similarity?

A third possibility is that schooling is involved. Those doing well at the task attended English schools; those doing poorly either did not go to school or attended inadequate lower-class schools. But can schooling be a more important influence than either social class or culture?

Another interpretation still, which Goodnow originally offered, is that IQ is the important factor. She found that groups superior in the combinations task had higher IQs than the groups who did poorly on it. If the effect of IQ is eliminated by statistical means, then there are no major differences among the groups. But the IQ interpretation is ambiguous, too. What do IQ scores in foreign cultures mean? And are not the IQ findings confounded with social-class differences, the high IQ subjects being middle class and the low, lower class? As you can see, each interpretation is complex.

Furthermore, there is the possibility that some combination of factors—not just a single one—is involved. Perhaps lack of schooling and social class and culture are all related to the observed differences.

My second comment is that it is hard to see why there were no group differences on the conservation tasks, while there were differences on the combinations test. Whatever the factor—culture, social class, schooling, or IQ—responsible for the group differences in the combination tasks, why should it not affect conservation tasks as well?

Further research clarifies some of these issues. Price-Williams (1961) found that West African children from 5 to 8 years of age showed roughly the same progression as European children in the development of conservation of continuous and discontinuous quantities.

These children were not in school, nor were they of European culture. The study indicates, then, that neither schooling nor Westernization is necessary for successful conservation in these cases.

Vernon (1965a) gave a battery of Piagetian tests, in a standardized fashion, to 100 British and 50 West Indian boys. All children attended school and were from 10½ to 11 years. The middle and lower classes were represented in each cultural group. First, consider overall cultural differences on the Piaget tasks. On several tests there were negligible or small differences between British and West Indian children: conservation of substance, conservation of volume, inclusion relations (classification), and imagery. The largest differences occurred in the case of conservation of continuous quantities, where 6 percent of the English children and 18 percent of the West Indian children were wrong on the standard problem; conservation of length, where 5 percent of the English and 40 percent of the West Indians were incorrect; conservation of area, where the error rates were 7 percent for the English and 18 for the West Indians. Of the three "large" differences, only conservation of length seems important. The Vernon results must be viewed with caution since the method of administration was extremely inflexible. Nevertheless, the findings suggest that on most of the tasks, with the possible exception of conservation of length, West Indian and British children perform at roughly equivalent levels. In a second paper (1965b), Vernon reports that West Indian boys of different social classes did not differ on the Piagetian tasks. (He does not give social-class data for the English.)

Greenfield (1966) studied the conservation of liquid in West African children (Senegal). There were three groups: village children who did not attend school, village children who did, and urban children who attended school. In all groups there were three age levels: 6 to 7 years; 8 to 9; and 11 to 13. The results showed that the schooled children, both rural and urban, followed the typical course of development with regard to conservation: relative success at age 6 or 7 and almost perfect performance by the age of 11 to 13. By contrast, the unschooled rural Senegalese failed to improve after the age of 8 or 9; only about 50 percent succeeded at this age level and at ages 11 to 13. Thus culture does not affect the development of conservation; the urban-rural distinction is not important, either. What seems to matter is schooling.

Opper (1971) has performed what I think is the most thorough study in this area. Her aim was to examine Thai children's acquisition of the intellectual stages and types of reasoning described by Piaget. She studied two groups, one involving 142 children from the city of Bangkok, and the other involving 140 children from a small rural community engaged mainly in rice farming. The children in both samples ranged from 6 to 16 years of age. Opper administered to all children from 6 to 11 years of age a battery of 10 Piagetian tasks measuring concrete operational thought: class inclusion, conservation of length, conservation of liquid, one-to-one correspondence, and seriation. They also received tasks of mental imagery. In addition, she administered to children from 6 to 16 years of age two tests of formal operational thinking: conservation of volume and permutations. In testing the children, the examiners, who were native speakers of Thai, used Piaget's clinical method. This procedure produces data both on the children's stage of cognitive development (for example, whether or not they can conserve volume) and on the mental processes used to solve the problems. Too few studies of cross-cultural differences in cognition have employed the clinical method to examine the mental processes themselves.

Consider first the results concerning concrete operational tasks. On each task, both the urban and rural samples showed the same three-stage progression described by Piaget and displayed by Western children. Furthermore, at each stage of development, the Thai children used the same types of reasoning shown by Swiss children and often verbalized the reasoning in identical words.

In the tasks of mental imagery, there was a slight difference between the Thai and Swiss children. The Thai children do approximately as well on both static and dynamic problems, whereas Swiss children find the static tasks easier. Nevertheless, Thai children develop each type of imagery in the manner Piaget describes and in general make the same types of errors as do Swiss children.

In the case of formal operational tasks, Thai children again show the pattern of development described by Piaget.

In general, the similarities between Thai and Swiss children are remarkable when one considers the stages of development, and the similarities are especially striking when one considers the types of reasoning. Children from Geneva and children raised in rice paddies in central Thailand often justify their solution of a conservation problem in precisely the same manner!

At the same time, there were some differences between Thai and Swiss children. The rural Thai children develop at a slower rate than do either Genevan or urban Thai children. In general, the urban Thai and Swiss children acquired the various concepts at about the same age (although there were a few exceptions) whereas the rural Thai children acquired these concepts about 2 or 3 years later. Opper presents some evidence suggesting that the older the child, the less the lag between rural Thai children and the others. Thus, as the rural Thai child grows older, he becomes more similar to the urban Thai and Swiss child.

In brief, Opper's research shows overwhelming similarities in stages of development and types of reasoning between Thai and Swiss children (who are of course quite similar to American and other Western children). The major difference is in the age of acquisition of the various concepts: rural Thai children acquire them at a later age than do the others. Unfortunately there is no simple explanation for the Thai urban-rural difference in rate of cognitive development. Both groups go to school; both speak the same language. Presumably, some as yet unidentified differences in environment or experience can explain the results.

Table 1 summarizes the results from various studies. What do they show? First, consider the hypothesis that culture produces important differences in certain cognitive skills. The evidence does not support this hypothesis. Goodnow found minimal effects of culture; Price-Williams showed that conservation develops "normally" in West African children; Vernon found that culture had little effect on many tasks; and Greenfield's data indicate that schooled African children are similar to Europeans in performance on the conservation task. There were a few exceptions to the general rule: Goodnow found some differences, possibly attributable to culture, in a combinatorial reasoning task; and Vernon found West Indians to be inferior in conservation of length. These results need to be replicated; all we can say now is that the bulk of evidence indicates little effect of cultural factors on the Piagetian tasks investigated.

Is social class a crucial factor? In general, the evidence seems to show that it is not. Goodnow found no such effects in the case of conservation, although social class might underlie some of the obtained differences in the combinatorial task. Vernon found no social-class differences on Piagetian tasks and neither did Greenfield (if one interprets the urban-rural factor as social class). The only discrepant finding is Opper's. She found social-class differences in

Table 1   Cross-Cultural Studies of Cognitive Development

I. Goodnow (1962), Hong Kong.
Groups: Middle-class Europeans; middle-class Chinese attending English Language School; lower-class Chinese attending Chinese School; lower-class Chinese with a minimum of education.
Tasks: Conservation of weight, area, volume, and combinatorial reasoning.
Results: All groups were about the same on conservation tasks. On the combinatorial task, the middle-class European and Chinese were superior to the lower-class Chinese, schooled or unschooled.

II. Price-Williams (1961), West Africa.
Groups: Unschooled African children of various ages.
Tasks: Conservation of continuous and discontinuous quantities.
Results: Performance is similar to what is found in Europeans.

III. Vernon (1965a, b), England and West Indies.
Groups: Middle- and lower-class British and West Indian children.
Tasks: A battery of conservation, classification, and imagery tasks.
Results: There were negligible differences in the case of conservation of substance and volume, inclusion relations, and imagery. There were small differences in the case of conservation of continuous quantities and area. The West Indian children did poorly on the conservation of length. There were no social-class differences within the West Indian group.

IV. Greenfield (1966), Senegal.
Groups: Urban schooled, rural schooled, rural unschooled.
Tasks: Conservation of continuous quantity.
Results: The schooled groups showed the normal pattern of development, and the unschooled group did poorly.

V. Opper (1971), Thailand.
Groups: Urban schooled, rural schooled.
Tasks: Concrete operational, imagery, formal operational.
Results: Both groups were similar to the Swiss in developmental stages and types of reasoning. The rural group acquired the concepts at a later age than did the urban Thai or Swiss, both of which were similar.

Thai children (if one interprets the urban-rural factor in this way). Of course, social-class differences in cognition may exist for tasks not yet studied or for groups within Western countries; not enough research has been done to rule out this possibility. Nevertheless, much of the evidence does not support the hypothesis.

Consider next the effects of schooling. Here the situation is ambiguous. Goodnow finds that schooling may make a difference for the combinatorial problem but not the conservation tasks. Price-Williams finds no effect of schooling in the case of conservation. Greenfield, however, shows that lack of schooling has marked effects on conservation. On the other hand, in Opper's study, both groups were schooled and yet there was a difference between urban and rural children. The picture seems confusing; schooling may or may not have an effect.

Finally, there is the hypothesis that IQ can account for observed cultural differences in cognitive development. Since the observed differences seem minor, this hypothesis has little work to do.

It should be pointed out that the cross-cultural studies, while in some respects illuminating, suffer from a major weakness. Much of the research does not obtain a clear measure of the reasoning process used in the solution of various problems. The conservation problem, for example, can be solved in a variety of ways, and Piaget is not interested so much in the fact that a child solved it, but in his method of doing so. He repeatedly points out that even complex problems, like Goodnow's combination task, can be solved by ontogenetically primitive modes of thought. To rule out this possibility, one must probe the child's thought by administering several problems in a flexible way. Only Opper's study does this. Such research is the only hope for clarifying some of the ambiguities posed by cross-cultural studies—for example, that West Indian children do well on conservation of substance but not length. If we had some idea of the reasoning process employed in both cases, we might be able to interpret the confusing results.

WESTERN STUDIES

What does Piagetian research tell us about social-class differences within Western culture? Several studies have compared the social classes on various Piagetian tasks. The results may be summarized as follows. Some studies find no social-class differences; some find minor ones; none of the research shows that lower-class children entirely lack the skills Piaget describes.

Here are a few examples of research showing a social-class difference. Beilin, Kagan, and Rabinowitz (1966) studied visual imagery in 7-year-olds. . . . They found significant social-class and racial differences in the imagery problems. Unfortunately, the writers do not tell us how large the differences were or whether lower-class or black subjects are completely deficient in the skills under consideration.

Rothenberg and Courtney (1969) investigated social-class differences in the conservation of number. Table 2 shows the percentage of children passing four different conservation of number problems. The table shows that few young children (2–5 to 3–4) of either social class are consistent conservers and that at ages 3–5 to 4–4 a significantly greater percentage of middle-class children conserve consistently than do lower-class children. Of course, the study has nothing to say about what occurs after the age of 4–4. Do poor children eventually catch up?

Table 2 Percentages of Responses to Four Conservation Problems

Problems	Lower class		Middle class	
	2–5 to 3–4	3–5 to 4–4	2–5 to 3–4	3–5 to 4–4
1. CONS[a]	0.0	13.3	0.0	17.1
CNC	10.0	30.0	37.5	58.5
INC	90.0	56.7	62.5	24.4
2. CONS	3.3	10.0	6.3	31.7
CNC	10.0	23.3	12.5	24.4
INC	86.7	66.7	81.2	43.9
3. CONS	0.0	6.7	0.0	17.1
CNC	10.0	16.7	31.3	56.1
INC	90.0	73.3	68.7	24.4
4. CONS	0.0	3.3	0.0	12.2
CNC	6.7	26.7	37.5	56.1
INC	90.0	66.7	56.2	29.3

Source: Rothenberg and Courtney, 1969, p. 497.
[a]CONS means consistent conserving, CNC means consistent nonconserving, and INC means inconsistent.

Consider next a few studies showing no social-class differences. Beilin (1964) studied lower- and middle-class children's performance on a task analogous to Piaget's problem of the conservation of area. According to Beilin, "performance in the MC Kindergarten [about age 5] is not appreciably different from that of the LC Kindergarten groups on all measures" (p. 221).

What happens in the case of older children? Mermelstein and Schulman (1967) investigated the effect of lack of schooling on lower-class children's conservation performance. These writers studied 6- and 9-year-old Negro children. About half of the subjects at each age level were from a lower-class background in the American South and did not attend school. Another group (again both 6 and 9 years of age) was from a similar background in the North and did attend school. The question was whether the first group's lack of schooling affected its performance on the conservation of continuous quantity. The results showed that both groups performed at about the same level: by 9 years of age, children from both the North and South did well at the conservation problem. The data are given in Table 3. They plainly show that on the various forms of the conservation tasks, poor 6-year-olds, schooled or unschooled, do badly, whereas a high proportion of older children show evidence of an ability to conserve. The results are of interest in two ways. They show first that extremely deprived black children in the South eventually acquire conservation and, second, that attendence in school apparently makes no difference for this aspect of development.

Table 3   Number of Schooled and Unschooled Children Showing
Conservation or Its Lack on Five Conservation Tasks

Task	6-year-olds	
	Unschooled	Schooled
1 Nonconservers (NC)	17	23
Conservers (C)	9	6
2 NC	25	28
C	4	1
3 NC	27	29
C	3	1
4 NC	24	26
C	6	4
5 NC	24	29
C	3	0
	9-year-olds	
1 NC	6	5
C	24	25
2 NC	17	14
C	9	13
3 NC	13	14
C	14	14
4 NC	6	5
C	21	20
5 NC	8	9
C	21	18

Source: Mermelstein and Schulman, 1967, p. 47.

CONCLUSIONS

In general, the available research supports Piaget's views. The cross-cultural studies show that the basics of cognitive functioning, at least as Piaget describes it, are quite similar in a variety of cultures throughout the world. The ages at which children master the Piagetian tasks may not be precisely the same in Geneva as in Hong Kong, but in both cases cognitive development seems to follow the same general course. In view of this, it seems unlikely that the minds of lower-class children within Western societies differ in remarkable ways from those of middle-class children. The available research supports this conjecture. Some studies show no social-class differences in intellect; other studies show minor differences.

The bulk of the evidence suggests that certain aspects of cognition are universal: all children acquire certain basic categories of thought. This is not to deny that there may be individual and social-class differences in other aspects of thought. Surely the *content* of poor children's thought must include unique features. Poor children in the ghetto often know about the numbers racket, whereas middle-class children may think of numbers in the context of adding lolli-pops.

Perhaps, too, poor children's *patterns* of thinking (not the content) are in some ways unique. The Lesser research suggests that this may be true of different ethnic groups. But as yet we know little about this possibility, however plausible it may be. As I pointed out earlier, the tests used in the Lesser research were rather super-ficial. To detect subtle differences in thought, we need subtle re-search—research which attempts to measure fine aspects of the reasoning process. It will benefit us little simply to tabulate the number of problems on which middle- and lower-class children are correct or incorrect. We should save wasted effort by attempting to measure instead the types of reasoning that both kinds of children employ.

So there must be social-class differences in the content of thought, and there may be some social-class differences in the pat-tern of thought. But we must not permit these differences to obscure the basic similarities—the cognitive universals. Taking this per-spective we see that much current theory concerning poor children's intellect is often misleading and incorrect: poor children do not suffer from massive deficiencies of mind. If this is so, then a basic question remains. How do poor children develop powerful intel-lectual skills despite an apparently deprived environment?

part IV
compensatory education

compensatory education

HELEN L. BEE

WHAT IS COMPENSATORY EDUCATION ANYWAY?

Several years ago, while I was traveling on sabbatical and looking at day-care and preschool facilities in other countries, I was invited by the United States Embassy in Belgrade, Yugoslavia, to give a talk to the local educators. Compensatory education in the United States was one of the subjects I'd indicated I could talk about, and that's the topic the local people wanted to hear. I proceeded to give my usual presentation (translated into Serbo-Croatian!), but from the puzzled look on everyone's face as I progressed, it was clear that something was wrong. When it came time for questions, I discovered that for them "compensatory education" meant special classes or programs after regular school hours for children whose parents both work. And there I had been, talking about preschool programs for "disadvantaged children" for an hour and a half. The experience persuaded me that I should never be too blithe about assuming that we all use terms in the same fashion, and that some definition of this phrase was in order.

The term "compensatory education" obviously suggests some kind of educational program designed to compensate for some lack in the child's life. In the Yugoslav's case the program compensated for the lack of parental supervision after school hours. In the United States we are attempting to compensate for the apparent lack of readiness for school on the part of millions of children, primarily those from poverty backgrounds.

The impetus for the development of various kinds of experimental and nationwide compensatory programs in this country came from the growing realization that many children, particularly those from poverty environments, were simply not equipped to take advantage of the normal elementary school education. Since equal opportunity in our society is offered primarily through the educational system, it seemed crucial (and still does) for all children to have an equal chance in the school system. If the school system wasn't working in a way that provided equal opportunity, then something was wrong. Obviously, the next step is to ask why some children are "ready" when they come to school and others are not. Since the three kinds of answers to that question were discussed at some length in Part III, I need merely list them here. First, one can assume that some children, because of lack of environmental stimulation, inadequate diet, or some other environmental factor, simply do not acquire the needed intellectual skills during the first years of life. They cannot learn in the average school because they do not possess the knowledge and the thinking tools that are required. Second, one can assume that the observed deficits in knowledge and thinking tools come not from environmental deficits, but from basic genetic differences; poor children do not do as well in school because inherently they are not as smart. Third, following Ginsburg's argument, one can assume that the typical school requires not only intellectual skill, but also a particular kind of motivation and attitude. Many children with perfectly well developed intellectual competencies may do poorly in school simply because the system of intellectual achievement emphasized there does not fit well with their motivational system.

Obviously, the solution you seek depends heavily on which of these three explanations you favor. If you favor a genetic view, there is essentially no solution. If you favor Ginsburg's view, you may argue for new "open classrooms," in which each child has an opportunity to develop at his own pace and with his own motivations. Compensatory education, as we know it, comes from neither of these, but rather arises virtually exclusively from the "deficit" views of the problem. It was assumed by those who designed compensatory projects that children from poverty environments had particular kinds of definable cognitive and educational deficits, and that these deficits could be overcome by the appropriate kind of early intervention.

But what sort of intervention is best? How do you go about compensating for what are presumed to be lacks in the child's environment? How do you help the child catch up intellectually to his more advantaged peers? To date, two general kinds of strategies have been attempted. The first, and by far the most widespread, is to enroll poverty-level children in preschools for one or two years prior to regular kindergarten classes. The notion of using preschool as a place in which to train cognitive skills was a relatively novel one, or at least was a return to an idea that had been prevalent in the 1930s and hadn't been heard of since. Between the 1930s and 1960 or so, virtually all preschools were for the middle class and focused almost exclusively on social and emotional development. But the "traditional" preschools did at least provide an operating model; there were many people who knew something about the mechanics of running a nursery school. What was needed, it appeared, was to add academic content to the curriculum in order to use the preschool format to reach the poverty-level child.

In the early 1960s several experimental programs were begun that did precisely that: They took the preschool format and added a heavy dose of cognitive training and stimulation, particularly verbal training, to the curriculum. Three of the best known of these early programs are Deutsch's in New York City (Deutsch, 1963, 1969), Weikart's in Ypsilanti, Michigan (Weikart, 1967, 1969, 1972), and Gray and Klaus's program in Tennessee (Gray and Klaus, 1965, 1970; Klaus and Gray, 1968). The early results from such studies were very encouraging, showing large initial gains in IQ for poverty children between the beginning and end of the program. In part because of these encouraging results, in 1965 a national program (Head Start) was begun, at first only with summer programs and then very quickly with all-year programs, modeled very generally after the experimental programs then available. Other experimental programs were also begun at about this time (Karnes, Teska, and Hodgins; 1970; Bereiter and Englemann, 1966), with each group of investigators attempting to design the curriculum that would have the greatest impact.

Most commonly, the compensatory preschool has been patterned after the "traditional" preschool. Children generally come for two and a half to three hours, either in the morning or in the afternoon, in a group of about 12 to 15 children. Usually, there are three adults (sometimes four). One is a trained teacher, and the others are less well trained aides of some variety. In Head Start the children begin the program when they are four years old, although in most of the experimental programs, children begin the preschool when they are three and continue for two years.

Past this very general format, however, the manner in which the material is presented differs a good deal from one program to another. (Carl Bereiter discusses this at some length in the paper included in the selections.) The continuum along which the variation occurs seems to be from highly structured to nonstructured, or from programs having a "strong instructional emphasis" (to borrow Bereiter's phrase) to those having a weak instructional emphasis.[1] On one end of this continuum are programs like Bereiter and Englemann's (1966), in which each moment of the child's time in the preschool is organized. Behavioral goals are clearly spelled out in sequential fashion. The children are given drills in the various skills. In these drills the teacher asks questions and prompts; the child responds; and the teacher rewards. Although the activities are done in a group, each child is expected to meet the basic behavioral criteria. In this type of program emphasis has been on language training, but such programs also train in elementary mathematics and reading. Other programs that are also strong in instructional emphasis include less drill, but are nonetheless fully planned and quite structured. (See Weikart, 1972; Gray and Klaus, 1965; Klaus and Gray, 1968.)

At the other end of the continuum lie the old-style "child-centered" preschools, attended primarily by the middle-class child. Head Start programs, although designed as compensatory efforts, nonetheless took many ideas and plans from the traditional nursery schools as well as from the more intellectually oriented experimental programs. Most Head Start programs are thus substantially less intensive and instructionally oriented than are programs such as Bereiter and Englemann's or Weikart's. Montessori preschools, although maintaining a more cognitive orientation than traditional American preschools, are also less highly structured; children are expected to explore and learn much more on their own than is the case in the more heavily structured compensatory programs. Obviously, then, when we talk of "compensatory education," it is not a single entity. One of the interesting questions, to which research has been directed recently, is the relative effectiveness of the several varieties of preschool programs.

There is another, altogether different, kind of compensatory program, which has become more common in just the past four to five years, namely intervention with the family rather than with the child. The argument goes something like this: If the deficits we observe result from some characteristics in the child's home environment, putting him in a two-hour-a-day preschool is only a stopgap measure. Every time he goes home to his normal environment, the preschool effect may be undone. Then, too, what about the younger brothers and sisters? If the fundamental difficulty is at home, we will need to provide a preschool program for each new child in the family, which is a costly and time-consuming process. But what if we can change the home environment directly? Wouldn't that have a far greater effect on the individual child,

---

[1]There are currently all sorts of arguments in the literature about the appropriate way to label this continuum, but "structure" and "instructional emphasis" seem to me at the moment to be equally good.

and potentially on the younger children in the family as well? Might it be cheaper in the long run?

A number of such programs have been attempted. Most commonly, social workers or "facilitators" of some kind are sent into the home on a regular basis. They provide the mother with new toys for her to use with the child, play with the child to demonstrate how the toy might be used, and interact with the mother in a way that encourages her to use positive reinforcement, questions, expanded sentences, and so on. (See Levenstein and Sunley, 1968; Levenstein, 1970; Schaefer, 1969). Weikart has combined home-visit programs with the child's preschool experience (Weikart and Lambie, 1969), as have Susan W. Gray and Rupert A. Klaus in the study included in the selections. In another paper included in the selections, Merle B. Karnes, James A. Teska, Audrey S. Hodgins, and Earladeen D. Badger have taken a somewhat different tack: They have worked directly with the mothers in out-of-the-home classes and have not dealt with the children at all. In every instance, however, regardless of the specifics of the program, the intent of family intervention is to make some lasting change in the child's inanimate environment (by adding new toys, for example) and to alter the animate environment by changing the manner in which the mother interacts with and teaches her child.

DO COMPENSATORY PROGRAMS WORK?

First off, how do you tell if a given program has "worked"? What are the criteria by which you judge the success or failure of a particular program? In general, you look first at the goals set for the particular program and then compare the results with the goals. Since virtually every compensatory program in existence was designed to improve the poverty-level child's chances of achieving adequately in school, success in school is one of the appropriate criteria. But to check the success of a program on the basis of a child's later school success means you have to wait for years. What do you do in the meantime? How do you know if you're on the right track? Normally, you make the interim judgment by testing the child on standard measures of intellectual performance, such as an IQ test, or on a measure of vocabulary such as the Peabody Picture Vocabulary Test. Since we know that scores on these tests predict later school performance, an increase in the score at least suggests the possibility that there will be a later improvement in school performance. The long-term follow-up is a better criterion, given the intent of the programs, but when the follow-up of the children has not yet been done, we must be content with examinations of the child's current intellectual performance.

There are many people (including me) who are made uncomfortable by the sort of evaluation strategy I've just described. This discomfort has two related facets. First, as Glick (1968) has pointed out so cogently, IQ tests or achievement tests inevitably are measures of *performance*. We ordinarily assume that such performances reflect competence, but that is an assumption (and an assumption that may be considerably less valid for a child from a poverty environment than for the middle-class children on whom the test was largely standardized). When the IQ score changes, as it does in most children who have been in compensatory education programs, can we be sure that the changes result from changes in fundamental competence? Or have the children only learned "how to take tests"—that is, how to improve their performance without altering their competence? To be sure, improving performance is not a negligible thing, since it is the child's performance and not his competence that the teacher sees and responds to and that the child responds to in developing his own self-image. If, however, what we are aiming to do with a compensatory program is to improve the fundamental competencies of the children (which are assumed to be deficient), we need tests that more nearly assess changes in competence. Perhaps tests based on Piagetian theory would be useful, although to my knowledge, they have not been used as assessment devices in evaluations of compensatory programs.

A second, related discomfort about the customary evaluation procedure arises from the fact that the IQ test is too broad a measure of performance. It doesn't tell us enough about the specific areas in which the child may have improved or not improved (White, 1968). Even if we accept the fact that we are largely measuring changes in performance, it is still useful and important to have measures that give us a finer-grained analysis of the impact of the program. In the more recent programs there has been some attempt to include more specific kinds of tests, such as the Illinois Test of Psycholinguistic Ability, but heavy reliance is still placed on the IQ tests as the major evaluation tool, as you will see in the results I've presented below and in the studies included in the selections.

You may wonder why measures of the child's motivation, his emotional health, or other noncognitive features of his functioning are not included. It is not because such factors are thought to be unimportant; they are not measured simply because alterations in motivation or emotional maturity are not part of the primary goals of most compensatory programs, and because well-standardized measures of such characteristics are not available. Some attempts have been made, as in Weikart's program (Weikart, 1972), but the major focus is on changes in the children's intellectual status.

So what are the results? Do the various kinds of programs make a difference in the short-term and long-term intellectual performance of children from poverty environments? The findings can be quite simply summarized (although it may take me several more pages to give you the details): Short-term gains are found by nearly everyone, almost without regard to the characteristics or content of the intervention program; long-term gains are much less common and are only moderate even in the best of programs. Let's look at the preschool programs first.

Short-term gains—that is, gains made during the year or months that the child actually attends the preschool—vary from about 8 points of IQ gain, which is common in Head Start programs, to as high as 30 points in some experimental programs (Weikart, 1969). The short-term results reported in the Gray and Klaus paper are reasonably typical: Their T1 group, after the first summer of preschool intervention, showed a mean IQ gain of 15.6 points, compared to a gain of 2.8 points for the nearby control group (T3). This initial large gain is not maintained, however. After a year the experimental groups had dropped 7.6 points, and they continued to drop in IQ over the years of the study. By the time the subjects were in the fourth grade, the experimental groups' IQs were in fact lower than they had been to start with. Even so, by the fourth grade the experimental groups were still significantly higher in IQ than were the control groups simply because the IQs of the control group subjects dropped more than did the experimental subjects'. So in one sense the effect of this program was to maintain the experimental groups at the level they were at to start with; the intervention prevented the progressive decline in IQ that is common among children from poverty environments.

Similar results may be found in another long-term study, this one by Weikart in Ypsilanti, Michigan. (See Table 1). He reports the same magnitude of initial gain for the experimental groups (16.1 points) compared to a gain of only 4.3 points for the control. The two groups differed significantly from one another in IQ through the first grade, after which there was no difference. As in the Gray and Klaus study, the experimental subjects showed a decline from their highest IQ, but in this case the control subjects showed an increase, rather than a decline, through the third grade. By the third grade the two groups were not distinguishable on IQ scores. They were distinguishable, however, on school achievement scores and on the teachers' ratings of the children's academic, emotional, and social development (Weikart, 1972): The experimental group children achieved significantly higher scores on standard achievement tests as late as third grade.

Other long-term experimental projects (such as Deutsch's, 1969) provide evidence of similar small differences between the experimental and control subjects after five to seven years. So at least there is some indication that the original goal was met in some of the programs: Children who attended compensatory preschools did achieve somewhat better in school. In general, Head Start follows-ups do not show such long-term gains, however. (Westinghouse Learning Corporation, 1969).

So the answer to whether compensatory preschools have worked is Yes and No. They have not had the massive effect that was hoped for them, but some of the better experimental programs have shown that short-term intervention before school can have a small effect that lasts well into elementary school. This brings us to the next question taken up by researchers and theorists, a question that is addressed extensively in Carl Bereiter's paper in the readings. Which *kinds* of programs work? What is it about the experimental programs that is different from Head Start and that produces the small but lasting effect? What researchers were hoping for was a simple answer to this question. It would have been nice if there were some "magic ingredient," some specific kind of curriculum that did the trick while others did not. Like most things, however, the answer is not simple. In fact, it looks as if *any* kind of curriculum and teaching strategy works fine as long as it is reasonably structured and intensive. Among those programs that are structured and intensive, there is little to choose from; they all seem to "work" about equally well. Head Start programs, on the whole, were not highly structured and intensive; they had inherited from the 30 years of middle-class preschool tradition some emphasis on social and emotional development and a tendency to organize the child's day so as to leave room for a good deal of free play or semi-structured play. Although such a structure is appropriate for meeting other kinds of goals, it does not seem to have done the job as far as altering the children's school prognosis.

What about programs with mothers? Have they done any better? As yet we do not have any long-term follow-ups for home intervention programs, only short-term results. The short-term results look very much like the findings from the good experimental preschool studies. In two studies, one of which is included in the readings, Karnes and her associates (Karnes, Teska, Hodgins, and Badger, 1970; Karnes, Studley, Wright, and Hodgins, 1968) have demonstrated that children of mothers who have been enrolled in training programs have post-intervention IQ scores about 15 points higher than control subjects, whose mothers have not been involved in the training program. Levenstein has found very similar results in two studies in which a visitor went directly into the home once a week (Levenstein and Sunley, 1968; Levenstein, 1970): The experimental group children showed an IQ gain of 17 points during a seven-month period, whereas the control subjects showed a gain of only 2 points. But do these gains last? Do children from these families do better in school? To date there is no

Table 1 Results from Weikart's Long-term Follow-up of Compensatory Education Subjects: Stanford-Binet IQ Results, Experimental vs. Control

| | Time of data collection | | | | | | |
	Fall, entering year, age 3	Spring, entering year, age 3½	Spring, second year, age 4½	Spring, kindergarten	Spring, first grade	Spring, second grade	Spring, third grade
Group size[a]							
Experimental	58	58	44	45	33	21	13
Control	65	65	49	52	37	24	15
Group IQ means							
Experimental	79.7	95.8	94.7	90.5	91.2	88.8	89.6
Control	79.1	83.4	82.7	85.4	83.3	86.5	88.1
F ratio	<1	39.78	25.36	4.58	8.26	<1	<1
Significance	n.s.	<.01	<.01	<.05	<.01	n.s.	n.s.

Source: Weikart (1972), p. 58.
[a]The group size declines over ages because the subjects who began the program in the later years have not yet reached elementary school.

long-term follow-up of subjects from such a study, although Leven-stein has reported (personal communication) that the IQ differences she saw after seven months of intervention were still present a year later. The hope, of course, is that the mother's behavior may have been permanently changed and that she, in turn, will help to bring about a permanent change in the child. But the data to support that hope are not available as yet.

SOME ANCILLARY
RESULTS

What about nonacademic or nonintellectual gains? Or what about intellectual gains for people other than the participants in the project?

One of the intriguing findings in the Gray and Klaus study, which you will read, is that the younger siblings of children enrolled in the experimental preschool showed some long-term effects. Gray and Klaus call this vertical diffusion and suggest that it may be an impor-tant, though usually unmeasured, result of preschool compensatory projects. Another kind of "diffusion" effect is apparent in the Karnes et al. paper in the readings: The mothers who were enrolled in the training program not only apparently changed their mode of inter-action with their child; they showed other changes in their behavior as well, including increase in leadership, initiative, and self-confidence.

Changes in the social or emotional behavior of the target children are harder to assess, and there has been less interest in this aspect of the problem. There are some data, however. I've already reported that Weikart (1972) found that his experimental subjects were rated by teachers as having better social, emotional, and academic develop-ment. Others have noted increases in cooperative play, self-confidence, and motivation to achieve in school during the Head Start experience. The fact that these variables are less often measured and harder to assess does not make change any the less important, and what little evidence we have suggests that some changes in affect, motivation, and interpersonal relationships have indeed been effected by inter-vention programs.

I must also mention improvements in medical status. One of the goals of Head Start, in addition to the academic goals, was to identify and treat medical and dental problems in the poverty-level child. The program has been eminently successful in this respect. Large num-bers of both medical and dental problems have been identified, and in most cases the children have received appropriate treatment. In addi-tion, most of the children have received vaccinations, been tested for hearing and vision problems, and generally been given the kind of *preventive* treatment common in the middle class.

WHERE DO WE
GO FROM HERE?

I suspect that after reading everything I've said, and after you have looked over the material in the readings, you will agree with Harry Beilin's statement: "The most disappointing fact to face about pre-school compensatory education is its inability to live up to the high expectations set for it" (Beilin, 1972, p. 165). You will find similar sentiments in the papers by Carl Bereiter and by Susan Gray and Rupert Klaus. Compensatory programs simply have not compensated for all of the initial performance deficits, at least not in the long run. They have had some effect, but not the big effects we had envisioned.

How are we to interpret such modest results of such massive, expensive projects? There are several ways we can go from here. First, we can accept the discrepancy between our expectations and the results as a sign of our original naïveté and arrogance. We thought we were sufficiently knowledgeable, both about the characteristics of the children and about intellectual development in general, to design programs that would cure what we perceived to be the problem. Furthermore, we expected that somehow with a two-hour-a-day intervention period when the child was four we could make a lasting difference, despite all the other things going on in the child's environment during the intervention period and despite all the things that would occur later in his educational experience. That's quite an expectation. In retrospect, now that we have a better understanding of the vast number of other factors influencing the child's intellectual performance, it seems amazing that any effect at all lasts as long as seven years.

Of course, an alternative interpretation of the lack of large permanent changes harks back to the genetic view: Perhaps we have had so little effect because we are dealing with children who are fundamentally and inevitably less competent. This is the position taken by Jensen in his controversial and hotly debated paper (Jensen, 1969), and it is a view that will no doubt be with us for a long time to come. I've discussed the complexities of the problem in the introduction to Part III, so I needn't review them here, but we must face up to the issue. If the small effect of compensatory programs is due to genetic differences, there is little reason to pursue such programs further. On the other hand, if the lack of effect arises because our intervention is too little, too late, or maybe just plain misdirected, then we should continue to search for other programs or procedures that will have the effects we were hoping for in the first place. We cannot prove unequivocally that the differences are *not* genetic, but we can point to the effects that comparatively minor environmental changes have had: Some of the children who have been in compensatory programs have gone on to achieve considerable success in school (Weikart estimates that 50 percent of the children in his programs show marked improvement in school performance), and data from the current home intervention programs suggest that the impact there may be greater. All of which, to me, justifies a "cautious optimism" about the usefulness of continuing with an environmental hypothesis.

What is needed now, in my opinion, is the exploration of some new questions. Bereiter suggests one such question: "What things can we teach a child of four or five that can then be built upon in the first grade and after?" (Bereiter, 1972, p. 16). I would suggest another: What kind of first grade builds upon the things the four- or five-year-old poverty child has learned, either at home or in preschool? If particular kinds of preschools make more of a difference than others, perhaps particular kinds of elementary schools make more of a difference for this same group of children. There are hints in both the Gray and Klaus and the Bereiter papers that such variations may make a difference. The results of project Follow-Through, a nationwide program involving planned variations in kindergarten and early elementary school programs, may give us some of the answers. Also needed is good research on the kinds of "open schools" advocated by Ginsburg and others. If, as Ginsburg has suggested, the poverty child's "deficits" are mostly illusory, then in a more open environment, in which the child is permitted to learn at his own pace and in his own sequence, the children will perform at about the same level in the long run. Ginsburg has himself done one study that appears to support such a conclusion (Ginsburg, Wheeler, and Tulis ,1971, cited in Ginsburg, 1972). More are needed.

QUESTIONS FOR POSSIBLE DEBATE AND DISCUSSION

1. In light of the evidence presented, should the government (federal or local) subsidize compensatory programs. If not, why not? If yes, what kind? What are the expected benefits?
2. What has been the impact of theories of cognitive development on the design of compensatory education projects?

ADDITIONAL REFERENCES USEFUL IN PREPARATION
FOR DEBATE OR DISCUSSION

Bereiter, C., and Englemann, S. *Teaching disadvantaged children in the preschool.* Englewood Cliffs, N.J.: Prentice Hall, 1966.
    A description of one controversial and highly effective compensatory program.

Ginsburg, H. *The myth of the deprived child.* Englewood Cliffs, N.J.: Prentice Hall, 1972.

See particularly pages 190–195, in which Ginsburg describes the usual assumptions underlying compensatory education projects and gives his own views about the validity of those assumptions.

Glick, J. Some problems in the evaluation of pre-school intervention programs. In R. Hess and R. Bear (Eds.), *Early education.* Chicago: Aldine, 1968, pp. 215–221.

An excellent discussion of the problem of distinguishing competence from performance.

Hess, R., and Bear, R. (Eds.) *Early education.* Chicago: Aldine, 1968.

A book including selections from many authors. It includes descriptions of a number of compensatory programs, as well as some theoretical discussions.

Kohlberg, L. Early education: A cognitive developmental view. *Child Development,* 1968, **39,** 1013–1062.

A really good and well-reasoned presentation of the Piagetian view of compensatory education. A very good theoretical overview of the role of theory in the design of educational programs.

Stanley, J. C. (Ed.) *Preschool programs for the disadvantaged.* Baltimore: Johns Hopkins University Press, 1972.

Another collection of papers, including the Bereiter paper that is in the selections. The other papers in the book are all current and excellent.

Westinghouse Learning Corporation. The impact of Head Start: An evaluation of the Head Start experience on children's cognitive and affective development. Westinghouse Learning Corporation, Ohio University, 1969.

The final report on the single largest evaluation of the impact of Head Start.

REFERENCES

Beilin, H. The status and future of preschool compensatory education. In J. C. Stanley (Ed.), *Preschool programs for the disadvantaged.* Baltimore: Johns Hopkins University Press, 1972, pp. 165–181.

Bereiter, C. An academic preschool for disadvantaged children: Conclusions from evaluation studies. In J. C. Stanley (Ed.), *Preschool programs for the disadvantaged.* Baltimore: Johns Hopkins University Press, 1972.

Bereiter, C., and Englemann, S. *Teaching disadvantaged children in the preschool.* Englewood Cliffs, N.J.: Prentice Hall, 1966.

Deutsch, M. The disadvantaged child and the learning process. In A. H. Passow (Ed.), *Education in depressed areas.* New York: Teachers College Press, 1963, pp. 163–179.

Deutsch, M. Happenings on the way back to the forum: Social science, IQ and race differences revisited. *Harvard Educational Review,* 1969, **39,** 523–557.

Ginsburg, H. *The myth of the deprived child.* Englewood Cliffs, N.J.: Prentice-Hall, 1972.

Glick, J. Some problems in the evaluation of preschool intervention programs. In R. D. Hess and R. M. Bear (Eds.), *Early education.* Chicago: Aldine, 1968, pp. 215–221.

Gray, S. W., and Klaus, R. A. An experimental preschool program for culturally deprived children. *Child Development,* 1965, **36,** 887–898.

Gray, S. W., and Klaus, R. A. The early training project: A seventh-year report. *Child Development,* 1970, **41,** 909–924.

Jensen, A. R. How much can we boost IQ and scholastic achievement? *Harvard Educational Review,* 1969, **39,** 1–123.

Klaus, R. A., and Gray, S. W. The early training project for disadvantaged children: A report after five years. *Monographs of the Society for Research in Child Development,* 1968, **33**(Whole No. 120).

Karnes, M. B., Studley, W. M., Wright, W. R., and Hodgins, A. S. An approach for working with mothers of disadvantaged preschool children. *Merrill-Palmer Quarterly,* 1968, **14,** 174–184.

Karnes, M. B., Teska, J. A., and Hodgins, A. S. The effects of four programs of classroom intervention on the intellectual and language development of 4-year-old disadvantaged children. *American Journal of Orthopsychiatry,* 1970, **50,** 58–76.

Karnes, M. B., Teska, J. A., Hodgins, A. S., and Badger, E. D. Educational intervention at home by mothers of disadvantaged infants. *Child Development,* 1970, **41,** 925–935.

Levenstein, P. Cognitive growth in preschoolers through verbal interaction with mothers. *American Journal of Orthopsychiatry,* 1970, **40,** 426–432.

Levenstein, P., and Sunley, R. Stimulation of verbal interaction between disadvantaged mothers and children. *American Journal of Orthopsychiatry,* 1968, **38,** 116–121.

Schaefer, E. Home tutoring, maternal behavior and infant intellectual development. Paper presented at the annual meeting of the American Psychological Association, Washington, D.C., 1969.

Weikart, D. P. Preschool programs, Preliminary findings. *Journal of Special Education,* 1967, **1,** 163–181.

Weikart, D. P. A comparative study of three preschool curricula. Paper presented at the biennial meeting of the Society for Research in Child Development, Santa Monica, Calif., March, 1969.

Weikart, D. P. Relationship of curriculum, teaching, and learning in preschool education. In J. C. Stanley (Ed.), *Preschool programs for the disadvantaged*. Baltimore: Johns Hopkins University Press, 1972, pp. 22–66.

Weikart, D. P., and Lambie, D. Z. *Ypsilanti-Carnegie infant education project progress report. Department of Research and Development.* Ypsilanti Public Schools, Ypsilanti, Michigan, 1969.

Westinghouse Learning Corporation. *The impact of Head Start: An evaluation of the Head Start experience on children's cognitive and affective development.* Westinghouse Learning Corporation, Ohio University, 1969.

White, S. H. Some educated guesses about cognitive development in the preschool years. In R. D. Hess and R. M. Bear (Eds.), *Early education*. Chicago: Aldine, 1968, pp. 203–214.

the early training project: a seventh-year report*

SUSAN W. GRAY
RUPERT A. KLAUS
George Peabody College for Teachers, Nashville, Tennessee

The Early Training Project has been a field research study concerned with the development and testing over time of procedures for improving the educability of young children from low-income homes. The rationale, the general design and methodology, and findings through the second year of schooling have been reported in some detail by Klaus and Gray (1968). A briefer report, up to school entrance, is given in Gray and Klaus (1965). The purpose of this report is to present the findings at the end of the fourth grade, 3 years after all experimental intervention has ceased.

The major concern of the Early Training Project was to study whether it was possible to offset the progressive retardation observed in the public school careers of children living in deprived

From *Child Development*, 1970, **41**. Copyright © 1970 by the Society for Research in Child Development, Inc. By permission.

*Major financial support for this study was received from the National Institute of Mental Health, under Health Project grant 5-R11-MH-765. Additional support for research staff during the later phases of the study was made possible through grant HD-00973 from the National Institute of Child Health and Human Development, from the Office of Education, contract OEC 3-7-070706-3118, and grant 9174 from the Office of Economic Opportunity. Susan Gray's address: Box 30, George Peabody College, Nashville, Tennessee 37203.

circumstances. In addition, the writers undertook to study the spill-over effect upon other children in the community and upon other family members.

The general research strategy was one of attempting to design a research "package" consisting of variables which—on the basis of research upon social class, cognitive development, and motivation—might be assumed to be relevant to the school retardation which is observed in deprived groups and which at the same time might be subject to the effects of manipulation. Because this was a problem with major social implications, we also tried to design a general treatment approach which would be feasible to repeat on a large scale in the event that the procedure proved successful.

Subjects were 88 children born in 1958. Sixty-one of these lived in a city of 25,000 in the upper South. The remaining 27, who served as a distal control group, resided in a similar city 65 miles away. The children were all Negro. When we initiated the study the schools of the city were still segregated; we chose to work with Negro children because in this particular setting we had reason to believe that our chances of success were greater with this group.

The children were selected on the basis of parent's occupation, education, income, and housing conditions. At the beginning of the study, incomes were considerably below the approximate $3,000 used as the poverty line for a family of four. Occupations were either unskilled or semiskilled; the educational level was eighth grade or below; housing conditions were poor. The median number of children per family at the beginning of the study was five; in about one-third of the homes there was no father present.

From the 61 children in the first city three groups were con-stituted by random assignment. The first group (T1) attended, over a period of three summers, a 10-week preschool designed to offset the deficits usually observed in the performance of children from disadvantaged homes. In addition, this group had 3 years of weekly meetings with a specially trained home visitor during those months in which the preschool was not in session. The second group (T2) had a similar treatment, except that it began a year later; the chil-dren received two summers of the special preschool and 2 years of home visits. The third group (T3) became the local control group, which received all tests but no intervention treatment. The fourth group (T4), the distal control group, was added to the design because of the somewhat ghetto-type concentration of Negroes in the first city. The local and distal control groups also made possible the study of spillover effects upon children and parents living in proximity to the experimental children. The general layout of the experimental design is given in Table 1. By reading down the columns, one may see the particular treatment and testing sequence followed for each

Table 1 Layout of General Research Design

Treatment time	Three Summer Schools (T1)	Two summer Schools (T2)	Local Controls (T3)	Distal Controls (T4)
First winter (1961–1962)	Criterion development, curriculum planning, general tooling up			
First summer (1962)	Pretest, summer school, posttest	Pretest, posttest	Pretest, posttest	Pretest, posttest
Second winter (1962–1963)	Home visitor contacts	—	—	—
Second summer (1963)	Pretest, summer school, posttest	Pretest, summer school, posttest	Pretest, posttest	Pretest, posttest
Third winter (1963–1964)	Home visitor contacts	Home visitor contacts	—	—
Third summer (1964)	Pretest, summer school, posttest	Pretest, summer school, posttest	Pretest, posttest	Pretest, posttest
Fourth winter (1964–1965)	Home visitor contacts	Home visitor contacts	—	—
Fourth summer (1965)	Follow-up tests	Follow-up tests	Follow-up tests	Follow-up tests
Fifth summer (1966)	Follow-up tests	Follow-up tests	Follow-up tests	Follow-up tests
Seventh summer (1968)	Follow-up tests	Follow-up tests	Follow-up tests	Follow-up tests

of the four groups. Periodic testing is continuing for the children through elementary school.

THE INTERVENTION PROGRAM

The overall rationale for the intervention program grew out of the literature on child-rearing patterns in different social classes, plus the writers' own observations in low-income homes. On the basis of this study, the intervention program for children was organized around two broad classes of variables: attitudes relating [to] achievement, and aptitudes relating to achievement. Under attitudes we were particularly interested in achievement motivation, especially as it concerns school type activities, in persistence, in ability to delay gratification; generally interested in typical school materials, such as books, crayons, puzzles, and the like. We were also concerned with the parents' attitude toward achievement, particularly in their aspirations for their children, especially as they related to schooling.

In the broad class of aptitude variables relating to achievement, we were particularly interested in perceptual and cognitive development and in language. Children from low-income homes have been shown to have deficits in these areas, all of which appear closely related to school success in the primary grades.

In the summer months, for 10 weeks the children met in assembled groups. Each of the two experimental groups had a head teacher, who was an experienced Negro first-grade teacher. There were, in addition, three or four teaching assistants. These assistants were divided about equally as to race and sex.

The work with the parents in the project was carried on largely through a home-visitor program in which a specially trained preschool teacher made weekly visits to each mother and child. Both the home program and the school program are described in considerable detail in Gray, Klaus, Miller, and Forrester (1966) and in Klaus and Gray (1968).

Prior to and after each summer session, children in all four groups were tested on several instruments. From the first summer certain standardized tests of intelligence and language were used, along with a number of less formal instruments. At the end of first grade, achievement tests were added. This testing schedule is shown in Table 1. In general the .05 level of significance was used.

RESULTS

The detailed results of the testing program through May 1966, the end of the second grade for the children, are given in Klaus and Gray (1968). This paper gives the results as they relate to the spring and summer testings of 1968 with some additional information on performance of younger siblings. The same kinds of analyses were used for the 1968 data as were used in the earlier paper.

In 1968 the following tests were administered to all children still residing in middle Tennessee: the Stanford-Binet, the Peabody Picture Vocabulary Test, and the Metropolitan Achievement Test. The analyses here reported are based only upon those children available for testing with the exception of one child in the distal control group.

The Stanford-Binet scores are given in Table 2, and are portrayed graphically in Figure 1. A Lindquist (1953) Type 1 analysis of the results of 1962–1968, in terms of IQ, gave a significant F of 4.45

Table 2 Mean Stanford-Binet MA and IQ Scores for the Four
Treatment Groups at Each Administration

Date of administration	T1($N = 19$)		T2($N = 19$)		T3($N = 18$)		T4($N = 23$)	
	MA (Mo)	IQ	MA (Mo)	IQ	MA (Mo)	IQ	MA (Mo)	IQ
May 1962	40.7	87.6	43.8	92.5	40.3	85.4	40.3	86.7
August 1962	50.7	102.0	46.9	92.3	44.3	88.2	43.4	87.4
May 1963	55.6	96.4	56.0	94.8	53.2	89.6	50.4	86.7
August 1963	59.3	97.1	60.6	97.5	55.0	87.6	52.3	84.7
August 1964	68.0	95.8	71.6	96.6	62.3	82.9	59.4	80.2
August 1965	83.8	98.1	86.3	99.7	79.4	91.4	77.0	89.0
June 1966	88.7	91.2	93.4	96.0	86.8	87.9	82.9	84.6
July 1968	106.0	86.7	111.4	90.2	104.7	84.9	96.2	77.7

for the four group, F of 16.81 for repeated measures, and F for interaction of groups over time of 3.51. All of these were significant at the .01 level or beyond. Next an analysis was made by the use of orthogonal comparisons. These are given in Table 3. Here it may be seen that the two experimental groups remained significantly superior to the two control groups. The comparison of the first and the

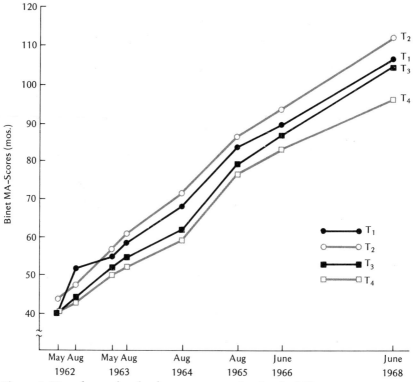

Figure 1 Mental ages for the four groups on the Stanford-Binet test.

Table 3 Orthogonal Comparisons of Treatment-Group Sums for Stanford-Binet IQ Scores for the Eight Administrations

Date of administration	Hypothesis: T1 = T2 + T3 + T4		Hypothesis: T2 = T3 + T4		Hypothesis: T3 = T4	
	F-ratio	Conclusion	F-ratio	Conclusion	F-ratio	Conclusion
August 1962	12.67[a]	T1 > T2 + T3 + T4	1.44	T2 = T3 + T4	<1.00	T3 = T4
May 1963	2.91	T1 = T2 + T3 + T4	3.36	T2 = T3 + T4	<1.00	T3 = T4

Date of administration	Hypothesis: T1 + T2 = T3 + T4		Hypothesis: T1 = T2		Hypothesis: T3 = T4	
	F-ratio	Conclusion	F-ratio	Conclusion	F-ratio	Conclusion
May 1962	2.07	T1 + T2 = T3 + T4	1.53	T1 = T2	<1.00	T3 = T4
August 1963	18.53[a]	T1 + T2 > T3 + T4	<1.00	T1 = T2	<1.00	T3 = T4
August 1964	29.94[a]	T1 + T2 > T3 + T4	<1.00	T1 = T2	<1.00	T3 = T4
August 1965	11.12[a]	T1 + T2 > T3 + T4	<1.00	T1 = T2	<1.00	T3 = T4
June 1966	5.99[a]	T1 + T2 > T3 + T4	1.18	T1 = T2	<1.00	T3 = T4
July 1968	7.50[a]	T1 + T2 > T3 + T4	<1.00	T1 = T2	3.53	T3 = T4

[a] $p < .05$; $F_{.95} = 3.97$.

Table 4 Mean PPVT Mental Age Scores and IQ Equivalents for the Four Treatment Groups for the 10 Administrations

Date of administration	Test form	T1(N = 19) MA (Mo)	IQ	T2(N = 19) MA (Mo)	IQ	T3(N = 18) MA (Mo)	IQ	T4(N = 23) MA (Mo)	IQ
May 1962	A	30.0	69.5	30.6	70.1	29.4	66.4	32.2	74.0
August 1962	B	36.8	75.3	33.1	63.9	32.7	65.8	30.7	62.8
May 1963	A	44.8	79.0	40.7	69.6	39.1	69.3	39.5	69.8
August 1963	B	45.0	78.4	50.7	83.6	38.4	64.0	37.6	63.8
May 1964	B	55.6	81.2	60.1	85.5	45.8	65.4	48.7	70.9
August 1964	A	59.1	83.0	62.0	87.0	50.6	72.4	48.7	69.6
June 1965	B	74.2	89.0	76.2	90.3	67.6	83.0	67.3	84.0
August 1965	A	70.6	86.2	76.5	91.8	65.4	80.2	66.3	83.4
June 1966	A	78.1	86.7	81.9	89.3	75.4	83.9	71.2	80.7
July 1968	A	96.4	84.5	100.3	86.7	91.7	81.8	89.3	78.7

second experimental groups for 1968 showed an F of less than 1.00. The comparison of the two control groups, however, yielded an F that, although not conventionally significant, was still large enough (3.52 where $F_{.95} = 3.96$) to be suggestive of a sharper decline in the distal than in the local control group. As was true of earlier analyses, the larger part of the variance appeared to be carried by the second experimental group and the distal control group.

The scores across the 10 administrations of the Peabody Picture Vocabulary Test are given in Table 4 in MA and IQ form. A Lindquist (1953) Type 1 analysis of variance was performed for the MA scores. For groups F was 5.16, indicating a significant effect of the experimental treatment upon the children's performance. For repeated testings F was 376.73, an effect that would be clearly expected when MA scores were used. These were selected in preference to IQ scores on this particular test since the IQ scores appear to lack discrimination at certain levels. The interaction between groups and time was nonsignificant. Orthogonals were next used. Here [it] was found that T1 + T2 was significantly greater than T3 + T4 up until 1968, in which year differences were not significant. As may be seen from Table 4, differences in mean scores were still apparent. Heterogeneity had increased over time, however, so that differences were no longer significant. In no analysis at any point of time was either experimental group significantly superior to the other. Nor did either control group show itself to be significantly superior to the other one.

The results for the Metropolitan Achievement Test are given in Table 5. A Lindquist (1953) Type 1 analysis was performed on each subtest, and orthogonal comparisons made. In the interest of brevity a table of orthogonal comparisons is not given. In 1965, at the end of first grade, the experimental children were significantly superior on three of the four tests used at that time: word knowledge, word discrimination, and reading. For arithmetic computation scores, F was less than 1.00. The local controls were also somewhat superior to the distal controls on these tests, an indication possibly of horizontal diffusion or, either in interaction or independently, a somewhat better instructional program. In 1966 five subtests were given. This time only two were significant, word knowledge and reading. On the other three tests, however, the F's ranged from 2.69 to 2.84, suggesting probabilities at about the .10 level. In neither year was T1 significantly superior to T2. The highest F was 1.16, where $F_{.95}$ is 3.97. In the comparisons of T3 and T4, T3 was superior to T4 on reading and arithmetic computation. On word knowledge, word discrimination, and spelling the F's ranged from 3.19 to 3.85, suggesting probabilities beyond the .10 level ($F_{.90} = 2.77$). At the end of the fourth year no significant effects were found with the single ex-

Table 5 Metropolitan Achievement Test Grade Equivalent Mean Scores for the Various Subtests for the Three Administrations

Subtest and year	T1	T2	T3	T4
Word knowledge:				
1965	1.69	1.73	1.79	1.37
1966	2.32	2.47	2.29	1.98
1968	3.58	3.90	3.54	3.27
Word discrimination:				
1965	1.68	1.81	1.82	1.37
1966	2.64	2.73	2.65	2.20
1968	3.73	3.95	3.76	3.47
Reading:				
1965	1.72	1.82	1.84	1.46
1966	2.52	2.75	2.56	2.11
1968	3.52	3.89	3.72	3.10
Arithmetic computation:				
1965	1.52	1.62	1.54	1.43
1966	2.41	2.55	2.49	2.05
1968	3.92	4.07	4.06	3.79
Spelling:				
1966	2.42	2.85	2.60	1.99
1968	4.26	4.69	4.24	3.67
Language:				
1968	3.52	4.00	3.63	3.17
Arithmetic problem solving and concepts:				
1968	3.31	3.54	3.75	3.26

ception of reading, on which T3 was superior to T4. There is some suggestion of residual effect since, in six of the seven possible comparisons of experimentals and controls, the experimentals were superior. Also, on all seven possible comparisons the local control group was superior to the distal control group.

The Stanford-Binet was administered in all four groups to those younger siblings who were of testable age. This was first done in 1964 and again in 1966. Since the 1966 findings have not been previously reported, they are presented here in Table 6. In 1964, 57 children were tested. Fifty of these same children were tested again in 1966, along with 43 additional siblings who were too young to test in 1964.

An analysis of covariance was performed on these scores, with the IQs at first testing of the target-age children used as the covariable. Also, where there were two younger siblings in the same family, one was dropped, so that the analysis was based on 87 children. Separate analyses were also performed for the 1964 and the 1966 results of all children who were retested. In addition, an analysis was performed on the 1966 results for those children who were being tested for the first time.

Table 6 Initial Stanford-Binet Scores of Treatment Group
Children and Younger Siblings in Two Testings

Testing and groups	Mean scores (first testing, 1962) for treatment group children with younger siblings			Mean scores for younger siblings		
	N	CA	IQ	N	CA	IQ
1964 testing of younger siblings born in 1959 and 1960:						
T1	12	47	82	13	54	82
T2	16	46	89	21	53	83
T3	7	50	84	9	54	71
T4	12	48	88	14	62	74
1966 retesting of younger siblings initially tested in 1964:						
T1	12	47	82	13	78	85
T2	14	46	92	19	76	85
T3	5	46	82	7	76	78
T4	11	48	86	13	77	75
1966 testing of younger siblings born in 1961 and 1962:						
T1	10	44	87	11	58	84
T2	9	47	91	10	52	87
T3	7	48	83	9	56	76
T4	12	47	88	15	55	84
1966 testing of all younger siblings						
T1	15	50	84	24	69	84
T2	17	46	91	29	68	86
T3	8	47	84	16	65	77
T4	15	47	86	28	63	80

On all younger siblings tested in 1966 F between groups was
not significant at the .05 level ($F = 3.97$). It was significant beyond
the .10 level, and therefore we made further analyses. Orthogonal
comparisons were used, with the hypotheses shown in Table 7. This
is the same general approach as used with the target children. All
orthogonal comparisons showed significant differences for the testing of all younger siblings in 1966: the combined experimental
group siblings were superior to the combined control group siblings;
the T1 siblings were superior to the T2 siblings; and the T3 siblings
were superior to the T4 siblings. When the children who were
tested for the first time are separated out, it is clear, both in the
1966 and the 1964 data, that most of the variance was being carried
by younger siblings closer in age to the target-age children. There
are some interesting implications of these general results on younger
siblings which will be examined in more detail in the Discussion.

Table 7 Orthogonal Comparisons of Stanford-Binet Scores of Younger Siblings

	HO:[a] T1 + T2 = T3 + T4		HO: T1 = T2		HO: T3 = T4	
	F-ratio	Conclusion	F-ratio	Conclusion	F-ratio	Conclusion
All younger siblings 1966	3.48	T1 + T2 = T3 + T4	0.75	T1 = T2	0.00	T3 = T4
Younger siblings first tested in 1966	0.77	T1 + T2 = T3 + T4	0.04	T1 = T2	0.80	T3 = T4
Younger siblings retested in 1966:						
1964 results	8.13[b]	T1 + T2 > T3 + T4	0.74	T1 = T2	0.01	T3 = T4
1966 results	4.72[b]	T1 + T2 > T3 + T4	5.11[b]	T1 > T2	2.07	T3 = T4

[a]HO = hypothesis.
[b]$p < .05$; $F\ .95 = 3.97$.

DISCUSSION

The results on the one test of intelligence which was used consistently, from the initiation of the program in 1962 until the testing at the end of the fourth grade in 1968, are very much in line with what might be expected. For this was an intervention program that used a broad-gauge approach and which was relatively successful in terms of improving the educability of young children from low-income homes. Intervention caused a rise in intelligence which was fairly sharp at first, then leveled off, and finally began to show decline once intervention ceased. The control groups on the other hand tended to show a slight but consistent decline with the single exception of a jump between entrance into public school and the end of first grade. Differences between experimentals and controls on Stanford-Binet IQ were still significant at the end of the third year after intervention ceased. All four groups have shown a decline in IQ after the first grade, but the decline, as shown in Figure 1, tended to be relatively parallel. Perhaps the remarkable thing is that with the relatively small amount of impact over time differences should still be significant. After all, the child experienced only five mornings of school a week for 10 weeks for two or three summers, plus weekly home visits during the other 9 months for 2 or 3 years. This suggests that the impact was not lost. It was not sufficient, however, to offset the massive effects of a low-income home in which the child had lived since birth onward.

The results on the PPVT showed a pattern that is not dissimilar. There was a rise during intervention, including the first grade, then a leveling off and a slight decline. Here, however, difference between groups, although consistent, was no longer significant.

The importance of the school situation for the maintenance or loss of a gain should be weighed. The children for the most part remained in schools in which the entire population was Negro. Eight of the local children at the end of first grade did enroll in schools that had previously been all white. Four more changed during the next 2 years. None of the distal children attended schools with white children. Since in this area, as in many places, race tends to be confounded with social class, the children in the study did not in general have the advantage of classmates with relatively high expectancies. There is some evidence that in both of the all-Negro schools the general teaching-learning situation, although fair, was less adequate than in the schools that have formerly been all white. This, plus the continuing effect of the home situation and the immediate community, took its toll. There are some data on achievement-test scores to be presented later which suggest the impact of the two all-Negro schools which most of the children attended.

On the one achievement battery administered from first to fourth grade, the Metropolitan Achievement Test (Table 5), significant differences did not appear in 1968 on any of the subtests with [the] sole exception of the reading score, in which the local control group was superior to the distal control group. The experimentals had been superior to the controls on three tests in 1965 and on two tests in 1966. One might interpret this as showing that the intervention program did have measurable effects upon test performance at the end of first grade, but that by the end of fourth grade, the school program had failed to sustain at any substantial level the initial superiority. Although disappointing, this is perhaps not surprising in a test battery so dependent upon specific school instruction.

An interesting sidelight is thrown on this matter by looking at the performance on the Metropolitan Achievement Test of the eight children from the local school who enrolled in previously all-white schools at the end of first grade. An attempt was made, on the basis of first-grade achievement tests and home ratings of educational aspirations, to match these eight children with eight who remained in the Negro school. Admittedly, this is a chancy business, and one which should not be taken too seriously. Table 8 presents the gains in grade equivalents on the Metropolitan Achievement Tests from the end of first grade to the end of fourth grade. On the four subtests common to both grade levels, the picture is a clear one of more gain in the children who changed schools, varying from .8 to 1.4 years' greater gain. These data did not seem appropriate for subjection to statistical analysis. They do suggest, however, the fairly obvious: that performance on achievement tests is directly related to school experience. The children who

Table 8   Mean Gains on the MAT over a 3-Year Period for Eight ETP Children in Integrated Schools and Matches in Negro Schools

	Mean gains 1965–1968			
	Word knowl- edge	Word discrimi- nation	Read- ing	Arith- metic
ETP Ss in integrated schools beginning fall 1965	3.1	2.8	2.7	2.9
ETP Ss in Negro schools matched to the first group on spring 1965 MAT and on verbal rating by home visitor	1.7	2.0	1.6	1.7
Difference	1.4	0.8	1.1	1.2

changed schools have made approximately "normal" gain for their 3 years; the children who did not change have gained 2 years or less during the 3 years from first through fourth grade.

The results on the younger siblings are to the writers among the most interesting findings of the study. We have termed the process by which such results are achieved and the product of that process "vertical diffusion," to suggest that this is a spread of effect down the family from the mother and possibly the target-age child to a younger child. In this study the effects of the older sibling and the mother upon the younger child were confounded. Some research currently being carried on under the direction of one of the writers has made possible the separation of the influence of mother and older siblings. Results so far indicate that most of the effect is coming from the mother. It is plausible to assume that the role of the mother was the more influential since considerable effort was expended by the home visitor over a period of 3 years with the first experimental group and over 2 years with the second experimental group. The emphasis of the home intervention was on making the mother a more effective teacher, or more generally, an effective educational change agent for her target-age child. Also worthy of note is the finding that vertical diffusion appeared more clearly in the younger siblings born in 1959 and 1960, who were within $1-2\frac{1}{2}$ years in age to the older siblings. The siblings born in 1961 and 1962, when pulled out for separate analysis, did not show an effect which approached statistical significance. Vertical diffusion also appeared more operative in the first than in the second experimental group. A plausible explanation is that intervention lasted a year longer with the first group and began a year earlier. There is also in the data some suggestion of a process we have examined in more detail elsewhere (Klaus and Gray 1968), one that may be termed horizontal diffusion, the spread of effect from one family to another. This we have in general analyzed by comparing the local and distal control groups. Here we find that the younger siblings in the local control group showed themselves to be superior to the distal control group.

To the extent that the findings on vertical diffusion have generality, they seem to point to the efficacy of a powerful process in the homes, presumably mediated by the parent, which may serve to improve the educability of young children. Before a second conclusion is reached by the reader, however, to the effect that "parent education" is the answer, we would like to point out that our procedure was clearly parent education with a difference. It was conducted in the homes; it was done by skilled preschool teachers with some experience in working in the homes; it was highly concrete and specific to a given mother's life situation; it was continuous over a long period of time. Indeed, parent education probably is the answer, but in low-income homes a very different kind of parent education from that usually provided may be needed.

Seven years after the Early Training Project began, in 1969, intervention programs for young children from low-income homes were nationwide. These programs differ tremendously in the length and timing of the intervention, in the objectives and consistency with which they are followed, in the degree of specificity of the program, and in the length and extent of follow-up study of the sample.

It is hardly surprising, with the wild heterogeneity of such programs, that nationwide assessment of programs, such as the Westinghouse Survey of Project Head Start (1969), would find relatively small evidence of positive effects upon the child's achievement and personal adequacy. Leaving aside all the problems of measuring personal adequacy and even achievement in young children, such lack of results is only to be expected in situations where the bad or inappropriate so cancels out the good that little positive effect can be found, especially if the evaluation is somewhat premature.

At this point in time it seems appropriate to look more closely at those programs which have clearly followed an adequate research design, specified and carefully monitored their treatments, and conducted adequate follow-up study of the sample. Such programs are relatively few in number, for their history is short.

In the Early Training Project we have been more fortunate than most. The study was initiated nearly 4 years before the tidal wave of interest in such early intervention that came about through such nationwide programs as Project Head Start and Titles I and III of the Elementary and Secondary Education Act. We have worked in a setting in which we have been free from administrative pressures either to change our procedures or to make premature conclusions from our data. The two communities in which [the] families live have had little outward mobility; even at the end of 7 years attrition is only a minor problem. For these reasons we believe the data collected over 7 years with our four groups of children do shed some light upon the problem of progressive retardation and the possibility that it can be offset.

Our answer as to whether such retardation can be offset is one of cautious optimism. The effects of our intervention program are clearly evidenced through the second year of public schooling, 1 year after intervention ceased. There is still an effect, most apparent in the Stanford-Binet, after 2 more years of nonintervention. Our data on horizontal and vertical diffusion, especially the latter, give us some hope that intervention programs can have a lasting effect that goes beyond the children that were the target of that intervention program.

Still, it is clear from our data, with a parallel decline across the four groups in the second through fourth grades, that an intervention program before school entrance, such as ours, cannot carry the entire burden of offsetting progressive retardation. By some standards the Early Training Project might be seen as one of relatively massive intervention. And yet a colleague of ours (Miller 1970) has estimated that in the years prior to school entrance the maximum amount of time that the children in the project could have spent with the Early Training Project staff was approximately 600 hours, less than 2 percent of their waking hours from birth to 6 years. Perhaps the remarkable thing is that the effect lasted as well and as long as it did. In a similar vein, we have estimated the amount of these contacts in the home as a maximum of 110 hours, or about 0.3 percent of the waking hours of the child from birth to 6 years. Surely it would be foolish not to realize that, without massive changes in the life situation of the child, home circumstances will continue to have their adversive effect upon the child's performance.

In 1968 we wrote:

> The most effective intervention programs for preschool children that could possibly be conceived cannot be considered a form of inoculation whereby the child forever after is immune to the effects of a low-income home and of a school inappropriate to his needs. Certainly, the evidence on human performance is overwhelming in indicating that such performance results from the continual interaction of the organism with its environment. Intervention programs, well conceived and executed, may be expected to make some relatively lasting changes. Such programs, however, cannot be expected to carry the whole burden of providing adequate schooling for children from deprived circumstances; they can provide only a basis for future progress in schools and homes that can build upon that early intervention.

In 1969 we saw no reason to alter this statement. Our seventh-year results only serve to underscore its truth.

REFERENCES

Gray, S. W., and Klaus, R. A. An experimental preschool program for culturally deprived children. *Child Development*, 1965, **36**, 887–898.

Gray, S. W.; Klaus, R. A.; Miller, J. O.; and Forrester, B. J. *Before first grade.* New York: Teachers College Press, Columbia University, 1966.

Klaus, R. A., and Gray, S. W. The early training project for disadvantaged children: a report after five years. *Monographs of the So-*

ciety for Research in Child Development, 1968, **33,** (4, Serial No. 120).

Lindquist, E. F. *The design and analysis of experiments in psychology and education.* Boston: Houghton Mifflin, 1953.

Miller, J. O. Cultural deprivation and its modification; effects of intervention. In C. H. Haywood (Ed.), *Social-cultural aspects of mental retardation.* New York: Appleton-Century-Croft, 1970.

Westinghouse Learning Corporation. *The impact of Head Start: an evaluation of the Head Start experience on children's cognitive and affective development.* Westinghouse Learning Corporation, Ohio University, 1969.

educational intervention at home by mothers of disadvantaged infants*

MERLE B. KARNES
JAMES A. TESKA
AUDREY S. HODGINS
EARLADEEN D. BADGER
University of Illinois, Urbana

Operation Head Start has, of course, generated widespread concern with compensatory education for disadvantaged preschool children, but it has also created an interest of a somewhat different sort: an interest in preventive programs of very early intervention which might forestall the developmental deficiencies characteristic of disadvantaged children by the age of 3 or 4 (Karnes, Hodgins, and Teska 1969; Karnes, Studley, Wright, and Hodgins 1968; Kirk 1969; Radin and Weikart 1967; Schaefer 1969; Weikart 1969). This investigation is based on similar assumptions of preventive programming through early intervention together with the notion that the mother might

From *Child Development*, 1970, **41.** Copyright © 1970 by the Society for Research in Child Development, Inc. By permission.
*This study was part of a larger research project at the University of Illinois supported by the U.S. Office of Education, Bureau of Research, grant 5-1181, contract OE6-10-235, and by the Office of Economic Opportunity, grants CG 8884 and CG 8889. Address reprint requests to: Dr. Merle B. Karnes, Department of Special Education, University of Illinois, Urbana, Illinois 61801.

well serve as the primary agent of that intervention. During weekly meetings, mothers in disadvantaged families were provided a sequential educational program to use at home in stimulating the cognitive and verbal development of their children and were instructed in principles of teaching which emphasized positive reinforcement. In addition to these child-centered activities, a portion of each meeting was devoted to mother-centered goals related to fostering a sense of dignity and worth as the mother demonstrated self-help capabilities within the family-setting and the community at large.

METHOD

RECRUITMENT

Twenty mothers (including two grandmothers responsible for the care of the child) with infants between the ages of 12 and 24 months were recruited from the economically depressed neighborhoods of Champaign-Urbana, a community of 100,000 in central Illinois. Staff workers at the offices of Aid to Dependent Children (ADC) and the Public Health Department were primary referral sources. In addition, an interviewer canvassed acutely disadvantaged sections of the city to locate families new to the community or otherwise unknown to the referring agencies. Sixteen of the 20 mothers who comprised the original training group were ADC recipients. The families of the remaining four children met the OEO poverty definition acceptable for Head Start admission.

During these initial contacts, the mother was asked if she was willing to attend a 2-hour meeting each week where she would be instructed in teaching techniques to use with her infant at home. In order to make appropriate baby-sitting arrangements for her children, she would be paid $1.50 an hour to attend these meetings. Transportation would also be provided. She was asked, further, to agree to apply these teaching techniques with her infant each day. She would not be paid for this work at home, but the toys used to implement the instructional program would be given to her baby. Finally, it was explained that the infant would be tested to determine how successful the mother had been as a teacher. Although the mothers readily acknowledged the importance of education to their children, they did not recognize their contribution to that enterprise. The suggestion that they could learn ways to stimulate the cognitive and language development of their babies at home was received with skepticism, and many mothers agreed to participate with only a limited commitment.

CHARACTERISTICS OF THE MOTHERS

Fourteen Negro and one Caucasian mother completed the 15-month training program. Five of these mothers had been born in the North (Illinois), and the others had migrated from the South, principally from Mississippi but also from Arkansas. The ages of these mothers ranged from 22 to 55 years, with a median of 26 years. Their educational levels ranged from 5 to 13 years, with a mean of 9.5 years. These mothers had from one to 12 children, with a mean of 4.9 children. Only two mothers were employed on a full-time basis outside the home. With one exception (a family in which the mother worked a 16-hour day at a factory assembly-line job and an evening food-service job), the annual income of these families did not exceed $4,000.

The average attendance of the 15 mothers who continued in the program was more than 80 percent. The five mothers who left the program had an average attendance of less than 60 percent during the first 7 months.

INITIAL CHARACTERISTICS OF THE CHILDREN

The initial mean chronological age of the 15 infants who completed the intervention was 20 months, with a range of 13 to 27 months. Five of these subjects were female and 10 were male. No child attended a day-care center or was enrolled in a preschool prior to or during this 2-year study.

A control (no intervention) group could not be maintained over the 2-year period, and the effectiveness of the mother training program is evaluated through comparisons between the scores on standardized instruments of the 15 children in the experimental group and 15 children of similar age with similar background characteristics chosen from a group of over 50 disadvantaged children who had been tested prior to intervention in the larger research project. The age range (31 to 44 months) within the experimental group at the conclusion of the program was divided into approximate thirds, and each third was comparably represented in the control group so that the ages of the control subjects would closely match those of the experimental children in range as well as mean. Within these age groupings, each experimental child was matched by a control child of the same race and sex. Further, the control child closely approximated his experimental match in the following family background characteristics: number of children in the family, working mother, birthplace of mother, educational level of mother, presence of father or father surrogate, and welfare aid (ADC) to the family. Since the effect of the interactions of these factors on the develop-

Table 1 Background Characteristics

Variable	Experimental group	Control group
Mean Binet CA (months)	37.9	38.3
Race:		
Negro	14	14
Caucasian	1	1
Sex:	10	10
Male		
Female	5	5
Mean number of children	4.9	4.7
Working mother	2	2
Mother's birthplace:		
Illinois	5	4
Mississippi	7	6
Other South	3	5
Mean educational level of mother (years)	9.5	9.1
Father (or surrogate) present	11	7
ADC	10	9

ment of the child is unknown, background characteristics were matched on an individual rather than a group basis. A summary of these characteristics for both groups appears in Table 1.

In spite of the careful effort to establish a comparable control group, a conspicuous variable remains uncontrolled. The mothers of the experimental children demonstrated a concern for the educational development of their children by participating in the training program over a 2-year period. A parallel level of motivation cannot be established for the mothers of the control children. This variable is, however, controlled in a second comparison. Six children in the experimental group had older siblings for whom test scores were available at similar chronological ages (within 12 months) and prior to the mothers' enrollment in the training program. The experimental child and his sibling control were not necessarily the same sex, but there were four males and two females in each group. Further, *all* data—the scores for the six experimental children and their sibling controls as well as the scores for the 15 experimental children and their matched controls—were obtained within a 3-year period; thus, family dynamics and community milieu remained relatively constant.

EVALUATION PROCEDURE

At the conclusion of the program, the 15 children in the experimental group received the Stanford-Binet Intelligence Scale, form L-M, and the experimental edition of the Illinois Test of Psycholinguistic Abilities (ITPA). The matched control and the sibling control children had been tested with these instruments in connection with recruitment for the larger research project. All tests were administered by qualified psychological examiners at a school site.

THE INTERVENTION

FIRST YEAR

To encourage discussion, the 20 mothers met in two groups of 10 throughout the 7-month intervention of the first year. The weekly meetings were divided between child- and mother-centered activities. The first category, the presentation of educational toys and materials with an appropriate teaching model, required strong staff leadership. The mother-centered activities involved group discussion with the intention that the group would provide its own vehicle for attitude change through interactions among the members. Two staff members conducted these weekly 2-hour meetings; one functioned as a group leader while the other served as a recorder. After the meeting, both staff members made a written evaluation of the content presented and the interactions within the group. Staff members made monthly (more often when necessary) home visits to reinforce the teaching principles introduced at the meetings and to help each mother establish a positive working relationship with her baby. They observed the appropriateness of the infant curriculum as well as the mother's effectiveness in communicating teaching strategies. Certain principles of teaching were repeated often at the weekly meetings and were encouraged during home visits:

1. If you have a good working relationship with your child, you can become an effective teacher. A good relationship is based on mutual respect.

2. Be positive in your approach. Acknowledge the child's success in each new task, even when the child simply tries to do as he is instructed. Minimize mistakes, show the right way immediately, have the child attempt the task again, and praise him.

3. Break a task into separate steps. Teach one step at a time, starting with the simplest. Do not proceed to the next step until the child is successful with the first.

4. If the child does not attend or try to do as instructed (and you are absolutely sure he can do what is asked), put the toys away until later. Do not scold, beg, or bribe. This time together should be fun for both of you.

Toys were the instructional media for the intellectual and language stimulation of the infant but were, of course, equally important as the media in which a positive interaction between mother and child occurred; they included nested cans and boxes, snap and string beads, graduated rings, a form box, and masonite shapes in various colors and sizes. The materials used in the Kirk tutorial study served as an initial guide and are described in Painter (1968). In addition, art materials (crayons, scissors, play dough, and chalk and slate), inexpensive books, a lending library of wooden inlay puzzles (three to 12 pieces), simple lotto games, toys for unstructured play (pounding bench, busy box, and musical ball), and toys to demonstrate transfer of learning (a stack tower and interlocking cubes) were provided. A home project which proved very successful in stimulating verbal responses was a picture scrapbook. The mother or older children in the family cut pictures from magazines which the infant was able to identify by naming or pointing and pasted these pictures in the scrapbook. "Reading" this book together fostered a sense of accomplishment shared by mother and child. A child's table and chair and a laundry basket for toy storage were supplied to encourage organization and good work habits. While the books were intended to foster language interactions between mother and child, all program toys created opportunities for verbal development. As the leader demonstrated teaching techniques with each new toy, she used key words which the mothers were to use and which they were to encourage their children to say. Initial work periods for mother and child were 10 minutes but lengthened as the child's attention span grew and the selection of toys increased.

The choice of discussion topics for the mother-centered portion of the meetings was guided by response to previous material. Child discipline, birth control, and the generation gap were among the topics which stimulated discussion. On occasion, pamphlets or magazine excerpts were distributed for reading prior to discussion sessions. Several films (*Guess Who's Coming to Dinner?* and *Palmour Street*) and speakers (a black-power advocate and a family-planning counselor) were included as were a trip to the public library to obtain library cards and to explore the resources of the children's library and a visit to a demonstration nursery school.

A more detailed description of the instructional program implemented by the mothers during the first year and a discussion of certain critical variables in mother participation and child performance can be found in Karnes and Badger (1969).

SECOND YEAR

The structure of the program the second year was patterned after that of the first year, and 15 of the original 20 mothers continued to attend weekly 2-hour meetings over an 8-month period. They were again paid to attend these sessions and transportation was provided. The group met as a single unit with only one staff member, with the exception of a group-leader trainee who participated during the last 2 months. Program responsibilities (note-taking during meetings, group leadership, program planning, and home visits) were shared by the mothers to develop their leadership capabilities.

Many of the child-centered activities of the second year extended those initiated the first year. Form perception, introduced the first year with the form box and the masonite shapes, was reinforced the second year with masonite templates. Most children were able to recognize and name three shapes and to distinguish big, little, and middle-sized. Matching skills acquired in the first year in object lotto games were incorporated into classification activities the second year. All children regularly used the art materials and pasted their own projects (snowmen, geometric shapes, collages) into a scrapbook. The lending library of wooden inlay puzzles was enlarged to include puzzles of 20 pieces.

New concepts and activities expanded the instructional goals of the first year. Each mother and child received a set of three books from which regular assignments were given, and mothers were encouraged to model the presentations offered by the teacher. A sequence of visual-motor activities from the Frostig Program for the Development of Visual Perception (Frostig and Horne 1964) was used to emphasize left-to-right progression and visual-motor coordination. Children learned to sort objects or pictures into two categories, and older children were able to sort by six categories at the same time. The ability to distinguish among the alphabet letters *A* through *F* was also developed in this manner. Rubber counting units and felt cutouts of familiar figures were used in patterning experiences. All children learned to sequence colored rods of five lengths and were exposed to seriational and dimensional vocabulary. Mothers encouraged the children to match concrete objects with pictured objects in inexpensive word books. Color and number concepts were emphasized with all program materials. In addition, a lending library of toys and materials which included picture files, puppets, beaded numeral cards, pegboards, blocks, and children's books was available for shared used.

The mother-centered aspect of the meetings during the second year emphasized topics related to programs of community involvement. Interactions during meetings were consistently lively. Mothers volunteered suggestions during the instructional demonstrations and offered comment on the teaching principles presented by the staff leader. Such spontaneous contributions had not been evident the first year and indicated improved self-confidence. Compared with their first-year reactions to guest speakers, the mothers seemed more receptive. Leadership capabilities emerged within the group during the year. Five mothers presented talks and moderated the discussion that followed. One mother served as notetaker at meetings for the year. Four mothers were trained to carry out home visits and performed ably. The group planned and presented a demonstration meeting for visitors from an out-of-state teachers college. Four mothers presented a taped panel discussion on family planning, and one mother arranged for a speaker on black history.

The confidence and capabilities demonstrated by the mothers within the program were reflected in increased community involvement. Four mothers assumed responsibility in the summer recruitment of Head Start children, and one was hired as an assistant teacher and promoted later to the position of head teacher. Two mothers spoke of their experiences in the mother training program at a Head Start parent meeting. Finally, total group involvement was demonstrated at a local Economic Opportunity Council meeting called to discuss the possibility of establishing a parent-child center in the community. Twelve of the 15 mothers attended this meeting and were, in fact, the only persons indigenous to the neighborhood in attendance.

RESULTS

THE MATCHED CONTROL COMPARISON

On both standardized measures, the performances of the experimental group were significantly superior to those of the control group (Table 2). The mean Binet IQ of the children whose mothers had worked with them at home was 16 points above that of the children who had received no intervention. The ITPA performance of the experimental group closely approximated its mean chronological age, and that of the control group was nearly 6 months below its chronological age. Since seven of the 15 control subjects scored below the normative range of the ITPA total and were arbitrarily assigned the lowest normative age score, the mean of this group is artificially inflated.

THE SIBLING CONTROL COMPARISON

Greater differences in intellectual functioning and language development were found between the experimental subjects and their siblings than between the matched groups. The 28-point difference in Binet IQ between the six experimental children and their sibling controls was, in spite of the small sample, significant (Table 3). Virtually no overlap in the range of IQ scores was found between the two groups. In the experimental group, scores ranged from 99 to 134, and in the sibling control group, from 71 to 102. Three of the six experimental subjects obtained scores of 124 or above. The experimental group achieved a mean acceleration in language develop-

Table 2 Experimental (N = 15) and Matched Control
(N = 15) Groups, Stanford-Binet and ITPA

Variable	Binet CA (months)		Binet MA (months)		Binet IQ		ITPA total language-age difference score (months)[a]	
	Exp.	Control	Exp.	Control	Exp.	Control	Exp.	Control
Mean	37.9	38.3	41.8	35.5	106.3	90.6	−0.8	−5.9
Standard deviation	3.92	3.45	6.84	5.43	12.46	9.87	6.59	5.42
Difference	0.4		6.3		15.7		5.1	
t[b]	0.24		2.72		3.70		2.25	
Level of significance	N.S.		.01[b]		.0005[b]		.025[b]	

[a]To relate ITPA language age and chronological age and to compensate for slight differences in mean chronological ages between groups, a language-age *difference score* was computed by subtracting each child's chronological age at the time of testing from his language-age score. For example, a child who was 36 months old with a total language-age score of 32 months received a difference score of −4 months. All ITPA data are presented in this form. Children who scored below the norms provided for the ITPA total were arbitrarily assigned the lowest total language-age score (30 months). This scoring convention was required in three instances in the experimental group and in seven instances in the matched control.

[b]One-tailed test.

Table 3 Experimental (N = 6) and Sibling Control
(N = 6) Groups, Stanford-Binet and ITPA

Variable	Binet CA (months)		Binet MA (months)		Binet IQ		ITPA total language-age difference score (months)[a]	
	Exp.	Control	Exp.	Control	Exp.	Control	Exp.	Control
Mean	38.2	40.3	46.5	36.7	116.7	89.0	3.0	−3.8
Standard deviation	3.33	3.20	6.95	5.76	12.43	10.28	7.68	7.73
Difference	2.1		9.8		27.7		6.8	
t[b]	0.86		3.00		5.90		2.54	
Level of significance	N.S.		.05		.01		.10	

[a]Children who scored below the norms provided for the ITPA total were arbitrarily assigned the lowest total language-age score (30 months). This scoring convention was not employed for any of the six experimental children used in the sibling comparison but was applied to one of the six sibling controls.

[b]For correlated pairs of means.

ment (ITPA) of 3 months, while the sibling control group scored nearly 4 months below its mean chronological age. The t for this difference approaches significance at the .05 level.

DISCUSSION

The comparability of a control group established after the intervention interval may be open to serious question. In this study, family background and mother motivation variables were of particular concern. Mother motivation, demonstrated to be high in the experimental group, may well have been lower in the matched control group, and differences in performance between these groups might, therefore, have been magnified. On the basis of this assumption, smaller differences would have been found between sibling groups than between matched groups. Such was not the case. In the sibling comparison, where mother motivation and family background characteristics were controlled, differences between experimental and control subjects were larger than those between matched groups and suggest that the comparison with the matched control group was legitimate.

The results of this study endorse the effectiveness of the mother training program in altering in positive ways the development of disadvantaged children before the age of 3. The 16-point Binet IQ difference between the infants whose mothers worked with them at home and the control infants nearly equals the 17-point Binet IQ difference between the experimental and control subjects in the Schaefer study, where the educational intervention was carried out by college graduates who served as tutors, visiting the child at home for 1 hour a day, 5 days a week, over a 21-month period. In the Kirk study, where professional tutors were used in a similar way over a 1-year period, the mean Binet IQ of the experimental group was seven points higher than that of the control. Since at-home intervention by mothers can be budgeted at a fraction of the cost of tutorial intervention, the direction for further research in preventive programs of very early intervention seems clear. Further, programs which train the mother to serve as the agent for intervention hold potential for developing her self-help capabilities and sense of personal worth, pivotal factors in effecting broader changes within the disadvantaged family. Not only may the mother represent the ideal agent for fostering an improved school prognosis for the young disadvantaged child, but through group interaction she may extend this sense of responsibility for infant, self, and family to the wider community in which they live.

The encouraging implications of this study must be interpreted with caution. Three-year-old disadvantaged children have been found to make gains in a structured preschool setting (Karnes, Hodgins, Stoneburner, Studley, and Teska 1968) comparable to the difference between the experimental and control subjects in this study. The superiority of intervention before the age of 3 is not demonstrated unless earlier gains are more stable than the disappointingly transitory gains attained in preschools for the disadvantaged. It may be that gains obtained by intervention through the mother that affects the child's total environment on a sustained basis will prove more stable and will be reflected in later school competency. Conclusions based on the performance of 3-year-old children are obviously premature, but the results of this study suggest that a program of mother training can do much to prevent the inadequate cognitive and linguistic development characteristic of the disadvantaged child.

REFERENCES

Frostig, M., and Horne, D. *The Frostig program for the development of visual perception.* Chicago: Follett, 1964.

Karnes, M. B., and Badger, E. Training mothers to instruct their infants at home. In M. B. Karnes, Research and development program on preschool disadvantaged children, Vol. 1. Final Report, May 1969, Project No. 5-1181, Contract No. OE6-10-235, Bureau of Research, Office of Education, U.S. Department of Health, Education, and Welfare. Pp. 245–263.

Karnes, M. B.; Hodgins, A. S.; Stoneburner, R. L.; Studley, W. M.; and Teska, J. A. Effects of a highly structured program of language development on intellectual functioning and psycholinguistic development of culturally disadvantaged three-year-olds. *Journal of Special Education,* 1968, **2,** 405–412.

Karnes, M. B.; Hodgins, A. S.; and Teska, J. A. The impact of at-home instruction by mothers on performance in the ameliorative preschool. In M. B. Karnes, Research and development program on preschool disadvantaged children. Vol. 1. Final Report, May 1969, Project No. 5-1181, Contact No. OE6-10-235, Bureau of Research, Office of Education, U.S. Department of Health, Education, and Welfare, Pp. 205–212.

Karnes, M. B.; Studley, W. M.; Wright, W. R.; and Hodgins, A. S. An approach for working with mothers of disadvantaged preschool children. *Merrill-Palmer Quarterly,* 1968, **14,** 174–183.

Kirk, S. A. The effects of early education with disadvantaged infants. In M. B. Karnes, Research and development program on preschool disadvantaged children. Vol. 1. Final Report, May 1969, Project

No. 5-1181, Contract No. OE6-10-235, Bureau of Research, Office of Education, U.S. Department of Health, Education and Welfare. Pp. 233–248.

Painter, G. *Infant education.* San Rafael, Calif.: Dimensions, 1968.

Radin, N., and Weikart, D. P. A. home teaching program for disadvantaged preschool children. In D. P. Weikart (Ed.), *Preschool intervention: a preliminary report of the Perry Preschool Project.* Ann Arbor, Mich.: Campus, 1967. Pp. 105–116.

Schaefer, E. S. A home tutoring program. *Children,* 1969, **16,** 59–61.

Weikart, D. P. Ypsilanti Carnegie Infant Education Project. Progress Report, Ypsilanti, Michigan, Ypsilanti Public Schools, Department of Research and Development, 1969.

an academic preschool for disadvantaged children: conclusions from evaluation studies

CARL BEREITER   The Ontario Institute for Studies in Education, Toronto, Ontario, Canada

I shall set forth here some generalizations about preschool education, based on evaluative research that has been done on the academic preschool for disadvantaged children, more familiarly known as the Bereiter-Engelmann program. To base general conclusions on what is essentially product-testing research is, of course, a highly speculative if not fanciful undertaking. There is no true separation of variables in product-testing research, only the single variable of product entity, and so it is difficult to defend any generalization beyond the products tested. Nevertheless, I think the effort is worth making for two reasons. The first is that there is not much else besides product-testing research to base inferences on when it comes to questions of what leads to what in preschool education. There are the careful studies of Carolyn Stern and Evan Keislar that investigate, for instance, the conditions under which verbalization does or does not facilitate learning in young children; but these studies stand largely alone. For the rest, we have either program evaluations that do not separate variables or laboratory experiments that are remote enough from real-life learning so that inferences from them are equally speculative.

Another reason for trying to draw inferences from product-testing research is that unless such general inferences can be drawn the research will have been largely in vain, since the products themselves change from one study to another and tend to be obsolete by the time the testing is completed—certainly by the time that long-term effects have been evaluated. Thus, in the case of the Bereiter-Engelmann program, the target of evaluation studies has never actually been the program as set forth in the 1966 book, *Teaching Disadvantaged Children in the Preschool*, but rather local modifications or subsequent revisions of it. And also the original program has since been superseded by the DISTAR program of Engelmann and others, the Conceptual Skills Program of Bereiter and others, and, most recently, the Open Court Kindergarten Program of Bereiter and Hughes, all of which differ from one another and from the original program on practically any dimension one might name. Thus even a simple statement of product evaluation requires judgments about what factors in a given program are central and about the extent to which these factors have been controlled.

Unfortunately, evaluation studies of preschool programs have with few exceptions compared a single program with a control condition, the control condition usually involving no treatment. Such studies, even when adequately designed to test treatment effects, allow only the most tenuous comparisons between one program and another, because each program is evaluated by a different experiment conducted in a different location with a different population, different testers, and so on.

There have, however, been several studies in which the Bereiter-Engelmann program has been compared with other programs or types of preschool education, using experimental procedures designed to maximize comparability of results for the various treatments. These studies, on which the remainder of this discussion will be based, are described here briefly.

1. *The Illinois study* (Karnes et al. 1969) was primarily concerned with comparison of the Ameliorative program originated by Karnes, the Bereiter-Engelmann program (called "Direct Verbal" in that study), and a Traditional program. However, related experiments evaluated a Montessori program and a treatment which merely involved placing disadvantaged children in various private nursery schools. Subjects for all the comparison groups were drawn by stratified random sampling from a common pool of children in Urbana-Champaign, Illinois, meeting Head Start eligibility criteria.

Stratification was by three levels of Binet IQ, and the children were between four and five years of age as of December 1 of the school year. All groups were tested by the same testers, although a blind procedure was not employed. It should be noted that this study, like most other preschool evaluation studies but unlike the studies to be described below, was a "home ball park" evaluation. That is to say, the Ameliorative and Direct Verbal treatments were carried out by the staffs that developed them.

2. *The Kalamazoo study* (Erickson et al. 1969) compared Bereiter-Engelmann, Traditional (called "Enrichment" in that study), and no-treatment control groups drawn from a common pool of Head Start-eligible four-year-olds by stratified random sampling according to geographical area. A novel feature of the evaluation was the employment of a cross-over design whereby the samples of children who had been in the two experimental preschool programs were each divided into two groups, one of which continued with the same treatment in kindergarten and one crossed over to the other treatment. Testing on the Stanford-Binet, the main dependent variable of the study, was blind.

3. *Ypsilanti Preschool Demonstration Project* (Weikart 1972) compares the Cognitively Oriented curriculum developed at Ypsilanti, the Bereiter-Engelmann program (called "Language Training" in that study), and a Traditional program (called "Unit-Based curriculum"). Subjects were randomly assigned to treatment from among three-year-old black children identified as functionally mentally retarded (low IQ but no discoverable organic impairment).

4. *The Louisville study* (Miller and Dyer 1970) compared Bereiter-Engelmann; the DARCEE program, developed at the George Peabody College for Teachers by Gray and Klaus (1968); Montessori; and Traditional. Over two hundred four-year-olds, almost all blacks, were involved in these experimental treatments. The design was not completely randomized, there being ten schools involved, with enough children for at most two different experimental treatments. This study included an extensive investigation of process variables as well as effect variables. Testing was carried out blind and with balancing to control effects of tester differences.

5. *The New York State study* (Di Lorenzo et al. 1969). Eight different preschool programs, each conducted in a different community, were included in this study. In effect there were eight separate experiments of the single treatment-versus-control group design, but the standardization of evaluation procedures and the centralized monitoring of program characteristics allows for somewhat more comparability than would be obtained from unrelated experiments. The most clearly identifiable treatments were the Bereiter-Engelmann, adaptations of which were used in two com-

munities, and the Montessori, which was used in one. One other community used a structured approach with cognitive emphasis, and the rest could be classed as traditional.

In describing the above studies, I have not indicated sample sizes, since they are a rather complex matter in every case. However, the size of the several studies can be approximated from the number of children in the Bereiter-Engelmann treatments of each study for whom end-of-preschool IQ scores were reported. The numbers are 29 for the Illinois study, 136 for the Kalamazoo study, 25 for the Ypsilanti study, 64 for the Louisville study, and 69 for the New York State study. The other experimental groups used in these studies were generally of similar size.

The fact that a number of independent researchers have chosen to deal with the Bereiter-Engelmann program in their investigations is easy to explain plausibly. It is not, I think, that they have found the program intrinsically interesting or appealing, but that they have seen it as representing an extreme on a dimension that they wished to study. As Erickson et al. (1969) put it, the program is "at the heart of one of the most burning issues in nursery school education today, namely, open-ended enrichment programs versus highly structured, detailed methods of instruction" (p. 3). If the issue is drawn as Erickson has stated it, then I think there would be little disagreement that the Bereiter-Engelmann program stands as the most extreme and clear-cut version of a "highly structured, detailed method of instruction."

I would, however, call special attention to the term "instruction." There are other highly structured programs and there are other detailed methods, but in no other preschool program, to my knowledge, are the instructional goals quite so clear-cut nor the procedures so exclusively devoted to achieving those goals in the most efficient manner. Although certain features of the program, such as pattern drill and the rapid pace of teaching, attract notice, I would assert that the program is not bound or distinguished by any particular methods, but is at bottom distinguished entirely by the degree to which content and method are combined into a fully engineered instructional program.

Accordingly, the kind of general inferences that can be drawn from evaluations of the Bereiter-Engelmann program are likely to be inferences about the value of deliberate instruction at the preschool level. The remainder of this paper is devoted to the discussions of three general conclusions related to this issue.

1. *The Bereiter-Engelmann program has clearly had more impact on IQ and achievement than the traditional, child-centered approach, but not necessarily more impact than other programs with a strong instructional emphasis.* This conclusion has been borne out

consistently by all the studies mentioned above. This is also the conclusion arrived at by Bissell (1970) in her reanalysis of data from the Illinois, Ypsilanti, and New York State studies. The results have been replicated widely enough and with a great enough variety of cognitive and achievement measures so that there is no serious problem in generalizing the conclusion to diverse populations of disadvantaged children or to diverse measures. The problem rather is to decide to what kinds of treatments the conclusions can be generalized: what are the limits of the categories *traditional, child-centered approach, and programs with a strong instructional emphasis?*

I have elsewhere (Bereiter 1970) discussed the common body of cognitive content that seems to be found in preschool programs of all types: identification of colors, shapes, numbers, letters, materials, parts of objects, uses, and actions, and the use of prepositions, comparisons, categories, and logical operators. This content has been dealt with in traditional preschool materials and activities and figures prominently in intelligence tests for young children. By programs with a strong instructional emphasis I mean ones in which the teacher's activities are specifically geared toward seeing to it that every child masters this content. In the traditional or child-centered approach the teacher's activities may be intended to promote learning of this content, but the teacher is not held responsible for seeing that the learning actually occurs.

Among the programs that emphasize instruction, there are conspicuous differences in method and less conspicuous ones in content. Some investigators have also tried to distinguish them on the basis of broad goals, but in the absence of observational evidence to the contrary, I regard such distinctions as purely rhetorical. Bissell (1970), for instance, distinguishes a structured-cognitive approach, exemplified by the Ameliorative program of Karnes, and a structured-informational program, exemplified by the Bereiter-Engelmann program—the former emphasizing cognitive processes and the latter supposedly ignoring these and concentrating upon "correct" responses. I observed these two programs operating side by side for two years and, while I could detect many differences in method and organization, I did not observe anything to support the distinction Bissell has made. Such distinctions derive, apparently, entirely from the kinds of theoretical ornamentation that program originators use to raise the tone of their reports.

This is not to say that the instructional programs are identical in effect. In comparison with other instructional programs, the Bereiter-Engelmann program has tended to show higher immediate IQ gains on the Stanford-Binet (Miller and Dyer 1970; Karnes et al. 1969; Weikart 1972). The Karnes program has shown higher gains in reading readiness, the DARCEE program on Peabody Picture

Vocabulary. These differences can be plausibly explained by differences in content emphasis. The Bereiter-Engelmann program contains relatively little work on vocabulary development or paper-and-pencil exercises of the kind used in readiness testing, but does entail more verbal reasoning and problem solving.

Having noted that different instructional programs appear to teach somewhat different things, we need not analyze the differences any further, as if to tease out all the differences and then weigh them up to decide which program offers the most of what. Such comparisons may be worth while if one is shopping for a program to install, but they are not instructive because there is very little evidence that learning one thing does more good than learning another. Gains on predictor variables are not necessarily predictive of gains on the criterion, as shown in studies of alphabet learning. Among preschool children, knowledge of the alphabet is a good predictor of future reading success, yet training in letter names did not transfer to subsequent reading achievement, although training in letter sounds did (Johnson 1970; Samuels 1970).

It would be helpful to have similar evidence on the relative value of vocabulary building versus training in the more precise and flexible use of words already known—on the transfer value, that is, of such learning to worthwhile tasks like reading. Merely to know that one kind of teaching yields better scores on a vocabulary test and the other on the Basic Concept Inventory is not much help. It is not known whether gains on these tests or on general intelligence or readiness tests are of any value.

From the data available on transfer of preschool treatment to later school learning, we have no grounds for distinguishing between programs with strong instructional emphasis. Again, they do better than the traditional, child-centered programs (Bissell 1970), but they do not differ noticeably from one another. Comparative data on transfer effects are much more scanty than on immediate effects, however. The only strictly comparable follow-up data are those for the Karnes and Bereiter-Engelmann programs (Karnes et al. 1969), where no differences in subsequent achievement appear, although both show achievement in first and second grades superior to that obtained with children in a traditional program.

One seemingly implausible conclusion that may be drawn from the studies to date is that all programs that have set out in a deliberate fashion to teach the core content of preschool education have succeeded, no matter how they have gone about it. The conclusion is probably not true, in that the programs under consideration here are ones that had enough success to have enjoyed continued funding for long enough to carry out extended evaluations and to have been investigated by researchers interested in comparative evaluation. On the other hand, I think it is reasonable to say that the core content mentioned earlier, consisting largely of everyday concepts, is not very hard to teach. It is not like phonics or fractions where, if the teacher is not careful, she can muddle the children's minds so that they not only don't learn it but they are rendered to some extent incapable of learning it thereafter. From this standpoint it may be said that the differences in *method* represented in the various instructional programs have not been put to adequate test. They would need to be applied to the teaching of something difficult. Reading and arithmetic have been taught in the Bereiter-Engelmann program. These are hard to teach, and they were taught with success: children at the end of kindergarten were averaging second-grade level in word recognition and in arithmetic computation (Bereiter 1968). Since the other programs have not tried to teach anything this difficult to children so young, there is no evidence to say they couldn't do it. I have only my own experience to go on in saying that I do not think that the more casual, unprogrammed kinds of instruction that characterize programs other than Bereiter-Engelmann are equal to the task of teaching anything difficult.

Special note must be taken of the showing made by Montessori classes. Three of the studies mentioned thus far included Montessori classes among the treatments compared (Di Lorenzo 1969; Karnes 1969; Miller and Dyer 1971). In all of these the Montessori classes produced results similar to those of traditional classes and thus inferior to those that I have been calling instructional approaches. In a study involving middle-class children (Bereiter 1966), Montessori-trained four-year-olds lagged far behind Bereiter-Engelmann-trained four-year-olds in reading, arithmetic, and spelling, although not in psycholinguistic skills. The Montessori method is so unusual, of course, that it is going to make a strange bedfellow no matter what category of program it is put into. Bissell (1970) labels it a "structured-environment" approach and puts it into a category with the "New Nursery School" of Nimnicht and Meier. Such a designation is reasonable, but doesn't take account of the very elaborate and systematic pedagogy of sense training and concept teaching which the Montessori method prescribes.

One source of difficulty in describing the Montessori program is that it is sequential, the infant program containing activities appropriate for children from three to five years or older. It is the higher-level activities, involving work with letters, numbers, and science concepts, that have drawn attention to the Montessori method as a possible vehicle for cognitive enrichment and acceleration, but it is entirely possible that disadvantaged preschool children, brought in for one year of Montessori schooling, never work their way up to these activities. The lower-level activities, which

center upon housekeeping skills and sense training, are not ones
that would be expected to produce noteworthy cognitive gains. As
for the higher-level activities, they differ from those in most instructional programs in being strictly tied to a few concrete representations of concepts. As Mussen, Conger, and Kagan (1969, pp. 432–33)
point out, such a method tends to produce failure to abstract in
young children.

2. The "traditional" nursery-school and kindergarten program
is not a serious contender as an educational program. Not only has
the "traditional" approach failed to achieve as good results in cognitive learning as the more instructional approaches, it has failed to
demonstrate any redeeming advantages. In the Kalamazoo and
Louisville studies a variety of motivation and adjustment measures
were taken; in the Kalamazoo study, teacher ratings of adjustment,
observer tabulations of deviancies, and records of attendance; in the
Louisville study, ratings by teachers, ratings by testers, and scores
on the Cincinnati Autonomy Battery. On none of these indicators
did the traditionally taught children show themselves to be better
off than those in the more instructional programs. In the Kalamazoo
study they were significantly lower, although superior to controls.

One of the cleanest sets of results is from the Kalamazoo study's
analysis of kindergarten attendance records. Here children who had
been in a Bereiter-Engelmann preschool showed higher kindergarten
attendance than those who had been in a traditional preschool, who
in turn showed higher attendance than those who had not been to
any preschool. But within each of these three groups, those who
attended a Bereiter-Engelmann kindergarten showed higher attendance than those who attended a regular kindergarten. Now it is not
at all clear what child characteristics attendance is an indicator of;
but the same may be said of any other available measure of childhood
personality and adjustment, impressive test labels notwithstanding.
One thing that can be said of attendance that cannot be said confidently of test variables is that it must indicate something important
and not some trivial instrument factor. School attendance would
seem to be a social indicator, a very gross index of how well things
are going with a child in relation to school. Its very lack of specificity guards it from the complaint that can be made against other
variables in the evaluation of preschool effects—that they do not
do justice to the broad socio-emotional goals of a child-centered program. I do not know any way to interpret a difference in school
attendance in favor of children in the Bereiter-Engelmann program
that is not damaging to the claims made for the traditional child-centered program.

Experimenters who have used a traditional program as one kind
of treatment have all evidenced difficulty in defining what such a

program is. The name itself, of course, isn't descriptive of what goes on and is regarded by many early childhood educators as pejorative. Yet even to find a name that distinguishes it from competing programs is difficult. Early childhood educators have also complained to me that there is no such thing as a traditional program or a "regular" Head Start approach, that they differ widely. Such differences, however, have always escaped my observation and apparently they also escape detection by systematic classroom observation. (Lois-ellin Datta [private communication] reports that efforts to study the effects of natural variations among Head Start programs have had little success because there simply was not enough variation to work with.)

Miller and Dyer, in the Louisville study, offered a systematic point-by-point comparison of the four types of programs they studied. The traditional approach, interestingly enough, is largely distinguished from the rest on the basis of things that are not done. The video-tape monitoring of teacher behavior in the same study provides striking support for the ideological distinction. Teachers in the traditional program are not so much distinguished by differences in the relative frequency of different kinds of teaching acts (as are teachers in the other three programs) as by the generally low frequency of teaching acts of any kind. The mean frequency of teaching acts of any kind among the traditional teachers is less than half that of teachers in the Bereiter-Engelmann classes (Miller and Dyer 1970, p. 53).

Furthermore, the only categories of behavior in which traditional teachers showed up as noticeably more active than teachers in the other programs were Contingent Negative Verbal Reinforcement, Conduct Modification, and Academic-Verbal Giving (lecturing).

The picture that emerges from these results is one that accords with my own observations. It is that the traditional approach does not represent a *different* way of teaching from those represented in newer programs but simply represents a lower order of program, one that is more custodial and less purposefully educational. The lesser overall amount of teaching behavior and the greater emphasis on behavior management suggest the custodial function. The greater use of straight verbal presentation as a way of giving information is entirely out of keeping with traditional doctrine if it is taken to indicate deliberate pedagogical method. It is quite understandable, however, on the assumption that instruction occurs only incidentally in traditional classrooms, without prior planning, so that the teacher is not prepared to communicate information in any other way than through just talking. To demonstrate or model a concept, to ask leading questions, to develop a concept through sequenced tasks—any of these require more preparation and a more deliberate intent to teach than is found in the traditional class.

It seems to me somewhat misleading to go on treating the traditional approach as one among a host of alternative approaches to teaching young children. It is better seen, not as a distinctive approach to teaching, but as a system of custodial child care that may incorporate to a greater or lesser extent various educational components similar to those found in instructional programs for young children, but that is primarily distinguished by its minimization of teaching. The true issue between the traditional approach and the various instructional approaches is not *how* young children should be taught but *whether*. This is still a live issue, far from having been settled by research. It is to this issue that I now turn.

3. *The long-term effects of preschool instruction are about as good as can be expected.* However impressive the immediate results of preschool compensatory instruction may be, and however much encouragement may be drawn from follow-up achievement data, the fact remains that no preschool program shows any promise of making, by itself, any *permanent* difference in the scholastic success of poor children.

The standard against which long-term results of preschool intervention are judged seems to be that of the Skeels (1966) experiment, where thirty years later the experimental subjects were leading successful lives and the control subjects were in miserable shape. This is a very unfair standard, however, for the Skeels intervention (taking children out of an institution and putting them in foster homes) was not only much more extreme, but it was an intervention that continued life long. Would anyone expect that putting children into foster homes at age five for one year and then sending them back to the institution would show such effects thirty years later?

To me it is quite remarkable that some preschool interventions are showing statistically significant effects for three years or more after the cessation of treatment. It is also noteworthy that these programs are the same kinds of instructional programs that produce the greatest immediate results.

To treat the eventual vanishing of preschool effects as failure is to imply either that preschool compensatory education is futile or that the effective method has yet to be discovered. Either of these conclusions *could* be true, but those who think they follow from current evidence are applying criteria of success to preschool education that are not applied in any other realm of human effort. They are asking the doctor for a pill they can take when they are ten that will prevent them from getting fat when they are fifty.

Reason would have it that if we have designed a preschool program that produces benefits lasting for three years, then instead of agonizing that they didn't last for five or ten, we should be concerned with what can be done in the years after preschool to produce further benefits. This, of course, is a popular notion, one that lies behind the entire Follow-Through program. It raises, however, some troubling questions concerning preschool education.

a. If it is granted that education for poor children must be improved over the whole span of school years, then is it any longer necessary or practical to invest heavily in preschool education for such children? In other words, is preschool education anything more than the stone in the stone soup?

b. Is there justification for heavy investment in a continued search for more effective methods of preschool education, or have the limits of effectiveness largely been reached?

Both of these are policy questions that have to be acted upon whether there is any pertinent evidence or not, and so whatever faintly valid evidence may be dredged out of evaluation studies is that much to the good.

The cross-over data from the Kalamazoo study afford some evidence that is directly pertinent to the first question. Put more crudely, the first question reads: If you are going to follow up anyway, does it make any difference what you follow up on? The Kalamazoo study found that children in regular kindergarten classes did better if they had been in a Bereiter-Engelmann preschool than if they had been in a traditional one, or had had no preschool at all. On the other hand, children from these three preschool conditions who went into a Bereiter-Engelmann kindergarten all ended up at about the same level of performance. If the Bereiter-Engelmann kindergarten is taken to represent follow-up—that is, the continuation of special treatment—then it would appear that it does not make much difference what one follows up on: the preschool treatments could have been eliminated without loss. On the other hand, when there was no follow-up—that is, when children were put into a regular kindergarten program—performance was highly dependent on the nature of preschool experiences.

This finding is pregnant with implications. Consider, for instance, how the results might have been interpreted if all the children from the three preschool conditions had gone into a Bereiter-Engelmann kindergarten, and if this kindergarten program had somehow gotten itself established as normal, so that no mention was made of what kind of kindergarten program it was. Then the data would have shown that preschool effects "washed out" when the children got to kindergarten. One might even have been tempted to blame the kindergarten for washing out those grand effects. Under the actual circumstances, however, with traditional kindergarten classes for comparison, it appears that the washing out of effects was a good thing, since it consisted of bringing those children with the less favorable preschool experience up to the level of those with the more favorable experience.

A rather more complex set of results from recent phases of the Louisville study (Miller and Dyer 1971; Miller et al. 1971) appears to support the same interpretation of "wash out." After completing the preschool treatments described previously, children were branched into either a regular kindergarten or into a Follow-Through kindergarten program described as "a highly academic, individualized program structured as a token-economy" (Miller and Dyer 1971, p. 4). Children who received the Follow-Through treatment did significantly better than those who went to regular kindergarten, regardless of their preschool experience. There was also a clear wash out of differences in the Follow-Through treatment, with children who had received no preschool education and those who had received a traditional one scoring as well as those who had received the more effective experimental treatments. On the other hand, in the regular kindergarten there were significant differences due to preschool experience. However, in contrast to the Kalamazoo findings, the differences were by no means a simple carry-over of differences observed at the end of preschool. On one of the main measures, the Metropolitan Readiness Test, the lowest scores were obtained by regular kindergarten children who had had Bereiter-Engelmann preschool. A number of other shifts in relative standing are puzzling as to what kinds of interactions with preschool experience actually took place in the regular kindergarten classrooms of this study; but the overall result, that an effective instructional program in kindergarten can wash out preschool differences in a favorable way while a conventional kindergarten does not do so, remains consistent with the Kalamazoo findings.

Extrapolated, these results would suggest that a highly effective program at any level of schooling will overcome the effects of variations in educational experience up to that level. The suggestion is probably not true, of course. If it were we could concentrate all our efforts on making a bang-up success of the last year of schooling and not worry about whether children learned anything in the years preceding. But so long as it appears true that an effective kindergarten program will overcome differences in preschool experience, we must question the wisdom of concentrating compensatory education on the preschool period.

The wise strategy for the present would seem to be to look for elementary school programs that are more successful than the present ones at washing out the effects of differences in earlier school experience. This strategy does not, however, preclude the continued search for more effective methods of preschool education. On this matter we have to ask ourselves what increased effects we would want or have any reason to expect were possible.

Such a question invites visionary responses à la George Leonard (1966). Generalizing from what we have been able to teach in our experimental programs, however, I am inclined toward the more pedestrian position that existing technology already enables us to teach young children far more than they can benefit from. What we need to do is not discover ways to teach them more but rather construct articulated educational programs that permit us to teach in the preschool what will be of use later and to teach later what builds upon what was learned in the preschool.

Thus I do not believe we need to be devoting resources to developing a better preschool program because we are in no position to say what a preschool program ought to accomplish that present ones do not. As we noted previously, the various effective instructional programs do not accomplish precisely the same things, but there is no basis for saying that the accomplishment of one is more valuable than that of another. I think, therefore, that we are at a point where development of preschool programs, if it is to proceed any further, has to be joined to elementary school curriculum design. The two questions: "What does a child need to know in order to be ready for first grade?" and "What does a child need to know in order to get the most out of being four years old?" have about yielded their all. The first has yielded the core content of preschool education mentioned previously and the second has yielded such things as handling a paint brush and putting on a coat (to mention only objectives that can be acted on; the second question also gives rise to an abundance of fine sentiments). Only by joining preschool education with elementary school curriculum can we begin plausibly asking the potentially much more productive question: "What things can we teach a child of four and five that can then be built upon in the first grade and after?"

My attitude toward the failure of preschool programs to produce lasting gains is perhaps cavalier. I realize that the more accepted behavior, which I have on occasions engaged in myself, is to express sincere regrets that things haven't turned out better and then offer an explanation which, while vague and speculative, makes it clear that I am not at fault. It is also possible to find cause for optimism in follow-up results. Verbal reports from Karnes and Erickson indicate that Bereiter-Engelmann children continue to show achievement advantages over control and traditionally taught children as far as the third grade. Weikart children, from his original experimental treatment, show achievement advantages as late as sixth grade. To me, however, the most parsimonious hypothesis to account for these persisting advantages is that there was a degree of continuing differential treatment given to experimental group children—by virtue of their being assigned to different streams on entry into regular school. I know this to have been the case in the Illinois study, where the schools used IQ and other scores from the research testing to place children in first grade streams. Differential treatment in the Ypsilanti study may have been even more marked, judging from Weikart's verbal report of a substantially larger proportion of control group children being assigned to special classes for the mentally retarded.

The data on long-term effects of preschool intervention are disillusioning but not, to me at least, discouraging. The illusion that they serve to dispel is that there is some magic in the early years of intellectual development, such that a little difference there will make a lot of difference later. What we seem to be finding instead is that a lot of difference there may just possibly make a little difference later. Weakening of the "magic years" illusion will, I hope, render more credible the position that Engelmann and I have argued from the beginning, that learning in young children is just learning: some things can be taught to young children and some cannot; some of the things that can be taught will prove useful later and some will not; what will prove useful later is not determined by some innate chain of development but by the actual course of real-life events. The corollary that I have argued in this section is that one way to make preschool learning more useful is to alter the actual course of subsequent school events so as to make use of it.

IMPLICATIONS FOR DAY CARE AND FOR EARLY CHILDHOOD EDUCATION RESEARCH

Because of the twin concerns of the Hyman Blumberg Memorial Symposium with the providing of day care services for children of working parents and with research in early childhood education, it seems appropriate to comment specifically on the implications that the foregoing conclusions have for these two concerns.

With respect to day care I am an outsider, and I make the following observations without pretending to know the complexities of the enterprise. It appears that the main thing wrong with day care is that there is not enough of it, and the main reason there is not enough of it is that it costs too much. At the same time, those who are professionally dedicated to advancing day care seem to be pressing continually to make it more costly by setting certification requirements for day care workers and by insisting that day care should be educational and not just high-quality institutionalized baby-sitting.

What the previous discussion should suggest is that producing a measurable educational effect in young children is far from easy, that it requires as serious a commitment to curriculum and teaching as does education in older children. I cannot imagine day care centers on a mass basis carrying out educational programs of the kind needed to produce measurable effect. If they cannot do so, then it will prove in the long run a tactical blunder to keep insisting that day care must be educational. Sooner or later those who pay for it will begin demanding to see evidence that educational benefits are being produced, and there will be no evidence.

It would seem to me much wiser to seek no more from day care than the sort of high-quality custodial care that a child would receive in a well-run home, and to seek ways to achieve this level of care at a cost that would make it reasonable to provide for all those who need it. One should not have to justify day care on the grounds that it will make children do better in school, any more than one should seek such justification for a hot lunch program. A child has a right to a square meal regardless of whether or not it helps him read better.

A well-run and well-equipped day care center resembles very closely a traditional preschool—which I have argued is also primarily custodial in its function. The traditional preschool has managed to flourish, with its clientele of upper-middle-class families willing to pay, without having to promise educational benefits. It has earned a place for itself simply by providing a wholesome experience for children in pleasant surroundings and in the company of other children. I do not see why day care centers should have to promise more in order to justify their existence.

Early childhood education has been a thriving area of research and development during the past five years. High expectations and availability of money combined to draw talented investigators into the area. Both the expectations and the money are likely to diminish and with them, no doubt, the special attractiveness of the field. The likely result, however, is that early childhood education research will merge more with educational research in general. There is much to be done in the early childhood field, for instance in the discovery of the critical variables in instructional treatment and in the closer analysis of particular learning problems; but there is no reason why such research should stand apart from the main body of research into classroom learning. Abandonment of the "magic years" illusion should have, in the long run, beneficial effects on research as well as on educational practice.

REFERENCES

Bereiter, C. 1966. *Acceleration of intellectual development in early childhood.* Washington, D.C.: U.S. Office of Education.

———. 1968. A nonpsychological approach to early compensatory education. Pp. 337–46 in M. Deutsch et al. (eds.). *Social class, race, and psychological development.* New York: Holt, Rinehart & Winston.

———. 1970. Designing programs for classroom use. Pp. 204–7 in F. F. Korten et al. (eds.), *Psychology and the problems of society.* Washington, D.C.: American Psychological Association.

Bereiter, C., and Engelmann, S. 1966. *Teaching disadvantaged children in the preschool.* Englewood Cliffs, N.J.: Prentice-Hall.

Bissell, J. S. 1970. *The cognitive effects of pre-school programs for disadvantaged children.* Bethesda, Maryland: National Institute of Child Health and Human Development, June 1970 (mimeographed).

Di Lorenzo, L., Salter, R., and Brady, J. J. 1969. *Prekindergarten programs for educationally disadvantaged children.* Washington, D.C.: U.S. Office of Education.

Erickson, E. L., McMillan, J., Bennell, J., Hoffman, L., and Callahan, O. D. 1969. *Experiments in Head Start and early education: Curriculum structures and teacher attitudes.* Washington, D.C.: Office of Economic Opportunity, Project Head Start.

Gray, S. W., and Klaus, R. A. 1968. The Early Training Project and its general rationale. Pp. 63–70, in R. D. Hess and R. M. Bear (eds.), *Early Education.* Chicago: Aldine.

Johnson, R. J. 1970. The effect of training in letter names on success in beginning reading for children of differing abilities. Paper presented at annual meeting of the American Educational Research Association, Minneapolis, Minnesota, March 1970.

Karnes, M. B., Hodgins, A. S., Teska, J. A., and Kirk, S. A. 1969. *Research and development program on preschool disadvantaged children.* Vol. I. Washington, D.C.: U.S. Office of Education.

Leonard, G. B. 1968. *Education and ecstacy.* New York: Delacorte Press.

Miller, L. B., and Dyer, J. L. 1970. Experimental variation of Head Start curricula: A comparison of current approaches. Annual progress report, June 1, 1969–May 31, 1970. Louisville, Kentucky: University of Louisville, Department of Psychology.

———. 1971. Two kinds of kindergarten after four types of Head Start. Louisville, Kentucky: University of Louisville, Department of Psychology.

Miller, L. B., et al. 1971. Experimental variation of Head Start curricula: A comparison of current approaches. Progress Report No. 9, March 1, 1971–May 31, 1971. Louisville, Kentucky: University of Louisville, Department of Psychology.

Mussen, P. H., Conger, J. J., and Kagan, J. 1969. *Child development and personality* (3rd ed.). New York: Harper & Row.

Samuels, S. J. 1970. Letter-name versus letter-sound knowledge as factors influencing learning to read. Paper presented at annual meeting of the American Educational Research Association, Minneapolis, Minnesota, March 1970.

Skeels, H. M. 1966. Adult status of children with contrasting early experiences. *Monograph of the Society for Research in Child Development*, 51, no. 3.

Weikart, D. P. 1972. Relationship of curriculum, teaching, and learning in preschool education. Pp. 22–66, in [J. C. Stanley (ed.), *Preschool programs for the disadvantaged*. Baltimore: Johns Hopkins University Press].

part V
fathers

on the importance of fathers

HELEN L. BEE

With more and more attention being paid, in these days of the women's liberation movement, to the characteristics of the male and female roles in our society, it is of increasing interest to look particularly at the roles of adults as mothers and fathers. One of the contentions of the women's lib movement is that women have been "kept at home." It's held that our society's notions that a mother is the only one who can bring up a child, and that a woman's only fulfillment is in bringing up children, have created a situation in which only the mother-wife role is available to a woman. Whether or not one agrees with the notion that women have somehow been tyrannized into accepting the wife and mother role, it is certainly true that as far as child rearing goes, we are a highly matriarchal culture. (See Nash, 1965, for a discussion of this, including some cross-cultural comparisons.) Both in society at large and among psychologists who study child rearing, the mother is seen as the figure of primary importance for the child.

For example, one of the typical conclusions drawn from studies of institutionalized (orphanage) children is that they suffer from "maternal deprivation," and that this deprivation is the cause of their cognitive retardation and emotional difficulties. But what about "paternal deprivation"? Children in institutions do not have father figures either; in fact, one could argue that there is a greater paternal than maternal deprivation, since virtually all caretakers in such institutions are female. The child at least has a female model or two, but he or she may have no male model at all.

Similarly, virtually all studies of "parent-child interaction" really do not examine "parent-child" interaction; rather they study "mother-child" interaction. In part the emphasis on mothers in such studies is reasonable, particularly for young children, since the mother in the "typical" intact family spends far more time with the child than does the father. In addition, there is the simple practical fact that it is much easier to study mothers with children than fathers with children, since fathers are rarely available during times when the young child is awake. (Having done some observations of mother-father-child inter-actions in the home, I can attest to the difficulties involved in arranging for such observations. See Bee, 1967.) Whatever the reasons, however, there has clearly been a neglect of the fathering role, both in the psychological literature and in society at large; indeed "parenting" has been equated with "mothering." The father is ordinarily seen some-how as an appendage to the family, his duties being primarily eco-nomic.

It seems to me that whether we retain a matriarchal child-rearing system or not, it is important to know a good deal more about the role of fathers with children. If we are moving toward a more equali-tarian family arrangement, with fathers and mothers sharing more of the child-rearing role, it becomes even more crucial for us to know about fathers, their relationships with young children, and the effect variations in such relationships have on the child's development. Hence a section on fathers in a book devoted to "social issues."

Obviously, since we know comparatively little about the roles or impact of fathers, most of what I can do here is to raise questions. But there *is* a body of research worth examining, and some selections from that research literature, which are worth your reading, have been included in this section.

METHODOLOGICAL QUESTIONS

Before we go on to examine the literature, there is one major meth-odological question we need to take up: How do you determine the effect the father has on the child? What kind of behaviors in the child do you look at? Of major concern in nearly all of the studies to date is the question of the father's impact on the development of a "mascu-line" sex role in the son and a "feminine" sex role in the daughter. But how does one define "masculine" and "feminine"? And how does one measure them? In virtually every case masculinity and femininity are defined in terms of the commonly accepted stereotypes in our society, namely that the masculine role is primarily an "instrumental" one (competent, effective, strong), and the feminine role is primarily an "expressive" one (affectionate, warm, emotional). (I have borrowed these terms from Hetherington and Deur's review paper, 1972.) Given these definitions, the research questions usually asked are: What kind of father or what kind of father-availability leads to a son who, as an adult, fits into the accepted male role and a daughter who fits into the accepted female role? And what kind of father leads to a son or daughter who does *not* fit into the traditional roles? The measurement techniques used reflect the emphasis on stereotype; most measures assess simply whether the child's interests or activities match those that are typical for his or her own sex and age. (See, for example, Rabban, 1950; Anastasiow, 1965; Rosenberg and Sutton-Smith, 1959).

I must emphasize strongly, though, that the use of masculine and feminine stereotypes as the basis for measuring masculinity and femininity does not imply that the authors of the tests, or the particular researchers involved, necessarily think the stereotypes are either accurate or desirable. The accuracy and desirability of such stereotypes about male and female behavior are really not at issue. The fact is that such stereotypes exist (Rosenkrantz, Vogel, Bee, Broverman, and Broverman, 1968); thus it becomes a legitimate question to ask what kinds of rearing practices result in children who are typical or atypical for their sex. That's not the only question we might be interested in, but it's a legitimate question, nonetheless. With that in mind, we can go on to an examination of the literature.

STUDIES OF ABSENT FATHERS

Most of what we know about the impact of fathers comes from studies of *absent* fathers. This may seem to be a backward way to go about it, but presumably one can get some estimate of the effect of the father's presence by looking at what happens to a child when the father is absent during various periods in the child's early years.[1] The three studies of father absence included in the selections illustrate most of the major conclusions that can be drawn from an examination of the literature on father absence, namely:

1. The impact of an absent father is greater on the boy than on the girl. In virtually all the research done on father absence, the clear

[1]The fatherless families are of interest in their own right, too, if only because they are so numerous. In 1969 there were *7 million* children under age 14 who were being raised in families without fathers (Profiles of Children, 1970).

finding is that the boy is affected more than the girl is. More specifically, the greatest effect of father absence seems to be a kind of "feminization" of the boy, in the sense that the boy shows fewer typically male behaviors and more typically female behaviors. The first selection by E. Mavis Hetherington illustrates this; she finds father-absent boys to be less aggressive than father-present boys, and aggression is clearly a "masculine" characteristic. Lyn Carlsmith notes a different kind of feminization, a feminization of cognitive skills. The father-absent boys showed the typically female intellectual pattern of greater skill at verbal tasks than at quantitative tasks, and the father-present boys showed the more typical masculine pattern of greater quantitative than verbal skill.

There is some evidence, however, that girls too are affected, but in a different way. Hetherington (1972) has done one study of father-absent adolescent girls, in which she found that the father-absent adolescent girl showed one of two kinds of disruption of her heterosexual behaviors. Either she was very shy and anxious around males, or she was promiscuous and "inappropriately assertive" with males. These same girls, however, had no difficulty in their relationships with other girls.

For the boy, then, it would appear that the lack of a father deprives him of a masculine role model; his mother becomes his major role model, and his behavior is thus feminized. In the case of the girl, as Hetherington and Deur put it, "the critical function of the father in the feminine development of daughters may be in providing a learning situation in which, through the use of contingent reinforcement, he shapes the daughter's skills for interacting with males" (Hetherington and Deur, 1972, p. 310).

2. The impact of father absence, on the boy at least, can be seen in both personality and cognition. In both areas we see a feminization of the boy's behavior. Again, the first Hetherington paper and the Carlsmith paper in the selections illustrate the point.

3. The age at which the separation occurs seems to be crucial, with early separation (before age five) having by far the greatest effect. In fact, Mavis Hetherington's data and B. Sutton-Smith, B. G. Rosenberg, and Frank Landy's suggest that father absence after age five may have very little effect—at least on the sort of behaviors measured in the typical studies.

4. The feminizing effects of father absence on the boy can be mitigated if male figures are available to the child. The alternative male figure may be a brother, as Sutton-Smith, Rosenberg, and Landy's paper shows; they found that in a family of two boys father absence had the least effect, compared to families with a boy and a girl.

All of this information from studies of absent fathers is of interest, since it certainly suggests the importance of the father's presence for the "normal" development of the boy (and to a lesser extent, the girl) in our society. If a boy is to adopt the traditional male role, he has to have available to him a model who occupies that role. It is also of interest because the greater impact of the father's absence on the boy is what we would expect from most kinds of theories of identification. (See Carlsmith's paper for a discussion of this question.)

SOME REMAINING ISSUES

Studies of absent fathers do not tell us much about the positive effects of father presence; nor do they tell us much about what may be the result of various new patterns of parental involvement with children, or the effects of the presence of fathers who do *not* adopt the traditional masculine role. More specifically, we need to know more about three questions.

1. What is the impact of *maternal* absence? There is an enormous literature on the question of total and partial separation of the mother and child, but practically none on the effect of a family constellation in which the mother is absent and the children are reared by the father. The one major study of "motherless families" that I know of was done recently in England (George and Wilding, 1972) and is really a study of the impact of wifelessness on the father; George and Wilding collected no data on the impact of motherlessness on the children. Of course, there is a good reason for the scarcity of such studies: There are exceedingly few cases. The death of a mother with young children is comparatively rare, and even when it occurs, the children are often reared by some female relative, rather than by the widowed father. And in the vast preponderance of divorce cases, either by the choice of the two parents or by decree of the court, the custody of minor children goes to the mother. George and Wilding estimate that for the English population, approximately 1 percent of children are reared by their fathers alone, and a similar percentage is estimated for the United States.

The situation may be changing, however. In Seattle recently there was a widely discussed case—reported in the national press as well— of a woman who left her husband and children in order to pursue a career, leaving her husband to rear the children. Given the current *Zeitgeist,* there are bound to be more such cases. In addition, there is some indication that the courts have substantially relaxed their bias in favor of mothers in divorce cases. Leon Friedman, in a recent article in the *New York Times* (1973), cited a study in Minneapolis showing that in 38 percent of the contested custody cases custody was granted to the father. In California, Colorado, Minnesota, and Florida the state laws have been changed to eliminate any preference for the mother in custody cases.

What all of these changes suggest is that over the next decades, we can expect to see many more "motherless families," which makes it even more important for us to know something about the potential impact on the child of being reared by a father alone. What would we expect the result of this to be? Would it have the same effect on the girl as father absence does on the boy? That is, would there be a "masculinization" of the girl? It's reasonable to expect that there would be. It is probably also true, however, that the father's being the major child rearer involves a greater change in the traditional male role than the mother's being the sole parent does for the female role (particularly if the mother is not working). So both son and daughter in a mother-absent family may well be exposed to a very different kind of masculine figure—one who is expressive as well as instrumental. Will this result in a feminization of the boy along with more masculinization of the girl? That is, will the two sexes come out acting more alike? We have some hint that such an outcome might result from studies of families in which the mother works. In particular, take a look at Vogel, Broverman, Broverman, Clarkson, and Rosenkrantz's paper in Part II. They found that college age males and females whose mothers work now or have worked have less clearly differentiated stereotypes of the male and female roles than do students of the same age whose mothers have not worked. It appears that when the mother adopts more of the attributes of the traditional male role, the sons and daughters *both* have less stereotyped views of male and female roles. It's conceivable that one would find a similar effect in family situations in which the father adopts more of the female role, as in families with an absent mother.

Additional evidence suggesting the same conclusion comes from research on intact families in which the father adopts some of the aspects of the traditional female role, such as cooking and performing household chores, and in which both mother and father share in decision making. Bronfenbrenner (1958), in a review of the few such studies available, finds that such a role pattern on the part of the father *is* associated with "less masculine" interests in the son.

2. What is the impact of the father's caretaking when the family unit is intact, but the father does all or a considerably greater part of the child caretaking than is usual? For example, if both parents work and share the caretaking, or if the mother works and the father is the major caretaker, what is the impact on the child?

One of the old assumptions about child development is that there is something necessarily special about mothers with infants. The mother is thought to have some special attachment to the infant that the father does not have. It's true that only the mother can breast-feed the infant, and that in the feeding situation important reciprocal relationships between the adult and the infant are developed. Infants do not have to be breast-fed, however; they can be fed by bottle, and bottle feeding can be done by a father as well as by a mother. Does the infant become as attached to a male caretaker? Evidence from animal studies would suggest that they can. Harlow's work (1958) with monkeys shows clearly that the infant monkey attaches itself not to the person or object that gives milk, but to the person or object that provides "contact comfort." So perhaps the person who holds, cuddles, and strokes the infant is the one the infant becomes primarily attached to—and fathers ought to be able to perform this function as well as mothers.

What about the father being attached to the infant? Is the "mothering instinct" present only in mothers? Is it an instinct at all? Again we have some evidence from animal studies that mothering is not an instinct among female monkeys. Harlow's studies of female monkeys who have been reared without an adult female model (Harlow, Harlow, Dodsworth, and Arling, 1966) show that these motherless monkeys are themselves inadequate mothers, at least with their first infants (although they seem to do better with later infants). These findings suggest that mothering may be a pattern of behavior that one learns through experience and observation, and such learning ought to be equally available to males and females in our society. One recent study with humans also suggests that some aspects of maternal behavior are not instinctual. Leifer, Leiderman, Barnett, and Williams (1972) studied mothers of prematures, who were separated from their infants for up to two months while the infant was in an incubator, and compared these mothers with a group of mothers of full-term infants, who were separated from the infant only sporadically during the first several days. When the mothers in the two groups were later compared in the degree of their attachment to their infant, the full-term mothers were found to show greater attachment; they smiled at the infant more and held the baby close to their body more often. They were also more confident about their ability to care for the infant than the mothers of the prematures. And among mothers of prematures, those who had had an opportunity to hold the infant while in the incubator and share in some of the caretaking while the infant was in the hospital were more confident about their caretaking skills than were mothers who had been able only to look at the infant during the hospitalization. Whether the full-term mother's greater attachment for the infant is due to the greater amount of early contact or to some kind of hormonal state that is present immediately after birth but not several months later, we can't say at this point. But Leifer et al.'s research does suggest the possibility that attachment to an infant may require physical contact with that infant from very early in the infant's life. Since fathers rarely have extensive physical contact with the newborn, it's at least conceivable that their presumed lesser attachment comes from too little contact. What is needed, of course, is some research on the effects of various amounts of early contact on fathers' attachment to their infants. Until such research is done, we have only speculation.

What all the speculation does suggest, at any rate, is that fathers undoubtedly *could* perform the mothering role without detriment to the child, although as I've discussed, such caretaking on the part of the father would probably affect the sex-role adoptions and stereotypes of the children.[2]

3. What is the father's impact in the currently more typical family arrangement, in which the father works and the mother is at home? For example, what is the effect of the roles that the father and the mother adopt within the family on the children's role development? I've already mentioned the limited amount of research done on families in which the father and mother share both the housekeeping and the decision making. The related evidence is from research on families in which the fathers are clearly dominant in decision making. The second selection by E. Mavis Hetherington is an example of such research. She found that boys from father-dominant homes were more masculine than boys from mother-dominant homes, and this finding is typical.

There is other evidence that the quality of the father-son relationship affects the boy's adoption of the father's role. In particular, warm, nurturant fathers (that is, fathers who have a positive, affectionate relationship with their sons) seem to have sons who are more likely to model themselves after their father. So if the father is high in traditional masculinity and is warm and nurturant, the son is likely to be high in traditional masculinity as well. What we don't know is whether a warm nurturant father who adopts a nontraditional masculine role will have a nontraditional son as well (Sears, 1953; Mussen and Distler, 1959; Bronson, 1959). The traditionally masculine father who simul-

[2]As a delightful example of the sort of role perceptions that might arise out of a family situation in which the mother works and the father does the major caretaking, witness the following conversation (overheard by a student of mine and passed on to me) between Carl and Monica, both children of families with "reversed" roles:
The two children, aged four and three, were playing house:
Carl: "Good-bye wife. I'm going to work now."
Monica: "See you tonight, sweetheart. Don't forget I have to go to work early. Be home to take Ruth swimming . . . Oh, and feed the cat."
Carl: "Okay. Don't forget to buy tires and get the oil changed." Loud motor noises. "I'll buy the baby food."

taneously emphasizes appropriate feminine behaviors for the daughter also has a daughter who in fact adopts a more traditionally female role (Mussen and Rutherford, 1963). If you put these findings together, it appears that a warm, affectionate father who has clear stereotypes about appropriate masculine and feminine behavior and who epitomizes the masculine stereotype is likely to have children who adopt the traditional male and female roles.

In all of this, of course, it is difficult to sort out the effect of the father from the effect of the family constellation, since the father with the more traditional role expectations is likely to have married a woman who is willing to adopt the more traditional female role. So the son and daughter of the family have clearly differentiated role models available to them.

Obviously, what's missing in this entire area is good research on atypical families. Of greatest interest—to me at least—would be research on families in which the father is the primary caretaker. Such families *do* exist. In Sweden a man who adopts this role is called the househusband, and I presume that if a word exists to describe the situation, it must be at least moderately frequent. In the United States approximately 15 percent of all children under 14 whose mothers work either full- or part-time are cared for by their father while the mother works. So the cases are there, but the research is lacking.

I'm sure you can think of other relevant questions that should be asked about the role of the father in the family. Among other things, it's obviously important that we begin to look at the impact of fathering on other things besides the child's adoption of "appropriate" sex roles. With our increased sensitization to the importance of fathers and to their potentially increased role in child rearing, I suspect this whole area will be a fruitful one for research over the next few years. By the time this book is revised, perhaps we will have more answers and fewer questions.

QUESTIONS FOR DEBATE AND DISCUSSION

1. If you were a judge charged with deciding whether children in divorce proceedings should live with the father or the mother, what conclusions would you draw from the material presented in this section? Would the child's age or sex affect your decision? If so how?

2. In Sweden some families have arranged their lives so that the wife works and supports the family, and the husband stays home and takes care of the children and the housework. Based on your reading of this section, what do you think would be the social and psychological implications of such an arrangement? Would you choose such an arrangement for yourself?

ADDITIONAL REFERENCES USEFUL IN PREPARATION
FOR DEBATE OR DISCUSSION

Biller, H. B., and Borstelmann, L. J. Masculine development: An integrative review. *Merrill-Palmer Quarterly,* 1967, **13,** 253–294.

A review of all the material on factors affecting the development of masculinity, including all the material on the impact of fathers' roles on sons' masculinity development.

Biller, H. B., and Weiss, S. D. The father-daughter relationship and the personality development of the female. *Journal of Genetic Psychology,* 1970, **116,** 79–93.

Another good review of a different facet of the problem.

Hetherington, M., and Deur, J. The effects of father absence on child development. In W. W. Hartup (Ed.), *The young child: Reviews of research.* Vol. 2. Washington, D.C.: National Association for the Education of Young Children, 1972, pp. 303–319.

Excellent review of father absence.

Nash, J. The father in contemporary culture and current psychological literature. *Child Development,* 1965, **36,** 261–297.

A good review of all the literature on fathers.

REFERENCES

Anastasiow, N. S. Success in school and boys' sex role patterns. *Child Development,* 1965, **36,** 1053–1066.

Bee, H. L. Parent-child interaction and distractibility in 9-year-old children. *Merrill-Palmer Quarterly,* 1967, **13,** 175–190.

Bronfenbrenner, U. The study of identification through interpersonal perception. In R. Tagiuri and L. Petrillo (Eds.), *Person perception and interpersonal behavior.* Stanford, Calif.: Stanford University Press, 1958, pp. 110–130.

Bronson, W. C. Dimensions of ego and infantile identification. *Journal of Personality,* 1959, **27,** 532–545.

Friedman, L. "Fathers don't make good mothers," said the judge. *The New York Times,* January 28, 1973.

George, V., and Wilding, P. *Motherless families.* London: Routledge & Kegan Paul, 1972.

Harlow, H. F. The nature of love. *American Psychologist,* 1958, **13,** 673–685.

Harlow, H. F., Harlow, M. K., Dodsworth, R. O., and Arling, G. L. Maternal behavior of rhesus monkeys deprived of mothering and peer association in infancy. *Proceedings of the American Philosophical Society,* 1966, **110,**(1).

Hetherington, E. M. Effects of father absence on personality development in adolescent daughters. *Developmental Psychology*, 1972, **7**, 313–326.

Hetherington, M., and Deur, J. The effects of father absence on child development. In W. W. Hartup (Ed.), *The young child: Reviews of Research*. Vol. 2. Washington, D.C.: National Association for the Education of Young Children, 1972, pp. 303–319.

Leifer, A., Leiderman, P. H., Barnett, C. R., and Williams, J. A. Effects of mother-infant separation on maternal attachment behavior. *Child Development*, 1972, **43**, 1203–1218.

Mussen, P. H., and Distler, L. Masculinity, identification and father-son relationships. *Journal of Abnormal and Social Psychology*, 1959, **59**, 350–356.

Mussen, P. H., and Rutherford, E. Parent-child relations and parental personality in relation to young children's sex-role preferences. *Child Development*, 1963, **34**, 589–607.

Nash, J. The father in contemporary culture and current psychological literature. *Child Development*, 1965, **36**, 261–297.

Profiles of children. (1970 White House Conference on Children) Washington, D.C.: United States Government Printing Office, 1970.

Rabban, M. Sex-role identification in young children in two diverse social groups. *Genetic Psychology Monographs*, 1950, **42**, 31–158.

Rosenberg, B. G., and Sutton-Smith, B. The measurement of masculinity and femininity in children. *Child Development*, 1959, **30**, 373–380.

Rosenkrantz, P., Vogel, S., Bee, H. L., Broverman, I. K., and Broverman, D. M. Sex role stereotypes and self concepts in college students. *Journal of Consulting and Clinical Psychology*, 1968, **32**, 287–295.

Sears, P. S. Child rearing factors related to playing of sex-typed roles. *American Psychologist*, 1953, **8**, 431. (Abstract)

Vogel, S. R., Broverman, I. K., Broverman, D. M., Clarkson, F. E., and Rosenkrantz, P. S. Maternal employment and perception of sex roles among college students. *Developmental Psychology*, 1970, **3**, 384–391.

effects of paternal absence on sex-typed behaviors in negro and white preadolescent males

E. MAVIS HETHERINGTON   *University of Wisconsin*

This study investigated the effects of father absence on the development of sex-role preferences, dependency, aggression, and recreational activities of Negro and white preadolescent boys. All children had mothers but no father substitutes present in the home and no contact with the fathers subsequent to separation.

In previous studies of the effects of father absence on the development of children, total and final absence of the father usually had not occurred. The father was either temporarily away due to war (Bach, 1946; Sears, Pintler, and Sears, 1946) or to occupational demands (Lynn and Sawrey, 1959; Tiller, 1958). An exception to this is the McCord, McCord, and Thurber (1962) study of boys from broken homes. These studies frequently indicated disruption of masculine identification in boys whose fathers were absent. Boys with fathers absent from the home tended to be less aggressive in doll-play situations (Sears et al., 1946), had father fantasies more similar to those of girls (Bach, 1946), and were more dependent (Stolz et al., 1954; Tiller, 1958) than boys whose fathers were living

E. Mavis Hetherington, Effects of paternal absence on sex-typed behaviors in negro and white preadolescent males. *Journal of Personality and Social Psychology*, **4**, 1966, 87–91. Copyright © 1966 by the American Psychological Association, and reproduced by permission.

in the home. In contrast to these findings McCord et al. found no differences in dependency between boys from homes in which the father was absent and those in which the father was present and found the former group was more aggressive. The Lynn and Sawrey study also indicated that boys deprived of regular contact with their fathers made stronger strivings toward masculine identification shown by preference for a father versus a mother doll in a Structured Doll Play Test, and manifested an unstable compensatory masculinity. They found no differences between boys whose fathers were absent and those whose fathers were present in ratings of dependency in the doll-play situation and attribute this to a "compensatory masculine reluctance to express dependency [p. 261]."

It might be expected that if boys with absent fathers in contrast to those with a father present manifest compensatory masculinity they would score high on behaviors associated with masculinity such as independence, aggression, masculine sex-role preferences, and participation in activities involving force and competition. Moss and Kagan (1961) suggested that for boys, participation and skill in sports is closely involved with maintenance of sex-role identification. However, if father absence results in a direct expression of a failure to establish masculine identification, boys without fathers would be rated low on the previous variables.

The age at which separation from the father occurs could differentially affect the form of disrupted identification in boys. Early separation may result in greater disruption of sex-typed behaviors than would later separation when identification is well under way or completed. Early separation might result directly in less masculine sex-role behaviors since identification with the father has never developed. In contrast later separation may have little effect on these behaviors or result in exaggerating masculine behavior in an attempt to sustain the already established masculine identification with the major role model, the father, absent.

It might also be expected that the effects of father absence would interact with the race of the family. It has frequently been suggested that the Negro family structure is basically matriarchal (Karon, 1958). Maternal dominance has been demonstrated to have a disruptive effect on sex typing in boys (Hetherington, 1965; Mussen and Distler, 1959). In such mother-dominated families, absence of the father might be expected to have a less disruptive effect on sex-typed behavior of boys than it would in a father-dominant family.

Kardiner and Ovesey (1951) suggest that Negroes have strong inhibited aggressive needs which are displaced and expressed in competitive sports. It would therefore be predicted that Negroes would be rated lower in overt social aggression than would white boys, but would show a marked preference for aggressive, competitive activities.

METHOD

Subjects were 32 Negro and 32 white first-born boys between the ages of 9 and 12, who were attending a recreation center in a lower-class urban area. Sixteen of the boys in each group were from homes in which both parents were present, and 16 from homes in which the father was absent. In half of the father-absent homes for Negro and white families, separation had occurred at age 4 or earlier, and in half, after age 6. Father separation was caused by desertion, divorce, death, and illegitimacy. No father substitutes lived in the home. There were no significant differences in causes of father separation between groups, although illegitimacy was a cause only in the early groups.

Forty-nine of the subjects were only children, seven subjects had a younger male sibling, and eight subjects had a younger female sibling. These subjects were distributed approximately evenly across groups, although there was a slightly larger proportion of only children in the group of children whose fathers left early than in the groups whose fathers were present or had left the home after age 6.

PROCEDURE

Two male recreation directors who had known the subjects for at least 6 months rated them on 7-point scales measuring dependence on adults, dependence on peers, independence, aggression, and on an activities test. The scales ranged from 1, very rarely and without persistence, to 7, very often and very persistently. Interrater reliabilities ranged from .85 to .94. All subjects were also individually administered the It Scale for Children (ITSC; Brown, 1956).

MEASURES

Scales for dependence and independence were based upon those used by Beller (1957). The aggression scale was based on that of Sears, Whiting, Nowlis, and Sears (1953). Behaviors involved in each scale were more fully elaborated as in Beller (1957), but used behaviors appropriate to the age group of the present study. A total rating for each of these three scales was obtained.

Rating Scale for Dependence on Adults was comprised of ratings of:

1. How often does the boy seek physical contact with adults?
2. How often does the boy seek to be near adults?
3. How often does the boy seek recognition (any form of praise and punishment) from adults?

4. How often does the boy seek attention from adults?

Rating Scale for Dependence on Peers was composed of the same items as dependence on adults oriented toward children.

Rating Scale for Independence involved the following four of Beller's autonomous achievement-striving scales:

1. How often does the boy derive satisfaction from his work?

2. How often does the boy take the initiative in carrying out his own activity?

3. How often does the boy attempt to overcome obstacles in the environment?

4. How often does the boy complete an activity?

Rating Scale for Aggression involved the following items:

1. How often does the boy act to necessitate correction, scolding, or reminding?

2. How often does the boy ask for special privileges?

3. How often does the boy attack other children or their property to show envy?

4. How often does the boy threaten adults?

5. How often does the boy threaten other children?

6. How often does the boy destroy the property of the Center or of other children?

7. How often does the boy derogate others?

8. How often does the boy quarrel with other children?

9. How often does the boy display undirected aggression?

10. How often does the boy attack other children physically?

11. How often does the child exhibit displaced aggressive attacks?

The Activities Test was comprised of ratings on a 7-point scale ranging from 1, very rarely participates in this activity, to 7, very often and persistently participates in the activity. Five activities in each of four categories were rated. In standardizing the Activities Test three recreation directors were asked to sort a group of 48 activities into the following four categories. Only those in which the three judges agreed were retained.

1. Physical skill involving contact—boxing, wrestling, football, basketball, battle ball.

2. Physical skill not involving contact—footracing, bowling, horseshoes, table tennis, darts.

2. Nonphysical competitive games—dominoes, checkers, Scrabble, Monopoly, cards.

4. Nonphysical, noncompetitive games—reading, watching television, building things, working on puzzles, collecting things.

Total ratings for each of the four types of activities were obtained.

The ITSC (Brown, 1956) is a test of sex-role preference which presents the child with an ambiguous figure (It) and asks the child to select from a group of toys and objects those that "It" prefers. A high score indicates masculine preference.

RESULTS

Separate two-way analyses of variance involving race and father status (early absent, late absent, and present) were calculated for each scale. When significant F ratios were obtained, t tests between means were calculated. Table 1 presents the means for all groups on all variables.

The analysis of variance of total dependence on adults yielded no significant differences; however, the analysis of dependence on peers yielded a significant F ratio $(F = 10.18, p < .005)$ for father status. Subsequent t tests indicated that both early-separated and late-separated boys were significantly more dependent on peers than were the boys with fathers living in the home $(t = 2.23, p < .05; t = 2.90, p < .005)$.

No significant differences were found between groups on total independence scores.

The analysis of total aggression scores indicated a significant effect of father status $(F = 10.39, p < .005)$ on aggressive behavior. Both boys who were deprived of their fathers after age 6 and boys whose fathers [were] present manifested more aggression than boys who were deprived of their fathers at an early age $(t = 3.20, p <' .005; t = 2.21, p < .05,$ respectively).

The results of the ITSC also yielded a significant effect for father status $(F = 4.966, p < .025)$. Boys experiencing late separation from the father and boys from unbroken homes have more mas-

Table 1 Means for Father Separation Early, Father Separation Late, and Father Present, Negro and White Boys

	Father present		Early		Late	
	White	Negro	White	Negro	White	Negro
Dependency on adults	15.69	15.19	14.25	14.00	12.75	13.00
Dependency on peers	15.31	15.50	17.62	18.25	18.25	19.12
Independence	15.75	15.69	18.25	15.37	15.25	18.25
Aggression	39.87	47.06	32.00	30.75	51.00	52.12
ITSC	67.56	70.69	53.50	55.00	65.12	73.25
Physical contact	20.62	23.62	14.87	18.87	21.50	21.87
Physical noncontact	21.06	18.75	15.37	17.50	21.12	17.00
Nonphysical, competitive	21.44	20.81	16.87	18.62	20.12	17.62
Nonphysical, noncompetitive	17.69	16.62	24.25	22.37	21.37	19.12

culine sex-role preferences than early-separated boys ($t = 2.32$, $p <$ .05; $t = 3.14$, $p < .005$).

The Activities Test indicates that early-separated boys play fewer physical games involving contact than do either late-separated boys or boys with fathers living in the home ($t = 2.06$, $p < .05$; $t = 2.60$, $p < .025$). Negro boys tend to play more games of this type than do white boys ($t = 2.22$, $p = .05$). It should be noted that this is the only significant racial difference found in the entire study. No significant effects were obtained in the analysis of physical activities involving no contact or in nonphysical competitive activities. However, a significant effect ($F = 8.236$, $p < .005$) for father status was found in nonphysical, noncompetitive activities. Early-separated boys spend more time in these activities than do boys living with both parents.

It seemed possible that the obtained differences between early- and late-separated boys were a result of the total time elapsed since the father left the home, rather than the developmental stage at which separation occurred. The early-separated children may have had more time for a loss of cathexis on masculine behaviors. In order to investigate this possibility, an attempt was made to compare subjects in the early- and late-separation groups who had been deprived of their fathers [for] 6 years. The resulting Ns in each group were too small to permit an adequate analysis of the scores ($N = 4$ in early separated, $N = 3$ in late separated); however, the results appeared to parallel those of the total early- and late-separated groups.

The small sample size and predominance of only children did not permit satisfactory analysis of the effects of family size and sex of siblings on the behavior studied.

Table 2 presents the intercorrelations among all variables studied for all subjects.

Dependence on adults but not on peers is negatively related to independence. Masculine sex-role preferences, aggressive behavior, and participation in physical activities cluster together. Conversely, it appears that boys who enjoy nonphysical, noncompetitive activities are low in masculine sex-role preferences, aggression, and in participation in activities involving physical contact or nonphysical competition.

DISCUSSION

The results of the study indicate that absence of the father after age 5 has little effect on the sex-typed behaviors of boys. These boys in most respects do not differ from boys who have their fathers present.

Table 2 Correlations Among All Variables for All Subjects

	1	2	3	4	5	6	7	8	9
1. Dependency on adults	1.00	.02	-.25[b]	.06	.04	.04	.06	.11	-.06
2. Dependency on peers		1.00	-.10	.06	.04	-.02	.03	-.26	.10
3. Independence			1.00	.05	.02	-.01	.11	.17	-.17
4. Aggression				1.00	.21[a]	.40[d]	.22[a]	-.01	-.33[c]
5. ITSC					1.00	.38[c]	.02	.09	-.29[c]
6. Physical contact						1.00	.13	.03	-.59[d]
7. Physical noncontact							1.00	.17	-.16
8. Nonphysical, competitive								1.00	-.23
9. Nonphysical, noncompetitive									1.00

NOTE. Numbered variables in columns correspond to those in rows.
[a] $p = .10$.
[b] $p = .05$.
[c] $p = .01$.
[d] $p = .001$.

They are similar in their independence, dependence on adults, aggression, and sex-role preferences. In preferences for activities involving physical force or competition which might permit socially accepted expression of compensatory masculinity we again find no differences. An increased dependence on the adult all-male staff of the recreation center might have been expected if the boys lacking fathers were seeking attention from other adult males as father substitutes. This did not occur. It appears that any frustrated dependency needs which loss of a father might have produced do not generalize to other adult males. In fact there was a trend for boys with no fathers to be less dependent on adults ($F = 2.56$, $p < .10$). The greater dependence on peers of boys who had lost their fathers early or late is difficult to explain. It may be that loss or lack of a father results in a mistrust of adults with a consequent compensatory increase in dependence on peers. This general pattern of relations was reported by Freud and Burlingham (1944) in their studies of children separated from their parents by World War II. These children showed strong ties to their peers but few emotional ties to adult caretakers in institutions.

Boys who lost their fathers early, before identification can be assumed to have been completed, showed considerable deviation in sex-typed traits. They are less aggressive and show more feminine sex-role preferences than the other boys. They also participate less in physical games involving contact and more in nonphysical, noncompetitive activities. This preference for the latter type of activity could be considered an avoidance of activities involving the appropriate masculine behaviors of competition and aggressive play. An alternative explanation might be that it is a manifestation of social withdrawal since the activities in that category tend to be ones which involve a minimum of social interaction. It is difficult to accept this interpretation in view of the high dependency on peers ratings obtained by these boys. One could speculate that these boys make unsuccessful dependent overtures to peers, are rebuffed, and remain socially isolated.

The results suggest that adequate masculine identification has occurred by age 6 and that this identification can be maintained in the absence of the father. If the father leaves in the first 4 years before identification has been established, long-lasting disruption in sex-typed behaviors may result.

The predictions concerning racial differences were only partially confirmed. Differences between Negro and white boys in overt aggression which would be expected if Negroes inhibit direct expression of aggression were not obtained. However, the predicted high participation of Negroes in competitive activities involving contact was found. On the basis of this study it must be concluded that the behavior of Negro and white boys observed in the setting of a recreation center appears very similar.

REFERENCES

Bach, G. R. Father-fantasies and father typing in father-separated children. *Child Development*, 1946, **17**, 63–79.

Beller, E. K. Dependency and autonomous achievement-striving related to orality and anality in early childhood. *Child Development*, 1957, **29**, 287–315.

Brown, D. G. Sex-role preference in young children. *Psychological Monographs*, 1956, **70**(14, Whole No. 421).

Freud, A., and Burlingham, D. T. *Infants without families.* New York: International Universities Press, 1944.

Hetherington, E. M. A developmental study of the effects of sex of the dominant parent on sex-role preference, identification, and imitation in children. *Journal of Personality and Social Psychology*, 1965, 2, 188–194.

Kardiner, A., and Ovesey, L. *The mark of oppression.* New York: Norton, 1951.

Karon, B. P. *The Negro personality.* New York: Springer, 1958.

Lynn, D. B., and Sawrey, W. L. The effects of father-absence on Norwegian boys and girls. *Journal of Abnormal and Social Psychology*, 1959, **59**, 258–262.

McCord, J., McCord, W., and Thurber, E. Some effects of paternal absence on male children. *Journal of Abnormal and Social Psychology*, 1962, **64**, 361–369.

Moss, H. A., and Kagan, J. Stability of achievement and recognition seeking behaviors from early childhood through adulthood. *Journal of Abnormal and Social Psychology*, 1961, **62**, 504–513.

Mussen, P., and Distler, L. Masculinity, identification, and father-son relationships. *Journal of Abnormal and Social Psychology*, 1959, **59**, 350–356.

Sears, R. R., Pintler, M. H., and Sears, P. S. Effects of father-separation on preschool children's doll play aggression. *Child Development*, 1946, **17**, 219–243.

Sears, R. R., Whiting, J. W. M., Nowlis, H., and Sears, P. S. Some childrearing antecedents of dependency and aggression in young children. *Genetic Psychology Monographs*, 1953, **47**, 135–234.

Stolz, L. M., et al. *Father relations of war-born children.* Stanford: Stanford University Press, 1954.

Tiller, P. O. Father-absence and personality development of children in sailor families: A preliminary research report. *Nordisk Psykologi*, 1958, Monogr. No. 9.

effect of early father absence on scholastic aptitude*

LYN CARLSMITH   *Yale University*

Theories of identification, whatever their form, usually agree on two points: for the boy to identify successfully with the father, the father must be present during at least some portion of the boy's childhood; development of an appropriate masculine identity or self-concept is predicated upon the success of this early identification with the father. One of the most direct methods of investigating these general propositions is to study boys whose fathers were absent during their childhood. The present study, by considering a sample of boys whose home life was presumably normal in every respect except for the temporary absence of the father in World War II, seeks to answer two questions. First, are there lasting measurable effects due to the absence of the father at an early age? Second, is the age of the child during the father's absence an important variable in determining these effects?

Lyn Carlsmith, Effect of early father absence on scholastic aptitude. *Harvard Educational Review*, **34**, Winter 1964, 3–21. Copyright © 1964 by President and Fellows of Harvard College.
*The research for this paper was done at the Laboratory of Human Development at Harvard University. It is a part of a larger project on sex identity being carried on at the Laboratory under the direction of John W. M. Whiting. A more extensive report of this study appears in a Ph.D. thesis of the same title under the author's former name, Karolyn Gai Kuckenberg, which was accepted by the Department of Social Relations in June, 1963. The author is grateful to John W. M. Whiting, Beatrice B. Whiting, and J. Merrill Carlsmith for their generous assistance in the planning and execution of this research.

Previous studies on the effect of father absence during the first years of life represent three different approaches: 1) studies of the fantasy and behavior of children (Bach, 1946; Sears, 1946; Stolz, 1954; Lynn and Sawry, 1959; Tiller, 1957; D'Andrade, 1962); 2) retrospective accounts from the case histories of delinquents (Zucker, 1943; Glueck and Glueck, 1950; Rohrer and Edmonson, 1960); 3) studies of other cultures (Burton and Whiting, 1961). Each of these sources suggests that absence of the father significantly affects personality development and behavior in certain ways. The results of all these studies are generally consistent: father-absent boys show more underlying feminine traits and, at least in lower or working class families, they attempt to compensate by demonstrating extreme masculinity. However, the effect of the early experience of father absence on later development under normal circumstances has not been studied in this culture.

The study to be reported in this paper stems from an early and serendipitous finding that aroused considerable interest at the outset of this research on the effects of father absence. The finding was this: boys who experienced early separation from their fathers had a different pattern of aptitude scores on the College Board tests than boys who were not separated. Since the finding concerned the differential development of Mathematical and Verbal ability, it dovetailed into the current interest and research on the learning of mathematical or analytical modes of thought. It seemed possible that we had hit upon an unexpected antecedent variable—the presence or absence of the father in early childhood. Although the finding was initially based on a very small sample of Harvard students, it seemed sufficiently intriguing to explore further with a much larger group of students.

Whiting's (1960) theory of cross-sex identification provided the framework from which this study developed. This theory provides a set of explicit hypotheses concerning the development of cross-sex identification. However, it should be pointed out that the present study was not designed to discriminate between theories of identification; rather, it provides evidence relevant to any general theory of identification by showing certain strong effects of father absence at various ages.

Let us now consider the relevance of aptitude scores to sex-role identification. Accumulated evidence from a large number of studies on Math and Verbal aptitudes clearly demonstrates that females are generally superior to males in Verbal areas, while males are superior to females in quantitative pursuits, particularly numerical reasoning (e.g., McCarthy, 1954; Samuels, 1943; Heilman, 1933). These differences are well replicated and seem to hold over a broad age range, increasing from the elementary school years. Preferences for school subjects follow the same pattern. A particularly relevant study by Milton (1957) indicates a striking correlation between the problem-solving ability of adolescents and their scores on masculinity-femininity scales (MMPI and Terman-Miles). That is, both boys and girls who obtain a high masculinity score show superior problem-solving ability. In a retrospective study of the autobiographies of professional mathematicians, Plank and Plank (1954) report that female mathematicians have a "strong identification with a masculine figure in their lives. Parallel with it, seems to go a lack of feminine identification . . ." (p. 268). The lives of male mathematicians are characterized by a "loss of relationship to the mother."

These findings suggest that superior ability in mathematics reflects a typically masculine way of thinking or "conceptual approach." For the purposes of this study, the pattern of Math and Verbal aptitude scores from the College Entrance Examination Board seemed to provide a clear, objective measure of this sex-typed ability. That is, students who score relatively higher on Math aptitude than on Verbal aptitude tests have an aptitude pattern that is typical of a masculine conceptual approach; students who score relatively higher on Verbal aptitude tests have a more feminine conceptual approach.

Finally, there is considerable evidence that aptitude is a fairly stable characteristic, showing little variation with time (*College Board Score Reports*, 1960). A special mathematics teaching program which followed school children from fourth to seventh grade (Alpert, 1963) indicates that aptitude for mathematics is fairly well established by fourth grade and is highly resistant to change during subsequent school training. These data suggest that aptitude patterns are a useful index for the measurement of primary sex-role identity since they are apparently little influenced by the external pressures or expectations that occur in the subject's later experience. That is, while we would expect many indices of personality and behavior to be strongly influenced by our cultural norms for males and females, it is likely that aptitude patterns are both relatively free from and impervious to such expectations and that they are therefore a good indicator of the primary or underlying identity.

Children who were born during the war years (1941 to 1945) and whose fathers were away during their first years of life are now finishing school or attending college. This group offers a number of advantages for a study of the effects of early father absence on subsequent development. It is possible to locate students from stable families who have shared this common experience, the reason for father absence was socially acceptable and even desirable, the exact periods of father absence may usually be ascertained, and all other background factors (except the wartime separation) can be matched

Table 1 Length of Father Absence

Length of time father was absent after child's birth	Harvard class of 1963	Harvard class of 1964
Over 3 years	38	3
2–3 years	53	36
Less than 2 years	124	44
Not absent	666	224
	High school boys	High school girls
1–5 years	19	14
Less than 1 year	19	12
Not absent	99	109

in the two groups studied. The present study includes only boys from intact families (both parents living and not divorced) of middle or upper-middle class background. The majority of students were sophomores at Harvard College; one small sample includes high school seniors who planned to attend college the next year. Thus all students have achieved a relatively high level of academic success and have also made a reasonably satisfactory adjustment in terms of our social and cultural norms.

SAMPLES

Both college and high school students were subjects in this study. The college population consists of 881 Harvard freshmen in the class of 1963 and 307 Harvard freshmen in the class of 1964. The high school sample includes 137 boys and 135 girls from the 1961 senior classes at Concord, Lexington, and Newton South Public High Schools. All students in both college and high school samples are American-born and are from intact families (i.e., natural parents are not separated, divorced, or deceased). The high school sample is limited to those students on whom aptitude scores from the College Entrance Examination Board were available.

All students in the study were born during the war years, 1941 to 1945. Approximately one-third of their fathers served overseas and were separated from their wives and young children for varying lengths of time. Table 1 presents this distribution.

METHODOLOGY

In March, 1961, I administered a simple questionnaire on father absence to 450 Harvard freshmen (class of '64) who were voluntarily taking a series of interest-aptitude tests through facilities of the Harvard Testing Service. On this form, three questions were asked: was your father in the service during World War II; was he overseas during this time; if so, estimate the dates that he was overseas. Verbal and Math aptitude scores from the College Entrance Examination Board tests were then obtained on all students whose fathers had served overseas. Students whose fathers were in the service but did not go overseas were eliminated from the study because I felt it would be too difficult to ascertain the periods of father-separation for this group. Foreign-born students and those from broken homes (due to death, separation, or divorce) were also excepted. Finally, the median College Board aptitude scores for the entire freshman class were obtained.

A similar procedure was used with the high school students, except that the father-absence questionnaire was addressed to the parents to increase accuracy of the dates of the father's military service. Math and Verbal aptitude scores were then obtained for all students who had taken the College Entrance Examination Board tests. Since no other aptitude test had been uniformly administered in the high schools, the majority of high school students could not be included in this survey.

To further test the relationship between father absence and aptitude, I studied a second group of Harvard freshmen (class of '63). Questions on the father's military service had been included in the medical history record filled out by all entering students. Data on these students were provided by Dr. Stanley King from material collected in the Harvard Student Study.

SCHOLASTIC APTITUDE TEST (SAT)

This test is administered to high school juniors and seniors by the College Entrance Examination Board. The test yields two scores: a Verbal score and a Mathematical score. Norms for the test were established nationally over a period of years, and it is possible to make direct comparisons between students taking the test in different years. The reported reliability coefficient for the test is .91. In *College Board Score Reports* (1961), the average aptitude scores achieved by all high school seniors taking the test in a recent year are reported.

Average SAT scores

	Math	Verbal
Boys	527	479
Girls	467	486

The booklet also states: "In general girls do less well than boys on the Mathematical parts of the test and should not be surprised if their Mathematical scores are noticeably lower than their Verbal" (p. 8).

DATA ANALYSIS

In addition to mean Math and Verbal aptitude scores, a single Math-minus-Verbal score was computed for each subject. In this paper, the Math-minus-Verbal difference score will be represented by the term M-V. This single difference score is preferred for all comparisons between groups since it controls to some extent for general level of ability. That it, by considering only the relative superiority of Math to Verbal aptitude for each individual, differences in absolute level of ability between individuals are not weighted. For this reason, the single M-V difference score is used for all statistical comparisons between the Father-absent and Father-present groups. Several methods were used to test the significance of the difference between groups; these will be described with the presentation of results.

RESULTS

The independent variables considered here are: 1) length of the father's absence and 2) age of the child when the father left. Since each of the three samples included in this survey represents a different class year in school and different age group (by year of birth), there is considerable variation in the periods of father absence between groups. In addition, data on both independent variables were not available for one of the samples. Because of these limitations, it is not possible to combine groups or to present uniform tables on the dates of father absence for all groups. In the data analysis, father-absent categories for each sample are determined by the distribution of dates of father absence, sample size, and the information available for that group. All Math and Verbal scores presented in these tables are from the Scholastic Aptitude Test (SAT) of the College Entrance Examination Board.

HARVARD CLASS OF 1964

For the entire Harvard class of 1964 ($n = 1180$), the median Math aptitude score was 695; the median Verbal score was 677. Clearly the students in this class scored higher on the Math aptitude test

Table 2 A. Background Variables on Which Two
Groups of Students Were Matched

Fathers' occupations	Fathers' education	Subjects' education
8 physicians	14 advanced degrees	5 prep school—boarded at school
2 architects	5 attended college	5 prep school—lived at home
1 lawyer	1–4 years	10 public school—lived at home
1 minister	1 high school only	
1 professor		
4 business, managerial		
3 business, sales		

B. Other Background Variables: Subjects' Age,
Ordinal Position, and Parents' Age

	Father absent	Father present
Mean age of subjects	19.3	19.4
Only child	4	4
Oldest child	11	8
Second or third child	5	8
Mean age of fathers	53	55
Mean age of mothers	49	51
Age range of fathers	40–70	45–68
Age range of mothers	39–62	43–57

than on the Verbal aptitude test. The first evidence to be presented
on the effects of father absence comes from an attempt to compare
as extreme groups as possible. Twenty students whose fathers went
overseas before they were six months old and were away for at least
two years were chosen as the father-absent group. A matched sample
of twenty students whose fathers were not in the service at all were
selected as the control group. The two groups were matched on the
basis of father's occupation, education, marital status (both parents
living and not divorced), and on the student's previous academic
experience (public or private school). Table 2A shows the breakdown
on these background variables which are identical in both groups.
Table 2B gives the mean age and ordinal position of subjects as well
as the age of parents in the father-absent and father-present groups.[1]
Except for the wartime separation of the father-absent group, none
of the students in either group had been separated from his father
for more than two months during his childhood or adolescence. Five
students in each group attended boarding prep schools; all other students lived at home with both parents until college. During the war-

[1]Additional background information was obtained on this sample of students as
part of a more intensive interview study reported in Kuckenberg, Karolyn G.,
Effect of Early Father Absence on Scholastic Aptitude.

Table 3 Relationship of Math to Verbal Aptitude for a Selected Group of 20 Matched Pairs of Subjects, Harvard Class of 1964

	Aptitude scores	
	Verbal higher than math	Math higher than verbal
Father absent	13	7
Father not absent	2	18

time period, no other adults lived as permanent members in any of the family households of either group.

Table 3 compares these two matched groups, indicating the number of cases in which Verbal aptitude is superior to Math aptitude.

As Table 2 suggests, many doctors were sent overseas early in the war, and it is interesting to look at the findings for this single occupational group. A total of 18 doctors' sons were found to be included in the original sample of 450 students; 9 of these boys were separated from their fathers during the war years and 9 were not separated. Table 4 compares these groups of doctors' sons, again showing the number of cases in which Verbal aptitude is superior to Math aptitude.

In these matched samples, the performance of the control group is representative of the relative aptitude scores typically obtained by males, both nationally and at Harvard (i.e., Math superior to Verbal). However, the performance of the father-absent group is similar to the pattern typically achieved by girls (Verbal superior to Math).

To further explore the relationship between father absence and aptitude, the scores for the 83 students in the father-absent sample were analyzed. In Figure 1 the relationships between length of father absence, age of son when father left, and relative superiority of Math or Verbal aptitude are presented graphically. These drawings clearly show that both independent variables are systematically related to aptitude: the relative superiority of Verbal to Math aptitude increases steadily the longer the father is absent and the younger the child is when the father left. This effect is strongest for students

Table 4 Relationship of Math to Verbal Aptitude for 9 Matched Pairs of Doctors' Sons, Harvard Class of 1964

	Aptitude scores	
	Verbal higher than math	Math higher than verbal
Father absent	8	1
Father not absent	2	7

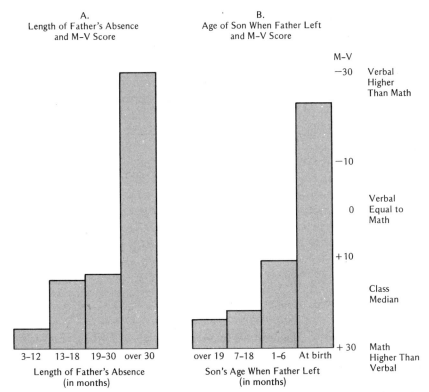

A.
Length of Father's Absence
and M-V Score

B.
Age of Son When Father Left
and M-V Score

M-V

−30   Verbal
Higher
Than Math

−10

0   Verbal
Equal to
Math

+10

Class
Median

+30   Math
Higher Than
Verbal

3-12   13-18   19-30   over 30   over 19   7-18   1-6   At birth
Length of Father's Absence   Son's Age When Father Left
(in months)   (in months)

Figure 1 Father-absent students, Harvard class of 1964. Relationship of Math to Verbal aptitude (SAT) (n = 83).

whose fathers were absent at birth and/or were away for over 30 months.

The interaction of the two independent variables with aptitude is presented in Table 5, which shows the mean Math and Verbal scores and the mean M-V difference scores for these students. The table employs a two-way break: age of the child when his father left (horizontal axis); total length of time the father was away after his son's birth (vertical axis). A minus sign preceding any of the M-V scores indicates that the mean Verbal score is higher than the mean Math score for that group.

To test the significance of the relationships shown here, a regression analysis was performed. This analysis showed that each variable was significantly related to the M-V aptitude scores ($p < .05$ for each). That is, in Table 5 each variable considered alone shows a significant effect on the M-V score. Because of the high correlation between age at absence and length of absence ($r = -.59$), neither variable added significantly to prediction of the M-V score when the other had already been taken into account.

Table 5   Father-Absent Students, Harvard Class of 1964 Mean Math, Verbal, and M-V Aptitude Scores (SAT) (n = 83)

Length of father's absence (in months)		Son's age when father left (in months)				
		Over 19	7–18	1–6	At birth	Total
	n	10	1	—	4	15
	Math	687	601	—	702	685
3–12	Verbal	643	685	—	694	660
	M-V	44	−84	—	8	25
	n	3	3	4	1	11
	Math	595	761	691	609	677
13–18	Verbal	623	704	670	615	661
	M-V	−28	57	21	−6	16
	n	1	22	8	9	40
	Math	708	696	697	665	689
19–30	Verbal	731	668	669	693	675
	M-V	−23	28	28	−28	14
	n	—	4	3	10	17
	Math	—	680	653	656	661
over 30	Verbal	—	685	696	690	690
	M-V	—	−5	−43	−34	−29
	n	14	30	15	24	—
	Math	669	697	687	665	—
Total	Verbal	645	674	674	689	—
	M-V	24	23	13	−24	—

HIGH SCHOOL CLASS OF 1961

A similar method of analysis was used for the sample of high school boys. Table 6 again shows a two-way break for length of father absence and age of son when father left.

There are two striking differences to be seen in this table. If the father left when his son was very young (0–12 months) and was away for a long time (1–5 years), the relative superiority of Math to Verbal aptitude shows a sharp decrease. This is consistent with the

Table 6   Concord, Lexington, Newton High School Boys, Class of 1961 Mean Math, Verbal and M-V Aptitude Scores (SAT) (n = 137)

Length of father's absence	Son's age when father left	n	Mean aptitude scores		
			Math	Verbal	M-V
3–12 months	1–5 years	12	633	536	97
	0–12 months	7	568	517	51
1–5 years	1–5 years	7	555	499	56
	0–12 months	12	517	505	12
	Not absent	99	576	529	47

finding for the Harvard sample. However, if the father left late in the boy's childhood and was gone for only a brief time, a reverse effect apparently takes place. The other two conditions show no strong effect. An analysis of variance shows the differences between the groups (on the M-V score) to be significant beyond the .001 level.

While this sample is too small and unstable to draw any firm conclusions, the second finding of a sharp increase in Math aptitude, relative to Verbal aptitude, for one of the father-absent groups is intriguing. Returning to Table 5, there are ten cases in a somewhat comparable cell in the upper left corner: again the father left relatively late in the boy's childhood (after he was 18 months old) and was gone for only a brief time (3-12 months). These ten cases show a noticeable superiority in Math ability and are the chief contributors to the mean total scores for their column. The mean M-V difference score for these 10 cases is 44; the comparable score for the entire class is 18. Although many more cases in this experimental condition are needed, these two findings suggest that there may be a reverse effect operating if the child first knows his father and then is briefly separated from him.

To summarize these findings in comparable form for both the high school and college samples, a simple breakdown on each of the independent variables is shown in Tables 7 and 8. These tables are a condensation of the data already presented for the two groups.

Despite the sizeable difference between the groups in range of aptitude scores, the effect of father absence is similar for both groups. Comparing the father-absent students with the control groups, these data indicate that if the father leaves early (before his son is 12 months old) and if he is gone for more than a year, the son's Verbal aptitude is relatively superior to his Math aptitude. However, both late and brief separation from the father are associated with a relative increase in Math ability.

Although the independent variables are presented separately in these tables, it should be noted that for both samples of students there is a high negative correlation between length of father's absence and son's age when father left. Thus the findings presented here should be considered as resulting from an interaction of the two variables, rather than as the result of either variable taken alone.

In addition to the high school boys, a small sample of girls from Lexington, Concord, and Newton High Schools (class of 1961) were also included in this survey. In general, the effect of father absence on aptitude appears to be the same for girls as for boys, with both early and long separation from the father being positively related to a relatively higher Verbal aptitude.

Table 7   Relationship Between Length of Father's Absence and
Aptitude for Both the College and High School Samples

| | Harvard class of 1964 | | | | High school classes of 1961 | | | |
| | | Mean aptitude scores | | | | Mean aptitude scores | | |
Length of father's absence	n	Math	Verbal	M-V	n	Math	Verbal	M-V
3–12 months	15	685	660	25	19	609	529	80
More than 12 months	68	680	677	3	19	532	503	29
Control[a] group	1180	695	677	18	99	576	529	47

Table 8   Relationship Between Son's Age When Father Left and
Aptitude for Both the College and High School Samples

| | Harvard class of 1964 | | | | High school classes of 1961 | | | |
| | | Mean aptitude scores | | | | Mean aptitude scores | | |
Son's age when father left	n	Math	Verbal	M-V	n	Math	Verbal	M-V
More than 12 months	21	683	658	25	19	604	522	82
0–12 months	62	682	679	3	19	536	509	27
Control[a] group	1180	695	677	18	99	576	529	47

[a]For the Harvard class of 1964, the scores for the control group are the median aptitude scores obtained by the *entire* class, and therefore include both father-absent and father-present students. For the high school classes, the control group includes only students who were not separated from their fathers at any time.

HARVARD CLASS OF 1963

As a further replication, available data on the Harvard class of 1963 were analyzed. This sample includes the entire freshman class with the exception of 1) foreign students, 2) students from broken homes, and 3) students whose fathers were in the service but did not go overseas. For this class, since it was not possible to determine the age of the child when the father left, only the duration of the father's absence will be considered here.

Table 9 compares the mean aptitude scores obtained by the father-absent and father-present groups; it also shows the relative superiority of Math to Verbal aptitude (M-V) for each group. As for the previous sample, the M-V difference score shows an orderly progression with length of time father was absent, indicating that father absence is related to relatively lower Math ability.[2]

[2]Since only the distribution of Math and Verbal aptitude scores were available for this sample, it was not possible to determine the M-V score for each individual subject, and thus an analysis of variance test could not be performed on these data.

Table 9 Harvard Class of 1963 Mean Math, Verbal
and M-V Aptitude Scores (SAT) (n = 881)

Length of father's absence	n	Math	Verbal	M-V
Less than 2 years	124	669	660	9
2–3 years	53	671	663	8
Over 3 years	38	649	646	3
Not absent	666	680	656	24

Throughout this paper, emphasis has been placed on the M-V difference scores rather than on the independent Math or Verbal scores. Although it is interesting to speculate whether a decrease in Math or an increase in Verbal ability is the chief contributor to the observed differences in the M-V scores of the father-absent students, it is impossible to tell from these data. In Table 9 the main effect of father absence seems to be a progressive depression of the Math score. However, for the first Harvard sample presented in Table 5, the principal effect of father absence appears to be an increase in Verbal ability. A careful study of these two tables strongly suggests that this discrepancy is an artifact resulting from different levels of ability between groups rather than a contradictory statement about the effects of father absence. For example, in Table 9 the group that was father-absent for over three years is considerably lower in both Math and Verbal aptitude than any of the other groups, which suggests a generally lower level of ability for this group. If we attempt to compensate for the lower ability of this group by adding 20 points to *both* their Math and Verbal aptitude scores, the M-V difference score remains unchanged, and the discrepancy between Tables 5 and 9 disappears.

This discrepancy between the two Harvard groups points up the danger of comparing Math or Verbal aptitude scores between groups, unless absolute level of ability is partialed [sic] out. From the data at hand, there is no reason to argue that father absence is consistently related to a lower level of intelligence.[3] The results do indicate however that father absence is consistently related to a discrepancy between Math and Verbal abilities and that the father-absent boys have a lower Math aptitude, relative to their Verbal aptitude, than do their father-present peers.

[3]Data from a recent study at Dartmouth College (Landauer and King, personal communication, 1963) indicate that the father-absent students (early wartime separation) scored *higher* than the class average on both the Math and Verbal aptitude tests of the College Entrance Examination Board. In the Dartmouth study, the M-V discrepancy between matched groups of father-absent and father-present control students is consistent with the findings reported here.

DISCUSSION

Two major questions were asked at the outset of this paper. First, are there lasting measurable effects due to the absence of the father at an early age? Second, is the age of the child during the father's absence an important variable in determining these effects? The evidence presented provides clearly affirmative answers to both questions.

Stated concisely, the results of the aptitude survey of father-absent and father-present students indicate: 1) early and long separation from the father results in relatively greater ability in Verbal areas than in Mathematics; 2) no separation produces relatively greater ability in Mathematics; and 3) late brief separation may produce an extreme elevation in Mathematical ability (relative to Verbal ability).

The first two findings are consistent with predictions derived from any general theory of sex-role identification. Although the third finding has intriguing theoretical implications, it is based on a small sample and therefore must be considered less reliable than the other two findings. Since we have no additional information on this latter group, further pursuit seems unprofitable until more stable findings are obtained on a larger sample.

While the findings reported here are provocative, they leave several questions unanswered. For example, is the principal effect of early separation from the father an acceleration of Verbal ability or a depression of Math ability? This question cannot be answered from the data presented here. However, the studies of problem-solving techniques used by children (e.g., Seder, 1955; Milton, 1957; Bieri, 1960) suggest that this may be an inappropriate question. More specifically, these studies suggest that Math and Verbal aptitude scores may simply reflect two aspects of a single, more general characteristic: conceptual style or approach to problem solving. In these studies, two styles of conceptualization are usually differentiated: an "analytic approach" which is characterized by clear discrimination between stimuli, a direct pursuit of solutions, and a disregard for extraneous material; a "global approach," characterized by less clear discrimination of stimuli and a greater influence from extraneous material. The first approach is more typically used by boys while the second is more typical of girls. It seems reasonable to assume that boys using the analytic approach to problem solving would score relatively higher on Math aptitude than on Verbal aptitude tests; boys using the global approach would show relatively greater ability on Verbal comprehension tests. Thus the relative superiority of Math or Verbal aptitude is, in effect, a single measure of the boy's conceptual style or approach to problem solving. It follows that any antecedent variable, such as presence or absence of the father, may directly influence conceptual approach (i.e., aptitude pattern), but only indirectly influences performance on a particular test.

A second query that is sometimes raised in response to the data reported here concerns the possible influence of anxiety on the Math aptitude of father-absent boys. It is argued that the early experience of father absence produces high anxiety and that anxiety has a more debilitating effect on proficiency in Mathematics than on Verbal skills. Data in support of this argument are drawn largely from studies of emotionally disturbed individuals which indicate that some aspects of Verbal ability are less vulnerable to stress and are therefore used as indicators of the "premorbid" level of intellectual functioning (e.g., Mayman et al., 1951). Contrary to this position is a directly relevant study by Alpert (1957) which relates a number of anxiety scales[4] with the Math and Verbal aptitude scores obtained on the College Board tests by a large sample of Stanford males. While most of the anxiety scales correlate negatively with both aptitude scores, the author states that "in *every* instance in which the data were significant, the correlations with mathematical aptitude were in the same direction as those with verbal aptitude but in no instance were they of as large magnitude" (p. 46). Several of the correlations between anxiety and Verbal aptitude are fairly high, but not one of the correlations with Math aptitude reaches an acceptable level of significance. Since none of the father-absent students in this study can be considered severely emotionally disturbed, there is no reason to suspect that extreme stress or anxiety is responsible for the observed differences in their aptitude scores. If anxiety had any effect at all, the Alpert study indicates that Verbal aptitude, rather than Math aptitude, would be expected to show the greater decrement. This is clearly contrary to the data reported here.

What other variables or conditions might be considered possible contributors to the aptitude differences between the father-absent and father-present groups? In the large high school and college samples, no attempt was made to match subjects on background variables (except, of course, that all subjects were from intact homes, academically successful, and from a reasonably homogenous population). In the small matched samples, however, such variables as age, occupation and education of parents, number and age of sib-

[4]Taylor Manifest Anxiety Scale; Welsh Anxiety Index; Freeman Anxiety Scale; Mandler-Sarason Test Anxiety Scale; Achievement Anxiety Scale.

lings, and high school experience of subject were considered and controlled for (cf. Table 2). Whether there may be some further variable correlated with father absence in World War II and capable of producing such large effects on Mathematical and Verbal aptitude cannot be answered from these data. It should be borne in mind, however, that any such variable would have to account not only for differences between father absence and father presence but also for the effects due to the age of the child at the time the father departed, as reported in this paper. Thus, such an explanatory variable would have to be correlated with the exact age of the child when the father was called into active duty as well as with the gross fact that the father was called overseas.

A final puzzling question is why conceptual approach or pattern of aptitudes should be so clearly sex-typed in our culture. An adequate explanation of this recurrent finding is not available, but several studies suggest that the masculine analytical approach is acquired through close and harmonious association with the father. Seder (1955) found that boys who used the global approach to problems had fathers who spent little time with them or who were very passive in their interaction with their sons. Bieri (1960) reports that boys who willingly accept authority and describe themselves as more similar to their mothers are poor performers on differentiation-analytic tasks. Levy (1943) reports the same finding for "maternally over-protected" boys. Finally, Witkin (1960) reports that boys who perform poorly on analytic problems perceive their fathers as dominating and tyrannical.

A study of male college students at Stanford University relates College Board aptitude scores with certain childhood experiences reported by the students (Maccoby, 1961). Boys who achieve a more feminine pattern of aptitudes (i.e., Math aptitude relatively lower than Verbal aptitude) than their peers report that in their childhood: 1) their fathers were away from home for one to five years; 2) they almost never talked about personal problems with their fathers; 3) they were often fearful of their fathers; and 4) they were punished exclusively by their mothers.

All of these studies consistently point to close, positive relationships between father and son as a prerequisite for development of a masculine conceptual approach. However, they still do not explain why the relationship exists or how this approach develops. Milton (1957), who reports a striking correlation between problem-solving skill and sex-role identification in both boys and girls, suggests simply that girls typically won't learn the necessary skills since problem solving is inappropriate to the female sex-role. This reasoning suggests that a conceptual approach is developed fairly consciously and probably not until after the child enters school. The accumulated evidence on learning of sex-role identity suggests that this occurs quite early in childhood through a largely unconscious process of imitation or identification with one of the parents. Whether the conceptual approach develops later as a result of sex-role identity (as Milton suggests) or early along with sex-role identity (through a similar process of identification) cannot be ascertained from the information available. However, studies of the problem-solving behavior of very young children may be designed to answer this part of the question. Studies of the interaction of mothers and fathers with their young children may also give us some ideas about the direct roles parents play in the development of a conceptual approach. At the present time, we can only say that aptitude patterns or conceptual approaches are related to both sex-role identity and to father-son relationships and that absence of the father during certain early periods of the child's life has an important effect on later cognitive development.

REFERENCES

Alpert, R. School mathematics study group: a psychological evaluation. 1963, in press.

Alpert, R. Anxiety in academic achievement situations: its measurement and relation to aptitude. Unpublished Ph.D. thesis, Stanford University, 1957.

Bach, G. R. Father-fantasies and father-typing in father-separated children. *Child Developm.*, 1946, **17,** 63–80.   •

Bieri, J. Parental identification, acceptance of authority, and within-sex differences in cognitive behavior. *J. abnorm. soc. Psychol.*, 1960, **60,** 76–79.

Burton, R. V. and Whiting, J. W. M. The absent father and cross-sex identity. *Merrill-Palmer Quarterly*, 1961, **7,** 85–95.

College board score reports. Princeton: Educational Testing Service, College Entrance Examination Board, 1960.

D'Andrade, R. G. Father-absence and cross-sex identification. Unpublished Ph.D. thesis, Harvard University, 1962.

Dember, W. N., Nairne, F. and Miller, F. J. Further validation of the Alpert-Haber achievement anxiety test. *J. abnorm. soc. Psychol.*, 1962, **65,** 427–428.

Glueck, S. and Glueck, E. *Unravelling juvenile delinquency.* N.Y.: The Commonwealth Fund, 1950.

Heilman, J. D. Sex differences in intellectual abilities. *J. educ. Psychol.*, 1933, **24,** 47–62.

Hill, J. P. Sex-typing and mathematics achievement. Unpublished thesis prospectus, Harvard University, 1962.

Landauer, T. K. and King, F. W. Personal communication, 1963.

Lynn, D. B. and Sawrey, W. L. The effects of father-absence on Norwegian girls and boys. *J. abnorm. soc. Psychol.*, 1959, **59,** 258–262.

Maccoby, Eleanor E., and Rau, Lucy. *Differential cognitive abilities.* Final report, U.S. Office of Education, Cooperative Research Project No. 1040, 1962.

Mayman, M., Schafer, R., and Rapaport, D. Interpretation of the Wechsler-Bellevue Intelligence Scale in personality appraisal. In H. H. Anderson and G. L. Anderson (eds.) *An introduction to projective techniques.* New York: Prentice-Hall, 1951.

McCarthy, Dorothea. Language development in children. In L. Carmichael (ed.) *Manual of child psychology.* New York: Wiley, 1954, pp. 492–630.

Milton, G. A. The effects of sex-role identification upon problem-solving skill. *J. abnorm. soc. Psychol.*, 1957, **55,** 208–212.

Milton, G. A. Five studies of the relation between sex-role identification and achievement in problem-solving. Technical Report, Office of Naval Research, Contract Nonr 609(20) (NR150-166). New Haven: Yale University, 1958.

Munroe, Ruth. The role of the father in the development of the child: a survey of the literature. Unpublished report, Harvard University, 1961.

Plank, Emma N. and Plank, R. Emotional components in arithmetical learning as seen through autobiographies. *The psychoanalytic study of the child.* Vol. IX, N.Y.: International Universities Press, 1954.

Rohrer, J. H. and Edmonson, M. S. *The eighth generation.* New York: Harper, 1960.

Samuels, F. Sex differences in reading achievement. *J. educ. Res.*, 1943, **36,** 594–603.

Sears, Pauline S. Doll play aggression in normal young children: influence of sex, age, sibling status, father's absence. *Psychol. Monogr.*, 1951, **65,** 1–43.

Sears, R. R., Pintler, M. H., and Sears, Pauline S. Effect of father separation on preschool children's doll play aggression. *Child Developm.* 1946, **17,** 219–243.

Seder, Joan A. The origin of difference in the extent of independence in children: developmental factors in perceptual field dependence. Senior Honors Thesis, Social Relations, Radcliffe College, 1955. (As reported by Witkin, H. A., The problem of individuality in development. *loc. cit.*)

Stolz, Lois M. *Father relations of war-born children.* Stanford, Calif.: Stanford University Press, 1954.

Tiller, P. O. Father absence and personality development of children in sailor families: a preliminary research report. Part II. In N. Anderson (ed.), *Studies of the family.* Vol. 2. Gottingen: Vandenhoeck and Ruprecht, 1957, pp. 115–137.

Tukey, J. W. The future of data analysis. *Annals Math Stat.,* 1962, **33,** 1–67.

Whiting, J. W. M. Social structure and child rearing: a theory of identification. Unpublished lectures presented at Tulane University as part of the Mona Bronsman Scheckman Lectures in Social Psychiatry, March, 1960.

Witkin, H. A. The problem of individuality in development. In Kaplan, B. and Wapner, S. (eds.), *Perspectives in psychological theory.* New York: International Universities Press, 1960.

Zucker, H. J. Affectional identification and delinquency. *Arch. Psychol.,* 1943, **40,** No. 286.

father-absence effects
in families of different
sibling compositions*

B. SUTTON-SMITH   *Teachers College, Columbia University*
B. G. ROSENBERG
FRANK LANDY
Bowling Green State University

While there have been studies of the deleterious effects of father absence upon children (Nash, 1965), there has not been any consideration of these father-absence effects in families of varying sibling composition. Koch's studies (1955, 1956, 1960) of sibling composition in the two-child family strongly suggest that sibling position will interact with other familial variables such as father absence. In our own studies we have shown that siblings in two-child families have systematic effects both upon each other and upon their parents (Rosenberg and Sutton-Smith, 1968).

The question raised by this paper, therefore, is whether father absence is equally deleterious for children from different sibling statuses and family sizes. It makes sense to argue that the effects of father absence will depend both on the length of his absence and upon the age period in the child's life during which he is absent.

From *Child Development*, 1968, **39**. Copyright © 1968 by the Society for Research in Child Development. By permission.
*This investigation was supported by grant MH 07994–04 from the National Institute of Mental Health.

The antecedent variables in this study, therefore, are: the length of father's absence, the child's age at the time of absence, and the type of sibling composition of which the subject was a member. Subjects in the eight two-child sibling positions were included. Also·included, at least as a group, were the members of the 24 categories of the three-child family. These various sibling groupings make it possible to compare subjects of first- and second-born status, subjects with like- and opposite-sex siblings, and subjects from only-child, two-child, and three-child families.

The consequent variable chosen for analysis is the subject's scores on the American College Entrance Examination (ACE). This is a test of quantitative and language abilities. An earlier study by Carlsmith (1964) has already shown that father absence has an effect upon mathematical and verbal aptitude scores taken at the college level.

METHOD

In order to obtain an adequate sample of father-absent subjects, sophomore members of a lower-division psychology course at Bowling Green State University were sampled over a 5-year period yielding an N of 295.[1] A comparable father-present sample was randomly obtained from the same course during this period (N = 760). The subjects for both groups were 19 years median age and did not differ significantly on the Warner scale of socioeconomic status (Warner, Meeker, and Eels, 1949). Similarly, there were no socioeconomic differences between sexes and between any of the various ordinal groups. All groups were characterized by a mixture of subjects of middle and lower-middle socioeconomic status.[2] Scores on the ACE (Berdie, Dressel, and Keslo, 1951), taken by all incoming freshmen at the university, were obtained from the Counseling Center. The norms for establishing percentile scores were developed and subsequently modified through use over a 12-year period at Bowling Green University by the Counseling Center.

The ACE is an instrument designed to measure aptitude for college study and has been widely used in many colleges and universities from 1942 to 1964 for the evaluation of freshmen. It is not

[1]This course is required for all education majors in the university. As a result, the ratio of females to males over the years has been approximately 2:1. Consequently, it is not surprising that our father-absent sample parallels this ratio (198 females, 97 males).

[2]Only 2 out of the 10 comparisons (8 two-child ordinal positions and 2 onlies) of father absence and father presence on socioeconomic status approached a significant difference (M1F and F1F). It may be concluded that the differences in ACE scores were not due to differences in socioeconomic status.

an intelligence test but a test of certain intellectual abilities that have been shown to be closely related to scholastic success. The examination consists of six tests of linguistic and quantitative abilities. The tests had been derived from wide use and extensive factor analyses to determine the most discriminating items. Three sets of norms for the interpretation of scores are available for (a) the Q score, which represents ability to think in quantitative terms; (b) the L score, which depends upon linguistic ability; and (c) the T score, or total score, which involves both abilities. Scores on the scales have been frequently correlated with college grades, and the median coefficients are generally in the range of +.50. The L score shows the highest relation with grades in English and social sciences, while the Q score shows the highest relation with performance in mathematics and chemistry. For statistical purposes, all ACE scores (reported in percentiles) were converted to standard scores, and t tests were employed in the analysis. Nevertheless, median scores are presented in the tables as they communicate more directly than standard scores.

With varying-sized N's and varying periods in which the father was reported absent, it was arbitrarily decided to include in the father-absent sample only those individuals whose father had been absent from the home for 2 or more consecutive years. To order the data, it was further decided to group together those subjects whose father was absent during the subject's early childhood (0–4 years), middle childhood (5–9 years), and adolescence (10+ years). Thus, there were two major breakdowns in addition to family size, sex of subject, and sex of sibling: (a) length of time of father absence from home (0–4, 5–9, and 10+ years) and (b) age of subject during father absence (0–4, 5–9, and 10+ years). Unfortunately, in order to obtain sufficient cell frequencies for the latter breakdown, it was necessary to collapse across categories. Thus, there was the early group of subjects, whose fathers had been absent only between 0 and 4 years (43 males, 89 females); the early and middle group, whose fathers had been absent during the overlapping period of 0–4 and 5–9 years or only for 5–9 years (20 males, 27 females); the middle and late group, whose fathers had been absent during the overlapping periods of 5–9 and 10+ years (16 males, 28 females); and the late group, whose fathers had been absent only from 10+ years (28 females). While this overlapping system of classification leaves much to be desired, it was the only one that would adequately match the actual father absences experienced by the available subjects.

The notation system for the ordinal positions refers to only males as M, only females as F, first-born boys with a younger brother as M1M, first-born boys with a younger sister as M1F, second-born boys with an older brother as MM2, and second-born boys with an older sister as FM2. The comparable female positions are FIF, FIM, FF2, and MF2.

There were insufficient numbers to permit the 24 three-child ordinal positions to be dealt with separately. In order to maximize the information from the total sample, the three-child data were included in the summary analysis.

RESULTS

Table 1 presents the median Q, L, and T scores for the entire sample. The T scores were obtained as a by-product of the administration of the test, though no relevant predictions were attempted. Since the N's were too small for the second-born boys with an older brother (MM2) or with an older sister (FM2), these categories, though presented in the table for inspection, were included in the overall analysis but omitted in the category comparisons.

SEX DIFFERENCES

While sex differences are not strictly pertinent to the present study, they are presented here because of their importance in the related literature. The results bearing on general sex differences for all subjects on quantitative and verbal abilities tend to be in the direction expected, with males directionally superior to females on Q ($p < .20$) and females directionally superior to males on L ($p < .20$). This finding is similar to those in our earlier studies of cognitive abilities in the two- and three-child families (Rosenberg and Sutton-Smith, 1964b, 1966) and to those in the study of the ACE by Berdie et al. (1951). In our earlier studies in the two-child families, girls were superior to boys on L ($p < .01$), while boys were directionally superior to girls on Q. In the three-child family, boys were found to be superior on Q ($p < .01$), while girls were directionally superior on L. The failure to achieve uniform male-quantitative, female-linguistic differences in the present study is parallel to these earlier demonstrations of the effects of sibling sex on cognitive scores. In the present study with one-child family subjects, the expected differences appear directionally ($p < .10$).

ENTIRE SAMPLE

It is apparent that father-absence effects are dramatic. For the majority of the sample, Q, L, and T scores on the ACE are lower for father-absent subjects than for father-present subjects, regardless of

Table 1 Comparison of Median Scores on the ACE for Father Absence–Father Presence for Total Sample

	Father absent				Father present				Differences (t test)		
	Q	L	T	N	Q	L	T	N	Q	L	T
M	53	54	47	(21)	56	45	48	(35)	—	.20	—
F	53	66	61	(46)	71	71	67	(51)	.05	.20	.10
M1M	49	38	44	(20)	67	54	56	(38)	.10	.10	.20
M1F	49	33	35	(17)	71	58	67	(34)	.01	.001	.001
MM2	(68)	(53)	(60)	(6)	(62)	(43)	(54)	(33)	—	—	—
FM2	(44)	(42)	(36)	(6)	(72)	(63)	(68)	(44)	—	—	—
F1F	56	67	61	(40)	60	61	56	(43)	—	—	—
F1M	49	69	60	(36)	71	61	68	(68)	—	—	—
FF2	64	58	68	(15)	59	63	59	(48)	—	—	—
MF2	60	70	67	(17)	71	61	66	(59)	.02	—	—
2-child males	49	38	41	(49)	71	56	63	(149)	.20	—	—
2-child females	56	65	61	(108)	67	63	63	(217)	.20	.001	.001
3-child males	57	30	39	(27)	69	48	58	(136)	.01	.001	.001
3-child females	53	65	61	(44)	66	63	66	(172)	.10	.001	.001
Total M's	53	49	44	(97)	71	55	63	(320)	.001	.001	.001
Total F's	56	65	61	(198)	67	54	66	(440)	.001	—	.20

the subject's stage in development or the length of time the father was away. This effect obtains more uniformly for males than females, whose language scores show a nonsignificant increment with father absence.

STAGE AND LENGTH OF ABSENCE

Tables 2 and 3 present the data concerning the length of time of the father's absence (Table 2) and the stage of development at which it occurred (Table 3). The number of years the father was absent does not show any significant effects for males or females. The period in development (the subjects' chronological ages) at which the father was absent does show a number of significant relations. Although males whose fathers were absent during the early and middle period (0–4, 5–9: No. 2 in Table 3) have lower total scores than males

Table 2 Median ACE Scores for the Number of Years of Father Absence

	Years absent		
	0–4	5–9	10+
	Males		
	(N = 6)	(N = 6)	(N = 15)
Q	55	58	54
L	36	50	38
T	38	54	38
	Females		
	(N = 17)	(N = 39)	(N = 37)
Q	54	58	54
L	68	68	57
T	59	65	50

Table 3 Median ACE Scores for Age of Subject When Father Absence Occurred

	Males				Females			
	Q	L	T	N	Q	L	T	N
1. Early (0–4)	59	43	46	43	59	66	62	89
2. Early and middle (0–4; 5–9)	38	34	35	20	37	64	54	27
3. Middle and late (5–9; 10+)	51	38	39	16	62	64	60	28
4. Late (10+)[a]	—	—	—		51	76	65	28
1 vs. 2[b]	—	—	.05		.02	—	.10	
1 vs. 3	—	—	—		—	—	—	
1 vs. 4	—	—	—		—	—	—	
2 vs. 3	—	—	—		.001	—	.05	
2 vs. 4	—	—	—		.05	.05	.05	
3 vs. 4	—	—	—		.05	.05	—	

[a]There were no male subjects in the sample that fit this category.
[b]The single significant difference obtained for males could well occur by chance.

whose fathers were absent during the early period (0–4: No. 1 in Table 3), the majority of the significant differences hold only for females. ACE scores for females categorized by the early and middle period (No. 2, Table 3) were, in general, lower than ACE scores for females categorized by the early (No. 1, Table 3), middle and late

(No. 3, Table 3), or late (No. 4, Table 3) periods. In addition, in one or two comparisons, ACE scores for females categorized by early (No. 1) or middle and late (No. 3) are lower than those scores falling in the late (No. 4) category. The larger number of significant findings for female subjects, however, may be due to the greater number of females in the sample depicted in Table 2 as well as Table 3.

Unfortunately, these data, which appear to show so clearly that the early and middle period is the most important in its relation to father absence and cognitive decrements, are contaminated by their cross-sectional nature. The major reason given for father absence by the 0–4-year group was war service (Korean War), and by all other groups it was divorce. The difference was highly significant ($p <$ .001). This finding does not remove the possibility that father absence interacts critically with the child's stage in development (it doesn't, for example, explain why the middle period has a greater influence than the late or adolescence periods with the female subjects), but it does mean that the present data are insufficient to confirm the critical character of this middle period.

FAMILY SIZE

Table 1 indicates that father-absence effects are strongest in three-child families, moderate in two-child families, and minimal in one-child families. While both sexes seem affected in three-child families, males are more affected in two-child families and females in one-child families.

SIBLING SEX-STATUS EFFECTS

The evidence from Table 1 shows fairly clearly that in the two-child family the greatest differences between father absence and presence are produced when the child has an opposite-sex sibling. Thus, first-born boys (M1M) with a younger male sibling differ only direction-ally on all scores when father absence and presence are compared. First-born boys (M1F) with a younger sister show a stronger and significant lowering of scores with father absence. Again, for females, the first-born girl (F1M) with a younger brother shows a significant lowering of quantitative scores with father absence, while first-born girls (F1F) with a younger sister show no such differences between the conditions. The comparisons of the male subgroups must, of course, be qualified somewhat by the cell sizes.

DISCUSSION

The results satisfy the major contention of this paper that father absence interacts with sibling status in its effects upon aptitude scores. There are, in addition, the findings that these effects vary with the age of the subjects during the father's absence, are in general more pervasive with males than with females, and increase in importance with family size (one-child, two-child, and three-child).

The central consideration for the present paper, however, is the reason for the difference between the affected and nonaffected subjects. The sibling composition of the unaffected females (on which there are data) suggests that the possession of a like-sex sibling modifies the effects of father absence. The boy with a younger brother is less affected than the boy with a younger sister, and the girl with a younger sister is less affected than the girl with a younger brother. Furthermore, an only girl is affected by the father's absence, but an only boy is not. Given the fact that the same cognitive outcomes often have functionally diverse antecedents in the two sexes, each of these conditions probably require a separate explanation (Sigel, 1965). Holding in mind that this is a relatively novel area of research and that there is little systematic literature on such parent-child and child-child interactions, we offer the following speculations.

First, it seems probable that, in the absence of a father, male siblings may act as mediators for male-sex-role values in a way that female siblings cannot. But boys do not have the same effect on girls; in fact, paradoxically, the girl who is affected deleteriously by the father's absence is the one with a younger brother (the boy with a younger brother is not affected). Koch (1955, 1956, 1960) demonstrated that at age 6 this same girl is the one most stimulated both intellectually and socially by her rivalry with the younger brother. We argued elsewhere that this is because she identifies with the father (Sutton-Smith and Rosenberg, in press). Without the father's presence, she may not have this stimulus, so that the major effect of the younger brother is instead a depressive one.

Of a somewhat more surprising character are the present findings that the only male is not strongly affected by the father's absence and that the only female is. We would expect the males to model after their father and the girls to model after their mother. The present finding suggests that the reverse process is occurring. That this may be the case is tentatively supported by two other studies in the literature showing that the only male is more "feminine" than other males and that the only female is more "masculine" than other females (Hooker, 1931; Rosenberg and

Sutton-Smith, 1964a). If the results of the present study and these other studies can be interpreted as an outcome of a feminine identification by the only male and a masculine identification by the only female, an interesting problem then arises: Why in these only-child families, where personal relationships and intimacies are likely to be most intense, does each child identify with the parent of the opposite sex rather than with the parent of the same sex?

We may sum up this discussion of father absence and sibling composition by stressing that, while the interactions between both are by no means clear, it is evident that this is a fruitful area for research. Father absence does have negative influence on cognitive activity, an effect modified by sibling composition.

REFERENCES

Berdie, R., Dressel, P., and Kelso, P. Relative validity of the Q and L scores of the ACE Psychological Examination. *Educational and Psychological Measurement*, 1951, **11**, 803–812.

Carlsmith, L. Effect of early father absence on scholastic aptitude. *Harvard Educational Review*, 1964, **34**, 3–21.

Hooker, H. F. The study of the only child at school. *Journal of Genetic Psychology*, 1931, **39**, 122–126.

Koch, H. The relation of certain family constellation characteristics and the attitudes of children toward adults. *Child Development*, 1955, **26**, 13–40.

Koch, H. Some emotional attitudes of the young child in relation to characteristics of his sibling. *Child Development*, 1956, **27**, 393–426.

Koch, H. The relation of certain formal attributes of siblings to attitudes held toward each other and toward their parents. *Monograph of the Society for Research in Child Development*, 1960, **25**(4, Serial No. 78).

Nash, J. The father in contemporary culture and current psychological literature. *Child Development*, 1965, **36**, 261–297.

Rosenberg, B. G., and Sutton-Smith, B. Ordinal position and sex role identification. *Genetic Psychology Monographs*, 1964, **70**, 297–328. (a)

Rosenberg, B. G., and Sutton-Smith, B. The relationship of ordinal position and sibling sex status to cognitive abilities. *Psychonomic Science*, 1964, **1**, 81–82. (b)

Rosenberg, B. G., and Sutton-Smith, B. Sibling association, family size, and cognitive ability. *Journal of Genetic Psychology*, 1966, **109**, 271–279.

Rosenberg, B. G., and Sutton-Smith, B. Family interaction effects on masculinity-femininity. *Journal of Personality and Social Psychology*, 1968, **8,** 117–120.

Sigel, I. E. Rationale for separate analyses of male and female samples on cognitive tasks. *Psychological Record*, 1965, **15,** 369–376.

Sutton-Smith, B., and Rosenberg, B. G. *The sibling.* New York: Holt, Rinehart, & Winston, in press.

Warner, W. L., Meeker, M., and Eels, K. *Social class in America.* Chicago: Science Research Associates, 1949.

a developmental study of the effects of sex of the dominant parent on sex-role preference, identification, and imitation in children

E. MAVIS HETHERINGTON   *University of Wisconsin*

Most theories of identification agree that identification is based on a process or processes whereby the child through imitation, modeling, or introjection acquires traits, characteristics, and values similar to the parent. In normal development the boy is assumed to identify with the father, and the girl with the mother which results in the preference for and adoption of appropriate sex-role behavior. Psychoanalytic theory has stressed the role of fear of punishment and identification with the aggressor, while learning theory has stressed the facilitating effects of reward in promoting identification. A third theory (Parsons, 1955) has emphasized the importance of total parental power in the development of identification. According to Parsons, the child identifies with the parent because he is powerful in his ability to dispense both rewards and punishments. Several recent experiments support the position that parental power or dominance plays a major role in identification (Hetherington and Brackbill, 1963; Mussen and Distler, 1959).

E. Mavis Hetherington. A developmental study of the effects of sex of the dominant parent on sex-role preference, identification, and imitation in children. *Journal of Personality and Social Psychology* 2, 1965, 188–194. Copyright © 1965 by the American Psychological Association, and reproduced by permission.

In identifying with parents, children may acquire traits and values which are particularly characteristic of either male or female roles in our society. This would be directly related to the formation of sex-role preferences. They may also imitate parental behaviors which are not sex typed but which are equally appropriate in males and females. It would be expected that the rate of development and type of sex-role preference would be related not only to parental behavior but also to social pressures to conform, and the status of a given sex in the culture. Parent-child similarity in traits which are not sex typed should have fewer extra familial social sanctions bearing on them and therefore should be more directly and consistently related to reinforcements and imitative models provided by the parents. Since the child has relatively few social contacts outside the family in the preschool years it would be expected that identification on both sex-typed and non-sex-typed measures would be closely related to family power structure in 4- and 5-year-old children. However in older children sex-typed behaviors should be increasingly influenced by social norms. Boys will be encouraged by peers and adults outside the family to develop masculine sex-role preferences and girls feminine sex-role preferences and these preferences should therefore be less directly related to parental dominance in older than in younger children. It would also be predicted that because of the greater prestige and privileges of males in our culture, girls will be slower and less consistent in developing appropriate sex-role preferences than boys (Brown, 1956, 1958). In contrast parent-child similarity on non-sex-typed traits should be closely related to parental dominance in both preschool and school aged boys and girls. This similarity would be expected to increase with age as identification is more fully established.

If children identify with the dominant parent and this parent is the same sex as the child this should facilitate the development of normal sex-role preferences. If the dominant parent is the opposite sex of the child this should strengthen cross-sex identification and may retard the development of normal sex-role preferences. This disruption in identification and sex-role preferences should be particularly marked in boys from mother-dominant homes since the acquiescing father supplies a socially inappropriate model for the son. In contrast, girls from father-dominant homes at least have parental models whose power relationships are appropriate for their culturally defined sex roles. Although it could be argued that a dominant mother does not provide a normal sex-role model for girls, maternal dominance may not preclude the mother having other feminine traits with which a daughter will identify.

If imitation is involved in identification, children's performance on an experimental task involving imitation of the parents and a measure of parent-child personality similarity should be positively related. Past research (Bandura, 1962; McDavid, 1959) suggests that although children tend to imitate the most powerful model there is a greater readiness for both boys and girls to imitate a male model. Thus children should imitate and have personality traits similar to the most dominant parent, particularly if it is the father. The findings of McDavid also suggest that girls will imitate increasingly with age while boys will imitate less.

The present study investigated the effects of parental dominance on sex-role preferences, parent-child trait similarity, and imitation of boys and girls of three different age levels.

METHOD

SUBJECTS

Subjects were three groups of 36 boys and 36 girls ages 4–5, 6–8, and 9–11 enrolled in nursery schools or in elementary schools in a public-school system. Half of the boys and girls in each group came from mother-dominant homes and half from father-dominant homes.

EXPERIMENTERS

Half of the subjects in each condition were run by male experimenters and half by female experimenters. Since no experimenter differences were found in a preliminary analysis of the data, this variable was not considered in the final analysis.

PARENTAL DOMINANCE MEASURE

The parental dominance measure was adapted from a procedure by Farina (1960). Farina's problem situations were modified to make them more suitable for all age levels in the present study. Each parent was seen individually in a quiet room in his own home. He was read 12 hypothetical problem situations involving child behavior and asked how he would handle them when he was by himself. Both parents were then brought together and asked to arrive at a compatible solution on handling these children's problems. The discussion of each problem continued until both parents said the terminating signal, "agreed." The experimenter participated only minimally in the discussion in order to clarify scoring responses. All interviews were tape-recorded and scored later.

The scoring procedure was identical with that used by Farina (1960) which involved seven indices of parental dominance. If six of the seven indices indicated paternal dominance the family was classified as father dominant; if six of the indices indicated maternal dominance the family was classified as mother dominant. A total of 326 couples were run in order to obtain the 108 mother-dominant and 108 father-dominant families for the study.

PROCEDURE

The study was comprised of three procedures: the It Scale for Children (ITSC; Brown, 1956), a parent-child similarity task, and an imitation task.

ITSC

The ITSC, a projective test of sex-role preference, was administered to each subject at school. In this test the child is presented with a drawing of an ambiguous child figure referred to as "It," and is asked to choose what It would like in a series of 36 picture cards of objects and figures identified with masculine or feminine roles. Scores can range from 0, exclusively feminine choices, to 84, exclusively masculine choices. It is assumed that "the child will project himself or herself into the It-figure on the basis of his or her own sex-role preference, and will attribute to It the child's own role preference" (Brown, 1956, p. 5).

PARENT-CHILD SIMILARITY MEASURE

A list of 130 adjectives was given to 10 advanced education students who were asked to categorize the adjectives as more characteristic of males, or females, or as neutral (equally applicable to both sexes). They were also asked to check whether each adjective was descriptive of the behavior of children or adults or both. Forty adjectives which had been rated as neutral by 90% of the judges and as descriptive of both adults and children by all were included in the final list (e.g., friendly, honest, imaginative, humorous, pleasant, capable, etc.). These adjectives appeared to give a broad view of non-sex-typed personality traits.

Parents were asked to give the name of someone who knew them well enough to rate them on the adjective check list. Different raters were used for each parent. The lists were sent to the raters with assurances of the confidentiality of the responses and were returned by mail to the experimenter. If the list was not returned in 2 weeks, raters were contacted by phone. Eleven of the raters refused to cooperate and others suggested by the parents were substituted. Children were rated on the same list by their teachers. In an attempt to control for response bias raters were asked to mark 15 adjectives which were most like the ratee X, 15 which were most unlike the ratee O, and to leave 10 blank.

The procedure was repeated on 45 of the families 1 month later. The test-retest reliabilities were .82 for ratings of mothers, .86 for fathers, and .79 for children.

Similarity scores were based on the number of identical responses in the mother and child, and father and child lists. Two blanks, X–X or O–O pairings on an item were scored as similar.

IMITATION TASK

Each child was run in his home on the imitation task twice, once with each parent as a model. The child was instructed that he and his parent were participating in a study attempting to evaluate what things people think are prettiest. While the child watched, the parent, who had been coached before the experimental session, was asked to indicate by pointing and naming which picture in each of 20 pairs of pictures he thought was prettiest. The parent repeated this procedure three times consistently selecting the predetermined prettiest pictures. The child then went through the series once selecting the pictures he thought were prettiest. One month later the same procedure was repeated with the other parent and a second series of pictures. Order of presentation of list and parent models was balanced for male and female children. An imitation measure of number of similar responses was derived for mother-child and father-child.

RESULTS

Separate analyses of variance were run on ITSC scores, parent-child similarity measures, and parent-child imitation scores. Differences between means were tested by Duncan multiple range tests; those reported are significant at $p < .05$.

SEX-ROLE PREFERENCE

The summary of an analysis of variance of ITSC scores for all subjects is presented in Table 1. As was expected, parental dominance influenced sex-role preference. More appropriate sex-role preferences occurred when the father [was] dominant than when the mother [was] dominant. Duncan range tests indicated that the differences in sex-role preferences for girls from mother- and father-dominant homes were nonsignificant, however these differences for boys were significant at all ages. Mother dominance was related to less masculine sex-role preferences in boys.

As predicted, girls were later in developing feminine sex-role preferences than were boys in masculine sex-role preferences. Boys

Table 1 Analysis of Variance of ITSC Scores

Source	df	MS	F
Parental dominance (D)	1	1,247.07	4.67[a]
Sex of child (S)	1	32,047.04	120.03[b]
Age (A)	2	2,055.70	7.70[b]
D × S	1	4,329.12	16.21[b]
D × A	2	265.29	<1
S × A	2	6,520.29	24.47[b]
D × S × A	2	154.92	<1
Error	204	267.00	—
Total	215	—	—

[a] $p < .05$.
[b] $p < .01$.

at age 4–5 had already developed a preference for the masculine role which continued and increased slightly but nonsignificantly through ages 9–11. In contrast, girls showed a significant increase in preference for the feminine role in the age 9–11 group. The means and standard deviations of ITSC scores for the three age groups of boys and girls from mother- and father-dominant homes are summarized in Table 2. A high score indicates masculine sex-role preference.

PARENT-CHILD SIMILARITY

A summary of the analysis of variance of mother-child and father-child similarity measures obtained from the adjective check list ratings by friends and teachers is presented in Table 3. Duncan range tests indicate that 4- and 5-year-old children obtained lower parent-child similarity ratings than the two older groups who did not differ from one another.

Dominance played an important role in parent-child similarity. Children tended to be more similar to the dominant parent than the passive parent. Mother dominance appeared to inhibit father-child similarity. This similarity was lower than mother-child similarity in father-dominant homes. The disrupted identification of boys was again particularly marked in mother-dominant homes. In father-

Table 2 Means and Standard Deviations of ITSC Scores

	Mother dominant				Father dominant			
	Boys		Girls		Boys		Girls	
Ages	M	SD	M	SD	M	SD	M	SD
4–5	52.4	14.3	41.8	15.9	67.3	13.1	44.8	16.9
6–8	53.7	22.3	55.1	14.3	66.9	14.9	44.6	16.1
9–11	61.0	20.9	24.1	15.9	74.2	12.7	19.1	15.9

Table 3   Analysis of Variance of Parent-Child Similarity Scores

Source	df	MS	F
Parental dominance (D)	1	498.38	18.06[b]
Sex of child (S)	1	2.38	<1
Age (A)	2	273.17	9.90[b]
D × S	1	107.98	3.91[a]
D × A	2	29.82	1.08
S × A	2	58.42	2.13
S × D × A	2	15.91	<1
Error (a)	204	27.59	—
Similarity (Sim)	1	564.90	20.43[b]
Sim × D	1	2,380.08	86.08[b]
Sim × S	1	630.74	22.81[b]
Sim × A	2	23.85	<1
Sim × D × S	1	158.92	5.75[a]
Sim × D × A	2	59.55	2.15
Sim × S × A	2	39.82	1.44
Sim × D × S × A	2	52.78	1.91
Error (b)	204	27.65	—
Total	431	—	—

[a] $p < .05$.
[b] $p < .01$.

dominant homes the boy identified significantly more with the father than the mother, however in mother-dominant homes this relation was reversed. In fact, the mother-son similarity in mother-dominant homes did not differ from the father-son similarity in father-dominant homes.

In contrast, girls in father-dominant homes identified equally strongly with both parents. Also their mother-daughter similarity did not differ from that in mother-dominant homes. On the other hand, girls in mother-dominant homes identified notably more with mother than father. The father-daughter similarity scores in mother-dominant homes were significantly lower than similarity scores in any other group. The means and standards deviations of parent-child similarity scores for all groups are summarized in Table 4.

PARENT-CHILD IMITATION

A summary of the results of the analysis of variance of imitation scores is presented in Table 5. In the child's imitation of the parent, as in sex-role preferences and parent-child similarity, parental dominance was a significant factor. Children of both sexes imitated the dominant parent more than the passive parent. The prediction that children would imitate the father more than the mother was not confirmed. There were no significant differences between imitation of the dominant mothers and fathers, or between passive mothers and fathers. As was expected on the basis of past research, girls imitated more than boys; however no differential trends with age

Table 4 Means and Standard Deviations of Parent-Child Similarity Scores

	Mother dominant						Father dominant					
Ages:	4–5		6–8		9–11		4–5		6–8		9–11	
Similarity	M	SD	M	SD	M	SD	M	SD	M	SD	M	SD
Mother-daughter	19.1	5.3	19.8	4.5	21.9	5.8	18.7	5.3	21.1	4.3	20.1	5.9
Mother-son	16.9	6.1	20.4	6.1	23.3	5.3	15.8	6.0	15.2	4.3	15.3	4.5
Father-daughter	11.6	4.1	12.0	4.6	12.7	3.6	18.2	5.8	19.5	6.0	18.3	6.3
Father-son	12.1	4.4	16.2	4.5	15.0	4.3	17.6	6.8	23.3	5.4	23.6	4.8

Table 5   Analysis of Variance of Parent-Child Imitation Scores

Source	df	MS	F
Parental dominance (D)	1	1.12	<1
Sex of child (S)	1	108.00	10.58[b]
Age (A)	2	5.56	<1
D × S	1	.01	<1
D × A	2	20.10	1.97
S × A	2	24.02	2.35
D × S × A	2	4.97	<1
Error (a)	204	10.21	—
Imitation (I)	1	1.56	<1
I × D	1	560.34	58.30[b]
I × S	1	15.57	1.62
I × A	2	23.16	2.41
I × D × S	1	6.25	<1
I × D × A	2	4.89	<1
I × S × A	2	3.71	<1
I × D × S × A	2	7.50	<1
Error (b)	204	9.61	—
Total	431	—	—

[a] $p < .05$.
[b] $p < .01$.

for the two sexes were found. The means and standard deviations of imitation scores are presented in Table 6.

RELATIONS AMONG MEASURES

The ITSC scores, father-child and mother-child similarity measures, and father-child and mother-child imitation scores were correlated separately for boys and girls in mother- and father-dominant homes for each age group. The results suggest that these measures are meaningfully related only for older girls from father-dominant homes. In this group, girls who imitate their mother are rated as being similar to them on the adjective check list ($r = .58$, $p < .01$) and have feminine sex-role preferences ($r = -.68$, $p < .01$). When these girls have feminine sex-role preference they are rated as similar to their mothers ($r = -.67$, $p < .01$), when they have masculine sex-role preferences they are rated as similar to their fathers ($r = .42$, $p < .05$). It appears that in homes where parents serve as culturally appropriate sex-role models with the father more dominant than the mother, girls' feminine sex-role preferences are closely related to imitation of the mother and similarity to the parents on other traits which are not sexually defined.

In contrast, there are few systematic or meaningful relationships for girls from mother-dominant homes or for boys from either mother- or father-dominant homes. There was a tendency for parent-child imitation to be related to parent-child similarity in these

Table 6 Means and Standard Deviations of Parent-Child Imitation Scores

	Mother dominant						Father dominant					
Ages:	4–5		6–8		9–11		4–5		6–8		9–11	
Imitation	M	SD	M	SD	M	SD	M	SD	M	SD	M	SD
Mother-daughter	13.3	3.4	13.4	3.7	14.7	3.1	11.7	2.6	11.3	3.6	10.7	3.8
Mother-son	12.3	3.2	12.0	2.6	12.3	4.5	10.9	2.8	10.1	3.8	9.1	2.9
Father-daughter	10.1	3.1	11.2	3.0	11.8	2.8	11.8	3.1	14.2	3.1	14.4	3.2
Father-son	10.1	2.8	10.8	3.1	11.1	2.9	13.1	2.8	12.8	3.1	11.9	3.7

groups, but there was little relationship between sex-role preference and the other measures. In fact, for boys there were no significant correlations between the ITSC and any other measures at any age.

DISCUSSION

The results appear to support partially a theory of identification based on parental power. Parental dominance influenced children in imitation of parents, sex-role preferences, and similarity to parents in non-sex-typed traits. Inversions of the normal parental dominance pattern were related to more disruption in the identification of boys than of girls. Boys from mother-dominant homes acquired non-sex-typed traits like the mother and also more feminine sex-role preferences than boys from father-dominant homes. Contrary to expectations these differences in sex-role preferences were present at ages 4–5 and were sustained through ages 9–11. The predicted decrease in the relationship between sex-role preference and parental dominance with age did not occur. It appears that later social pressures on boys to acquire masculine preferences do not adequately counteract the early developed more feminine preferences of boys in mother-dominant homes. The prediction of an increasing similarity of the child and dominant parent on non-sex-typed traits with age is supported. This similarity is significantly less in 4- and 5-year-olds than in older children. Since the period from 3 to 6 years is considered to be a critical formative one in which identification is rapidly changing and growing, this increase in similarity following the preschool years might be anticipated. After this marked increase in identification, a stabilizing of identification on non-sex-typed traits appears to occur early in the school aged years.

It was surprising that girls from mother- and father-dominant homes showed no difference in sex-role preference at any age, since it might be assumed that a dominant mother offers her daughter a rather "unfeminine" role model. However, it should be remembered that the measure of maternal dominance in this study was one of dominance relative to the spouse and not to other members of her own sex. Thus a mother could be more dominant than a passive husband and still not be dominant or "unfeminine" relative to other women. The significance of parental dominance relative to other members of the same sex remains to be investigated. It is possible that since the feminine role in our culture is less well defined, less highly valued (Lynn, 1959; McKee and Sherriffs, 1957), and later acquired than the male role, these factors attenuate any differences due to maternal dominance.

It could be argued that lack of appropriate paternal dominance rather than the presence of maternal dominance led to the obtained findings. If boys and girls initially both identify with the mother, the socially appropriate sex-role behavior of paternal dominance may be necessary to facilitate the shift in identification models for the boy. Since normal identification for girls involves sustaining and intensifying the mother-child relationship, father dominance may contribute only to cross-sex identification and do little to disrupt the girls' primary identification. Social pressures may also encourage the child to identify with the like-sexed parent unless his behavior is culturally inappropriate. Since the feminine role is less well defined than the masculine role, either dominant or passive behavior in mothers may be regarded as more acceptable than passivity in fathers. Evidence for this is provided not only by the different results for boys and girls on the ITSC, but also by the parent-child similarity on traits not influenced by sex typing. Paternal dominance facilitated cross-sex identification in girls but did not disturb like-sex identification. Thus the mother-daughter and father-daughter similarity in father-dominant homes, and mother-daughter similarity in mother-dominant homes did not differ significantly. However, neither the sons nor daughters in mother-dominant homes identified with the passive father.

This interpretation of the role of dominance in identification appears to be consistent with the psychoanalytic stress on the great importance of "identification with the aggressor" in boys' identification, and its lesser importance in the identification of girls.

REFERENCES

Bandura, A. Social learning through imitation. In M. R. Jones (Ed.), *Nebraska symposium on motivation: 1962.* Lincoln: Univer. Nebraska Press, 1962. Pp. 211–269.

Brown, D. G. Sex-role preference in young children. *Psychological Monographs*, 1956, **70**(14, Whole No. 421).

Brown, D. G. Sex role development in a changing culture. *Psychological Bulletin*, 1958, **55**, 232–242.

Farina, A. Patterns of role dominance and conflict in parents of schizophrenic patients. *Journal of Abnormal and Social Psychology*, 1960, **61**, 31–38.

Hetherington, E. Mavis, and Brackbill, Yvonne. Etiology and covariation of obstinacy, orderliness and parsimony in young children. *Child Development*, 1963, **34**, 919–944.

Lynn, D. B. A note on sex differences in the development of masculine and feminine identification. *Psychological Review*, 1959, **66**, 126–135.

McDavid, J. W. Imitative behavior in pre-school children. *Psychological Monographs*, 1959, **73**(16, Whole No. 486).

McKee, J. P., and Sherriffs, A. C. The differential evaluation of males and females. *Journal of Personality*, 1957, **25**, 356–371.

Mussen, P., and Distler, L. Masculinity, identification, and father-son relationships. *Journal of Abnormal and Social Psychology*, 1959, **59**, 350–356.

Parsons, T. Family structure and the socialization of the child. In T. Parsons and R. F. Bales (Eds.). *Family, socialization, and interaction process*. Glencoe, Ill.: Free Press, 1955, Pp. 35–131.

index

74　75　76　77　9　8　7　6　5　4　3　2　1